Always use / (? Key) to get Main Menu
Master Menu - Top Line
Sub-Menu - 2nd Line (Worksheet) (.

To Select Format - Choose Range 1st
To Save - /FS (Select File)
To Exit - Use quit option
To Name File - 8 Letters Before .

☐ Parallel

☐ Landscape

Alt-F7 - 1P
Configuration
Orientation
Landscape

◆ Learning to Use Microcomputer Applications: Lotus 1-2-3 Release 2.2

To Erase A Cell (Error) - Use /space of space bar
To Get New Worksheet - / - Worksheet - Erase - Y (after saving)
To Total Lengthy Columns - @ sum (C5.. C8) enter
To Copy Formula To New Column - /C - copy, enter, go to column, enter
To Subtract Columns - +1st column - 2nd column = answer (ie +D4-D5 = D6)
To Undo Command - Alt-FX

Learning to Use Microcomputer Applications: Lotus 1-2-3 Release 2.2

GARY B. SHELLY
THOMAS J. CASHMAN
JAMES S. QUASNEY

SHELLY
CASHMAN
SERIES

boyd & fraser publishing company

© 1992 by boyd & fraser publishing company
A Division of South-Western Publishing Company
One Corporate Place • Ferncroft Village
Danvers, Massachusetts 01923

Developed by Susan Solomon Communications

Manufactured in the United States of America

ISBN 0-87835-738-6

2 3 4 5 6 7 8 9 10 BC 6 5 4 3

◆ CONTENTS IN BRIEF

◆ CONTENTS

INTRODUCTION TO COMPUTERS

v

I N T R O D U C T I O N   T O   D O S

 PROJECT 1   Working with Files on Disks   DOS2

◆ **PROJECT 2   Managing and Organizing Files on Disks   DOS25**

S P R E A D S H E E T S   U S I N G   L O T U S   1-2-3   R E L E A S E   2.2

◆ PROJECT 1   Building a Worksheet   L2

PROJECT 2   Formatting and Printing a Worksheet   L44

 PROJECT 3   Enhancing Your Worksheet   L92

PROJECT 4   Building Worksheets with Functions and Macros   L153

◆ PROJECT 5   Graphing with 1-2-3 and Allways   L192

PROJECT 6   Sorting and Querying a Worksheet Database   L228

 APPENDIX—Command Structure Charts for Release 2.2   L257

◆ PREFACE

Congratulations! You are about to use a Shelly Cashman Series textbook. In doing so, you join millions of other students and instructors who have discovered why this is the best-selling computer education series of all time.

The Shelly Cashman Series offers superior materials from which to learn about computers. The series includes books on computer concepts, microcomputer applications, and introductory programming. No matter what you cover in your class, the Shelly Cashman Series provides the appropriate texts.

Traditionally bound series texts are shown in the table below. If you do not find the exact combination that fits your needs, boyd & fraser's unique Custom Editions Program allows you to choose from a number of options and create a text perfectly suited to your course. This exciting new program is explained in detail on page xiv of this preface.

Traditionally Bound Texts in the Shelly Cashman Series

Computer Concepts	*Essential Computer Concepts* *Complete Computer Concepts*
Computer Concepts Study Guide	*Workbook and Study Guide with Computer Lab Software Projects to accompany Complete Computer Concepts*
Computer Concepts and Microcomputer Applications	*Essential Computer Concepts with Microcomputer Applications: WordPerfect 5.0/5.1, Lotus 1-2-3 Release 2.2, and dBASE III PLUS* *Complete Computer Concepts and Microcomputer Applications: WordPerfect 5.1, Lotus 1-2-3 Release 2.2, and dBASE III PLUS* (also available in spiral bound edition) *Complete Computer Concepts and Microcomputer Applications: WordPerfect 5.1, Lotus 1-2-3 Release 2.2, and dBASE IV Version 1.1* (also available in spiral bound edition)
Computer Concepts and Programming	*Complete Computer Concepts and Microsoft BASIC* *Complete Computer Concepts and QuickBASIC*
Microcomputer Applications	*Learning to Use Microcomputer Applications: WordPerfect 5.1, Lotus 1-2-3 Release 2.2, and dBASE III PLUS* (also available in spiral bound edition) *Learning to Use Microcomputer Applications: WordPerfect 5.1, Lotus 1-2-3 Release 2.2, and dBASE IV Version 1.1* (also available in spiral bound edition)
Word Processing	*Learning to Use Microcomputer Applications: WordPerfect 5.1* *Learning to Use WordPerfect 4.2* (WordPerfect 4.2 Educational Version Software available) *Learning to Use Microsoft Word 5.0* *Learning to Use WordStar 6.0* (with WordStar 6.0 Academic Edition Software)
Spreadsheets	*Learning to Use Microcomputer Applications: Lotus 1-2-3 Release 2.3* *Learning to Use Microcomputer Applications: Lotus 1-2-3 Release 2.2* *Learning to Use Lotus 1-2-3 Release 2.01* *Learning to Use Microcomputer Applications: Quattro Pro* *Learning to Use Microcomputer Applications: Quattro with 1-2-3 Menus* (with Quattro Educational Version Software)
Database	*Learning to Use dBASE III PLUS* (dBASE III PLUS Educational Version Software available) *Learning to Use Microcomputer Applications: dBASE IV Version 1.1* *Learning to Use Microcomputer Applications: Paradox 3.5* (with Paradox Educational Version Software)
Programming	*Programming in Microsoft BASIC* *Programming in QuickBASIC*

CONTENT

◆ Shelly Cashman Series texts assume no previous experience with computers and are written with continuity, simplicity, and practicality in mind.

Computer Concepts

The Shelly Cashman Series computer concepts textbooks offer up-to-date coverage to fit every need. *Essential Computer Concepts* is a brief concepts text that covers the topics most commonly found in short courses on computer concepts. *Complete Computer Concepts* offers a more comprehensive treatment of computer concepts.

All Shelly Cashman Series computer concepts textbooks are lavishly illustrated with hundreds of photographs and carefully developed illustrations—features that have become a hallmark of the Shelly Cashman Series. The impact of microcomputers and the user's point of view are consistently addressed throughout these texts. In addition they include coverage of important topics to help students understand today's rapidly changing technology:

■ A chapter on Management Information Systems that presents information as an asset to organizations, discusses how computer-based systems effectively manage information, and addresses recent trends in decision support and expert systems.
■ An innovative approach to the phases of the Information System Life Cycle.
■ Up-to-date coverage of local area networks, pen-based and notebook computers, graphic user interfaces, multimedia, object-oriented programming, page printers, and desktop publishing.

Each concepts chapter concludes with:

■ A Chapter Summary to help students recall and comprehend key concepts.
■ Key Terms to reinforce terminology introduced in the chapter.
■ Review Questions to test students' mastery of the chapter content.
■ Controversial Issues to stimulate classroom discussion and critical thinking.
■ Research Projects to provide opportunity for in-depth investigation of chapter content.

Microcomputer Applications

The Shelly Cashman Series microcomputer applications textbooks include projects on DOS, word processing, spreadsheets, and database management. In each project students learn by way of a unique and time-tested problem-solving approach, in which problems are presented and then *thoroughly* solved in a step-by-step manner. Numerous, carefully labeled screens and keystroke sequences illustrate the exact order of operations. Using this approach, students are visually guided as they perform the various commands and quickly come up to speed.

The DOS materials are divided into two projects. Project 1 covers the essential commands on file management and Project 2 presents directory and subdirectory file management concepts.

Each word processing application contains six projects. After an introduction to the keyboard, students are guided through the word processing cycle—starting the software, creating a document, entering text, saving, viewing, printing, and exiting to DOS. To reinforce their understanding of the cycle, students restart the software, retrieve the document they created, revise the document, save the changes, print the document, and exit to DOS again. In subsequent projects students learn to use the speller and thesaurus; to format, move, search, and replace text; to merge documents, create footnotes, and to use windows. They learn these skills by creating memos, letters, reports, and resumes.

Each spreadsheet application contains six projects. In Project 1 students learn spreadsheet terminology and basic spreadsheet characteristics and apply this know-how to create a company's first quarter sales report. In Project 2 students continue to use this sales report, learning such skills as adding summary totals, formatting, changing column widths, replication, debugging, and printing. In Project 3 students create a more complex quarterly report using what-if analysis and other skills such as inserting and deleting rows and columns, changing default settings, and copying absolute cell addresses. Projects 4, 5, and 6 cover functions and macros, graphing, and database functions, respectively.

Each database application contains six projects. In Project 1 students design and create a database of employee records, which they use as an example throughout the remaining five projects. Project 2 teaches students how to display records in a database in a variety of ways and also how to use statistical functions. Sorting and report generation are taught in Project 3. Project 4 introduces the processes of adding, changing, and deleting records. Students change the structure of the employee database, and create and use indexes and views in Project 5. Finally, in Project 6 students create custom forms for data entry and learn how to generate applications.

In all of the microcomputer applications, two beneficial learning and review tools are included at the end of each project—the Project Summary, which lists the key concepts covered in the project, and the Keystroke Summary, which is an exact listing of each keystroke used to solve the project's problem.

Following the last project in each application, an easy-to-use Quick Reference is included for each project. The Quick Reference is divided into three parts—the activity, the procedure for accomplishing the activity, and a description of what actually occurs when the keys are pressed.

Finally, each project concludes with a wealth of Student Assignments. These include: true/false and multiple-choice questions; exercises that require students to write and/or explain various commands; a series of realistic problems for students to analyze and solve by applying what they have learned in the project; and minicases for the database projects.

Programming

The Shelly Cashman Series includes QuickBASIC and Microsoft BASIC programming textbooks. They are divided into six projects that provide students with knowledge that is central to a real programming environment. They present the essentials of the language as well as structured and top-down programming techniques. In each project a problem is presented and then *thoroughly* solved step by step with a program.

In Project 1 students learn the program development cycle, the basic characteristics of the programming language, and the operating environment. Project 2 presents computations, summary tools, report editing, and report printing. In Project 3 students learn about decision making. Topics include implementing If-Then-Else and Case structures, and the use of logical operators. Unlike the first three projects, which use the READ and DATA statements to integrate data into a program, Project 4 shows students how to use the INPUT statement to accomplish this task. Also included is coverage of how to use For loops to implement counter-controlled loops, and how to design top-down programs. Project 5 introduces students to creating and processing a sequential data file. In Project 6 students learn how to write programs that can look up information in tables; they are then acquainted with the most often used built-in functions and, if applicable, special variables, of the language. Finally, an appendix on debugging techniques introduces students to debugging features that are built into the language.

Each programming project includes one or more sets of Try It Yourself Exercises, paper-and-pencil practice exercises to help master the concepts presented. Each project concludes with challenging and field-tested Student Assignments. All programming assignments include a problem statement, sample input data, and sample output results. Also included is a Reference Card that lists all statements, functions, and features of the language.

SHELLY CASHMAN SERIES CUSTOM EDITIONS

◆ The Shelly Cashman Series provides a new textbook option so flexible that you can easily put together a unique, customized computer textbook reflecting the exact content and software requirements of your course. Because all of the Shelly Cashman Series materials use a consistent pedagogy, you can easily "mix and match" them while maintaining a clear, cohesive text. It has all been designed to work together in any combination.

When you order your custom edition, you will receive individually packaged text materials that you selected for your course needs. The customized materials arrive in a sealed box together with a durable spine binding and two covers ready for your students to assemble in seconds.

Features of the custom bound editions include:

- Text that reflects the content of your course.
- Shelly Cashman Series quality, including the same full-color materials and proven Shelly Cashman Series pedagogy found in the traditionally bound books.
- Flexibility so you can also include your own handouts and worksheets.
- Affordably priced so your students receive the Custom Edition at a cost similar to the traditionally bound books.
- Guaranteed quick order processing where your materials are sent to your bookstore within forty-eight hours of receipt of your order.
- Applications materials are continually updated to reflect the latest software versions.

The materials available in the Shelly Cashman Series Custom Edition program are listed below.

Materials Available for Shelly Cashman Series Custom Editions

Concepts	*Introduction to Computers* *Essential Computer Concepts* *Complete Computer Concepts*
Operating Systems	*Introduction to DOS* (all versions using commands) *Introduction to DOS 5.0* (using menus)
Word Processing	*Word Processing Using WordPerfect 5.1* *Word Processing Using WordPerfect 4.2* *Word Processing Using Microsoft Word 5.0* *Word Processing Using WordStar 6.0*
Spreadsheets	*Spreadsheets Using Lotus 1-2-3 Release 2.3* *Spreadsheets Using Lotus 1-2-3 Release 2.2* *Spreadsheets Using Lotus 1-2-3 Release 2.01* *Spreadsheets Using Quattro Pro* *Spreadsheets Using Quattro with 1-2-3 Menus*
Database	*Database Management Using dBASE IV Version 1.1* *Database Management Using dBASE III PLUS* *Database Management Using Paradox 3.5*
Programming	*Programming in Microsoft BASIC* *Programming in QuickBASIC*

SUPPLEMENTS

 Ten available supplements complement the various textbooks in the Shelly Cashman Series.

Workbook and Study Guide with Computer Lab Software Projects

This highly popular supplement contains completely new activities to enhance the concepts chapters and to simulate computer applications that are not usually available to beginning students. Included for each chapter are:

- Chapter Objectives that help students measure their mastery of the chapter content.
- A Chapter Outline that guides students through the organization of the chapter.
- A Chapter Summary that helps students recall and comprehend key concepts.
- Key Terms with definitions that reinforce terminology introduced in the chapter.
- Six projects which range from self-testing on paper and communications skills activities to on-line computerized testing with self-scoring. Answers are included for all projects and exercises.

The Computer Lab Software Projects simulate the following applications in an interactive environment:

- Home banking
- Airline reservations
- On-line information services
- Electronic mail
- Desktop publishing
- Presentation graphics

Instructor's Manual to accompany the Workbook and Study Guide with Computer Lab Software Projects

The Instructor's Manual to accompany the workbook includes answers and solutions for the entire workbook, and the software for the on-line, self-testing projects as well as for the Computer Lab Software Projects.

Educational Versions of Applications Software

Free educational versions of WordPerfect 4.2, WordStar 6.0, Quattro 1.01, Paradox 2.04, and dBASE III PLUS are available to adopting institutions. This software is available for IBM or IBM compatible systems.

Instructor's Guide Including Answer Manual and Test Bank

The Instructor's Guide and Answer Manual includes Lesson Plans for each chapter or project. The Lesson Plans begin with behavorial objectives and an overview of each chapter or project to help instructors quickly review the purpose and key concepts. Detailed outlines of each chapter and/or project follow. These outlines are annotated with the page number of the text on which the outlined material is covered; notes, teaching tips, and additional activities that the instructor might use to embellish the lesson; and a key for using the Transparency Masters and/or Color Transparencies. Complete answers and solutions for all Exercises, Discussion Questions, Projects, Controversial Issues, Student Assignments, Try It Yourself Exercises, and Minicases are also included.

This manual also contains three types of test questions with answers and is a hard copy version of MicroSWAT III (see below). The three types of questions are—true/false, multiple choice, and fill-in. Each chapter or project has approximately 50 true/false, 25 multiple choice, and 35 fill ins.

MicroSWAT III

MicroSWAT III, a microcomputer-based test-generating system, is available free to adopters. It includes all of the questions from the Test Bank in an easy-to-use, menu-driven package that allows testing flexibility and customization of testing documents. For example, with MicroSWAT III a user can enter his or her own questions and can generate review sheets and answer keys. MicroSWAT III will run on any IBM or IBM compatible system with two diskette drives or a hard disk.

Transparency Masters

Transparency Masters are available for *every* illustration in all of the Shelly Cashman Series textbooks. The transparency masters are conveniently bound in a perforated volume; they have been photographically enlarged for clearer projection.

Color Transparencies

One hundred high-quality, full-color acetates contain key illustrations found in *Complete Computer Concepts*. Each transparency is accompanied by an interleaved lecture note.

Instructor's Data Disks

The Instructor's Data Disks contain the files used in the DOS projects; the letters and memos, and the final versions of documents used to teach the word processing projects; the project worksheets and Student Assignment worksheet solutions for the spreadsheet projects; the databases that students will create and use in the database Minicases; the data for the employee database example, and program solutions to all of the programming assignments.

HyperGraphics®

This software-based, instructor-led classroom presentation system is available to assist adopters in delivering top-notch lectures. It allows instructors to present much of the text's content using graphics, color, animation, and instructor-led interactivity. It requires an LCD projection panel, a microcomputer, and an overhead projector.

ACKNOWLEDGMENTS

◆ The Shelly Cashman Series would not be the success it is without the contributions of many outstanding publishing professionals, who demand quality in everything they do: Jeanne Huntington, typographer; Ken Russo, Anne Craig, Mike Bodnar, John Craig and Julia Schenden, illustrators; Janet Bollow, book design and cover design; Sarah Bendersky, photo researcher; Becky Herrington, director of production and art coordinator; Virginia Harvey, manuscript editor; Susan Solomon, director of development; and Thomas K. Walker, publisher and vice president of boyd & fraser publishing company. We hope you will find using this text an enriching and rewarding experience.

Gary B. Shelly
Thomas J. Cashman

Introduction
to Computers

INTRODUCTION

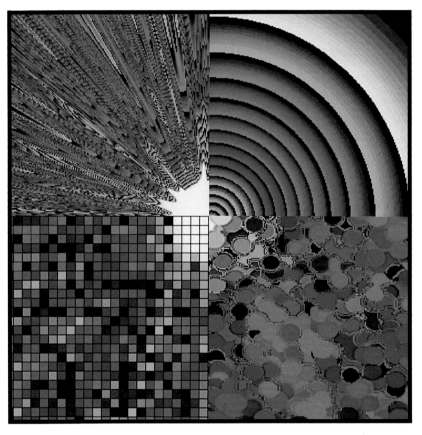

OBJECTIVES

◆ Define computer and discuss the four basic computer operations: input, processing, output, and storage

◆ Define data and information

◆ Explain the principal components of the computer and their use

◆ Describe the use and handling of diskettes and hard disks

◆ Discuss computer software and explain the difference between application software and system software

The computer is an integral part of the daily lives of most individuals. Small computers, called microcomputers or personal computers (shown on the next page in Figure 1), have made computing available to almost everyone. Thus, your ability to understand and use a computer is an important skill. This book teaches you how to use a computer by teaching you how to use software applications. Before you learn about the application software, however, you must understand what a computer is, the components of a computer, and the types of software used on computers. These topics are explained in this Introduction.

FIGURE 1
Microcomputers: The Apple
Macintosh IIsi (left) and Compaq Deskpro 386/25e (right)
are two examples of popular
microcomputer systems.

WHAT IS A COMPUTER?

A **computer** is an electronic device, operating under the control of instructions stored in its own memory unit, that accepts input or data, processes data arithmetically and logically, produces output from the processing, and stores the results for future use. All computers perform basically the same four operations:

1. **Input operations**, by which data is entered into the computer for processing.
2. **Processing operations**, which manipulate data by arithmetic and logical operations. **Arithmetic operations** are addition, subtraction, multiplication, and division. **Logical operations** are those that compare data to determine if one value is less than, equal to, or greater than another value.
3. **Output operations**, which make the information generated from processing available for use.
4. **Storage operations**, which store data electronically for future reference.

FIGURE 2
This microprocessor is
shown packaged and ready
for installation in a
microcomputer.

These operations occur through the use of electronic circuits contained on small silicon chips inside the computer (Figure 2). Because these electronic circuits rarely fail and the data flows along these circuits at close to the speed of light, processing can be accomplished in millionths of a second. Thus, the computer is a powerful tool because it can perform these four operations reliably and quickly.

WHAT ARE DATA AND INFORMATION?

◆ The four operations that can be performed using a computer all require data.
Data refers to raw facts, including numbers and words, given to a computer during the
input operation. Examples of data include the hours posted to a payroll time card or the
words comprising a memo to the sales staff. A computer accepts data, processes data
and, as a result of the processing, produces output in the form of useful information.
Information can therefore be defined as data that has been processed into a form that
has meaning and is useful.

WHAT ARE THE COMPONENTS OF A COMPUTER?

◆ To understand how computers process data into information, you need to examine
the primary components of the computer. The four primary components of a computer
are:

1. input devices
2. processor unit
3. output devices
4. auxiliary storage units

Figure 3 illustrates the relationship of the various components to one another.

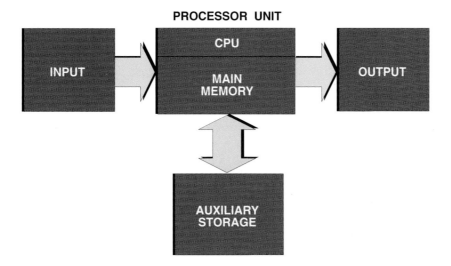

FIGURE 3
The four components
of a computer

Input Devices

Input devices enter data into main memory. Many input devices exist. The two most
commonly used are the keyboard and the mouse.

The Keyboard　The input device you will most commonly use on computers is the
keyboard, on which you manually *key in* or type the data. The keyboard on most computers is laid out in much the same manner as a typewriter. Two styles of IBM keyboards: the original standard keyboard and a newer enhanced keyboard are shown on
the next page in Figures 4⟨a⟩ and 4⟨b⟩. Although the layouts are somewhat different,
the use of the keys is the same.

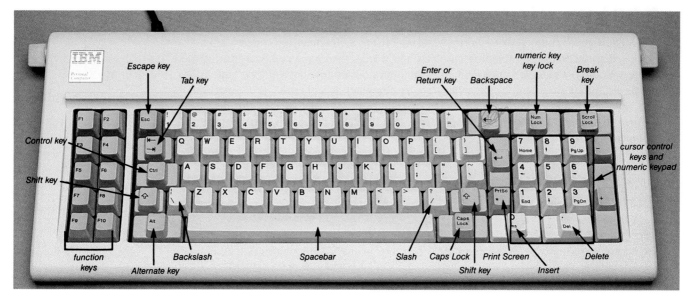

FIGURE 4a   The IBM standard keyboard

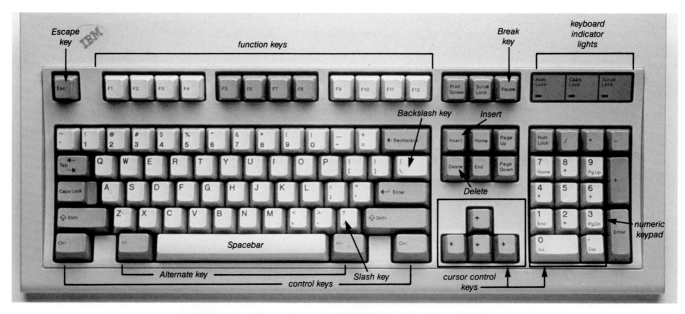

FIGURE 4b   The enhanced IBM PS/2 keyboard; notice the different placement of the function and cursor keys.

A **numeric keypad** in the 10-key adding machine or calculator-key format is located on the right side of both keyboards. This arrangement of keys allows you to enter numeric data rapidly. To activate the numeric keypad you press and engage the Num Lock key located above the numeric keypad. The **Num Lock** key activates the numeric keypad so that when the keys are pressed numeric characters are entered into the computer memory and appear on the screen. On the enhanced keyboard, a light turns on at the top right of the keyboard to indicate that the numeric keys are in use.

The **cursor** is a symbol, such as an underline character, which indicates where you are working on the screen. The **cursor control keys**, or **arrow keys**, allow you to move the cursor around the screen. Pressing the **Up Arrow** ↑ key causes the cursor to move upward on the screen. The **Down Arrow** ↓ key causes the cursor to move down;

the **Left Arrow** ← and **Right Arrow** → keys cause the cursor to move left and right on the screen. On the keyboards in Figures 4⟨a⟩ and 4⟨b⟩, cursor control keys are included as part of the numeric keypad. The enhanced keyboard has a second set of cursor control keys located between the typewriter keys and the numeric keypad. To use the numeric keypad for cursor control, the Num Lock key must be disengaged. If the Num Lock key is engaged (indicated by the fact that as you press any numeric key-pad key, a number appears on the screen), you can return to the cursor mode by pressing the Num Lock key. On an enhanced keyboard, the Num Lock light will be off when the numeric keypad is in the cursor mode.

The other keys on the keypad—Page Up, Page Down, Home, and End—have various uses depending on the software you use. Some programs make no use of these keys; others use the **Page Up** and **Page Down** keys, for example, to display previous or following pages of data on the screen. Some software uses the **Home** key to move the cursor to the upper left corner of the screen. Likewise, the **End** key may be used to move the cursor to the end of a line of text or to the bottom of the screen, depending on the software.

Function keys on many keyboards can be programmed to accomplish specific tasks. For example, a function key might be used as a help key. Whenever that key is pressed, messages appear that give instructions to help the user. Another function key might be programmed to cause all data displayed on the screen to be printed on a printer whenever the key is pressed. In Figure 4⟨a⟩, ten function keys are on the left portion of the standard keyboard. In Figure 4⟨b⟩, twelve function keys are located across the top of the enhanced keyboard.

Other keys have special uses in some applications. The **Shift** keys have several functions. They work as they do on a typewriter, allowing you to type capital letters. The Shift key is always used to type the symbol on the upper portion of any key on the keyboard. Also, to temporarily use the cursor control keys on the numeric keypad as numeric entry keys, you can press the Shift key to switch into numeric mode. If, instead, you have pressed the Num Lock key to use the numeric keys, you can press the Shift key to shift temporarily back to the cursor mode.

The keyboard has a Backspace key, a Tab key, an Insert key and a Delete key that perform the functions their names indicate.

The **Escape (Esc)** key also has many different uses. In some computer software it is used to cancel an instruction but this use is by no means universally true.

As with the Escape key, many keys are assigned special meaning by the computer software. Certain keys may be used more frequently than others by one piece of software but rarely used by another. It is this flexibility that allows you to use the computer in so many different applications.

The Mouse An alternative input device you might encounter is a mouse. A **mouse** (Figure 5) is a pointing device that you can use instead of the cursor control keys. You lay the palm of your hand over the mouse and move it across the surface of a table or desk. The mouse detects the direction of your movement and sends this information to the screen to move the cursor. You push buttons on top of the mouse to indicate your choices of actions from lists displayed on the screen.

FIGURE 5
A mouse can be used to move the cursor and select items on the computer screen.

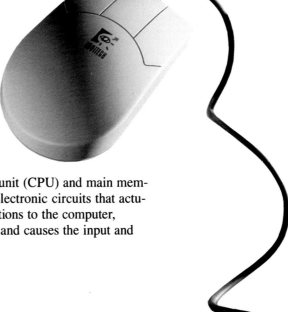

The Processor

The **processor unit** is composed of the central processing unit (CPU) and main memory (Figure 3). The **central processing unit** contains the electronic circuits that actually cause processing to occur. The CPU interprets instructions to the computer, performs the logical and arithmetic processing operations, and causes the input and output operations to occur.

Main memory consists of electronic components that store numbers, letters of the alphabet, and characters such as decimal points or dollar signs. Any data to be processed must be stored in main memory.

The amount of main memory in computers is typically measured in kilobytes (K or KB), which equal 1,024 memory locations. A memory location, or byte, usually stores one character. Therefore, a computer with 640K can store approximately 640,000 characters. The amount of main memory for computers may range from 64K to several million characters, or more. One million characters is called a **megabyte (MB)**.

Output Devices

Output devices make the information resulting from processing available for use. The output from computers can be presented in many forms, such as a printed report or color graphics. When a computer is used for processing tasks, such as word processing, spreadsheets, or database management, the two output devices most commonly used are the **printer** and the televisionlike display device called a **screen**, **monitor**, or **CRT** (cathode ray tube).

FIGURE 6
This Panasonic dot matrix printer is popular for use with personal computers.

FIGURE 7
On a dot matrix printer with a nine-pin print head, the letter E is formed with seven vertical and five horizontal dots. As the print head moves from left to right, it fires one or more pins into the ribbon, which makes a dot on the paper. At print position 1, it fires pins 1 through 7. At print positions 2 through 4, it fires pins 1, 4, and 7. At print position 5, it fires pins 1 and 7. Pins 8 and 9 are used for lowercase characters such as p, q, y, g, and j that extend below the line.

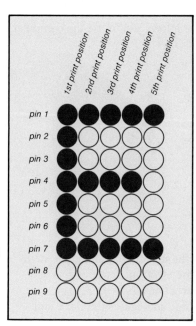

Printers   Printers used with computers can be either impact printers or nonimpact printers. An **impact printer** prints by striking an inked ribbon against the paper. One type of impact printer often used with microcomputers is the dot matrix printer (Figure 6). To print a character, a **dot matrix printer** generates a dot pattern representing a particular character. The printer then activates vertical wires in a print head contained on the printer, so that selected wires press against the ribbon and paper, creating a character. As you see in Figure 7, the character consists of a series of dots produced by the print head wires. In the actual size created by the printer, the characters are clear and easy to read.

Dot matrix printers vary in the speed with which they can print characters. These speeds range from 50 characters per second to over 400 characters per second. Generally, the higher the speed, the higher the cost of the printer.

Many dot matrix printers also allow you to choose two or more sizes and densities of character. Typical sizes include condensed print, standard print, and enlarged print. In addition, each of the three print sizes can be printed with increased density, or darkness (Figure 8).

Another useful feature of dot matrix printers is their capability to print graphics. The dots are printed not to form characters, but rather to form graphic images. This feature can be especially useful when you are working with a spreadsheet program to produce graphs of the numeric values contained on the worksheet.

```
CONDENSED PRINT - NORMAL CHARACTERS
CONDENSED PRINT - EMPHASIZED CHARACTERS


STANDARD PRINT - NORMAL CHARACTERS
STANDARD PRINT - EMPHASIZED CHARACTERS


ENLARGED PRINT - NORMAL CHARACTERS
ENLARGED PRINT - EMPHASIZED CHARACTERS
```

Nonimpact printers, such as ink jet printers and page printers, form characters by means other than striking a ribbon against paper (Figure 9). An **ink jet printer** forms a character by using a nozzle that sprays drops of ink onto the page. Ink jet printers produce relatively high-quality images and print between 150 and 270 characters per second.

FIGURE 8
These samples show condensed, standard, and enlarged print. All these can be produced by a dot matrix printer.

FIGURE 9
Two nonimpact printers: a laser printer (left) and an ink jet printer (right)

FIGURE 10
Sample output from a laser printer

Page printers convert data from the computer into a beam of light that is focused on a photoconductor, forming the images to be printed. The photoconductor attracts particles of toner that are fused onto paper to produce an image. Advantages of using a page printer are that it can print graphics and it can print in varying sizes and type styles. The output it produces is very high quality (Figure 10), with the images resembling professional printing rather than typewritten characters. Page printers for microcomputers can cost from $1,000 to over $8,000. They can print four to sixteen pages of text and graphics per minute. **Laser printers** are the most popular type of page printers.

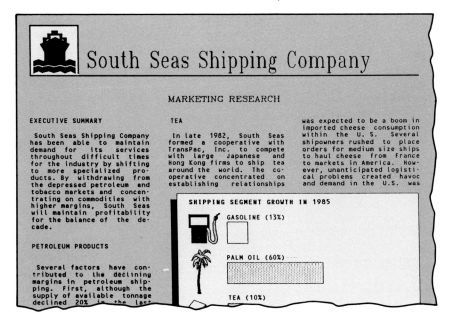

South Seas Shipping Company

MARKETING RESEARCH

EXECUTIVE SUMMARY

South Seas Shipping Company has been able to maintain demand for its services throughout difficult times for the industry by shifting to more specialized products. By withdrawing from the depressed petroleum and tobacco markets and concentrating on commodities with higher margins, South Seas will maintain profitability for the balance of the decade.

PETROLEUM PRODUCTS

Several factors have contributed to the declining margins in petroleum shipping. First, although the supply of available tonnage declined 20% in the last

TEA

In late 1982, South Seas formed a cooperative with TransPac, Inc. to compete with large Japanese and Hong Kong firms to ship tea around the world. The cooperative concentrated on establishing relationships

was expected to be a boom in imported cheese consumption within the U. S. Several shipowners rushed to place orders for medium size ships to haul cheese from France to markets in America. However, unanticipated logistical problems created havoc and demand in the U. S. was

SHIPPING SEGMENT GROWTH IN 1985

GASOLINE (13%)

PALM OIL (60%)

TEA (10%)

Computer Screens

The computer you use probably has a screen sometimes called a monitor or CRT (cathode ray tube). The **screen** displays the data entered on the keyboard and messages from the computer.

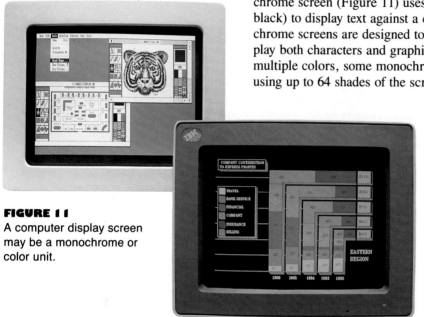

Two general types of screens are used on computers. A monochrome screen (Figure 11) uses a single color (green, amber, white, or black) to display text against a contrasting background. Some monochrome screens are designed to display only characters; others can display both characters and graphics. Although they cannot display multiple colors, some monochrome screens simulate full-color output by using up to 64 shades of the screen's single color.

The second type of screen is a color display. These devices are generally capable of displaying 256 colors at once from a range of more than 256,000 choices.

Computer graphics, charts, graphs, or pictures, can also be displayed on a screen so that the information can be easily and quickly understood. Graphics are often used to present information to others, for example, to help people make business decisions.

FIGURE 11
A computer display screen may be a monochrome or color unit.

Auxiliary Storage

Main memory is not large enough to store the instructions and data for all your applications at one time, so data not in use must be stored elsewhere. **Auxiliary storage** devices are used to store instructions and data when they are not being used in main memory.

Diskettes   One type of auxiliary storage you will use often with your computer is the **diskette**. A diskette is a circular piece of oxide-coated plastic that stores data as magnetic spots. Diskettes are available in various sizes. Microcomputers most commonly use diskettes that are 5¼ inches or 3½ inches in diameter (Figure 12).

To read data stored on a diskette or to store data on a diskette, you insert the diskette in a disk drive (Figure 13). You can tell that the computer is reading data on the diskette or writing data on it because a light on the disk drive will come on while read/write operations are taking place. Do not try to insert or remove a diskette when the light is on as you could cause permanent damage to the data stored on it.

The storage capacities of disk drives and the related diskettes can vary widely (Figure 14). The number of characters that can be stored on a diskette by a disk drive depends on three factors: (1) the number of sides of the diskette used; (2) the recording density of the bits on a track; and (3) the number of tracks on the diskette.

FIGURE 12
The most commonly used diskettes for personal computers are 5¼ inch (left) and 3½ inch (right). An advantage of the 3½-inch size is its rigid plastic housing, which helps prevent damage to the diskette.

Early diskettes and disk drives were designed so that data could be recorded on only one side of the diskette. These drives are called **single-sided drives**. **Double-sided diskettes**, the typical type of diskette used now, provide increased storage capacity because data can be recorded on both sides of the diskette. Disk drives found on many microcomputers are 5¼-inch, double-sided disk drives that can store from 360,000 bytes to 1.25 million bytes on the diskette. Another popular type is the 3½-inch diskette, which, although physically smaller, stores from 720,000 to 1.44 million bytes. An added benefit of the 3½-inch diskette is its rigid plastic housing, which protects the magnetic surface of the diskette.

The second factor affecting diskette storage capacity is the **recording density** provided by the disk drive. (The recording density is stated in technical literature as the bpi—the number of bits that can be recorded on a diskette in a one-inch circumference of the innermost track on the diskette.) For the user, the diskettes and disk drives are identified as being **single density**, **double density**, or **high density**. You need to be aware of the density of diskettes used by your system because data stored on high-density diskettes, for example, cannot be processed by a computer that has only double-density disk drives.

The third factor that influences the number of characters that can be stored on a diskette is the number of tracks on the diskette. A **track** is a very narrow recording band forming a full circle around the diskette (Figure 15). The width of this recording band depends on the number of tracks on the diskette. The tracks are separated from each other by a very narrow blank gap. Each track on a diskette is divided into sectors. **Sectors** are the basic units for diskette storage. When data is read from a diskette, it reads a minimum of one full sector. When data is stored on a diskette, it writes one full sector at one time. The

FIGURE 13
A user inserts a diskette into the disk drive.

DIAMETER (INCHES)	DESCRIPTION	CAPACITY (BYTES)
5.25	Single-sided, double-density	160KB/180KB
5.25	Double-sided, double-density	320KB/360KB
5.25	Double-sided, high-density	1.25MB
3.5	Double-sided, double-density	720KB
3.5	Double-sided, high-density	1.44MB

FIGURE 14
Types of diskettes and their capacities

FIGURE 15
Each track on a diskette is a narrow, circular band. On a diskette containing 40 tracks, the outside track is called track 0 and the inside track is called track 39. The distance between track 0 and track 39 on a 5¼-inch diskette is less than one inch. The disk surface is divided into sectors. This is a diskette with nine sectors.

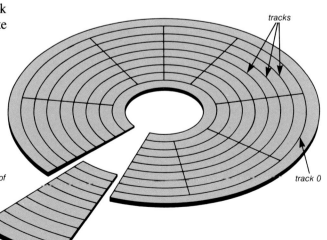

tracks

sector 1 of track 0

track 0

sector 1

tracks and sectors on the diskette and the number of characters that can be stored in each sector are defined by a special formatting program that is used with the computer.

Data stored in sectors on a diskette must be retrieved and placed into main memory to be processed. The time required to access and retrieve data, called the **access time**, can be important in some applications. The access time for diskettes varies from about 175 milliseconds (one millisecond equals 1/1000 of a second) to approximately 300 milliseconds. On average, data stored in a single sector on a diskette can be retrieved in approximately 1/5 to 1/3 of a second.

Diskette care is important to preserve stored data. Properly handled, diskettes can store data indefinitely. However, the surface of the diskette can be damaged and the data stored can be lost if the diskette is handled improperly. A diskette will give you very good service if you follow a few simple procedures (Figure 16):

FIGURE 16

Guidelines for the proper care of a 5¼-inch diskette. Most of the guidelines also apply to a 3½-inch diskette.

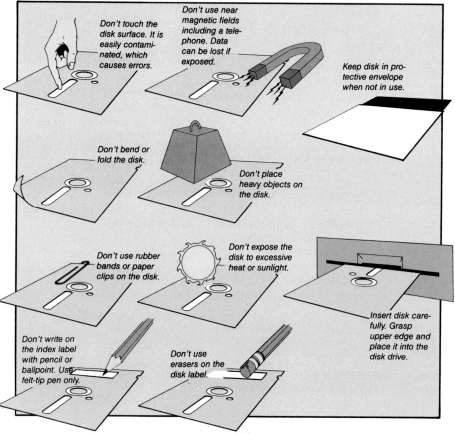

Don't touch the disk surface. It is easily contaminated, which causes errors.

Don't use near magnetic fields including a telephone. Data can be lost if exposed.

Keep disk in protective envelope when not in use.

Don't bend or fold the disk.

Don't place heavy objects on the disk.

Don't use rubber bands or paper clips on the disk.

Don't expose the disk to excessive heat or sunlight.

Insert disk carefully. Grasp upper edge and place it into the disk drive.

Don't write on the index label with pencil or ballpoint. Use felt-tip pen only.

Don't use erasers on the disk label.

1. Store a 5¼-inch diskette in its protective envelope when you are not using it. This procedure is necessary because the 5¼-inch diskette has an oval opening, the **access window**, which permits the read/write heads to access the diskette but also allows the diskette to be easily damaged or soiled.

2. Keep diskettes in their original box or in a special diskette storage box to protect them from dirt and dust and prevent them from being accidentally bent. Store the container away from heat and direct sunlight. Magnetic and electrical equipment, including telephones, radios, and televisions, can erase the data on a diskette so do not place diskettes near such devices. Do not place heavy objects on a diskette, because the weight can pinch the covering, causing damage when the disk drive attempts to rotate the diskette.

3. To affix one of the self-adhesive labels supplied with most diskettes, write or type the information on the label *before* you place the label on the diskette. If the label is already on the diskette, *do not* use an eraser to change the label. If you must write on the label after it is on the diskette, use only a felt-tip pen, *not* a pen or pencil, and press lightly.

4. To use the diskette, grasp the diskette on the side away from the side to be inserted into the disk drive. Slide the diskette carefully into the slot on the disk drive. If the disk drive has a latch or door, close it. If it is difficult to close the disk drive door, do not force it—the diskette may not be inserted fully, and forcing the door closed may damage the diskette. Reinsert the diskette if necessary, and try again to close the door.

The diskette **write-protect** feature (Figure 17) prevents the accidental erasure of the data stored on a diskette by preventing the disk drive from writing new data or erasing existing data. On a 5¼-inch diskette, a **write-protect notch** is located on the side of the diskette. A special **write-protect label** is placed over this notch whenever you want to protect the data. On the 3½-inch diskette, a small switch can slide to cover and uncover the write protection window. On a 3½-inch diskette, when the window is uncovered the data is protected.

window open

window closed

write protected disks

writable disks

write-protect notch covered

write-protect notch open

FIGURE 17

Data cannot be written on the 3½-inch diskette on the upper left because the window in the corner of the diskette is open. A small piece of plastic covers the window of the 3½-inch diskette on the upper right, so data can be written on this diskette. The reverse situation is true for the 5¼-inch diskettes. The write-protect notch of the 5¼-inch diskette on the lower left is covered and, therefore, data cannot be written to the diskette. The notch of the 5¼-inch diskette on the lower right, however, is open. Data can be written to this diskette.

Hard Disk   Another form of auxiliary storage is a hard disk. A **hard disk** consists of one or more rigid metal platters coated with a metal oxide material that allows data to be magnetically recorded on the surface of the platters (Figure 18). Although hard disks are available in cartridge form, most hard disks cannot be removed from the computer. As with diskettes, the data is recorded on hard disks on a series of tracks. The tracks are divided into sectors when the disk is formatted.

The hard disk platters spin at a high rate of speed, typically 3,600 revolutions per minute. When reading data from the disk, the read head senses the magnetic spots that are recorded on the disk along the various tracks and transfers that data to main memory. When writing, the data is transferred from main memory and is stored as magnetic spots on the tracks on the recording surface of one or more of the disk platters. Unlike diskette drives, the read/write heads on a hard disk drive do not actually touch the surface of the disk.

read/write head

spindle

disc surface

access arm

FIGURE 18

The protective cover of this hard disk drive has been removed to show the recording platters and the access arm that extends over the top platter. Other access arms extend over the top and bottom surfaces of the other recording platters. At the end of each access arm is a read/write head used to retrieve or record data on the surface of the platter.

The number of platters permanently mounted on the spindle of a hard disk varies from one to four. On most drives, each surface of the platter can be used to store data. Thus, if a hard disk drive uses one platter, two surfaces are available for data. If the drive uses two platters, four sets of read/write heads read and record data from the four surfaces. Storage capacities of fixed disks for microcomputers range from 20 million characters to over 300 million characters.

FIGURE 19
A computer system

printer

display screen

diskette drive

hard disk

processor unit

keyboard

SUMMARY OF THE COMPONENTS OF A COMPUTER

◆ The components of a complete computer are illustrated in Figure 19. (Compare this illustration to the computer you will be using.) Input to the computer occurs through the keyboard. As data is keyed on the keyboard, the data is transferred to main memory. In addition, the keyed data is displayed on the computer display screen. The output can be printed on a printer or can be displayed on the computer screen.

The processor unit, which contains main memory and the central processing unit (CPU), consists of circuit boards inside a housing called the **system unit**. In addition to the CPU and main memory, circuit boards inside the system unit contain electronic components that allow communication with the input, output, and auxiliary storage devices.

Data can be transferred from main memory and stored on a diskette or a hard disk. Computers can have a single diskette drive, two diskette drives, one diskette drive and one hard disk drive, or several other combinations. The keyboard, system unit, printer, screen, and auxiliary storage devices are called **computer hardware**.

WHAT IS COMPUTER SOFTWARE?

◆ A computer's input, processing, output, and storage operations are controlled by instructions collectively called a **computer program**, or **software**. A computer program specifies the sequence in which operations are to occur in the computer. For example, a program may give instructions that allow data to be entered from a keyboard and stored in main memory. Another time, the program might issue an instruction to perform a calculation using data in main memory. When a task has been completed, a program could give instructions to direct the computer to print a report, display information on the screen, draw a color graph on a color display unit, or store data on a diskette. When directing the operations to be performed, a program must be stored in main memory. Computer programs are written by computer programmers.

Most computer users purchase the software they need for their computer systems. The two major categories of computer software are (1) application software and (2) system software.

Application Software

Application software allows you to perform an application-related function on a computer. A wide variety of programs is available, but for microcomputers, the three most widely used types of application software are word processing, spreadsheet, and database management.

Word Processing Software **Word processing software** enables you to use a computer to create documents. As you use a word processing program, words are keyed in, displayed on the screen, and stored in main memory. If necessary, you can easily correct errors by adding or deleting words, sentences, paragraphs, or pages. You can also establish margins, define page lengths, and perform many other functions involving the manipulation of the written word. After you have created and corrected your text, you can print it and store it on auxiliary storage for reuse or future reference.

Spreadsheet Software **Spreadsheet software** is used for reporting and decision making within organizations. At home, you can use a spreadsheet program for budgeting, income tax planning, or tracking your favorite team's scores. You might choose spreadsheet software to enter the values and formulas you need to perform these calculations. One of the more powerful features of spreadsheet application software is its capability to handle what-if questions such as, *What would be the effect on profit if sales increased 12% this year?* The values on the worksheet could easily be recalculated to provide the answer.

Database Software **Database software** is used to store, organize, update, and retrieve data. Once stored in the database, data can be organized and retrieved in the manner you specify. For example, in a database containing employee information, you could request a report showing an alphabetical list of all employees in the accounting department.

System Software

System software consists of programs that start up the computer—load, execute, store, and retrieve files—and perform a series of utility functions. A part of the system software available with most computers is the operating system. An **operating system** is a collection of programs that provides an interface between you or your application programs and the computer hardware itself to control and manage the operation of the computer.

System software, including operating systems, available on computers performs the following basic functions: (1) booting, or starting, the computer operation, (2) interfacing with users, and (3) coordinating the system's access to its various devices.

Booting the Computer When a computer is turned on, the operating system is loaded into main memory by a set of instructions contained internally within the hardware of the computer. This process is called **booting** the computer. When the operating system is loaded into main memory, it is stored in a portion of main memory.

Interface with Users To communicate with the operating system, the user must enter commands that the operating system can interpret and upon which it can act. The commands can vary from copying a file from one diskette to another, to loading and executing application software.

Coordinating System Devices   Computer hardware is constructed with electrical connections from one device to another. The operating system translates a program's requirements to access a specific hardware device, such as a printer. The operating system can also sense whether the devices are ready for use, or if there is some problem in using a device, such as a printer not being turned on and, therefore, not ready to receive output.

SUMMARY OF INTRODUCTION TO COMPUTERS

As you learn to use the software we teach in this book, you will also become familiar with the components and operation of your computer system. You can refer to this introduction when you need help understanding how the components of your system function.

SUMMARY

1. A **computer** is an electronic device operating under the control of instructions stored in its memory unit.
2. All computers perform basically the same four operations: **input**, **processing**, **output**, and **storage**.
3. **Data** may be defined as the numbers, words, and phrases that are given to the computer during the input operation and processed to produce information.
4. The four basic components of a computer are input unit, processor unit, output unit, and auxiliary storage units.
5. **Information** can be defined as data that has been processed into a form that has meaning and is useful.
6. The **keyboard** is the most common input unit. It consists of typewriter like keys, a numeric keypad, cursor control keys, and programmable function keys.
7. The computer's **processing unit** consists of the **central processing unit (CPU)** and **main memory**.
8. Output units consist primarily of printers and screens. **Printers** can be impact or nonimpact. **Screens** can be monochrome or color.
9. A **dot matrix printer** forms characters by printing a series of dots to form the character.
10. **Page printers** produce very high-quality text and graphic output. **Laser printers** are the most popular type of page printers.
11. **Auxiliary storage** on a personal computer is generally disk storage. Disk storage may be on a 5¼-inch or 3½-inch **diskette**, or it may be on a **hard disk**.
12. New diskettes must be formatted before they can be used to store data.
13. Computer software can be classified as either **system software**, such as the **operating system**, or as **application software**, such as a word processing, spreadsheet, or database program.

STUDENT ASSIGNMENTS

STUDENT ASSIGNMENT 1: True/False

Instructions: Circle T if the statement is true and F if the statement is false.

T F   1. The basic operations performed by a computer system are input operations, processing operations, output operations, and storage operations.

T F   2. Data can be defined as numbers, words, or phrases suitable for processing to produce information.

T F   3. A commonly used input unit on most personal computers is the keyboard.

T F   4. A mouse is a hand-held scanner device for input.
T F   5. The central processing unit contains the processor unit and main memory.
T F   6. A computer with 640K can store approximately 64,000 characters.
T F   7. Auxiliary storage is used to store instructions and data when they are not being used in main memory.
T F   8. The diskette is considered to be a form of main memory.
T F   9. A commonly used 5¼-inch double-sided, double-density diskette can store approximately 360,000 characters.
T F 10. Diskettes can normally store more data than hard disks.
T F 11. A computer program is often referred to as computer software.
T F 12. A computer program must be permanently stored in main memory.
T F 13. Programs such as database management, spreadsheet, and word processing software are called system software.
T F 14. The cursor is a mechanical device attached to the keyboard.
T F 15. Page Up, Page Down, Home, and End are function keys.
T F 16. A laser printer is one form of impact printer.
T F 17. A dot matrix printer forms characters or graphics by forming images as a closely spaced series of dots.
T F 18. Application software is the type of program you will use to perform activities such as word processing on a computer.
T F 19. The operating system is a collection of programs that provides an interface between the user, the application program, and the computer equipment.

STUDENT ASSIGNMENT 2: Multiple Choice

Instructions: Circle the correct response.

1. An operating system is considered part of _____.
   a. word processing software
   b. database software
   c. system software
   d. spreadsheet software
2. The four operations performed by a computer include _____.
   a. input, control, output, and storage
   b. interface, processing, output, and memory
   c. input, output, processing, and storage
   d. input, logical/rational, arithmetic, and output
3. Data can be defined as _____.
   a. a typed report   c. a graph
   b. raw facts   d. both a and c
4. Logical operations compare data to determine if one value is _____.
   a. less than another value
   b. equal to another value
   c. greater than another value
   d. all of the above
5. A hand-held input device that controls the cursor location is _____.
   a. the cursor control keyboard
   b. a mouse
   c. a scanner
   d. the CRT
6. A printer that forms images without striking the paper is _____.
   a. an impact printer   c. an ink jet printer
   b. a nonimpact printer   d. both b and c
7. A screen that displays only a single color is _____.
   a. a multichrome monitor
   b. an upper-lower character display
   c. a 7-by-9 matrix screen
   d. a monochrome screen
8. Auxiliary storage unit is the name given to _____.
   a. the computer's main memory
   b. disk drives
   c. instruction storage buffers
   d. none of the above
9. A diskette is _____.
   a. a nonremovable form of storage
   b. available in 5¼- and 3½-inch sizes
   c. a form of magnetic data storage
   d. both b and c
10. The amount of storage provided by a diskette is a function of _____.
    a. whether the diskette records on one or both sides
    b. the recording pattern or density of bits on the diskette
    c. the number of recording tracks used on the track
    d. all of the above
11. Diskettes have an access window that is used to _____.
    a. pick up and insert the diskette into a disk drive
    b. provide access for cleaning
    c. provide access for the read/write head of the disk drive
    d. verify data stored on the diskette

12. When not in use, diskettes should be _____.
    a. stored away from magnetic fields
    b. stored away from heat and direct sunlight
    c. stored in a diskette box or cabinet
    d. all of the above
13. A hard disk is _____.
    a. an alternate form of removable storage
    b. a rigid platter coated with a metal oxide material
    c. a storage system that remains installed in the computer
    d. both b and c

14. Storage capacities of hard disks _____.
    a. are about the same as for diskettes
    b. range from 80,000 to 256,000 bytes
    c. range from 20 million to over 300 million characters
    d. vary with the type of program used
15. Software is classified as _____.
    a. utility and applied systems
    b. application and system software
    c. language translators and task managers
    d. word processing and spreadsheet programs

PROJECTS

Instructions: Complete the following projects.

1. Popular computer magazines contain many articles and advertisements that inform computer users of the latest in computing trends. Review a few recent articles and report on the apparent trends you have found. Discuss which hardware features seem to be the most in demand. What are the differences between the alternative hardware choices?
2. According to your reading of computer magazines, what software innovations seem to have the greatest promise? Which specific software features seem to offer new computing capabilities? Discuss any particular program that seems to be a style setter in its field.
3. Visit local computer retail stores to compare the various types of computers and supporting equipment available. Ask about warranties, repair services, hardware setup, training, and related issues. Report on the knowledge of the sales staff assisting you and their willingness to answer your questions. Does the store have standard hardware packages, or are they willing to configure a system to your specific needs? Would you feel confident about buying a computer from this store?

◆ INDEX

Photo Credits: *Opening Page*, Digital Art/West Light; *Figure 1*, (left) Courtesy of Apple Computer, Inc.; (right) Reprinted with permission of Compaq Computer Corp. All rights reserved.; *Figure 2*, Intel Corp.; *Figure 4⓪*, Curtis Fukuda, *4⓫*, International Business Machines Corp.; *Figure 5*, Logitech, Inc.; *Figure 6*, Courtesy of Panasonic Communications and Systems Company; *Figure 9*, (left and right) Hewlett-Packard Company; *Figure 11*, (left) Wyse Technology; (right) International Business Machines Corp.; *Figure 12*, Jerry Spagnoli; *Figure 13*, Greg Hadel; *Figure 17*, Jerry Spagnoli; *Figure 18*, Courtesy of Microscience International Corp.; *Figure 19*, International Business Machines Corp.

Introduction to DOS

PROJECTS

D O S

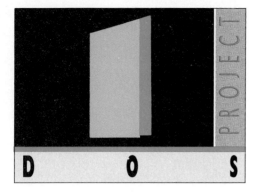

Working with Files on Disks

OBJECTIVES

You will have mastered the material in this project when you can:

◆ Boot your computer
◆ Enter the time and date, if required
◆ Establish the default disk drive
◆ Use file specifications for files stored on disk
◆ Distinguish between internal and external commands
◆ Format disks
◆ Clear the screen
◆ Copy files from one disk to another disk and to the same disk
◆ List a disk directory
◆ Rename files
◆ Display a file's contents and print a screen image
◆ Remove files

INTRODUCTION

An **operating system** is a collection of programs that controls and manages the operation of the computer. These programs allow you, the computer equipment, and the application software to communicate. To use a computer to print a memo, for example, you first use the operating system to start the computer. You next enter a command that the operating system processes to start the word processing program. When you instruct the word processing program to print the memo, the operating system finds the memo file on disk, retrieves the data from the disk, and routes the output to the printer. The operating system is not part of the application software itself, but it provides essential services that the application software uses to perform its functions for you.

When you use an application program, such as a word processor, a spreadsheet, or a database manager, the application program handles the interaction with the operating system. If you are not using an application program, however, and want to list or view your disk files, for example, you must directly interact with the operating system. To use your computer effectively, you need to know when and how to interact with the operating system. In Project 1 you will learn how to use the operating system called DOS to work with your disk files.

Operating Systems for IBM PCs

Microsoft Corporation developed the operating system known as **DOS** (pronounced doss, not dose), an acronym for **Disk Operating System**. DOS has been used since 1981 in IBM PC and IBM-compatible microcomputers. **PC-DOS** is the name for versions of DOS distributed by IBM for its Personal Computer and Personal System/2 lines of microcomputers. All IBM-compatible microcomputers use versions of DOS distributed by Microsoft under the name **MS-DOS**. PC-DOS and MS-DOS are essentially the same. We use the term DOS to refer to any of the various editions of PC- or MS-DOS and cover information applicable to all versions of DOS.

DOS Versions

The numbers following the abbreviation DOS indicate the specific version and release of the product (Figure 1-1). The **version** number is the whole number and signifies a major improvement of the product. The **release** number is the decimal number and identifies minor changes or corrections to a version of the product. For example, DOS 1.1 corrected some minor problems with DOS 1.0.

DOS VERSION RELEASE	MAJOR FEATURES SUPPORTED	YEAR
5.0	Improved Memory Management, Task Switching	1991
4.0	Hard Disks Larger than 32MB, File Manager Shell, Memory Support Beyond 640KB	1988
3.3	Introduction of IBM PS/2	1987
3.2	Token-Ring Networks, 3.5" Diskette Drive	1985
3.1	Addition of Networking, 1.2MB 5.25" Diskette Drive	1984
3.0	Introduction of IBM PC/AT	1984
2.0	Introduction of IBM PC/XT	1983
1.1	Enhancements to 1.0	1982
1.0	Introduction of IBM PC	1981

FIGURE 1-1 DOS versions and releases with their major supported features

Software developers try to maintain **upward compatibility**, that is, that all the features of an earlier version and release remain supported by a later one. Downward compatibility, however, is not common. Programs or equipment that require the features of DOS 3.3, for example, will not function with DOS 3.2 or earlier versions.

Disk Configurations

You will likely use a computer with one of three common disk configurations. The first configuration has a hard disk and one diskette drive (Figure 1-2). Each drive has a **drive name**, which is a unique one-letter name preassigned to the drive. The hard disk drive name is C, and the diskette drive name is A.

The second configuration has two diskette drives and no hard disk (Figure 1-3). Drive A is the top or left drive, and drive B is the bottom or right drive.

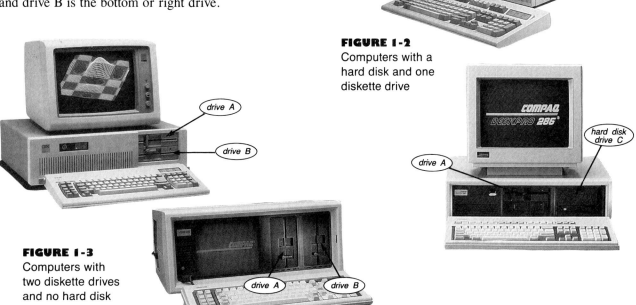

FIGURE 1-2
Computers with a hard disk and one diskette drive

FIGURE 1-3
Computers with two diskette drives and no hard disk

The third configuration connects your computer through a local area network with other computers (Figure 1-4).

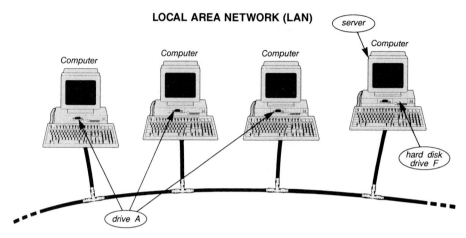

LOCAL AREA NETWORK (LAN)

FIGURE 1-4   Computers connected through a local area network (LAN)

A **local area network**, or **LAN**, is a collection of connected computers that share data. One special computer on the LAN, called the **server**, has a high-capacity hard disk that contains files that you can access from your computer. The server hard disk is usually drive F. Your computer would typically have a drive A with or without a drive C hard disk.

The DOS projects assume you have a drive A diskette drive and a drive C hard disk, unless otherwise noted. If you are using a computer with a different configuration, your instructor will instruct you on the changes you need to make for the DOS projects.

STARTING THE COMPUTER

DOS programs are stored on a hard disk or on a diskette. To begin using DOS, the operating system must be read into main memory, which is a process known as **booting**. How you begin to use the computer depends on your specific disk configuration and whether the computer has already been turned on.

On a LAN

If you are using a computer on a LAN, the laboratory attendant will have already booted your computer. You do not need to perform any start-up activities, unless your instructor gives you special instructions.

With Computer Power Off

Starting the computer by turning on the power switch is known as a **cold start**, or **cold boot**. The computer first runs some tests to diagnose its own circuitry and then loads DOS into main memory from the hard disk or your DOS diskette.

Hard Disk   If you are using a computer with a hard disk, DOS is available on the hard disk. Turn on the power switch and be certain you do not insert a disk in drive A. While DOS is booting, the hard disk status light flashes on and off for a few seconds as DOS is loaded into main memory.

Two Diskette Drives and No Hard Drive   If you are using a computer with two diskette drives and no hard disk, insert the DOS diskette in drive A and turn on the power switch. While DOS is booting, the status light for drive A flashes on and off, and drive A whirls for several seconds as DOS is loaded into main memory.

With Computer Power On

If the computer is already turned on, you can restart the computer without turning the power switch off and on. Restarting the computer in this way is called a **warm start**, **warm boot**, or **reset** because the computer power is already on. The warm start reloads DOS from disk but does not repeat the circuitry tests.

Hard Disk   If you are using a computer with a hard disk, be certain you do not insert a disk in drive A during a warm start. Hold down the Ctrl and Alt keys, press the Delete key, and then release all three keys to begin the warm start. During the warm start the hard disk status light flashes on and off for a few seconds as DOS is loaded into main memory.

Two Diskette Drives and No Hard Drive   If you are using a computer with two diskette drives and no hard disk, insert the DOS diskette in drive A before you begin a warm start. Hold down the Ctrl and Alt keys, press the Delete key, and then release all three keys to begin the warm start. During the warm start the status light for drive A flashes on and off, and drive A whirls for several seconds as DOS is loaded into main memory.

USING THE DISK OPERATING SYSTEM (DOS)

Setting the Date and Time

Many of today's computers have batteries that accurately maintain the date and time even when the computer power is off. Some computers, however, require that you enter the date and time and will display a message similar to Figure 1-5 after you boot DOS.

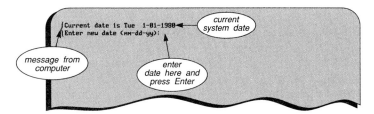

FIGURE 1-5   The request to enter the date

You would enter the month, day, and year as one-digit or two-digit numbers separated by hyphens (–), slashes (/), or, in DOS 3.3 and later versions, periods (.). If today is October 9, 1994, for example, you would type 10-9-94 and press the Enter key (Figure 1-6). Check with your instructor if you are not certain how to enter the date on your computer. If the date displayed is already correct, you do not need to enter the date. Instead, press the Enter key when the message "Enter new date: (mm-dd-yy):" appears on the screen.

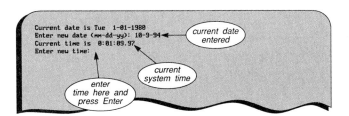

FIGURE 1-6   The request to enter the time

After you have entered the date, you enter the time in the format hh:mm:ss.xx, where hh stands for hours using the 24-hour system, mm stands for minutes, ss stands for seconds, and xx stands for hundredths of a second. If you need to enter the time, for practice, type the time as 11:50 and press the Enter key (Figure 1-7). When you do not include seconds and hundredths of seconds as in this case, DOS assumes a value of zero for them.

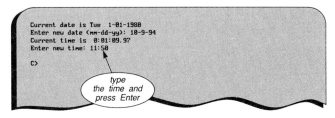

FIGURE 1-7   Date and time entered

The DOS Prompt

After the date and time messages and other messages tailored for your specific computer appear, DOS displays the **DOS prompt**, indicating that DOS is ready to receive your commands (Figures 1-8 through 1-10). The letter displayed before the > symbol shows which drive has been assigned as the default disk drive. The **default drive** is the drive that DOS assumes contains the disk where programs and data are located. Another term used for the default drive is **current drive** because it is the drive that is assumed to be currently used by DOS to first look at for files. If your DOS prompt is not exactly the same as one of those shown in Figures 1-8 through 1-10, your instructor will explain the difference to you.

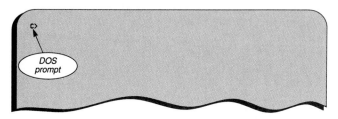

FIGURE 1-8   DOS prompt after booting from a hard disk

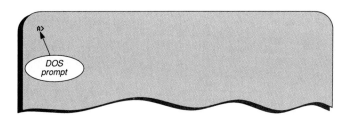

FIGURE 1-9   DOS prompt after booting from a diskette

FIGURE 1-10   DOS prompt after booting from a LAN

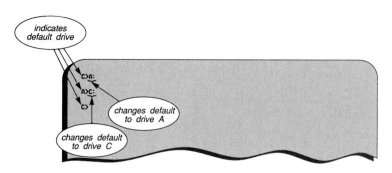

FIGURE 1-11   Changing the default drive using a hard disk

The Default Drive

The default drive assignment will vary depending on the specific hardware you are using. A hard disk computer assigns drive C as the default drive as shown in Figure 1-8. If your computer has two diskette drives and no hard disk, drive A is the default drive, and the prompt appears as shown in Figure 1-9. Drive F is usually the default drive on a LAN as shown in Figure 1-10.

At times you will need to change the default drive assignment. Before you do, be certain that the new drive is ready. If your computer has a hard disk, it is always installed and ready, as is the server hard disk on a LAN. A diskette drive on some computers, however, must have a diskette inserted before it can be assigned as the default drive.

To change the drive assignment, you would type the letter of the new drive to be used, followed by a colon (:), and then press the Enter key. If you have a hard disk with a DOS prompt of C >, change the default to drive A by placing a diskette in drive A, typing the letter A, followed by a colon, and then pressing the Enter key. The DOS prompt will now display drive A as the default drive. Now, change the default drive back to drive C by typing C : and pressing the Enter key (Figure 1-11).

In most of our examples, we assume a hard disk on your computer with drive C as the default drive and drive A as the second drive. If you have two diskette drives and no hard disk, drive A will be your default drive and drive B your second drive. On a LAN, drive F will be your default drive and drive A your second drive. We will point out when the *procedures* for a two-diskette or LAN configuration are different than those for a hard disk configuration. In most cases, the procedures are similar for each configuration with only the drive letters differing, so we will assume you will make the appropriate changes for your configuration.

Figure 1-12, for example, shows how to change the default drive with two diskette drives from drive A to drive B and back to drive A.

Figure 1-13, on the other hand, shows how to change the default drive on a LAN from drive F to drive A and back to drive F. For practice, follow Figure 1-11, 1-12, or 1-13 to complete these appropriate two steps for your computer.

Notice that you use a **drive specifier** consisting of the colon (:) with a one-letter disk drive name. Whenever you refer to a specific disk drive, type the letter designating the drive followed by the colon, such as A:, B:, C:, or F:.

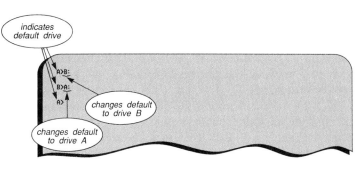

FIGURE 1-12 Changing the default drive on a two-diskette computer

Entering DOS Commands

Now that you have booted DOS, you can enter DOS commands. DOS includes a variety of commands, or instructions, to assist you in using the computer. Some commands might be called status, or informative, commands because they instruct DOS to give you information. Other commands direct DOS to perform functions for you. We show all DOS commands in capital letters for consistency. You can enter commands, drive names, and other entries to DOS, in any combination of uppercase and lowercase.

FIGURE 1-13 Changing the default drive using a LAN

ASSIGNING NAMES TO FILES

A **data file** is a collection of data created by application programs and used by the programs. For instance, the data can be figures used for a spreadsheet showing sales revenues, names and addresses in a database file, or a word processing document announcing the arrival of a new employee. A **program file** contains instructions that the computer follows to perform its tasks. The program might be a DOS program or one of the application programs such as a word processing or spreadsheet program.

DOS identifies a file on a disk through the file specification for the file (Figure 1-14). A **file specification** lets DOS know exactly where to search for a file and gives its exact name. A DOS file specification has four parts: (1) the drive specifier, which you already know as A:, B:, C:, or F:; (2) a path specification (explained later in Project 2); (3) the filename; and (4) the extension.

NAME	LEGEND	DEFINITION
1. Drive specifier	d:	A drive specifier consists of the one-letter drive name and a colon. The drive name specifies the drive containing the file you are requesting. For example, A: is the drive specifier for disk drive A. If you omit the drive specifier, DOS assumes the file is located on the default drive.
2. Path specification	\path	A path is an optional reference to a subdirectory of files on the specified disk. A backslash (\) separates the drive specifier from the path. Paths are discussed in Project 2.
3. Filename	filename	A filename consists of one to eight characters.
4. Extension	ext	A filename can contain an optional extension of one to three characters. A period separates the filename and the extension.

FIGURE 1-14 The four parts to a DOS file specification

Filenames

You must assign a filename to every data and program file you place on disk so that you can later retrieve it using that filename. A **filename** consists of one to eight characters and is used by DOS to identify each file. You can use any combination of characters except: period (.), quotation mark ("), slash (/), backslash (\), brackets ([]), colon (:), broken vertical bar (¦), less than (<), greater than (>), plus (+), equals (=), semicolon (;), comma (,), and space. DOS 5.0 also does not allow the question mark (?) and asterisk (*) in a filename.

In general, your filename should reflect the data stored in it. If your file contains employee records, for example, using the filename EMPLOYEE is more meaningful than using the filename FILE1, even though DOS will accept either filename.

Filename Extensions

A filename can also have an optional extension, which identifies a file more specifically or describes its purpose. An **extension** consists of one to three characters and is separated from the filename by a period. The same characters that are permitted for a filename are permitted for an extension. If you want to create a word processing document file containing a letter to Smith, for example, you could use the filename SMITH and the extension .DOC to identify the file as a document file. The entire name for the file would be SMITH.DOC. Many software packages automatically assign special extensions to the files they create.

INTERNAL AND EXTERNAL DOS COMMANDS

An **internal command** is part of DOS that is loaded into main memory when you boot. After you boot DOS, you can enter an internal command at the DOS prompt at any time. CLS, COPY, DEL, DIR, ERASE, and RENAME are examples of internal commands that you will use in Project 1.

External commands, are stored on the DOS disk as program files. They must be read from the DOS disk into main memory before they can be executed. This means that the DOS disk must be in the default drive or that you type the drive specifier so that the program can be found and loaded into main memory for execution. FORMAT and MORE are examples of external commands that you will use in Project 1.

All DOS external commands have the special extensions COM and EXE. Another special extension is BAT that is used for **DOS batch files** containing a series of DOS commands to be executed. Any DOS command with one of these three extensions (BAT, COM, and EXE) is an external command. To use external commands, simply type the filename (the extension is not required) with its required parameters and press the Enter key.

FORMAT COMMAND

You can buy disks that you can use immediately. Many disks, however, are blank and cannot be used until they have been formatted. You format a disk using the DOS **FORMAT** command. The **formatting** process establishes sectors on the disk and performs other functions that allow the disk to store data. Be careful when you select disks to use with the FORMAT command. *Formatting a disk destroys all the files previously stored on the disk.* You must be extremely careful, therefore, with the disks you format and how you type the FORMAT command. With a hard disk, take extra precaution to avoid losing files by formatting the hard disk accidentally. DOS versions 3.0 and later provide some protection against accidental formatting of a hard disk, but your own precautions are still the best insurance.

Disks vary by size and recording density, so your FORMAT command might differ from our description. If it does, your instructor will tell you what changes you need to make.

If you have a hard disk, the FORMAT program is stored on drive C, the hard disk. Be careful not to format drive C accidentally. To format a disk in drive A from a hard disk, type FORMAT A: at the C> prompt and press the Enter key (Figure 1-15).

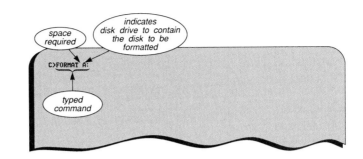

FIGURE 1-15
Entering the FORMAT com-
mand from a hard disk

If you are using a LAN, the FORMAT program is stored on drive F, the server hard disk. To format a disk in drive A using a LAN, type FORMAT A: at the F> prompt and press the Enter key (Figure 1-16).

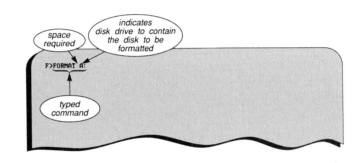

FIGURE 1-16
Entering the FORMAT com-
mand using a LAN

To format a disk on a two-diskette computer, place the DOS disk in drive A, making sure that drive A is the default drive. Type the command FORMAT B: and press the Enter key (Figure 1-17).

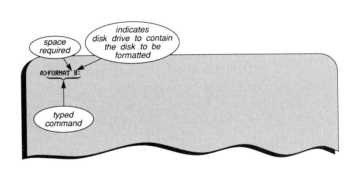

FIGURE 1-17
Entering the FORMAT com-
mand on a two-diskette
computer

When you press the Enter key, DOS loads the FORMAT program into main memory and executes the program. If you are using a hard disk, a message appears on the screen instructing you to "Insert new diskette for drive A: and strike ENTER when ready" (Figure 1-18). [For DOS 5.0 Users – The message will be "Insert new diskette for drive A: and press Enter when ready...".]

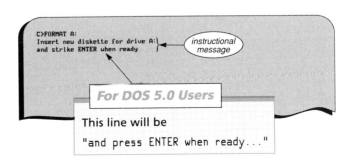

FIGURE 1-18
FORMAT message for inserting a disk using a hard disk

The responses for a LAN and two-diskette computer are shown in Figures 1-19 and 1-20, respectively.

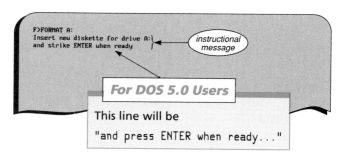

FIGURE 1-19
FORMAT message for inserting a disk using a LAN

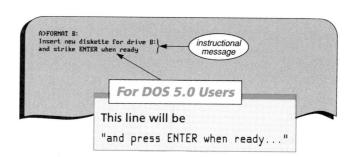

FIGURE 1-20
FORMAT message for inserting a disk on a two-diskette computer

To complete the format process, place the disk to be formatted into the appropriate drive (drive A for a computer with a hard disk or on a LAN; drive B for a two-diskette computer) and press the Enter key. While formatting occurs, a message appears on the screen indicating that the process is underway. Figure 1-21 shows the message on a computer with a hard disk or on a LAN, and Figure 1-22 shows the message from a two-diskette computer. Messages will differ slightly depending on the version of DOS and the type of disk you are using.

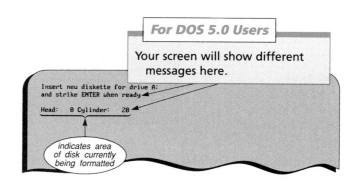

FIGURE 1-21
Message appearing when formatting using a hard disk or LAN

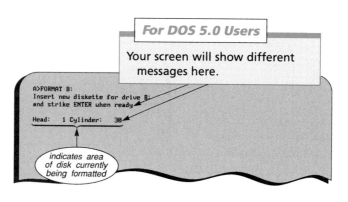

FIGURE 1-22
Message appearing when formatting using a two-diskette computer

When the formatting process is complete, the messages shown in Figure 1-23 appear. [For DOS 5.0 Users – Your screen will show different messages.] The FORMAT program reports that the disk is formatted for a total number of bytes and that all bytes are available for storage. The next FORMAT program prompt asks you if you want to format another disk. If you do, type the letter Y and press the Enter key to continue the formatting process. If you do not, type the letter N and press the Enter key to end the FORMAT program.

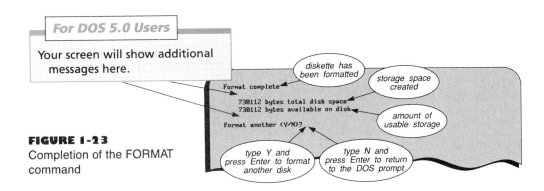

FIGURE 1-23
Completion of the FORMAT command

CLS COMMAND

Frequently, as you issue several commands or perform lengthy processes, the screen becomes cluttered. To clear the screen and place the DOS prompt on the first line of the screen, you can use the **CLS** (Clear Screen) command. Type the letters CLS and press the Enter key to execute the Clear Screen command (Figure 1-24).

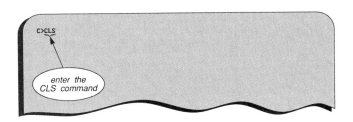

FIGURE 1-24
CLS (Clear Screen) command

COPY COMMAND

Once you have formatted a disk, you are ready to use it to store data or program files. You can use the **COPY** command to copy a file to the same disk or a different disk. You would often use the COPY command to make *working* copies of program and data disks. Copying original files from one disk creates a second disk that you can use for everyday work to protect the original disk from damage. A similar use for the COPY command is to make a **backup copy** of a disk to guard against accidental loss of data. One frequently used technique is to make a backup copy of a file whenever you revise an existing file. In fact, some application programs create a backup file automatically, using the filename extension BAK or BAC to indicate a backup file.

Copying a File from One Disk to Another Disk

Let's practice using the COPY command by copying files from drive C to drive A. Check to see that you still have your formatted disk in drive A. If you are using a two-diskette computer, place your formatted disk in drive B, and place the Data Disk provided to instructors in drive A. In this latter case, you will copy files from drive A to drive B.

Let's begin by copying the file DOSNOTES.DOC from drive C to drive A. Your instructor will make the DOSNOTES.DOC file available to you or will give you the name of another file to copy. Type COPY C:DOSNOTES.DOC A:DOSNOTES.DOC and press the Enter key (Figure 1-25). Notice that after the word COPY you left one or more spaces, then stated the file specification of the file to be copied. In DOS terminology, this file is called the **source file**. DOS looks for a source file with a filename of DOSNOTES and an extension of DOC on drive C.

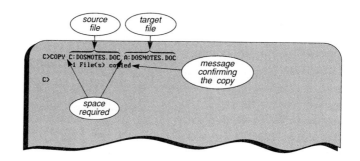

FIGURE 1-25
Copying a file to another disk

You leave one or more spaces after the source file. Then, you type the **target file**, which is the file specification of the file after it is copied. The drive specifier A: in Figure 1-25 indicates that the file is to be copied to a disk in drive A. The name of the file on drive A will be DOSNOTES.DOC. The message "1 File(s) copied" signals that the command is completed. You end up with a DOSNOTES.DOC file on both the disk in drive C and the disk in drive A.

When you copy a file from a disk in one drive to a disk in another drive, you can assign a new name to the target file. Let's copy the file DOSNOTES.DOC from drive C to the disk in drive A, giving the target file the name NOTECOPY.DUP on drive A. Type COPY C:DOSNOTES.DOC A:NOTECOPY.DUP and press the Enter key (Figure 1-26). You now have the two files with the names DOSNOTES.DOC and NOTECOPY.DUP on the disk in drive A.

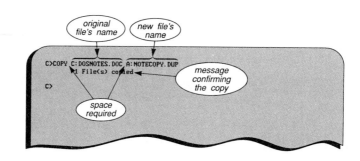

FIGURE 1-26
Coping a file to another disk using a different name for the target file

Copying a File to the Same Disk

You can copy a file to the same disk, but you must use a different name for the file. Let's copy the file named DOSNOTES.DOC stored on drive A onto the same disk. Give the filename DOSNOTES.BAK to the target file. Type the command COPY A:DOSNOTES.DOC A:DOSNOTES.BAK and press the Enter key (Figure 1-27).

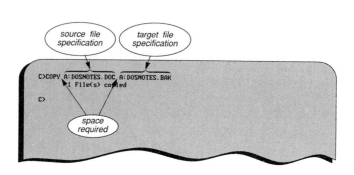

FIGURE 1-27
Copying a file to the same disk

When the COPY command is executed, the file DOSNOTES.DOC in drive A is copied to the same disk in drive A under the name DOSNOTES.BAK. The two different extensions of DOC and BAK are used to distinguish between the files.

What would happen if you use the same file specification to designate both the source and target files? Let's try it and see. Type COPY A:DOSNOTES.DOC A:DOSNOTES.DOC and press the Enter key (Figure 1-28).

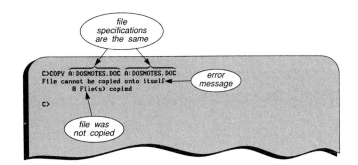

FIGURE 1-28
Error in attempting to copy a file onto itself

The messages "File cannot be copied onto itself" and "0 File(s) copied" indicate that DOS did not execute the COPY command. If you do want to make a copy of the source file, you have to reenter the COPY command using a different name for the target file.

ENTERING AND CORRECTING DOS COMMANDS

Even if you are an expert typist, you will sometimes make mistakes when you enter DOS commands. Fortunately, DOS provides several keys to allow you to correct the mistakes you make.

For example, you might want to enter the command COPY C:DOSNOTES.DOC A:DOSNOTES.BAC. Instead, type COOY. Now press the Backspace key twice to delete the OY, leaving just the CO following the DOS prompt. Pressing the **Backspace** key deletes the character to the left of the cursor and moves the cursor left one position.

Next, type PU V:DOSNOTES.DOC A:DOSNOTES.BAC, but do not press the Enter key. You could press the Backspace key several times to delete all the characters you typed except the COP, which are the first three typed characters on the line. Instead, press the **Esc** key once. A backslash (\) appears at the end of the typed line, and the cursor advances to the next line (Figure 1-29). You are now back at the beginning of the line and can begin over again; this is the same result as if you had pressed the Backspace key thirty-four times.

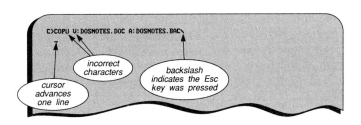

FIGURE 1-29
Using the Esc key

Let's now type COPY C:DOSNOTES.DOC A:DOSFILE.DOC and press the Enter key. You have just created a copy of the DOSNOTES.DOC file on drive C to drive A with a name for the target file of DOSFILE.DOC. Suppose you next want to recopy the same source file to drive A, but this time with a name of DOSFILE.BAK. Press the **F3** key once, and DOS automatically retypes the previous COPY command on the screen. Press the Backspace key three times, type BAK, and press the Enter key (on the next page in Figure 1-30). The F3 key retypes your previous command and is useful when you want to make minor changes at the end of your previous command.

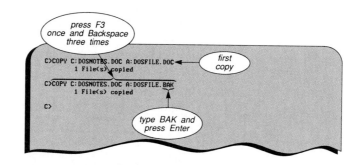

FIGURE 1-30
Using the F3 key

DIRECTORY COMMAND (DIR)

One of the functions of DOS is to store files containing programs and data on disks. To manage that file storage, DOS maintains a directory, or a list, of all the files stored on a disk. To display the directory of a disk, use the **DIR** command.

If you are using a hard disk or LAN, your disk should still be in drive A. Type DIR A: and press the Enter key. The directory of the disk in drive A displays as shown in Figure 1-31. [For DOS 5.0 Users – Your screen shows additional messages.]

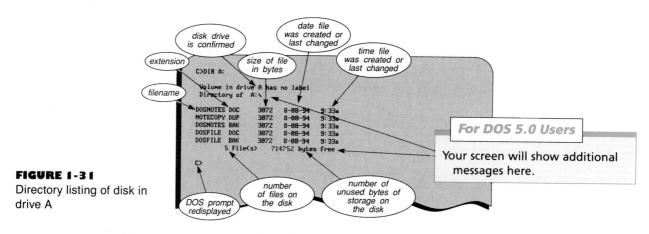

FIGURE 1-31
Directory listing of disk in drive A

The directory itself consists of the filenames and extensions of the files on the disk, the number of bytes used to store each file on the disk, the file creation date or the date of the last change to each file, and the file creation time or the time of the last change to each file. The message at the end of the directory listing indicates the number of files on the disk (in Figure 1-31 there are five files on the disk) and the remaining space available on the disk (714752 unused bytes remain on the disk in Figure 1-31, but your number might differ if your disk has a different recording density). At the end of the directory listing, the DOS prompt reappears on the screen, indicating that DOS is ready for your next command.

RENAME COMMAND

You use the **RENAME** command when you want to change the name of a file on a disk. For practice, let's change the filename NOTECOPY.DUP on drive A to NOTEFILE.DOC. Start by typing the command RENAME A:NOTECOPY.DUP NOTEFILE.DOC and pressing the Enter key (Figure 1-32). When you press the Enter key, the filename on the disk in drive A is changed from NOTECOPY.DUP to NOTEFILE.DOC. DOS does not display a message confirming a successful renaming of the file.

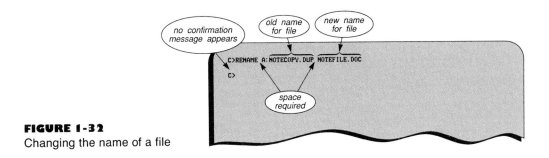

FIGURE 1-32
Changing the name of a file

You must be careful not to place a drive specifier on a file specification for the file's new name. Let's see what happens if you do. Type RENAME A:NOTEFILE.DOC A:NOTECOPY.DUP and press the Enter key (Figure 1-33). The message "Invalid parameter" appears because you typed the A: drive specifier for the new name for the file. DOS did not rename the file, so its name is still NOTEFILE.DOC.

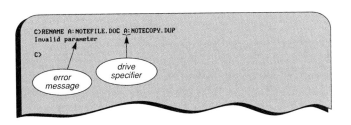

FIGURE 1-33
Error when renaming a file
and using a drive specifier on
the new name for the file

If you attempt to change a file's name to a name already used by a file on the disk, DOS displays an error message and does not change the name. Let's demonstrate this. Type the command RENAME A:NOTEFILE.DOC DOSNOTES.DOC and press the Enter key (Figure 1-34). The message "Duplicate file name or File not found" indicates that DOS found a file already on the disk with a name of DOSNOTES.DOC, so DOS did not change the name of the file.

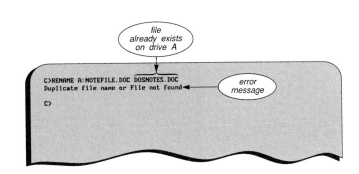

FIGURE 1-34
Error when renaming a file to
a name that already exists

DISPLAYING AND PRINTING FILES

◆ DOS allows you to display the contents of your files on the screen and to print screen images on your printer. You can use the MORE command to display files and the Print Screen key to print screen images.

MORE Command

You can use the **MORE** command to display the contents of a file on the screen. Because the MORE command is an external command, make sure you have the DOS diskette in drive A if you are using a two-diskette computer. For practice, let's display the contents of the file DOSNOTES.DOC located on drive A. Type MORE <A:DOSNOTES.DOC and press the Enter key (Figure 1-35); be certain that you type the less than symbol (<) immediately before A:DOSNOTES.DOC.

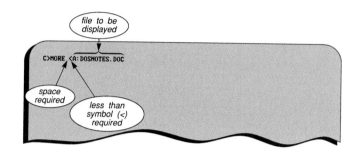

FIGURE 1-35
The MORE command to display a file's contents

After you press the Enter key, DOS displays the first full screen of lines from the file DOSNOTES.DOC (Figure 1-36). The message "-- More --" at the bottom of the screen indicates that more lines from the file remain to be displayed and that you should press any key to view the next screenful of lines from the file. Next, press any key to view the second screen of lines from the DOSNOTES.DOC file. DOS displays the second full screen of lines from the file, and the message "-- More --" again appears at the bottom of the screen. Once more press any key to display the next screen of lines from the file. This time you are returned to the DOS prompt, which indicates that you have viewed all the lines from the file.

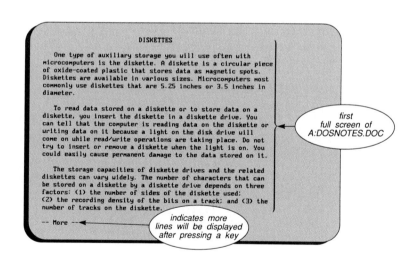

FIGURE 1-36
Display of a file using the MORE command

Print Screen

You can print the contents of the screen on the printer by using the **Print Screen** key (Shift-PrtSc on some key-boards). For practice, be sure your printer is turned on and that paper is inserted and properly aligned. Type MORE <A:DOSNOTES.DOC and press the Enter key. After the first full screen is displayed, press the Print Screen key. In response, DOS prints the contents of the screen on the printer. You can use the Print Screen key to generate a printed copy of any screen you want to study further or show to someone else.

ERASE AND DEL COMMANDS

Because a disk has limited space for storing your files, you should periodically remove unneeded files from your disks to make room for new files. The **ERASE** command will erase, or remove, a file from a disk. An alternative command that functions like the ERASE command is the **DEL** (delete) command. Take care when using the ERASE or DEL command because you do not want to inadvertently remove a file you mean to keep.

Removing a File

Let's remove the file NOTEFILE.DOC from the disk in drive A. Type ERASE A:NOTEFILE.DOC and press the Enter key (Figure 1-37). You could also use the DEL command instead by typing DEL A:NOTEFILE.DOC and pressing the Enter key. DOS does not display a message confirming the file's removal. To be sure that DOS has removed the file from the disk, type DIR A: and press the Enter key (Figure 1-37). [For DOS 5.0 Users – Your screen will show addi-tional messages.]

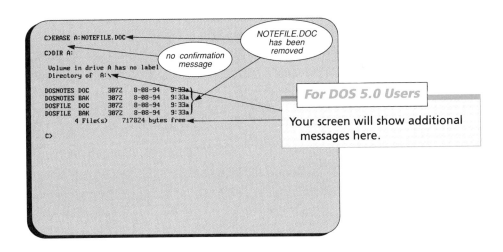

FIGURE 1-37
Removing a file from a disk

PROJECT SUMMARY

In Project 1 you learned how to boot DOS, name your files, and format disks using the FORMAT command. You also learned how to use these DOS commands to work with your files: COPY, CLS, DIR, RENAME, MORE, ERASE, and DEL. All the activities that you learned for this project are summarized in the Quick Reference following Project 2. The following is a summary of the keystroke sequence we used in Project 1.

SUMMARY OF KEYSTROKES — PROJECT 1

STEPS	KEY(S) PRESSED	RESULTS
1	Ctrl–Alt–Delete	Resets DOS.
2	10-9-94 ↵	Sets date.
3	11:50 ↵	Sets time.
4	A: ↵	Changes default drive.
5	C: ↵	Rechanges default drive.
6	FORMAT A: ↵	Formats a disk.
7	N ↵	Returns to DOS after formatting.
8	CLS ↵	Clears screen.
9	COPY C:DOSNOTES.DOC A:DOSNOTES.DOC ↵	Copies file.
10	COPY C:DOSNOTES.DOC A:NOTECOPY.DUP ↵	Copies file with new name.
11	COPY A:DOSNOTES.DOC A:DOSNOTES.BAK ↵	Copies file on same disk.
12	COPY A:DOSNOTES.DOC A:DOSNOTES.DOC ↵	Copies a file using erroneous same name.
13	COPY C:DOSNOTES.DOC A:DOSFILE.DOC ↵	Copies file.
14	F3 Backspace Backspace Backspace BAK ↵	Retypes command.
15	DIR A: ↵	Lists file directory.
16	RENAME A:NOTECOPY.DUP NOTEFILE.DOC	Changes file's name.
17	RENAME A:NOTEFILE.DOC A:NOTECOPY.DUP ↵	Renames with drive specifier error.
18	RENAME A:NOTEFILE.DOC DOSNOTES.DOC ↵	Renames with duplicate name error.
19	MORE <A:DOSNOTES.DOC ↵	Displays file contents.
20	Print Screen	Prints screen contents on printer. (Use Shift-PrtSc on some keyboards.)
21	ERASE A:NOTEFILE.DOC ↵	Removes file from disk.

The following list summarizes the material covered in Project 1.

1. An **operating system** is a collection of programs that controls and manages the operation of the computer.
2. The operating system known as **DOS**, an acronym for **Disk Operating System**, was developed by Microsoft Corporation. The operating system for an IBM Personal Computer is **PC-DOS**. Other compatible microcomputers use a similar operating system called **MS-DOS**.
3. The **version** number of DOS is the whole number and signifies a major improvement of the product. The **release** number is the decimal number and identifies minor changes or corrections to a version of the product.
4. **Upward compatibility** means that all the features of an earlier version and release of DOS remain supported by a later one.
5. A **drive name** is a unique one-letter name preassigned to each disk drive.
6. A **local area network**, or **LAN**, is a collection of connected computers that share data. The **server**, a special computer on a LAN, has a high-capacity hard disk that contains files that can be accessed from the other computers on the network.

7. **Booting** refers to the process of loading DOS from a disk into main memory.

8. A **cold start**, or **cold boot**, occurs when you turn on power to the computer and DOS boots from disk.

9. You can boot DOS without turning the power switch off and on by holding down the Ctrl and Alt keys and pressing the Delete key. This process is called a **warm start**, **warm boot**, or **reset**.

10. After DOS boots, you might be prompted to enter the date and time. Some computers have batteries that accurately maintain the date and time even when the computer power is off.

11. The **DOS prompt**, which typically consists of a drive name and a greater than (>) symbol, indicates that DOS is ready to receive your commands.

12. The **default drive**, or **current drive**, is the drive that DOS assumes contains the disk where programs and data are located. The default drive on a two-diskette computer is usually drive A. A computer with a hard disk generally uses drive C as its default drive. Drive F is usually the default drive on a LAN.

13. You can change the default drive by entering a valid drive specifier and pressing the Enter key. A **drive specifier** consists of the one-letter drive name, followed by a colon.

14. You can enter DOS commands in any combination of uppercase and lowercase letters.

15. A **data file** is a collection of data created by application programs and used by the programs. A **program file** contains instructions that the computer follows to perform its tasks.

16. A **file specification** lets DOS know exactly where to search for a file and gives its exact name. The file specification consists of a drive specifier, path specification, filename, and optional extension. Each **filename** is a one- to eight-character name, and each **extension** is a one- to three-character name; a period separates the filename and extension.

17. DOS has two types of commands: internal commands and external commands. **Internal commands** are a part of DOS that is loaded into main memory during booting and can be executed at any time. **External commands** are separate programs stored on the DOS disk, which must be available for the commands to execute. All DOS external commands have extensions of COM and EXE, while the BAT extension is used for **DOS batch files** containing a series of DOS commands to be executed.

18. Use the **FORMAT** command to prepare disks for storing data or program files. The **formatting** process establishes sectors on the disk and performs other functions that allow the disk to store data.

19. Use the **CLS** command to clear the screen and place the DOS prompt on the first line of the screen.

20. Use the **COPY** command to duplicate a file onto the same or another disk. Creating a working copy of a file helps protect the original file from damage. A **backup copy** of a file helps to guard against accidental loss of data.

21. A file to be copied is called the **source file**. The resulting copy is called the **target file**.

22. Use the **Backspace** key to delete the character to the left of the cursor and move the cursor one position to the left. The **Esc** key cancels the command you just typed. The **F3** key automatically retypes your previous command on the screen.

23. Enter the **DIR**, or directory, command to list the files on a disk.

24. Use the **RENAME** command to change a file's name.

25. Use the **MORE** command to display the contents of a file on the screen, one full screen at a time.

26. Press the **Print Screen** key (Shift-PrtSc on some keyboards) to print the screen's contents on the printer.

27. To remove a file from a disk, use either the **ERASE** or the **DEL** command.

STUDENT ASSIGNMENTS

STUDENT ASSIGNMENT 1: True/False

Instructions: Circle T if the statement is true and F if the statement is false.

T F   1. DOS is an example of application software.

T F   2. IBM developed DOS for use in IBM PCs.

T F   3. The DOS version number identifies minor changes or corrections to a release.

T F   4. The server hard disk on a LAN is usually drive C.

Student Assignment 1 (continued)

T F 5. During a cold start the computer first runs tests to diagnose its own circuitry.

T F 6. To begin a warm boot you hold down the Ctrl and Alt keys, press the Reset key, and then release all three keys.

T F 7. All computers require you to enter the date and time.

T F 8. The FORMAT command is an example of a DOS prompt.

T F 9. To change the default disk drive assignment to drive B, type B: and press the Enter key.

T F 10. All DOS commands must be entered in uppercase characters.

T F 11. A> is an example of a drive specifier.

T F 12. A DOS file specification can contain a filename of one to eight characters and an extension of one to three characters.

T F 13. Internal commands and external commands are the two types of DOS commands.

T F 14. The FORMAT command is an external command.

T F 15. If you are using a hard disk, you can format a diskette by entering the command FORMAT C:.

T F 16. More than one diskette can be formatted with one FORMAT command.

T F 17. To display a list of files stored on a disk, you must enter the CLS command.

T F 18. You use the Esc key to automatically retype your previous DOS command.

T F 19. The DIR command displays the remaining space available on the disk.

T F 20. When you use the RENAME command, you must enter the drive specifier as part of the file specification for the file's new name.

T F 21. The MORE command displays a file one screen at a time.

T F 22. The ERASE command can be used to remove a file from a disk.

STUDENT ASSIGNMENT 2: Multiple Choice

Instructions: Circle the correct response.

1. DOS was developed by _____.
   a. Disk Operating Systems
   b. IBM
   c. LAN
   d. Microsoft

2. The 3 in DOS 3.2 refers to the _____.
   a. default
   b. release
   c. version
   d. prompt

3. The symbol C> _____.
   a. is called the DOS prompt
   b. indicates the name of a program
   c. indicates the default disk drive
   d. both a and c

4. A file specification consists of all the following except the _____.
   a. extension
   b. drive specifier
   c. prompt
   d. filename

5. Examples of special DOS extensions are _____.
   a. BAT, COM, and EXE
   b. BAT, COM, and DOC
   c. BAT, DOC, and EXE
   d. COM, DOC, and EXE

6. The _____ command establishes sectors on a disk and performs other functions that allow the disk to store files.
   a. MORE
   b. DIR
   c. CLS
   d. FORMAT
7. Listing the files on a disk is accomplished by _____.
   a. typing MORE and pressing the Enter key
   b. typing LIST and pressing the Enter key
   c. typing DIR and pressing the Enter key
   d. typing DISPLAY and pressing the Enter key
8. To change the name of a file from FILEX.DOC to FILEA.DOC, type _____.
   a. ALTER FILEX.DOC FILEA.DOC
   b. ASSIGN FILEX.DOC FILEA.DOC
   c. CHANGE FILEX.DOC FILEA.DOC
   d. RENAME FILEX.DOC FILEA.DOC
9. To remove the file THISFILE.BAK from a disk, type _____.
   a. REMOVE THISFILE.BAK
   b. DEL THISFILE.BAK
   c. ERASE THISFILE.BAK
   d. either b or c

STUDENT ASSIGNMENT 3: Fill in the Blanks

Instructions: Fill in the blanks in the following sentences.

1. A(n) _____ is a collection of programs that controls and manages the operation of the computer.
2. Microsoft Corporation developed the operating system known as _____.
3. A(n) _____ is a unique one-letter name preassigned to a disk drive.
4. The _____ on a LAN has a high-capacity hard disk that contains files that you can access from your computer.
5. To change the default drive, you type the letter of the new drive to be used, followed by a _____.
6. In a file specification, C: is an example of a _____.
7. In a file specification, the _____ is optional and consists of one to three characters.
8. The _____ command establishes sectors on a disk and performs other functions that allow the disk to store data.
9. The _____ is the file specification of a file after it is copied.
10. The _____ key retypes your previous DOS command.
11. Use the _____ command to list the files stored on a disk.
12. Use the _____ command to change the name of a file on a disk.
13. Use the _____ command to display the contents of a file on the screen.
14. The _____ key prints the contents of the screen on the printer.

STUDENT ASSIGNMENT 4: Using DOS Commands

Instructions: Explain how to accomplish each of the following tasks using DOS.

Problem 1: Prepare a diskette using the FORMAT command and determine the amount of free space remaining on the disk.
Explanation: _____ _____

_____

_____

_____

Student Assignment 4 (continued)

Problem 2: List the files stored on the disk in drive A and determine the name of the most recently created or changed file.
Explanation: _____

_____

_____

_____

Problem 3: Create a backup copy on the default drive of the file DOCUMENT.IT using an extension of BAK and the same filename.
Explanation: _____

_____

_____

_____

Problem 4: Change the name of the file THISFILE.DUP to THATFILE.DOC on drive B.
Explanation: _____

_____

_____

_____

Problem 5: Print the current contents of the screen on the printer.
Explanation: _____

_____

_____

_____

Problem 6: Remove the file LETTER.DOC from the disk located in drive A.
Explanation: _____

_____

_____

_____

STUDENT ASSIGNMENT 5: Understanding DOS Options

Instructions: Explain what will happen after you perform each of the following DOS commands.

Problem 1: Type FORMAT A: at the C> prompt and press the Enter key.
Explanation: _____

_____

_____

Problem 2: Type DIR B: at the A> prompt and press the Enter key.
Explanation: _____

_____

_____

Problem 3: Type RENAME A:OLDFILE.ABC NEWFILE.XYZ at the A> prompt and press the Enter key.
Explanation: _____

_____

_____

Problem 4: Type MORE <A:DOSNOTES.DOC at the C> prompt and press the Enter key.
Explanation: _____

_____

_____

STUDENT ASSIGNMENT 6: Recovering from Problems

Instructions: In each of the following situations, a problem occurred. Explain the cause of the problem and how it can be corrected.

Problem 1: You started your two-diskette computer without a disk in drive A and a message appears that you don't recognize.
Cause of problem: _____

_____

Method of correction: _____

_____

Problem 2: When DOS instructs you to "Enter new date (mm-dd-yy):", you type 6\14\94, press the Enter key, and receive an "Invalid date" message from DOS.
Cause of problem: _____

_____

Method of correction: _____

_____

Problem 3: The default drive is drive A and you type B and press the Enter key to change the default drive. DOS responds with the message "Bad command or file name".
Cause of problem: _____

_____

Method of correction: _____

_____

Problem 4: You type COPY A:DOSNOTES.DOC A:MY FILE.DOC at the A> prompt and press the Enter key. DOS responds with the message "Invalid number of parameters".
Cause of problem: _____

_____

Method of correction: _____

_____

Problem 5: You type RENAME A:OLDFILE.BAK B:NEWFILE.NEW at the A> prompt and press the Enter key. DOS responds with the message "Invalid parameter".
Cause of problem: _____

_____

Student Assignment 6 (continued)

Method of correction: _____

_____

Problem 6: You type MORE A:NOTECOPY.OLD and press the Enter key. The cursor moves down the screen a few lines, but nothing is displayed on the screen, not even the DOS prompt.
Cause of problem: _____

_____

Method of correction: _____

_____

STUDENT ASSIGNMENT 7: Creating a Working Disk Copy

Instructions: At the DOS prompt perform the following tasks to create a working disk copy of the files you created in Project 1.

1. Format a new disk.
2. The disk on which you placed files in Project 1 should now contain four files. Copy these files onto your newly formatted disk.
3. Verify that both disks contain the same files.

STUDENT ASSIGNMENT 8: Booting DOS

Instructions: Perform the following tasks on the computer you used to complete Project 1.

1. If the computer is not on a LAN:
   a. Perform a cold boot.
   b. Perform a warm boot.
2. If the computer is on a LAN:
   a. Find out from your instructor if you are allowed to perform a cold boot. If so, perform a cold boot.
   b. Find out from your instructor if you are allowed to perform a warm boot. If so, perform a warm boot.

Managing and Organizing Files on Disks

OBJECTIVES

You will have mastered the material in this project when you can:

◆ Create subdirectories
◆ Change the current directory
◆ Change the DOS prompt
◆ Specify a path
◆ Use wildcard characters with DOS commands
◆ Copy all files from one diskette to another
◆ List a disk directory, using /P and /W
◆ Remove subdirectories
◆ Check the status of a disk
◆ Recognize common DOS error messages

In Project 1 you learned to boot DOS, assign names to files, and format disks. You also worked with files on disk by copying, listing, renaming, displaying, and removing files. In this project you will examine the COPY and DIR commands in greater detail, especially their use when working with a large number of files. You will also learn new topics in this project that will teach you how to organize your files by application or use and how to check the status of your disks and of main memory. Finally, we present a list of the common DOS error messages you might encounter.

THE ROOT DIRECTORY AND SUBDIRECTORIES

◆ Let's first further examine the file directory displayed by the DIR command. We will again assume you are using a hard disk and one diskette drive with the drive names C and A, respectively. If you are using a different disk configuration, check with your instructor for the changes you should make in Project 2.

Insert the disk you used in Project 1 in drive A. At the DOS prompt of C>, type DIR A: and press the Enter key (Figure 2-1). [For DOS 5.0 Users – Your screen will show additional messages.] The four files on the disk in drive A displayed by the DIR command are those you placed there during Project 1.

FIGURE 2-1
Directory listing of disk in drive A

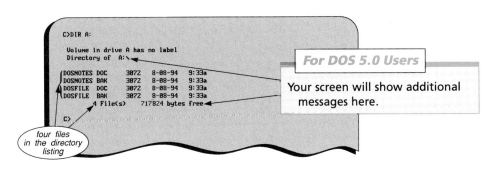

Root Directory

When you need to view your files on a disk, the computer does not actually read the entire disk looking for the files. Instead, it searches the file directory, which is an index of the files on the disk. This index, created when the disk is formatted, is a special file directory called the **root directory**. As an index, the root directory contains not only the information displayed by the DIR command, but also the physical locations of the files on the disk (Figure 2-2). [For DOS 5.0 Users – Your screen will show additional messages.]

FIGURE 2-2 Directory listing of disk in drive A and the root directory and its files

The root directory on a disk is limited in size. For example, a hard disk allows for up to 512 entries, while a 360KB diskette has room for 112 entries, and 1.2MB and 1.44MB diskettes hold 224 entries. This capacity might be sufficient on a diskette, but a hard disk with many millions of bytes of storage will likely have more files than can be stored in a single directory.

If you had a few hundred file entries in the root directory, you would have difficulty managing your disk files. Imagine scanning a directory listing of several hundred files to find the names of files you created months ago. It would be better if you could somehow divide your files into smaller logical groups — for example, all school documents together, all word processing personal letters together, and all spreadsheets together. DOS also takes longer to find a file you request when you have a larger number of files. Fortunately, DOS subdirectories allow you to create these smaller groups of files.

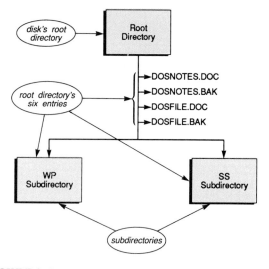

FIGURE 2-3
Root directory and the WP and SS subdirectories

Subdirectories

A **subdirectory** is a directory that you create on a disk. When you create a subdirectory, DOS places the subdirectory name in the root directory as one of its entries. You can subsequently place file entries either in the subdirectory or the root directory. Unlike the root directory, the number of files in a subdirectory is limited only by the amount of storage available on the disk. DOS users commonly refer to both the root directory and all subdirectories as directories, because a subdirectory is simply a directory within a directory by definition.

Let's assume we create two new subdirectories named WP, where we will place our word processing files, and SS, where we will place our spreadsheet files (Figure 2-3). The root directory would then contain six entries: the four files we placed there in Project 1, and the WP and SS subdirectories.

At a later time we might want to divide our WP sub-directory into two subdirectories: one for word processing program files, and the other for word processing data files. Since subdirectories themselves can have subdirectory entries, we could add a WPDOCS subdirectory to the WP subdirectory index (Figure 2-4).

MD COMMAND TO CREATE SUBDIRECTORIES

◆ You use the **MKDIR** command, usually abbreviated **MD**, to create a subdirectory. Let's create a subdirectory named DOS2 on your disk in drive A. Type MD A:\DOS2 and press the Enter key (Figure 2-5). [For DOS 5.0 Users – Your screen will show additional messages.] To see the DOS2 subdirectory entry in the root directory, next type DIR A: and press the Enter key. Notice in Figure 2-5 that the root directory now contains five files. The new fifth file is actually the DOS2 subdirectory and is identified as such by the " < DIR > " label in the directory listing.

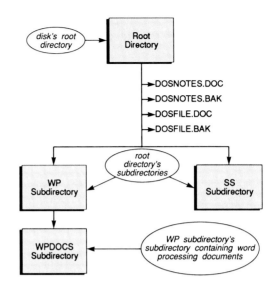

FIGURE 2-4 Root directory and the WP, SS, and WPDOCS subdirectories

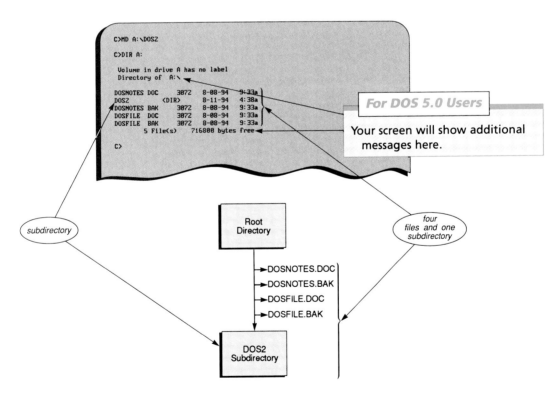

FIGURE 2-5 Root directory after creating the DOS2 subdirectory

When you use the MD command, you must follow four rules:

1. Start a subdirectory entry with the drive specifier. If the subdirectory is to be on drive A, for example, use A: to identify that drive. You can omit the drive specifier if you are creating the subdirectory on the default drive.
2. Following the drive specifier, type a backslash (\) character. In Figure 2-5 the message "Directory of A:\" indicates the root directory because the backslash alone following the drive specifier designates the root directory. When you typed MD A:\DOS2, you told DOS you wanted to create a subdirectory named DOS2 in the root directory of \ on drive A.
3. The subdirectory name, like any filename, can contain one to eight characters, followed optionally by a period and one to three characters for an extension. Subdirectory names, however, do not generally include extensions.
4. You can assign a subdirectory to an existing subdirectory.

Let's create a subdirectory named DOS2SUB and make it subordinate to the DOS2 subdirectory. Type MD A:\DOS2\DOS2SUB and press the Enter key (Figure 2-6). Just as A:\ identifies the root directory, A:\DOS2\ identifies the DOS2 subdirectory. This MD command, therefore, tells DOS to place the DOS2SUB subdirectory in the index for the DOS2 subdirectory.

FIGURE 2-6
Creating the DOS2SUB subdirectory subordinate to the DOS2 subdirectory

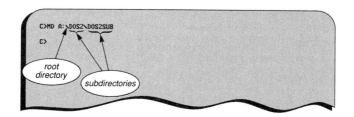

Next, type DIR A:\, which is an equivalent way of typing DIR A:, and press the Enter key (Figure 2-7). [For DOS 5.0 Users – Your screen will show additional messages.]

FIGURE 2-7
Directory listing of root directory after creating the DOS2 and DOS2SUB subdirectories

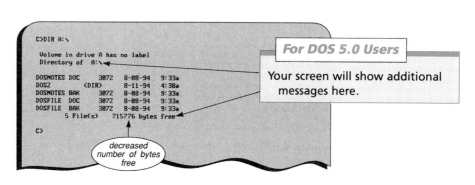

Notice that the directory listing for the root directory does not contain the DOS2SUB subdirectory. Something has happened, however, because the number of bytes free has changed from 716,800 to 715,776, which can be seen by comparing Figures 2-5 and 2-7. To see the entry for the DOS2SUB subdirectory, we need to view the directory listing for the DOS2 subdirectory.

To produce a directory listing for DOS2, type DIR A:\DOS2 and press the Enter key (Figure 2-8). [For DOS 5.0 Users – Your screen will show additional messages.] DOS displays the message "Directory of A:\DOS2" to tell you which directory it is listing. DOS lists the DOS2SUB subdirectory as an entry in the DOS2 index, but DOS also lists two other entries and labels them as directories: the . entry (pronounced dot), and the .. entry (pronounced dot-dot). The **dot** index entry refers to subdirectory DOS2 itself, and the **dot-dot** index entry refers to the root directory, which is the parent directory of DOS2, or the directory one level up from the DOS2 subdirectory.

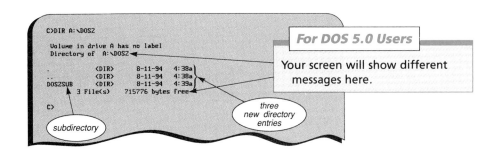

FIGURE 2-8
Directory listing of DOS2
subdirectory

CD COMMAND TO CHANGE DIRECTORIES

You use the **CHDIR** command, usually abbreviated **CD**, to move from one directory to another. Let's change from the root directory on drive A to the DOS2 subdirectory. Type CD A:\DOS2 and press the Enter key (Figure 2-9).

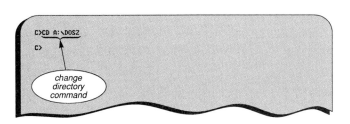

FIGURE 2-9
Changing from root directory
to DOS2 subdirectory

DOS does not display a confirmation message that it changed the directory to DOS2. Now, type DIR A: and press the Enter key, and DOS lists the DOS2 directory for you (Figure 2-10). [For DOS 5.0 Users – Your screen will show additional messages.]

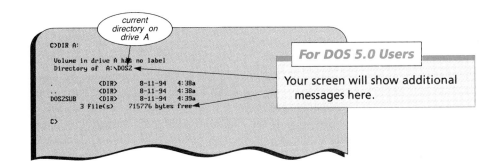

FIGURE 2-10
Directory listing of DOS2
subdirectory

The Current Directory

Just as there is a default, or current, disk drive, there is a current directory for each drive. The **current directory** for a drive is the directory on that drive in which you are currently working; that is, DOS looks by default for files on a drive in the current directory for that drive. When you first access a disk, the root directory is the current directory. You can, however, use the CD command to direct DOS to a subdirectory, which then becomes the current directory for that disk. Even if another drive is the default drive, your selected subdirectory remains the current directory for that drive until you change it to another directory. Drive C, for example, is our default drive, and the DOS2 subdirectory is the current directory on drive A. Whenever we access drive A, therefore, DOS looks at the DOS2 subdirectory.

So far we have used drive C as the default drive. Let's change the default drive to A; type A: and press the Enter key (Figure 2-11).

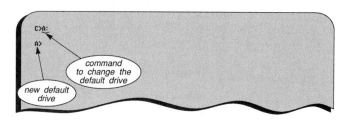

FIGURE 2-11
Changing default drive from
C to A

Notice that the DOS prompt has changed from C> to A>, which is the same prompt we would see if we were in the root directory on the A drive instead of the DOS2 subdirectory. Wouldn't it be better if DOS could somehow let us know what the current directory is for the drive?

PROMPT Command

You can use the **PROMPT** command to display the current directory on the default drive. Let's use the PROMPT command to change the DOS prompt; type PROMPT PG and press the Enter key (Figure 2-12).

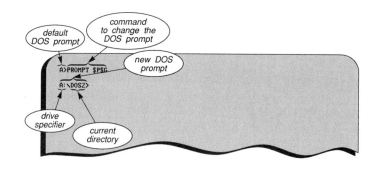

FIGURE 2-12
Changing the DOS prompt

The DOS prompt has changed from A> to A:\DOS2>. We now not only know that the default drive is A, but also that the current directory on drive A is DOS2. The PROMPT command **$P parameter** tells DOS to display the current directory as part of the DOS prompt, and the **$G parameter** tells DOS to display the > symbol as part of the DOS prompt. If you have been using a LAN, you might have been seeing this form of the DOS prompt all along because most installations use this form of the PROMPT command throughout their networks when they boot their computers. You can revert back to the A> prompt by entering the PROMPT command without parameters.

Let's further practice with the PROMPT command and with changing drives and directories. We will change the default drive to C and then back to A, change the DOS prompt to A> and then back to A:\DOS2>, change to the DOS2SUB directory and produce a directory listing for it, and then change back to the DOS2 subdirectory and produce a directory listing for it. The required commands are shown in Figures 2-13 and 2-14. [For DOS 5.0 Users – Your screen will show additional messages.]

First, let's change the default drive from A to C and back again to A. Type C: and press the Enter key to change the default drive to C (Figure 2-13). The C:\> prompt indicates that you are now in the root directory on drive C. Next, type A: and press the Enter key to change the default drive back to A (Figure 2-13). The A:\DOS2> prompt tells you that you are in the DOS2 directory on drive A.

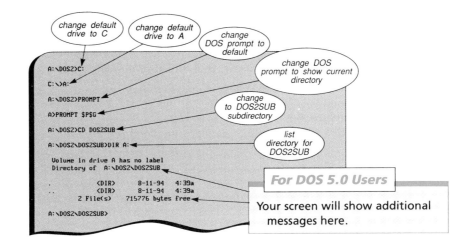

FIGURE 2-13

Changing default drives, DOS prompt, and current directories

Now, let's practice changing the DOS prompt. Type `PROMPT` and press the Enter key to change to the default DOS prompt of A> (Figure 2-13). Change back to the A:\DOS2> prompt by typing `PROMPT $P$G` and pressing the Enter key (Figure 2-13).

To change to the DOS2SUB directory, we could enter CD A:\DOS2\DOS2SUB, which is similar in syntax to the way we previously changed to the DOS2 directory. Because the default drive is now A, however, we do not need to enter the A:. Furthermore, because DOS2 is now the current directory on drive A, we can change to a subdirectory of DOS2 without entering the \DOS2. Consequently, type `CD DOS2SUB` and press the Enter key (Figure 2-13). The DOS prompt is now A:\DOS2\DOS2SUB>, which indicates that we have successfully changed to the DOS2SUB directory.

To list the files in the DOS2SUB directory, type `DIR A:` and press the Enter key (Figure 2-13). Once again we could have entered DIR A:\DOS2\DOS2SUB to request the directory listing, but did not need to do this because the default drive is A and the current directory on drive A is DOS2SUB. Notice that the DOS2SUB directory shows only the dot and dot-dot entries because we have not yet placed any files or subdirectories there.

To change back to the DOS2 directory, we could enter CD A:\DOS2. Instead, type `CD ..` and press the Enter key (Figure 2-14). The A:\DOS2> prompt indicates we successfully changed to the DOS2 directory. Recall that earlier we said that the dot-dot entry refers to the parent directory, or the directory that is one level up from the current subdirectory. In this case, DOS2 is the parent directory, so your CD command asked DOS to change from the DOS2SUB directory to the DOS2 directory.

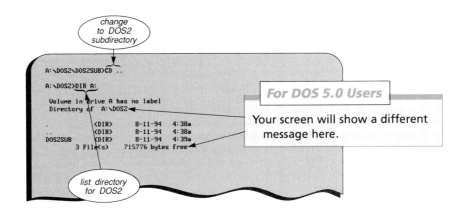

FIGURE 2-14

Changing current directory

Finally, type `DIR A:` and press the Enter key to list the DOS2 directory (Figure 2-14).

SPECIFYING A PATH TO DIRECTORIES AND FILES

When you use subdirectories you must learn to specify the path to a file. The **path** includes three components: (1) the drive specifier, (2) the name of the directory and the directories above it, and (3) the name of the file. The path specifies the route DOS is to take from the root directory through subdirectories leading to the file. You should specify the path whenever you want to access a file using the COPY, RENAME, ERASE, and other commands. Unless you specify the complete path, DOS might not find the file you want because it would search only the current directory of the default drive.

One way to specify the path is to include it in the command you are using. For example, let's copy the file DOSNOTES.DOC in the root directory of drive A to the DOS2 directory, using the same name for the target file. Type COPY A:\DOSNOTES.DOC A:\DOS2 and press the Enter key (Figure 2-15).

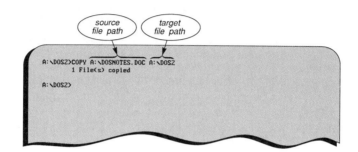

FIGURE 2-15
Specifying the path

Notice that the paths for both the source and target files have the drive specifier of A:. You also supplied the directory names of \ for the source file and \DOS2 for the target file. You entered the full name for the source file of DOSNOTES.DOC, but you did not enter the name for the target file. When you omit the filename and extension for a target file, DOS uses the filename and extension of the source file as the default. The file DOSNOTES.DOC now is in both the root and DOS2 directories.

Now you will remove the file DOSNOTES.DOC you just copied to the DOS2 directory, making sure you use the DIR command both before and after the ERASE command to verify the results of your work. Type DIR A: and press the Enter key; next, type ERASE DOSNOTES.DOC and press the Enter key; and finally, type DIR and press the Enter key (Figure 2-16). [For DOS 5.0 Users – Your screen will show additional messages.]

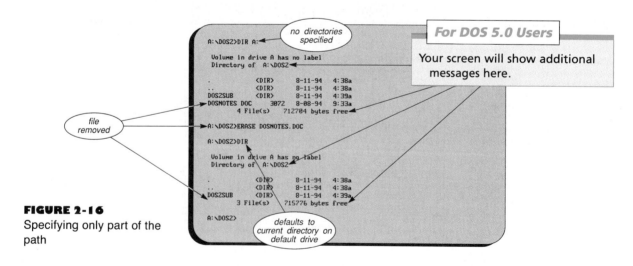

FIGURE 2-16
Specifying only part of the path

DIR A: is equivalent to DIR A:\DOS2 because DOS2 is the current directory on drive A. DIR is also equivalent to these other two forms of the DIR command because drive A is the default drive. Finally, you were able to use ERASE DOSNOTES.DOC instead of ERASE A:\DOS2\DOSNOTES.DOC because drive A is the default drive and DOS2 is the current directory on the default drive.

WILDCARD CHARACTERS

◆ You can access more than one file at a time when you use DOS commands such as COPY, RENAME, ERASE, and DEL. The wildcard characters of the asterisk (*) and the question mark (?) provide you with this multiple-file capability. You use a **wildcard character** in the file specification of a DOS command as a substitute for other characters. The asterisk represents one or more characters, whereas the question mark represents a single character.

The * Wildcard

You use the **asterisk** (*) wildcard character to represent one or more characters in a file's name. You can use the asterisk once in a filename and once in an extension. Wherever the asterisk appears, any character can occupy that position and all the remaining positions in the filename or the extension.

Let's illustrate the use of the wildcard asterisk by copying all the files from one directory to another directory. Check to be certain that your instructor has placed the DOS2 directory on your drive C hard disk. This directory contains 27 files that you will copy to the DOS2SUB subdirectory on drive A using a single COPY command. Type COPY C:\DOS2*.* A:\DOS2\DOS2SUB (Figure 2-17) and press the Enter key.

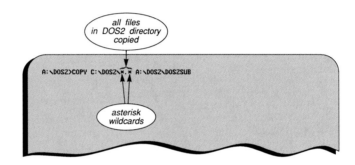

FIGURE 2-17
Copying using the * wildcard character

DOS lists the name of each source file as it makes the copy. The message "27 File(s) copied" is your final confirmation that DOS successfully copied all the files (Figure 2-18).

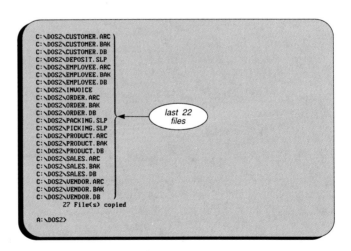

FIGURE 2-18
Copying 27 files with one COPY command

You can use the asterisk wildcard for just the filename portion or the extension portion of the file specification. DOS just copied three files with extensions of SLP to the DOS2SUB directory on drive A. Let's copy these three files to the DOS2 directory. Type COPY A:\DOS2\DOS2SUB*.SLP and press the Enter key (Figure 2-19). The asterisk for the filename asked DOS to copy any filename with an SLP extension in the DOS2SUB directory on drive A. Notice that you did not enter any target information, so all files were copied to the current directory of DOS2 on the default drive of A.

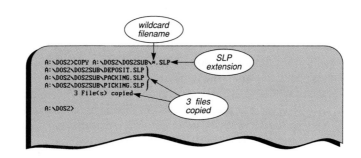

FIGURE 2-19

Using a wildcard filename and an extension of SLP to copy multiple files

DEPOSIT.SLP, PACKING.SLP, and PICKING.SLP are the three files you just copied to the DOS2 directory. Let's remove the last two files; type ERASE P*.SLP and press the Enter key (Figure 2-20). Then type DIR and press the Enter key to verify that only the DEPOSIT.SLP file remains (Figure 2-20). [For DOS 5.0 Users – Your screen will show additional messages.]

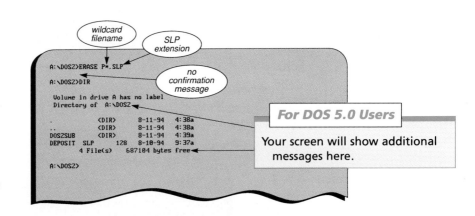

FIGURE 2-20

Using a wildcard filename to remove multiple files

The P*.SLP used in the ERASE command asked DOS to remove any file in the current directory of DOS2 on the default drive A whose extension is SLP and whose filename starts with the letter P.

The ? Wildcard

You use the **question mark (?)** wildcard character to represent any character occupying the position in which the wildcard character appears. Whereas the asterisk wildcard can represent one or more characters, the question mark wildcard represents only a single character replacement. You can use a single question mark or several in a command to identify files.

To use the question mark wildcard, type COPY A:\DOS2\DOS2SUB\P?CKING.SLP and press the Enter key (Figure 2-21).

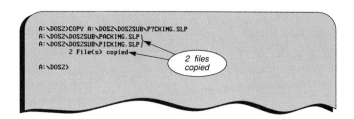

FIGURE 2-21
Using the ? wildcard to copy
multiple files

The two files of PACKING.SLP and PICKING.SLP met the model of the command and were copied to the DOS2 directory. Each has an extension of SLP, begins with the letter P, and has CKING in its third through seventh positions. Any character in the second position of the filename was allowed.

DIR COMMAND WITH A LARGE NUMBER OF FILES

Many directories contains many more files than can be displayed on the screen with the standard DIR command. For example, let's change to the DOS2SUB directory on drive A and produce its directory listing. Type CD DOS2SUB, press the Enter key, type DIR (Figure 2-22), and press the Enter key.

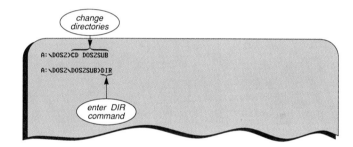

FIGURE 2-22
Changing directories and
entering the DIR command

Notice that the first few files scroll off the screen, and you can view only the last screenful of files (Figure 2-23).

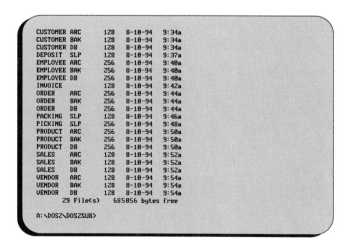

FIGURE 2-23
Last screen of DIR listing

The DIR command has two options to help in displaying large numbers of files. The first is the pause option and the second is the wide display option.

DIR Pause (/P) Option

The **DIR /P** command displays one screenful of files at a time and awaits your signal to show the next screenful. Try this option; type DIR /P (Figure 2-24) and press the Enter key.

FIGURE 2-24
Directory pause option

DOS lists the first screenful of files and pauses after displaying the message "Strike a key when ready . . ." at the the bottom of the screen (Figure 2-25). [For DOS 5.0 Users – Your screen will show a different message.]

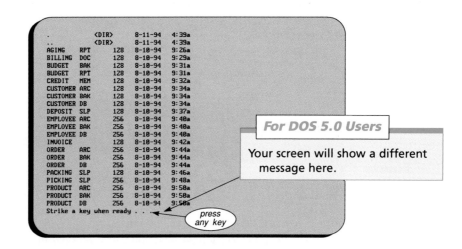

FIGURE 2-25
First page of directory pause option

When you are ready to view the next screenful of files, simply press any key (Figure 2-26). [For DOS 5.0 Users – Your screen will show additional messages.]

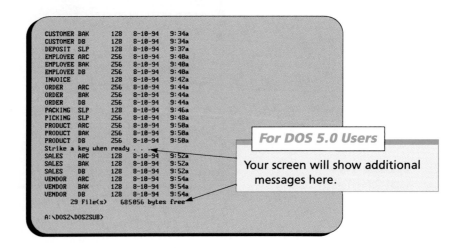

FIGURE 2-26
Last page of directory pause option

DIR Wide Display (/W) Option

The **DIR /W** command displays the directory information in a wide format to allow more files to fit on the screen. To try this option, type DIR /W and press the Enter key (Figure 2-27). [For DOS 5.0 Users – Your screen will show additional messages.] Notice that only the file and extension names appear; the size, time, and date of the files are not listed.

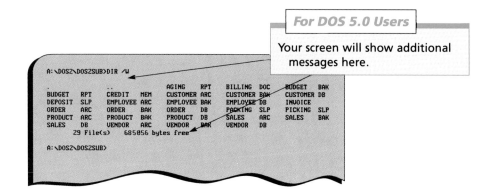

FIGURE 2-27
Directory wide display option

RD COMMAND TO REMOVE SUBDIRECTORIES

When you no longer need a subdirectory, you can remove, or delete, it. You use the **RMDIR** command, abbreviated **RD**, to remove a subdirectory from a disk.

Before you can remove a subdirectory, you must first remove all the files stored within it. This is a precaution that DOS takes to prevent your accidental removal of a directory containing files you need to keep. You can remove all the files by using the asterisk wildcard with the ERASE or DEL commands. You can issue this command from the subdirectory to be removed or from another directory if you give the full path. If you issue the command from another directory, make certain to use the correct subdirectory and path information or you might accidentally erase files from another part of the disk.

For practice, let's remove the DOS2SUB subdirectory. First, change to the DOS2 subdirectory and remove all files in the DOS2SUB subdirectory; type CD .. and press the Enter key. Next, type DEL A:\DOS2\DOS2SUB*.* and press the Enter key (Figure 2-28). In response to the message "Are you sure (Y/N)?", type the letter Y and press the Enter key.

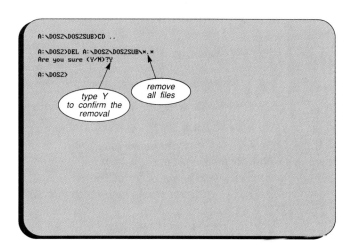

FIGURE 2-28
Removing all files from a directory

Now that you have removed all the files from the DOS2SUB subdirectory, you can also remove the subdirectory. To do this, type RD DOS2SUB and press the Enter key (Figure 2-29). No confirmation message appears, so you should use the DIR command to verify the removal of the subdirectory.

FIGURE 2-29
Removing the DOS2SUB directory

CHKDSK Command

Another useful command is the **CHKDSK** command, which checks the condition of your disk and reports the status of main memory to you. Because the CHKDSK command is an external command, you should change the default drive to C before you enter the command. To practice with the CHKDSK command, type C:, press the Enter key, type CHKDSK A:, and press the Enter key (Figure 2-30). [For DOS 5.0 Users – Your screen will show additional messages.]

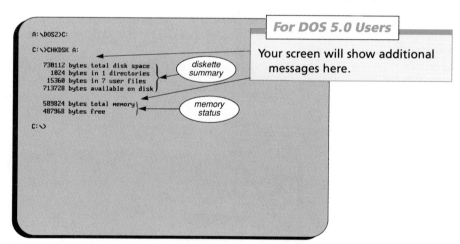

FIGURE 2-30
CHKDSK command listing

The CHKDSK command displays four lines of disk summary information. These lines indicate how many bytes can be stored on the disk, how much of this disk space is used by how many directories, how much of this disk space is used by how many files, and how much disk space is available for future storage. The CHKDSK command also reports how much main memory you have on your computer and how much is available, or free, for use by your programs.

If the CHKDSK command checks your disk and detects problems, it displays diagnostic messages instead of the status displays. If this occurs, ask for assistance from your instructor.

COMMON DOS ERROR MESSAGES

◆ When you make a mistake entering a command, DOS displays an error message that attempts to describe your specific mistake. You probably will not encounter most of the hundreds of different possible DOS error messages, but you are likely to see several of the common ones. You should refer to the DOS reference manual for a complete list of error messages and their explanations. In many cases a DOS error occurs because of a typing mistake, so your first means of correcting an error is to carefully verify the entire command you entered. The following is a list of the error messages you are likely to encounter and what each means.

ERROR MESSAGE	EXPLANATION
Bad command or file name	You used the wrong drive, path, or filename for the DOS command or application program.
Duplicate file name or File not found	You used the RENAME command and either the target filename already exists on the disk or the source filename could not be found.
Error reading drive	You do not have a diskette in the drive.
File allocation table bad	The disk might be defective and you might have to reformat it.
File cannot be copied onto itself	You used the same drive, path, and filename for both the source and target files.
File not found	You used the wrong drive, path, or filename.
Format failure	The disk you are attempting to FORMAT might be defective and unusable.
General failure	Your disk is not formatted or is not correctly inserted in the drive.
Insufficient disk space	Your disk does not have enough space to store the file.
Insufficient memory	You do not have enough usable main memory on your computer to execute the DOS command or application program.
Invalid date	You entered an invalid date.
Invalid filename or file not found	You tried to rename a file that could not be found.
Invalid number of parameters	You specified too few or too many options for the command.
Invalid parameter	You used an incorrect option for the command.
Invalid path or file name	You used an incorrect path or filename in your command.
Path not found	You entered a path that does not exist.
Program too big to fit in memory	You do not have enough usable main memory on your computer to execute the DOS command or application program.
Syntax error	Your DOS command is improperly typed.
Track 0 bad - Invalid media	You have a double-density disk in a high-density drive and entered the wrong FORMAT command.

PROJECT SUMMARY

In Project 2 you learned how to create, change, and remove subdirectories; change the current directory and specify the path; use the PROMPT and CHKDSK commands; use wildcard characters in commands; and use further options of the DIR command. All the activities that you learned for this project are summarized in the Quick Reference following Project 2.

The following is a summary of the keystroke sequence we used in Project 2.

SUMMARY OF KEYSTROKES — PROJECT 2

STEPS	KEY(S) PRESSED	RESULTS
1	DIR A: ↵	Lists file directory.
2	MD A:\DOS2 ↵	Creates subdirectory.
3	DIR A: ↵	Lists file directory.
4	MD A:\DOS2\DOS2SUB ↵	Creates subdirectory.
5	DIR A:\ ↵	Lists file directory.
6	DIR A:\DOS2 ↵	Lists file directory.
7	CD A:\DOS2 ↵	Changes directory.
8	DIR A: ↵	Lists file directory.
9	A: ↵	Changes default drive.
10	PROMPT PG ↵	Changes DOS prompt.
11	C: ↵ A: ↵	Changes default drive.
12	PROMPT ↵ PROMPT PG ↵	Changes DOS prompt.
13	CD DOS2SUB ↵	Changes directory.
14	DIR A: ↵	Lists file directory.
15	CD .. ↵	Changes directory.
16	DIR A: ↵	Lists file directory.
17	COPY A:\DOSNOTES.DOC A:\DOS2 ↵	Copies file.
18	DIR A: ↵	Lists file directory.
19	ERASE DOSNOTES.DOC ↵	Removes a file.
20	DIR ↵	Lists file directory.
21	COPY C:\DOS2*.* A:\DOS2\DOS2SUB ↵	Copies all files.
22	COPY A:\DOS2\DOS2SUB*.SLP ↵	Copies using wildcard.
23	ERASE P*.SLP ↵	Removes files.
24	DIR ↵	Lists file directory.
25	COPY A:\DOS2\DOS2SUB\P?CKING.SLP ↵	Copies using wildcard.
26	CD DOS2SUB ↵	Changes directory.
27	DIR ↵	Lists file directory.
28	DIR /P ↵	Pauses directory listing.
29	DIR /W ↵	Lists wide display directory.
30	CD .. ↵	Changes to parent directory.
31	DEL A:\DOS2\DOS2SUB*.* ↵ Y ↵	Removes all files.
32	RD DOS2SUB ↵	Removes directory.
33	C: ↵	Changes default drive.
34	CHKDSK A: ↵	Checks disk status.

The following list summarizes the material covered in Project 2.

1. The **root directory** is created by DOS during formatting and is an index of the files on the disk.
2. A **subdirectory** is a directory that you create on disk and is used to help organize your files.
3. Use the **MKDIR**, or the **MD**, command to create a subdirectory. The subdirectory entry for the MD command includes the drive specifier, a backslash, and the subdirectory name.
4. The **dot** index entry refers to its own subdirectory, and the **dot-dot** index refers to the subdirectory's parent directory.
5. Use the **CHDIR**, or **CD**, command to change from one directory to another.
6. The **current directory** for a drive is the directory on that drive in which you are currently working.
7. Use the **PROMPT** command to include the current directory as part of the DOS prompt. The prompt command **$P parameter** tells DOS to display the current directory, while the **$G parameter** tells DOS to display the > symbol.
8. The **path** to a file consists of the drive specifier, the name of the directory, and the name of the file. You use the path to specify the exact file you want to access.
9. You can use the **wildcards characters** of the **asterisk** and **question mark** in many DOS commands to replace specific characters in the file specification. Wildcards allow you to access multiple files with one command.
10. The **DIR /P** command produces a directory listing one screenful of files at a time. The **DIR /W** command displays directory information in a shorthand, wide format to allow more files to fit on the screen.
11. You remove a subdirectory by first erasing all the files in the subdirectory, then using the **RMDIR**, or **RD**, command to remove the subdirectory.
12. Use the **CHKDSK** command to verify the condition of your disk and to view a status of your disk and of main memory.

S T U D E N T   A S S I G N M E N T S

STUDENT ASSIGNMENT 1: True/False

Instructions: Circle T if the statement is true and F if the statement is false.

T F   1. The DIR A: command always produces a directory listing of the files in the root directory of drive A.
T F   2. Each disk directory keeps track of the physical locations of its files on the disk.
T F   3. The root directory has room to keep track of an unlimited number of files.
T F   4. A subdirectory can have subdirectories.
T F   5. A subdirectory name cannot have an extension.
T F   6. Only the default drive has a current directory.
T F   7. You can use only one wildcard question mark character in a command to identify files.
T F   8. The DIR /W command causes the directory listing to wait or pause after each screenful is displayed.
T F   9. Use the CHKDSK command to include the current directory as part of the DOS prompt.
T F 10. To move from one directory to another, use the MD command.
T F 11. The RD command removes a subdirectory and all its files.

STUDENT ASSIGNMENT 2: Multiple Choice

Instructions: Circle the correct response.

1. To move from one directory to another, you use the _____ command.
   - a. cd
   - b. md
   - c. rd
   - d. td
2. The _____ is the first entry in a path specification.
   - a. backslash
   - b. filename
   - c. subdirectory
   - d. drive specifier
3. Filenames are grouped on disks into _____.
   - a. index lists
   - b. source and target filename entries
   - c. internally labeled entries
   - d. directories and subdirectories
4. The _____ command uses the PG parameters.
   - a. CHKDSK
   - b. COPY
   - c. DIR
   - d. PROMPT
5. The _____ parameter tells the DIR command to display the maximum number of files on the screen.
   - a. /A
   - b. /G
   - c. /P
   - d. /W
6. The _____ command is an external command.
   - a. CHKDSK
   - b. COPY
   - c. PROMPT
   - d. RD

STUDENT ASSIGNMENT 3: Fill in the Blanks

Instructions: Fill in the blanks in the following sentences.

1. The special file directory that is created when a disk is formatted is called the _____ directory.
2. A(n) _____ is a directory that you create on a disk.
3. Use the _____ command to create a subdirectory.
4. The _____ character is used to represent the root directory.
5. Use the _____ command to move from one directory to another.
6. You can use the _____ wildcard character once in a filename and once in an extension.
7. Use the _____ parameter with the DIR command to display one screenful of files at a time.
8. Use the _____ command to delete a subdirectory.
9. You can use the _____ command to determine the amount of main memory your computer has.

STUDENT ASSIGNMENT 4: Using DOS Commands

Instructions: Explain how to accomplish each of the following tasks using DOS.

Problem 1: Copy all the files from the disk in drive B to the disk in drive A.
Explanation: _____

_____

_____

Problem 2: Verify how much free main memory you currently have on your computer.
Explanation: _____

_____

_____

Problem 3: Create a subdirectory named SUB1 on your diskette.
Explanation: _____

_____

_____

Problem 4: Erase the files in subdirectory SUB1, change to the root directory, and remove subdirectory SUB1.
Explanation: _____

_____

_____

STUDENT ASSIGNMENT 5: Understanding DOS Options

Instructions: Explain what will happen after you perform each of the following DOS commands.

Problem 1: Type COPY G*.* C: at the A> prompt and press the Enter key.
Explanation: _____

_____

_____

Problem 2: Type COPY D?S*.* A: at the C> prompt and press the Enter key.
Explanation: _____

_____

_____

Problem 3: Type PROMPT PG at the DOS prompt and press the Enter key.
Explanation: _____

_____

_____

STUDENT ASSIGNMENT 6: Recovering from Problems

Instructions: In each of the following situations, a problem occurred. Explain the cause of the problem and how it can be corrected.

Problem 1: You type COPY DOS**.* A: at the C> prompt and press the Enter key. DOS responds with the message "Invalid path or file name".

Cause of problem: _____

_____

Method of correction: _____

_____

Problem 2: You have the DOS disk in drive A, type CHKSDK A: at the A> prompt, and press the Enter key. DOS responds with the message "Bad command or file name".

Cause of problem: _____

_____

Method of correction: _____

_____

STUDENT ASSIGNMENT 7: Creating Subdirectories

Instructions: Perform the following tasks on the computer you used to complete Project 2 or on any other computer available to you.

1. Place a newly formatted disk in drive A and create these subdirectories in the root directory: SPSHEET, WORDPROC, GAMES, HOUSE, and MODEM.
2. Create two subdirectories in the SPSHEET directory: FINANCES and EXPENSES.
3. Create three subdirectories in the WORDPROC directory: WORKMEMO, PERSONAL, and WORDLIST.

STUDENT ASSIGNMENT 8: Managing Subdirectory Files

Instructions: Perform the following tasks on the computer you used to complete Project 2 or on any other computer available to you.

1. If you did not create the subdirectories in Student Assignment 7, do it now.
2. Make the HOUSE directory the current directory.
3. Copy two or more files into the HOUSE directory. You can use the files you copied onto your disk during Projects 1 and 2 or choose any other files.
4. Copy all these files from the HOUSE directory to the FINANCES directory.

STUDENT ASSIGNMENT 9: Removing Directories

Instructions: Perform the following tasks on the computer you used to complete Project 2 or on any other computer available to you.

1. If you did not create the subdirectories in Student Assignment 7, do it now.
2. Remove the GAMES directory from your disk.
3. Remove the SPSHEET directory from your disk.

STUDENT ASSIGNMENT 10: Using Wildcard Characters

Instructions: Perform the following tasks on the computer you used to complete Project 2 or on any other computer available to you.

1. If you did not create the subdirectories in Student Assignment 7, do it now.
2. Make the HOUSE directory the current directory.
3. Copy two or more files into the HOUSE directory using the ? wildcard in one or more positions of the source file-name. You can use the files you copied onto your disk during Projects 1 and 2 or choose any other files.
4. Copy two or more files into the HOUSE directory using the * wildcard in the source filename. You can use the files you copied onto your disk during Projects 1 and 2 or choose any other files.

STUDENT ASSIGNMENT 11: Subdirectories on a Hard Drive or LAN

Instructions: If you used a hard drive or LAN to complete Project 2, perform the following tasks on the computer you used to complete Project 2.

1. Determine which directories you have on drive C, if you are using a hard disk, or on drive F, if you are using a LAN.
2. Draw a diagram of this directory structure.

For each of the projects, we have provided the fundamental DOS activities in an easy-to-use quick reference format. This convenient reference tool is divided into three parts — activity, procedure, and description. All of the activities that you learn in each project are covered in the Quick Reference for that project. The numbers in parentheses that follow each activity refer to the page on which the activity is first discussed in the text.

You can use these Quick References as study aids or to quickly recall how you completed an activity. The Quick Reference is a valuable and time-saving tool, and we encourage you to use it frequently.

QUICK REFERENCE — PROJECT 1

ACTIVITY	PROCEDURE	DESCRIPTION
WARM START (DOS5)	Press Ctrl–Alt–Delete	Restart DOS if power is already on. Insert disk in drive A for two-diskette computer. Leave drive A empty for a hard disk or LAN.
SET DATE (DOS5)	Enter month Enter day Enter year Press ↵	Type one-digit or two-digit month, one-digit or two-digit day, and two-digit year, separating each with a hyphen or slash.
SET TIME (DOS5)	Enter hour Enter minute Enter second Press ↵	Type one-digit or two digit hour, one-digit or two-digit minute, and one-digit or two-digit second, separating each with a colon.
CHANGE DEFAULT DRIVE (DOS6)	Enter drive specifier Press ↵	Type single-letter drive name and a colon for the new default drive.
FORMAT DISK (DOS8)	Type format Press Spacebar Enter drive specifier	Initialize a diskette in the designated drive.
CLEAR SCREEN (DOS11)	Type cls Press ↵	Clear the screen and position DOS prompt to the top left.
COPY FILE (DOS11)	Type copy Press Spacebar Enter source file Press Spacebar Enter target file Press ↵	Duplicates the source file as the target file on the same disk or another disk.
RETYPE PREVIOUS COMMAND (DOS12)	Press F3	Automatically retype previous DOS command.
DISPLAY DIRECTORY (DOS14)	Type dir Press Spacebar Enter drive specifier Press ↵	Display file directory of the disk in the designated drive.
RENAME FILE (DOS14)	Type rename Press Spacebar Enter old file specification Press Spacebar Enter new file specification Press ↵	Change the name of the file (first filename) on the designated drive to another name (second filename).

QUICK REFERENCE — PROJECT 1 (continued)

ACTIVITY	PROCEDURE	DESCRIPTION
DISPLAY FILE (DOS15)	Type more Press Spacebar Type < Enter file specification Press ↵	Display the file's contents one screen at a time.
PRINT SCREEN (DOS17)	Press Print Screen	Print the contents of the screen on the printer.
REMOVE FILE (DOS17)	Type del or type erase Press Spacebar Enter file specification Press ↵	Delete the file from disk.

QUICK REFERENCE — PROJECT 2

ACTIVITY	PROCEDURE	DESCRIPTION
CREATE SUBDIRECTORY (DOS27)	Type md Press Spacebar Enter drive specifier Enter subdirectory name Press ↵	Create a new subdirectory.
CHANGE DIRECTORY (DOS29)	Type cd Press Spacebar Enter drive specifier Enter subdirectory name Press ↵	Change the current directory on a disk.
PAUSE DIRECTORY LISTING (DOS36)	Type dir Press Spacebar Enter path Type /p Press ↵	Display a directory listing one screenful at a time.
WIDE DIRECTORY LISTING (DOS37)	Type dir Press Spacebar Enter path Type /w Press ↵	Display a directory listing in a wide, condensed format.
REMOVE SUBDIRECTORY (DOS37)	Type rd Press Spacebar Enter drive specifier Enter subdirectory name Press ↵	Remove a subdirectory.
VERIFY DISK CONDITION (DOS38)	Type chkdsk Press Spacebar Enter drive specifier Press ↵	Verify and report a disk's condition.

DOS INDEX

Spreadsheets Using Lotus 1-2-3 Release 2.2

LOTUS 1-2-3 Release 2.2

PROJECTS

LOTUS 1-2-3 Release 2.2

Building a Worksheet

OBJECTIVES

You will have mastered the material in this project when you can:

◆ Start 1-2-3

◆ Describe the worksheet

◆ Move the cell pointer around the worksheet

◆ Enter labels, numbers, and formulas into a worksheet

◆ Save a worksheet

◆ Print the screen image of the worksheet

◆ Correct errors in a worksheet

◆ Use the UNDO command

◆ Answer your questions regarding 1-2-3 using the online help facility

◆ Quit 1-2-3

In Project 1 we will develop the worksheet illustrated in Figure 1-1. It contains a company's first quarter sales report. To build this worksheet, we will enter the revenues and costs for January, February, and March. 1-2-3 calculates the profit for each month by subtracting the cost from the revenue.

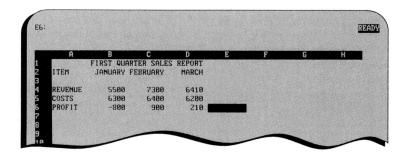

FIGURE 1-1   The worksheet we will build in Project 1.

STARTING 1-2-3

◆ Boot the computer following the procedures presented earlier in the *Introduction to DOS*. Next, follow the steps listed below if your computer has no fixed disk. If your computer has a fixed disk, follow the steps at the bottom of the next page. Several seconds will elapse while the 1-2-3 program is loaded from the disk into main memory. The status light on the disk drive turns on during this loading process. After 1-2-3 is loaded into main memory, it is automatically executed. The first screen displayed by 1-2-3 contains the copyright message shown in Figure 1-2. After a few seconds the copyright message disappears, leaving the worksheet illustrated in Figure 1-3.

Computer with No Fixed Disk Drive

To start 1-2-3 from a computer with no fixed disk drive, do the following:

1. Replace the DOS disk in drive A with the 1-2-3 system disk. If you have two disk drives, place your data disk in drive B.
2. At the A> prompt, type 123 and press the Enter key.
3. If you have only one disk drive, replace the system disk in drive A with your data disk after the program is loaded.

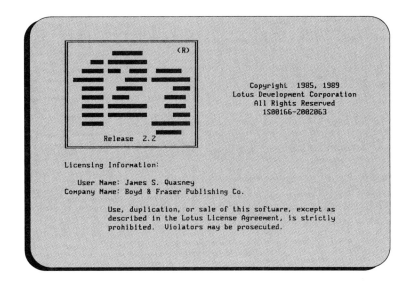

FIGURE 1-2
The copyright screen displays when you load 1-2-3.

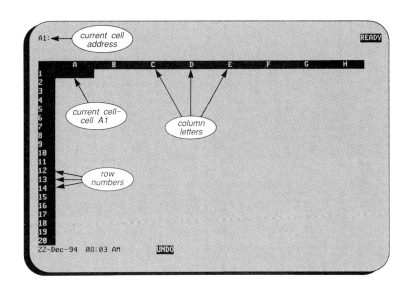

FIGURE 1-3
The worksheet

Computer with a Fixed Disk Drive

To start 1-2-3 from a fixed disk drive, do the following:

1. Use the DOS command CD to change to the subdirectory containing the 1-2-3 program.
2. Place your data disk in drive A.
3. At the DOS prompt, type 123 and press the Enter key.

THE WORKSHEET

The worksheet is organized into a rectangular grid containing columns (vertical) and rows (horizontal). In the border at the top, each **column** is identified by a column letter. In the border on the left side, each **row** is identified by a row number. As shown in Figure 1-3, eight columns (A to H) and twenty rows (1 to 20) of the worksheet appear on the screen.

Cell, Cell Pointer, and Window

Within the borders is the worksheet. It has three parts: cell, cell pointer, and window. A **cell** is the intersection of a column and a row. It is referred to by its **cell address**, the coordinates of the intersection of a column and a row. When you specify a cell address, you must name the column first, followed by the row. For example, cell address D3 refers to the cell located at the intersection of column D and row 3.

One cell on the worksheet is designated the current cell. The **current cell** is the one in which you can enter data. The current cell in Figure 1-3 is A1. It is identified in two ways. First, a reverse video rectangle called the **cell pointer** displays over the current cell. Second, the **current cell address** displays on the first of three lines at the top of the screen. It is important to understand the layout of the worksheet and how to identify all cells, including the current cell.

1-2-3 has 256 columns and 8,192 rows for a total of 2,097,152 cells. Only a small portion of the rectangular worksheet displays on the screen at any one time. For this reason, the area between the borders on the screen is called a **window**. Think of your screen as a window through which you can see parts of the worksheet as illustrated in Figure 1-4.

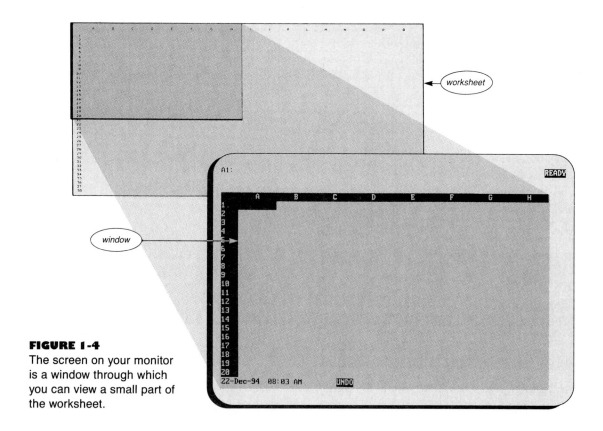

FIGURE 1-4
The screen on your monitor is a window through which you can view a small part of the worksheet.

The Control Panel and the Status Line

The three lines above the window at the top of the screen display important information about the worksheet. The three lines—mode line, input line, and menu line—are collectively called the **control panel**. Below the window, at the bottom of the screen, is the status line. These four lines are illustrated in Figure 1-5.

Mode Line   The first line in the control panel at the top of the screen is the **mode line**. It identifies the current cell address and displays the mode of operation. If data is already in the current cell, the mode line also shows the type of entry and its contents.

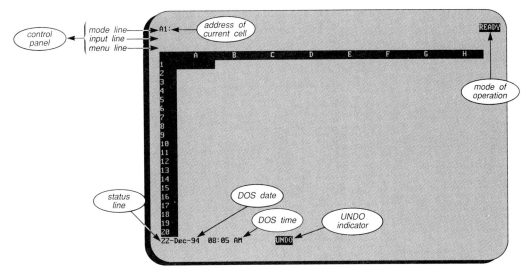

FIGURE 1-5 The control panel at the top of the screen and the status line at the bottom of the screen

The mode of operation displays on the right side of the mode line at the top of the screen. Mode indicators, like EDIT, ERROR, LABEL, MENU, POINT, READY, VALUE, and WAIT tell you the current mode of operation of 1-2-3. For now you should know that when READY displays (Figure 1-5), 1-2-3 is ready to accept your next command or data entry. When WAIT displays in place of READY, 1-2-3 is busy performing some operation that is not instantaneous, like saving a worksheet to disk.

Input Line   Just below the mode line is the input line. The **input line** displays one of three things: the characters you type as you enter data or edit cell contents; a menu of commands; or input prompts asking for additional command specifications.

Menu Line   The **menu line**, the third line in the control panel, displays information about the menu item highlighted on the input line when 1-2-3 is in MENU mode.

Status Line   The line at the very bottom of the screen is the **status line**. It displays three items: the date, the time of day as maintained by DOS, and the status indicators of 1-2-3. Status indicators, like UNDO, CALC, CAPS, CIRC, END, NUM, OVR, and SCROLL, tell you which keys are engaged and alert you to special worksheet conditions. Notice where the indicator UNDO appears at the bottom of Figure 1-5. When this indicator is on, you can use the UNDO command to restore the worksheet data and settings to what they were the last time 1-2-3 was in READY mode. We'll discuss this command in more detail later in this project.

MOVING THE CELL POINTER ONE CELL AT A TIME

◆ Before you can build a worksheet, you must learn how to move the cell pointer to the cells in which you want to make entries. Several methods let you easily move to any cell in the worksheet. The most popular method is to use the four arrow keys located between the typewriter keys and the numeric keypad. The arrow keys on a computer keyboard are illustrated on the next page in Figure 1-6.

Older keyboards do not include a separate set of arrow keys. With these older keyboards, the arrow keys are part of the numeric keypad. If you are using a keyboard without the separate arrow keys, then you must make sure that the Num Lock key is disengaged. You know that the Num Lock key is disengaged when the NUM indicator does not appear on the status line at the bottom of the screen.

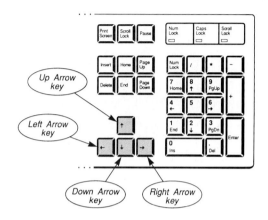

FIGURE 1-6 The arrow keys on the keyboard

We will use the separate set of arrow keys next to the typewriter keys. The arrow keys work as follows:

1. Down Arrow key (↓) moves the cell pointer directly down one cell.
2. Left Arrow key (←) moves the cell pointer one cell to the left.
3. Right Arrow key (→) moves the cell pointer one cell to the right.
4. Up Arrow key (↑) moves the cell pointer directly up one cell.

In the sample worksheet in Figure 1-1, the title FIRST QUARTER SALES REPORT begins in cell B1. Therefore, move the cell pointer from cell A1, where it is when 1-2-3 starts, to cell B1 so you can enter the title. Do this by pressing the Right Arrow key one time, as shown in Figure 1-7. Notice that the current cell address on the mode line in the upper left corner of the screen changes from A1 to B1. Remember, the current cell address on the mode line always identifies the current cell—the one in which the cell pointer is located.

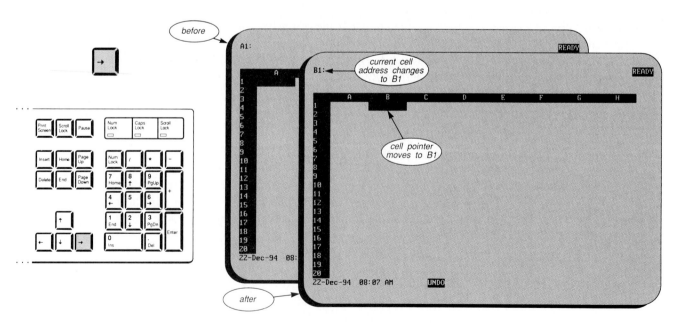

FIGURE 1-7 Press the Right Arrow key to move the cell pointer from A1 to B1.

ENTERING LABELS

◆ With the cell pointer on the proper cell (B1), you can enter the title of the worksheet. In the title FIRST QUARTER SALES REPORT, all the letters are capitals. Although it is possible to enter capital letters by holding down one of the Shift keys on the keyboard each time you type a letter, a more practical method is to press the Caps Lock key one time (Figure 1-8).

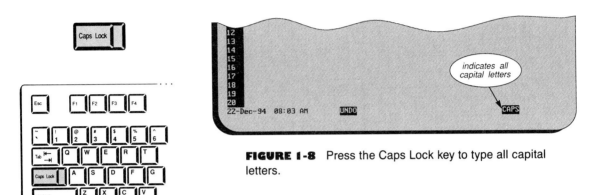

FIGURE 1-8 Press the Caps Lock key to type all capital letters.

The word CAPS on the status line at the bottom of the screen in Figure 1-8 tells you that the Caps Lock key is engaged. Therefore, all subsequent letters you type will be accepted by 1-2-3 as capital letters. Both uppercase and lowercase letters are valid in a worksheet, however, and the letters appear in the same case as you enter them. The Caps Lock key affects only the keys representing letters. Digit and special-character keys continue to transmit the lower character on the key when you press them, unless you hold down a Shift key while pressing the key. To enter a lowercase letter when the Caps Lock key is engaged, hold down the Shift key while typing the letter.

Labels That Begin with a Letter

Entering the title is simple. Just type the required letters on the computer keyboard. Type the words FIRST QUARTER SALES REPORT on the keyboard to get the display shown in Figure 1-9.

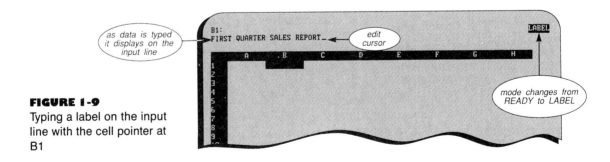

FIGURE 1-9

Typing a label on the input line with the cell pointer at B1

Figure 1-9 shows two important features. First, as soon as you enter the first character of the report title, the mode on the mode line changes from READY to LABEL. 1-2-3 determines that the entry is a **label** and not a number because the first character typed is a letter.

Second, as you type the report title, it displays on the input line followed immediately by the edit cursor. The **edit cursor** is a small, blinking underline symbol. It indicates where the next character you type will be placed on the input line.

Although the data appears at the top of the screen on the input line, it still is not in cell B1. To assign the title to cell B1, press the Enter key as shown in Figure 1-10. This causes the report title displayed on the input line to be placed in the worksheet beginning at cell B1, the cell identified by the cell pointer.

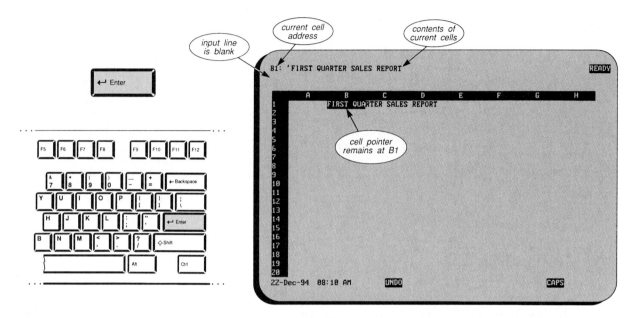

FIGURE 1-10 Pressing the Enter key assigns the label on the input line to cell B1. The cell pointer remains at B1.

If you type the wrong letter and notice the error while it is on the input line at the top of the screen, use the Backspace key (above the Enter key on the keyboard) to erase all the characters back to and including the ones that are wrong. If you see an error in a cell, move the cell pointer to the cell in question and retype the entry.

When you enter a label, a series of events occurs. First, the label is positioned left-justified in the cell where it begins. Therefore, the F in the word FIRST begins in the leftmost position of cell B1.

Second, when a label has more characters than the width of the column, the characters are placed in adjacent columns to the right as long as these columns are blank. In Figure 1-10, the width of cell B1 is nine characters. The words you entered have 26 characters. Therefore, the extra letters display in cell C1 (nine characters) and cell D1 (eight characters), since both cell C1 and cell D1 were blank when you made the 26-character entry in cell B1.

If cell C1 had data in it, only the first nine characters of the 26-character entry in cell B1 would show on the worksheet. The remaining 17 characters would be hidden, but the entire label that belongs to the cell displays in the upper left corner of the screen on the mode line whenever the cell pointer is moved to cell B1.

Third, when you enter data into a cell by pressing the Enter key, the cell pointer remains on the cell (B1) in which you make the entry.

Fourth, a label, in this case FIRST QUARTER SALES REPORT, appears in two places on the screen: in the cell and on the mode line, next to the cell address. Notice that 1-2-3 adds an apostrophe (') before the label on the mode line (Figure 1-10). This apostrophe identifies the data as a left-justified label.

With the title in cell B1, the next step is to enter the column titles in row 2 of the worksheet. Move the cell pointer from cell B1 to cell A2 by using the arrow keys (Figure 1-11). Press the Down Arrow key and then the Left Arrow key. Pressing the Down Arrow key once causes the cell pointer to move to cell B2. Then pressing the Left Arrow key once causes the cell pointer to move to cell A2. Remember that pressing an arrow key one time moves the cell pointer one cell in the direction of the arrow. The current cell address changes on the mode line from B1 to A2.

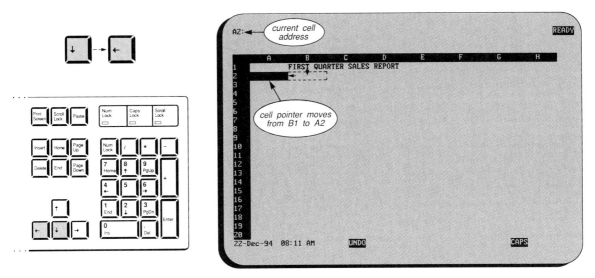

FIGURE 1-11 Moving the cell pointer from B1 to A2 using the arrow keys

With the cell pointer on A2, enter the label ITEM as shown on the input line in Figure 1-12. Since the entry starts with a letter, 1-2-3 positions the label left-justified in the current cell. To enter the label in cell A2 you could press the Enter key as you did for the report title in cell B1. But another way is to press any one of the four arrow keys, as shown on the next page in Figure 1-13. In this case, press the Right Arrow key. This is the better alternative because not only is the data entered into the current cell, but the cell pointer also moves one cell to the right. The cell pointer is at cell B2, the location of the next entry.

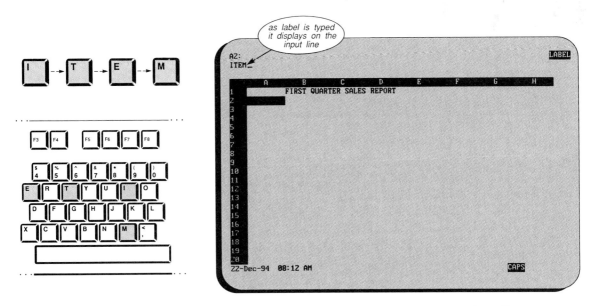

FIGURE 1-12 Typing a label on the input line

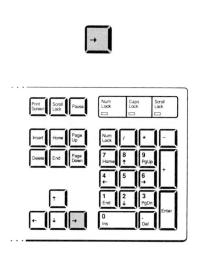

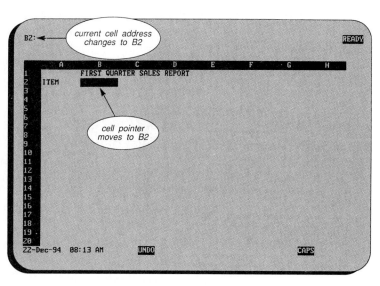

FIGURE 1-13 Pressing the Right Arrow key rather than the Enter key assigns the label on the input line to cell A2 and moves the cell pointer one cell to the right to B2.

Labels Preceded by a Special Character

The worksheet in Figure 1-1 requires that the column headings JANUARY, FEBRUARY, and MARCH be positioned right-justified in the cell, rather than left-justified. There are three different ways to position labels in a cell: left-justified, right-justified, or centered. Remember that the first character of the entry instructs 1-2-3 how to place the label in the cell.

If a label begins with a letter or apostrophe ('), 1-2-3 positions the label left-justified in the current cell. If a label begins with a quotation mark ("), it is positioned right-justified. Finally, if a label begins with a circumflex (^), it is centered within the cell. When the first character is an apostrophe, quotation mark, or circumflex, 1-2-3 does not consider the special character to be part of the label and it will not appear in the cell. However, the special character will precede the label on the mode line when the cell pointer is on the cell in question. Table 1-1 summarizes the positioning of labels in a cell.

TABLE 1-1   Positioning Labels within a Cell

FIRST CHARACTER OF DATA	DATA ENTERED	POSITION IN CELL	REMARK
1. Letter	ITEM	ITEM	Left-justified in cell.
2. Apostrophe (')	'9946	9946	Left-justified in cell. The label 9946 is a name, like the address on a house, and not a number.
3. Quotation Mark (")	"MARCH	MARCH	Right-justified in cell. This always results in one blank character at the end of the label in the cell.
4. Circumflex (^)	^MARCH	MARCH	Centered in the cell.

With the cell pointer located at cell B2, enter the column heading "JANUARY as shown in Figure 1-14, and then press the Right Arrow key. The word JANUARY appears, right-justified, in cell B2 and the cell pointer moves to cell C2 in preparation for the next entry (Figure 1-15).

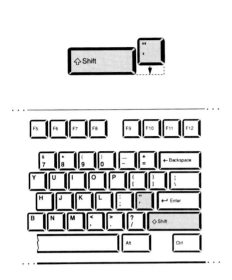

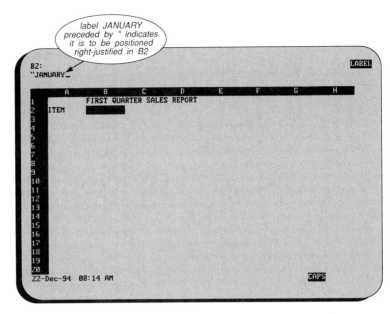

FIGURE 1-14 Begin a label with a quotation mark (") to make it right-justified.

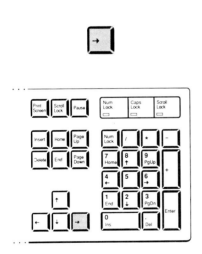

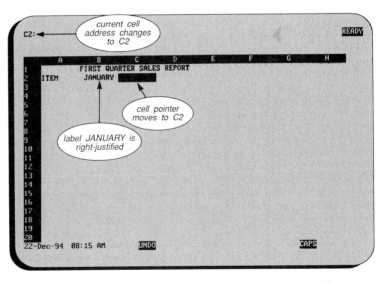

FIGURE 1-15 Pressing the Right Arrow key assigns the label on the input line to cell B2 and moves the cell pointer one cell to the right to C2.

Next, enter the month name "FEBRUARY in cell C2 and the month name "MARCH in cell D2. Enter both labels right-justified. That is, precede each month name with the quotation mark ("). Press the Right Arrow key after typing each label. With these latest entries, the worksheet appears as illustrated in Figure 1-16.

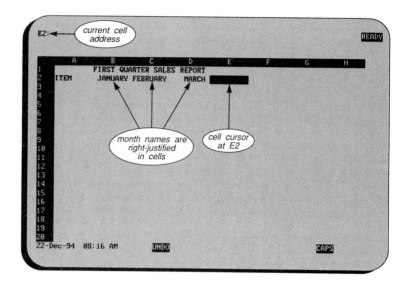

FIGURE 1-16
The three month names are
entered right-justified.

The cell pointer is now located at cell E2. According to Figure 1-1 no data is to be entered into cell E2. The next entry is the label REVENUE in cell A4. Move the cell pointer from cell E2 to cell A4. Press the Down Arrow key twice and the Left Arrow key four times, as shown in Figure 1-17.

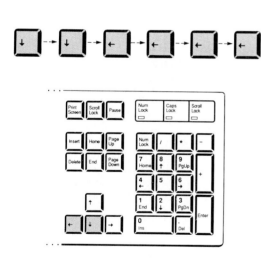

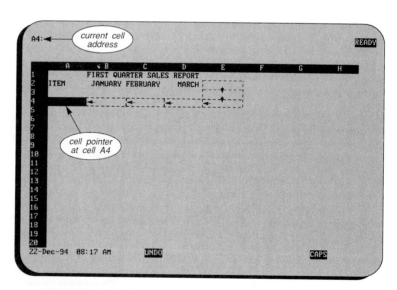

FIGURE 1-17   Using the arrow keys to move the cell
pointer from E2 to A4

With the cell pointer at A4, type the label REVENUE and press the Right Arrow key. The cell pointer moves to cell B4 as shown in Figure 1-18.

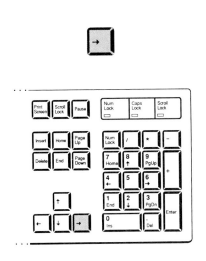

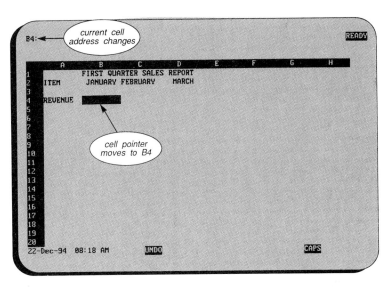

FIGURE 1-18 Pressing the Right Arrow key assigns the label on the input line to cell A4 and moves the cell pointer to B4.

ENTERING NUMBERS

◆ **Numbers** are entered into cells to represent amounts. Numbers are also called **values**. 1-2-3 assumes that an entry for a cell is a number or a formula if the first character you type is one of the following:

$$0\ 1\ 2\ 3\ 4\ 5\ 6\ 7\ 8\ 9\ (\ @\ +\ -\ .\ \#\ \$$$

Whole Numbers

With the cell pointer located at cell B4, enter the revenue amount for January. As shown in Figure 1-1, this amount is 5500. Type the amount 5500 on the keyboard without any special character preceding the number (Figure 1-19). Remember, the CAPS indicator affects only the keys that represent letters on the keyboard. Therefore, never hold down a Shift key to enter a number.

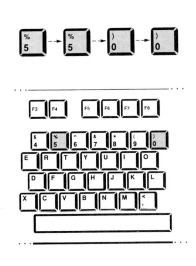

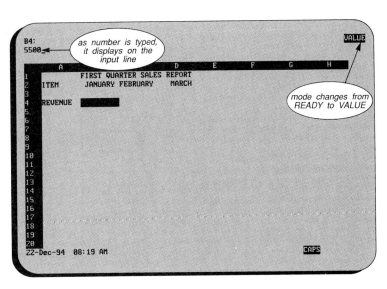

FIGURE 1-19 Entering a number on the input line

As soon as you enter the first digit, 5, the mode of operation on the mode line changes from READY to VALUE. As you type the value 5500, it displays in the upper left corner of the screen on the input line followed immediately by the edit cursor.

Press the Right Arrow key to enter the number 5500 in cell B4 and move the cell pointer one cell to the right. The number 5500 displays right-justified in cell B4 as shown in Figure 1-20. Numbers always display right-justified in a cell. As with right-justified labels, a blank is added to the right side of a number when it is assigned to a cell.

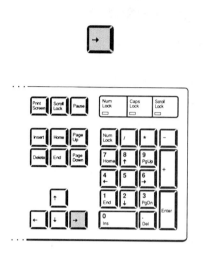

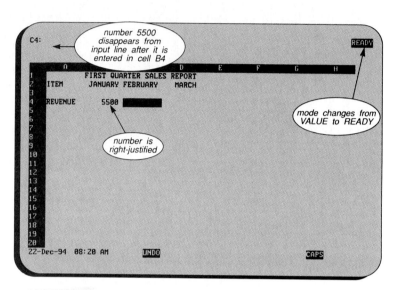

FIGURE 1-20 Pressing the Right Arrow key assigns the number on the input line to cell B4 and moves the cell pointer to C4.

After you enter the data in cell B4, the cell pointer moves to cell C4. At this point, enter the revenue values for February (7300) and March (6410) in cells C4 and D4 in the same manner as you entered the number 5500 into cell B4. After you make the last two revenue entries, the cell pointer is located in cell E4 as shown in Figure 1-21.

FIGURE 1-21
The revenues for the three months are entered into cells B4, C4, and D4.

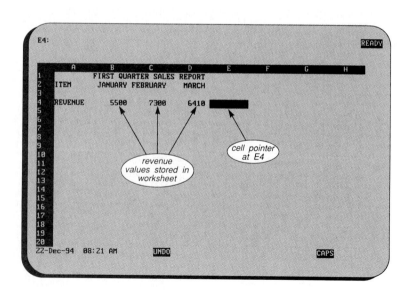

Decimal Numbers

Although the numeric entries in this project are all whole numbers, you can enter numbers with a decimal point, a dollar sign, and a percent sign. The dollar sign and percent sign will not appear in the cell, however. Other special characters, like the comma, are not allowed in a numeric entry. Table 1-2 gives several examples of numeric entries.

TABLE 1-2 Valid Numeric Entries

NUMERIC DATA ENTERED	CELL CONTENTS	REMARK
1.23	1.23	Decimal numbers are allowed.
32.20	32.2	Insignificant zero dropped.
320.	320	Decimal point at the far right is dropped.
$67.54	67.54	Dollar sign dropped.
47%	.47	Percent converted to a decimal number.

MOVING THE CELL POINTER MORE THAN ONE CELL AT A TIME

◆ After you enter the revenue values for the three months, the cell pointer resides in cell E4. Since there are no more revenue values to enter, move the cell pointer to cell A5 so that you can enter the next line of data. While you can use the arrow keys on the right side of the keyboard to move the cell pointer from E4 to A5, there is another method that is faster and involves fewer keystrokes. This second method uses the GOTO command.

The GOTO Command

The **GOTO command** moves the cell pointer directly to the cell you want. GOTO is one of many commands that you enter through the use of the function keys. As shown in Figure 1-22, each function key, except for F6, is assigned two commands — one when you press only the function key, and the other when you hold down the Alt key (or the Shift key) and then press the function key.

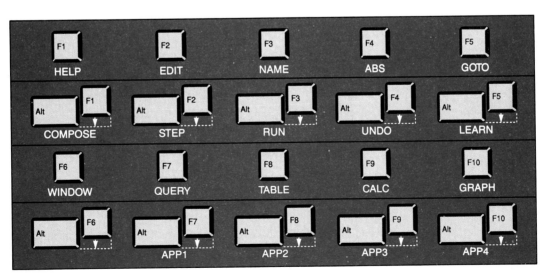

FIGURE 1-22 The commands associated with the function keys on the keyboard

The function keys may be located at the far left side or at the top of the keyboard. In either case, the function keys work the same. For these projects, we assume that the function keys are located at the top of the keyboard. Issue the GOTO command by pressing function key F5. 1-2-3 responds by displaying the message "Enter address to go to: E4" in the upper left corner of the screen and changing the mode from READY to POINT. This is illustrated in the top screen of Figure 1-23. When the mode is POINT, 1-2-3 is requesting a cell address.

Next, enter the cell address A5 as shown in the middle screen of Figure 1-23. Remember to enter the column letter first, followed by the row number. Now press the Enter key. The cell pointer immediately moves to cell A5 as shown in the bottom screen of Figure 1-23. Notice that not only does the cell pointer move, but also the current cell address on the mode line in the upper left corner changes from E4 to A5.

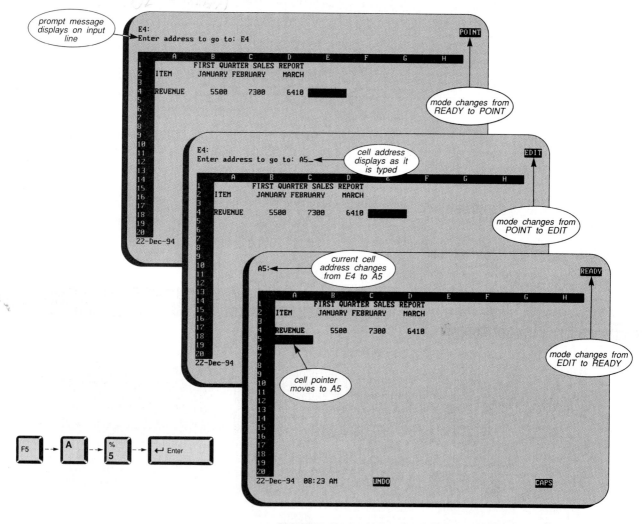

FIGURE 1-23   Using the GOTO command to move the cell pointer

With the cell pointer at cell A5, enter the label COSTS followed by the costs for January, February, and March in the same manner as for the revenues on the previous row. After entering the costs, enter the label PROFIT in cell A6. Figure 1-24 illustrates these entries.

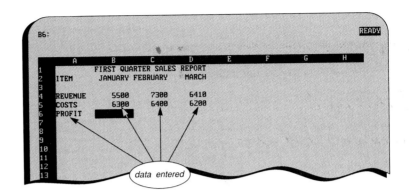

FIGURE 1-24
Costs for the three months
are entered into cells B5, C5,
and D5 and the label PROFIT
is entered into cell A6.

Summary of Ways to Move the Cell Pointer

Table 1-3 summarizes the various ways you can move the cell pointer around the worksheet. As we proceed through the projects in this book, this table will be a helpful reference. Practice using each of the keys described in Table 1-3.

TABLE 1-3   Moving the Cell Pointer Around the Worksheet

KEY(S)	RESULT
↓	Moves the cell pointer directly down one cell.
←	Moves the cell pointer one cell to the left.
→	Moves the cell pointer one cell to the right.
↑	Moves the cell pointer directly up one cell.
Home	Moves the cell pointer to cell A1 no matter where the cell pointer is located on the worksheet.
End	Moves to the border columns and rows of the worksheet in conjunction with the arrow keys.
F5	Moves the cell pointer to the designated cell address.
Page Down	Moves the worksheet under the cell pointer 20 rows down.
Page Up	Moves the worksheet under the cell pointer 20 rows up.
Tab	Moves the worksheet under the cell pointer one screenful of columns to the left.
Shift and Tab	Moves the worksheet under the cell pointer one screenful of columns to the right.
Scroll Lock	Causes the worksheet to move under the cell pointer when the cell pointer movement keys are used.

ENTERING FORMULAS

◆   The profit for each month is calculated by subtracting the costs for the month from the revenue for the month. Thus, the profit for January is obtained by subtracting 6300 from 5500. The result, –800, belongs in cell B6. The negative sign preceding the number indicates that the company lost money and made no profit in January.

One of the reasons why 1-2-3 is such a valuable tool is because you can assign a formula to a cell and it will be calculated automatically. In this example, the formula subtracts the value in cell B5 from the value in cell B4 and assigns the result to cell B6.

Assigning Formulas to Cells

In Figure 1-25, the cell pointer is located at cell B6. Type the formula +B4-B5 with no intervening spaces on the input line. This formula instructs 1-2-3 to subtract the value in cell B5 from the value in cell B4 and place the result in the cell to which the formula is assigned.

To Subtract
+ (1st column) + D4 - D5 =
- (2nd ") · D6 (number)

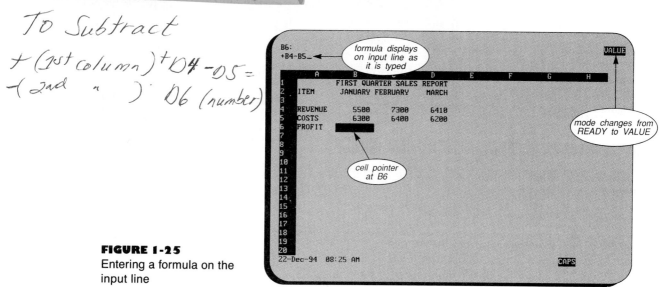

FIGURE 1-25
Entering a formula on the input line

The plus sign (+) preceding B4 is an important part of the formula. It alerts 1-2-3 that you are entering a formula and not a label. The minus sign (–) following B4 is the arithmetic operator, which directs 1-2-3 to perform the subtraction operation. Other valid arithmetic operators include addition (+), multiplication (∗), division (/), and exponentiation (^).

Pressing the Right Arrow key assigns the formula + B4–B5 to cell B6. Instead of displaying the formula in cell B6, however, 1-2-3 completes the arithmetic indicated by the formula and stores the result, –800, in cell B6. This is shown in Figure 1-26. Notice that the negative number displays in cell B6 with the minus sign on the left side of the number. Positive numbers display without any sign.

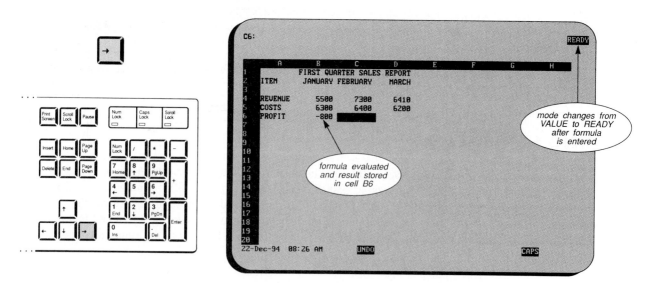

FIGURE 1-26   Pressing the Right Arrow key assigns the formula to cell B6 and moves the cell pointer to C6.

Formulas may be entered in uppercase or lowercase. That is, +b4–b5 is the same as +B4–B5. Like a number, a valid formula begins with one of the following characters: 0 1 2 3 4 5 6 7 8 9 (@ + – . # $. Otherwise, the formula is accepted as a label. Therefore, an alternative to the formula +B4–B5 is (B4–B5). The entry B4–B5 is a label and not a formula, because it begins with the letter B.

To be sure that you understand the relationship of a formula, the associated cell, and the contents of the cell, move the cell pointer back to cell B6. This procedure is shown in Figure 1-27. In the upper left corner of the screen, the mode line shows the assignment of the formula +B4–B5 to cell B6. However, in the cell itself, 1-2-3 displays the result of the formula (–800).

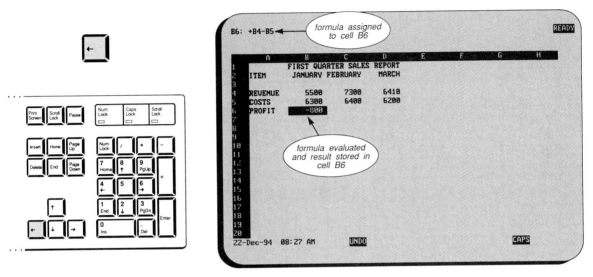

FIGURE 1-27 When the cell pointer is moved to a cell assigned a formula, the formula displays on the mode line.

Next, move the cell pointer to C6 and type the formula +C4-C5. As shown in Figure 1-28, the formula for determining the profit for February displays at the top of the screen on the input line.

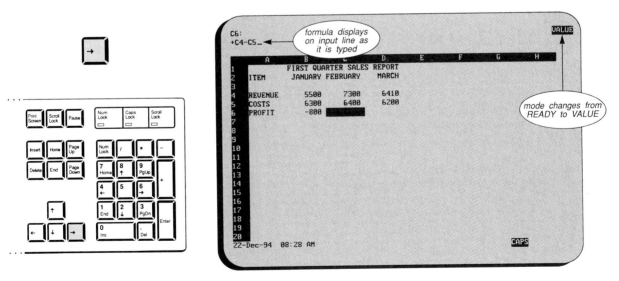

FIGURE 1-28 Entering the profit formula for February on the input line

Press the Right Arrow key. The value in cell C5 (February costs) is subtracted from the value in cell C4 (February revenue) and the result of the computation displays in cell C6 (February profit). The cell pointer also moves to cell D6, as shown in Figure 1-29. As you can see, the process for entering a formula into a cell is much the same as for entering labels and numbers.

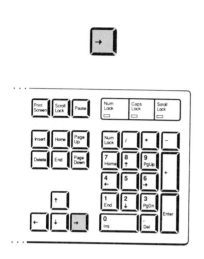

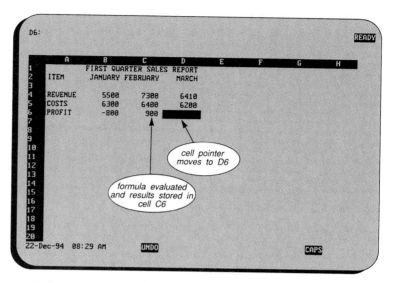

FIGURE 1-29   Pressing the Right Arrow key assigns the formula on the input line to cell C6 and the cell pointer moves to D6.

The same technique can be used to assign the formula +D4–D5 to cell D6. After pressing the Right Arrow key to conclude the entry in D6, the worksheet is complete, as illustrated in Figure 1-30.

FIGURE 1-30
Worksheet for Project 1 is complete.

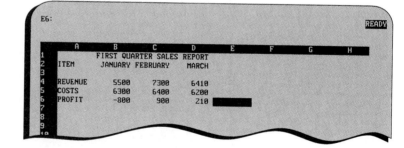

Order of Operations

The formulas in this project involve only one arithmetic operator, subtraction. But when more than one operator is involved in a formula, the same order of operations is used as in algebra. Moving from left to right in a formula, the **order of operations** is as follows: first all exponentiations ($\wedge$), then all multiplications ($*$) and divisions (/), and finally all additions ($+$) and subtractions (–). You can use parentheses to override the order of operations. Table 1-4 illustrates several examples of valid formulas.

TABLE 1-4 Valid Formula Entries

FORMULA	REMARK
+E3 or (E3)	Assigns the value in cell E3 to the current cell.
7*F5 or +F5*7 or (7*F5)	Assigns 7 times the contents of cell F5 to the current cell.
−G44*G45	Assigns the negative value of the product of the values contained in cells G44 and G45 to the current cell.
2*(J12−F2)	Assigns the product of 2 and the difference between the values contained in cells J12 and F2 to the current cell. It is invalid to write this formula as 2(J12−F2). The multiplication sign (*) between the 2 and the left parenthesis is required.
+A1/A1−A3*A4+A5^A6	From left to right: exponentiation (^) first, followed by multiplication (*) or division (/), and finally addition (+) or subtraction (−).

SAVING A WORKSHEET

◆ You use 1-2-3 either to enter data into the worksheet, as we did in the last section, or to execute a command. In this section we discuss the first of a series of commands that allows you to instruct 1-2-3 to save, load, modify, and print worksheets.

When a worksheet is created, it is stored in main memory. If the computer is turned off or if you quit 1-2-3, the worksheet is lost. Hence, it is mandatory to save to disk any worksheet that will be used later.

MENU Mode

To save a worksheet, place 1-2-3 in **MENU mode**. Do this by pressing the **Slash key** (/) as illustrated in Figure 1-31. First, notice in Figure 1-31 that the mode at the top right side of the screen is MENU. This means that 1-2-3 is now in MENU mode. Next, notice the menus on the input line and menu line in the control panel. A **menu** is a list from which you can choose. The Main menu appears on the input line when you first press the Slash key. A second-level menu appears immediately below on the menu line.

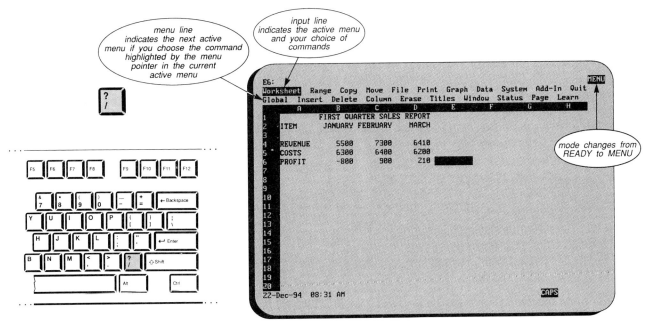

FIGURE 1-31 To save a worksheet to disk, first press the Slash key (/) to switch 1-2-3 to MENU mode.

The second-level menu lists the secondary commands that are available if you select the command highlighted by the menu pointer in the Main menu. The **menu pointer** is a reverse video rectangle that can be moved from command to command in the active menu on the input line, using the Right Arrow and Left Arrow keys. Although there are two menus on the screen, only the one on the input line is active. If you press the Right Arrow key four times, the menu pointer rests on the File command. This procedure is shown in Figure 1-32. Now compare Figure 1-31 to Figure 1-32. Notice that the second level of commands on the menu line has changed in Figure 1-32 to show the list of secondary commands that are available if you select the File command.

For a list of all the 1-2-3 commands, see the command structure charts in the Appendix following Project 6.

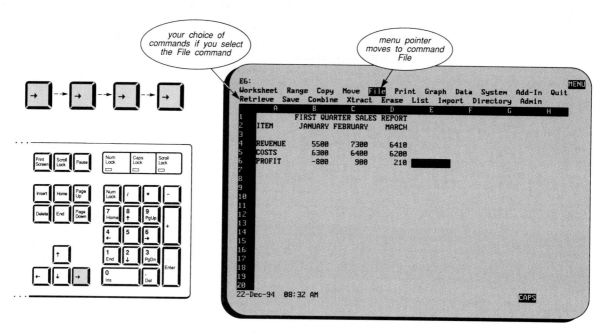

FIGURE 1-32 As you move the menu pointer to each command on the input line, the menu line indicates what the command can do.

Backing Out of MENU Mode

If you decide that you do not want to issue a command, press the **Esc key** until the mode of operation changes to READY. The Esc key, located on the top left side of the keyboard next to the digit 1 key, instructs 1-2-3 to exit MENU mode and return to READY mode.

Press the Esc key and the control panel changes from the one in Figure 1-32 to the one in Figure 1-30. Press the Slash key once and the Right Arrow key four times and the Main menu in Figure 1-32 reappears in the control panel. The Esc key allows you to *back out* of any command or entry on the input line. If you become confused while making any kind of entry (command or data), use the Esc key to reset the current entry. When in doubt, press the Esc key.

The File Save Command

To save a file, select the File command from the Main menu. There are two ways to select the File command.

1. Press the F key for File. Each command in the Main menu begins with a different letter. Therefore, the first letter uniquely identifies each command.
2. Use the Right Arrow key to move the menu pointer to the word File (Figure 1-32). With the menu pointer on the word File, press the Enter key.

Use the first method and press the F key as shown in Figure 1-33. This causes the File menu to replace the Main menu on the input line. The menu pointer is now active in the File menu.

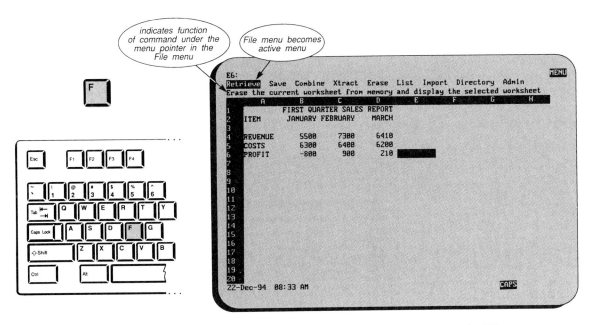

FIGURE 1-33 Typing the letter F moves the File menu
from the menu line to the input line.

Pressing the S key for Save causes the message "Enter name of file to save: A:\" followed by the blinking edit cursor to appear on the input line at the top of the screen. The mode also changes from MENU to EDIT. This procedure is shown in Figure 1-34.

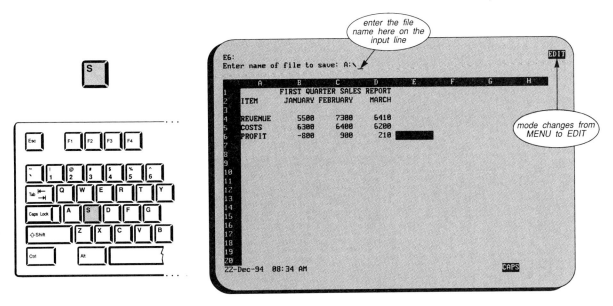

FIGURE 1-34 Typing the letter S for Save causes 1-2-3
to display the prompt message on the input line.

The next step is to select a file name. Any file name will do, provided it is eight or fewer characters in length and includes only the characters A–Z (uppercase or lowercase), 0–9, and the special characters described earlier in the *Introduction to DOS*. 1-2-3 automatically adds the file extension .WK1 to the file name. The file extension .WK1 stands for worksheet.

In this example, let's choose the file name PROJS-1. Type the file name PROJS-1 as shown in Figure 1-35. Next, press the Enter key. The file is stored on the A drive with the file name PROJS-1.WK1. Remember, 1-2-3 does not distinguish between uppercase and lowercase letters. Therefore, you can type PROJS-1 or projs-1 or ProJS-1. All three file names are the same.

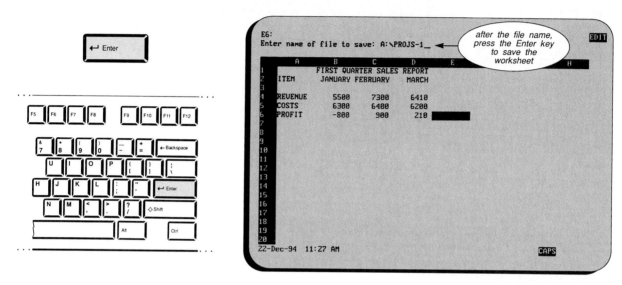

FIGURE 1-35 After you enter the file name on the input line, press the Enter key to complete the /FS command.

While 1-2-3 writes the worksheet on the disk, the mode changes from EDIT to WAIT. The status light on the A drive also lights up to show it is in use. As soon as the writing is complete, the status light goes off and 1-2-3 returns to the READY mode. This is shown in Figure 1-36.

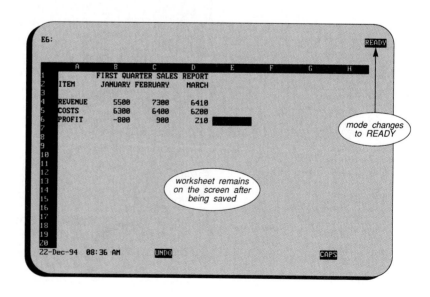

FIGURE 1-36
When the computer is finished saving the worksheet to disk, 1-2-3 returns to READY mode.

Saving Worksheets to a Different Disk Drive

If you want to save the worksheet to a different drive, enter the command /**F**ile **S**ave (/FS). Next, press the Esc key twice to delete the "A:*.wk1" from the prompt message "Enter name of file to save: A:*.wk1". Enter the drive of your choice followed by the file name. For example, to save the worksheet on the disk in drive B, enter B:PROJS-1 in response to the prompt "Enter name of file to save:". Do not attempt to save a worksheet to the B drive if it is unavailable.

To change the default drive permanently from A to B, enter the command /**W**orksheet **G**lobal **D**efault **D**irectory (/WGDD). That is, press the Slash key, then type the letters WGDD. Press the Esc key to delete the current default drive and type B: for drive B. Press the Enter key. Next, enter the commands Update and Quit (UQ). The Update command permanently changes the default drive in the 1-2-3 program. The Quit command quits the Default menu. The examples in the remainder of this book use the B drive as the default drive.

PRINTING A SCREEN IMAGE OF THE WORKSHEET

The **screen image** of the worksheet is exactly what you see on the screen, including the window borders and control panel. A printed version of the worksheet is called a **hard copy**.

Anytime you use the printer, you must be sure that it is ready. To make the printer ready, turn it off and use the platen knob to align the perforated edge of the paper with the top of the print head mechanism. Then turn the printer on. With the printer in READY mode, press the Print Screen key (Shift-PrtSc on older keyboards). The screen image of the worksheet immediately prints on the printer. When the printer stops, eject the paper from the printer and carefully tear off the printed version of the worksheet (Figure 1-37).

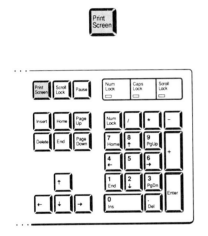

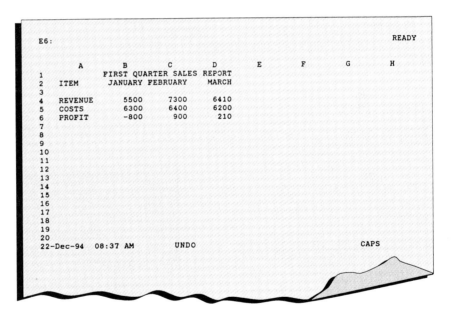

FIGURE 1-37 Press the Print Screen key to obtain a hard copy of the worksheet.

CORRECTING ERRORS

◆ There are several methods for correcting errors in a worksheet. The one you choose will depend on the severity of the error, and whether you notice it while typing the data on the input line or after the data is in the cell.

The error-correcting examples that follow are not part of the worksheet we are building in Project 1. However, you should carefully step through them since they are essential to building and maintaining worksheets.

Correcting Errors While the Data Is on the Input Line

Move the cell pointer to cell A5 and type the label COTTS, rather than COSTS, on the input line. This error is shown in Figure 1-38.

FIGURE 1-38
Incorrect data spotted on the input line

To correct the error, move the edit cursor back to position 3 on the input line by pressing the Backspace key three times (Figure 1-39). Each time you press the Backspace key, the character immediately to the left of the edit cursor is erased.

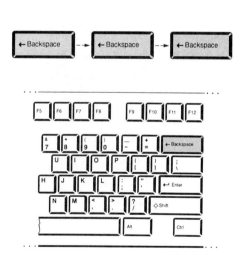

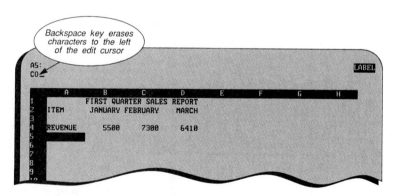

FIGURE 1-39 Press the Backspace key three times to erase the characters up to and including the first T in COTTS.

Then, as in Figure 1-40, type the correct letters STS. Now the entry is correct. Press the Right Arrow key to enter the label COSTS into cell A5.

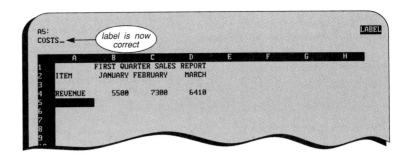

FIGURE 1-40
Enter the correct characters and press the Enter key or one of the arrow keys.

In summary, if you notice an error while the label, number, or formula is on the input line, you can do one of two things. You can use the Backspace key to erase the portion in error and then type the correct characters. Or, if the error is too severe, you can press the Esc key to erase the entire entry on the input line and reenter the data item from the beginning.

Editing Data in a Cell

If you spot an error in the worksheet, move the cell pointer to the cell with the error. You then have two ways to correct the error. If the entry is short, simply type it and press the Enter key. The new entry will replace the old entry. Remember, the cell pointer must be on the cell with the error before you begin typing the correct entry.

If the entry in the cell is long and the errors are minor, using the EDIT mode may be a better choice, rather than retyping. Move the cell pointer to cell A4 and enter the label GROSS PAY incorrectly as GRSS PSY. Figure 1-41 shows the label GRSS PSY in cell A4. You will have to insert the letter O between the letters R and S in GRSS and change the letter S in PSY to the letter A.

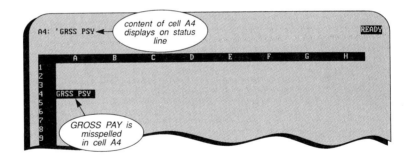

FIGURE 1-41
Error spotted in cell

The six steps in Figure 1-42 illustrate how to use the EDIT mode to correct the entry in cell A4. As shown on the next page in Step 1, first press function key F2 to switch 1-2-3 to EDIT mode. The contents of cell A4 immediately display on the input line, followed by the edit cursor. The contents of the cell can now be corrected. Table 1-5 on page L30 lists the edit keys available in EDIT mode and their functions.

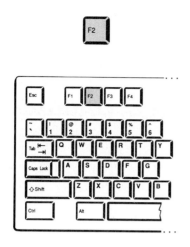

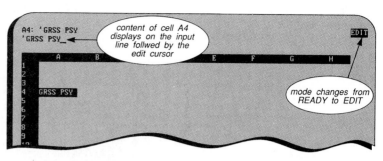

FIGURE 1-42 (Step 1 of 6) Press function key F2 to switch 1-2-3 to EDIT mode.

With 1-2-3 in EDIT mode, the next step in changing GRSS PSY to GROSS PAY is to move the edit cursor on the input line to the leftmost S in GRSS PSY. Press the Left Arrow key six times as shown in Step 2 of Figure 1-42.

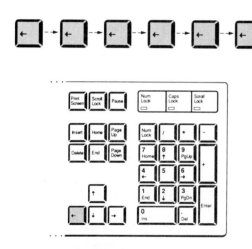

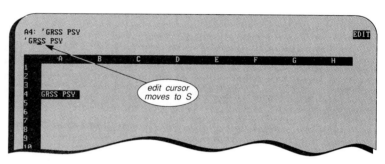

FIGURE 1-42 (Step 2 of 6) Press the Left Arrow key six times to move the edit cursor on the input line to the first S in GRSS PSY.

Next, type the letter O. Typing the letter O *pushes* the leftmost letter S and all the letters to the right of it to the right. The O is inserted as shown in Step 3 of Figure 1-42.

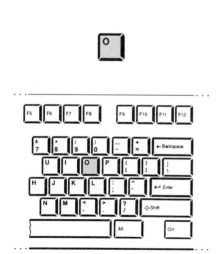

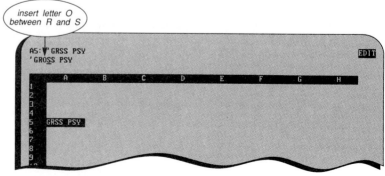

FIGURE 1-42 (Step 3 of 6) With the edit cursor on the first letter S in GRSS PSY, type the letter O.

The next step calls for moving the edit cursor to the S in PSY and changing it to the letter A. Use the Right Arrow key as shown in Step 4 of Figure 1-42. After moving the edit cursor, press the Insert key to switch from inserting characters to overtyping characters.

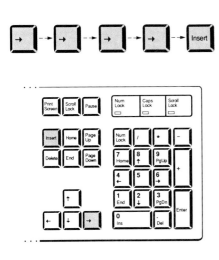

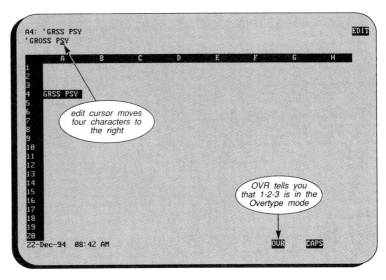

FIGURE 1-42 (Step 4 of 6) Press the Right Arrow key four times to move the edit cursor to the letter S in PSY. Press the Insert key to switch to overtype.

Type the letter A. The correct label GROSS PAY now resides on the input line (Step 5 of Figure 1-42).

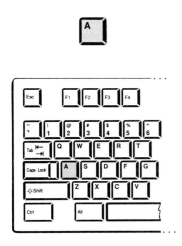

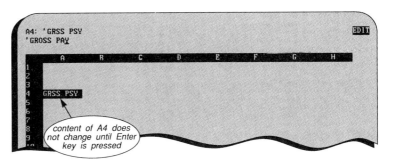

FIGURE 1-42 (Step 5 of 6) With the edit cursor on the letter S in PSY, type the letter A.

Press the Enter key to replace GRSS PSY in cell A4 with GROSS PAY. This is illustrated in Step 6 of Figure 1-42.

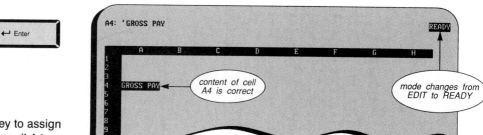

**FIGURE 1-42
(Step 6 of 6)**
Press the Enter key to assign
the edited value to cell A4.

Pay careful attention to the six steps in Figure 1-42. It is easy to make keyboard and grammatical errors. Understanding how to use the EDIT mode will make it easier to correct mistakes. Table 1-5 summarizes the keys for editing cell entries.

TABLE 1-5 Keys for Editing Cell Entries

KEY	FUNCTION
F2	Switches 1-2-3 to EDIT mode.
←	Completes entry. Up Arrow key or Down Arrow key also completes an entry. Either key also moves the cell pointer in the corresponding direction.
Backspace	Erases the character immediately to the left of the edit cursor.
Delete	Deletes the character on which the edit cursor is located.
Insert	Switches between inserting characters and overtyping characters. In EDIT mode, characters are inserted when the status indicator OVR does not display at the bottom of the screen. Characters are overtyped when the status indicator OVR displays at the bottom of the screen.
→	Moves the edit cursor one character to the right on the input line.
←	Moves the edit cursor one character to the left on the input line.
End	Moves the edit cursor to the end of the entry on the input line.
Home	Moves the edit cursor to the first character in the entry on the input line.

Undoing the Last Entry — The UNDO Command

As long as the UNDO indicator displays at the bottom of the screen (Figure 1-36), you can enter the UNDO command to erase the most recent cell entry. You enter the UNDO command by holding down the Alt key and pressing the function key F4 (Alt-F4).

To try the UNDO command, enter the value 7345.48 in cell B4. Before entering any other value into the worksheet, press Alt-F4. 1-2-3 erases the value 7345.48 from cell B4. To restore the value 7345.48 in B4, press Alt-F4 again. The second UNDO command *undoes* the first UNDO command.

UNDO is a time-saving command. It can be used to undo much more complicated worksheet activities than a single cell entry. For example, most commands issued from the Main menu can be undone if you enter the UNDO command before making any other entry after 1-2-3 returns from MENU mode to READY mode. The general rule is that the UNDO command can restore the worksheet data and settings to what they were the last time 1-2-3 was in READY mode.

Erasing the Contents of Any Cell in the Worksheet

It is not unusual to enter data into the wrong cell. In such a case, to correct the error, you might want to erase the contents of the cell. Let's erase the label GROSS PAY in cell A4. Make sure the cell pointer is on cell A4. Enter the command /Range Erase (/RE). That is, press the Slash key to display the Main menu, then press the R key for Range and the E key for Erase. When the message "Enter range to erase: A4..A4" appears on the input line at the top of the screen, press the Enter key. 1-2-3 immediately erases the entry GROSS PAY in cell A4.

Erasing the Entire Worksheet

Sometimes, everything goes wrong. If the worksheet is such a mess that you don't know where to begin to correct it, you might want to erase it entirely and start over. To do this, enter the command /Worksheet Erase Yes (/WEY). That is, first press the Slash key to display the Main menu. Next, type the letters W for Worksheet, E for Erase, and Y for Yes.

The /Worksheet Erase Yes (/WEY) ~~(after saving)~~ command does not erase the worksheet PROJS-1 from disk. This command only affects the worksheet in main memory. Remember that the /Worksheet Erase Yes (/WEY) command can also be a method for clearing the worksheet on the screen of its contents after you have saved it. This is especially useful when you no longer want the current worksheet displayed because you want to begin a new one.

ONLINE HELP FACILITY

◆   At any time while you are using 1-2-3, you can press function key F1 to gain access to the online help facility. When you press F1, 1-2-3 temporarily suspends the current activity and displays valuable information about the current mode or command. If you have a one-disk or two-disk system and no fixed disk drive, make sure the 1-2-3 system disk is in drive A before pressing the F1 key.

With 1-2-3 in READY mode, press the F1 key. The 1-2-3 Help Index screen shown in Figure 1-43 displays. Directions are given at the bottom of the help screen for accessing information on any 1-2-3 program subject. With the Help Index on the screen, use the arrow keys to select any one of the many 1-2-3 topics. To exit the help facility and return to the worksheet, press the Esc key.

If you press the F1 key while in any mode other than READY, 1-2-3 displays the appropriate help screen, rather than the 1-2-3 Help Index screen shown in Figure 1-43.

The best way to familiarize yourself with the online help facility is to use it. When you have a question about how a command works in 1-2-3, press F1. You may want to consider printing a hard copy of the information displayed on the screen. To print a hard copy, ready the printer and press the Print Screen key.

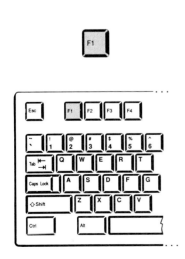

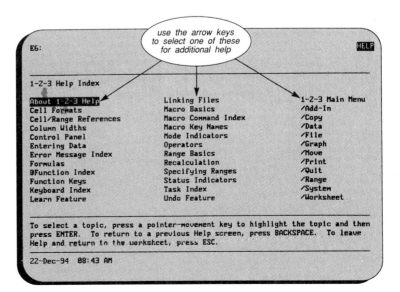

FIGURE 1-43   Press function key F1 to use the online help facility of 1-2-3.

QUITTING 1-2-3

 To exit 1-2-3 and return control to DOS, do the following:

1. Save the current worksheet if you made any changes to it since the last save.
2. If you loaded 1-2-3 from drive A, place the DOS disk in drive A.
3. Enter the Quit command (/Q). First, press the Slash key to display the Main menu. Next, type the letter Q for Quit.
4. When the message shown at the top of the screen in Figure 1-44 displays, type the letter Y to confirm your exit from 1-2-3.

If you made changes to the worksheet since the last time you saved it to disk, 1-2-3 displays the message "WORKSHEET CHANGES NOT SAVED! End 1-2-3 anyway?" Type Y to quit 1-2-3 without saving the latest changes to the worksheet to disk. Type N to return to READY mode.

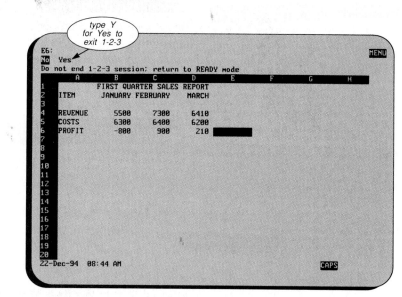

FIGURE 1-44
To quit 1-2-3 and return control to DOS, enter the command /Q and type the letter Y.

PROJECT SUMMARY

In Project 1 you learned how to move the cell pointer around the worksheet, enter data into the worksheet, save a worksheet, and print a hard copy using the Print Screen key. All the activities that you learned for this project are summarized in the Quick Reference following the Appendix. The following is a summary of the keystroke sequence we used in Project 1.

SUMMARY OF KEYSTROKES — PROJECT 1

STEPS	KEY(S) PRESSED	RESULTS
1	[Caps Lock]	Sets Caps Lock on.
2	→	Moves the cell pointer to B1.
3	FIRST QUARTER SALES REPORT ↵	Enters report heading.
4	↓ ←	Moves the cell pointer to A2.
5	ITEM →	Enters column heading.
6	"JANUARY →	Enters column heading.
7	"FEBRUARY →	Enters column heading.
8	"MARCH →	Enters column heading.
9	↓↓ ← ← ← ←	Moves the cell pointer to A4.
10	REVENUE →	Enters row identifier.
11	5500 →	Enters January revenue.
12	7300 →	Enters February revenue.
13	6410 →	Enters March revenue.
14	[F5] A5 ↵	Moves the cell pointer to A5.
15	COSTS →	Enters row identifier.
16	6300 →	Enters January costs.
17	6400 →	Enters February costs.
18	6200 →	Enters March costs.
19	[F5] A6 ↵	Moves the cell pointer to A6.
20	PROFIT →	Enters row identifier.
21	+B4-B5 →	Enters January profit formula.
22	+C4-C5 →	Enters February profit formula.
23	+D4-D5 →	Enters March profit formula.
24	/FS PROJS-1 ↵	Saves the worksheet as PROJS-1.
25	[Print Screen]	Prints the screen image of the worksheet.

The following list summarizes the material covered in Project 1.

1. The worksheet is organized in two dimensions—columns (vertical) and rows (horizontal).
2. In the border at the top of the screen, each **column** is identified by a column letter. In the border on the left side, each **row** is identified by a row number.
3. A **cell** is the intersection of a row and a column. A cell is referred to by its **cell address**, the coordinates of the intersection of a column and row.
4. The **current cell** is the cell in which data (labels, numbers, and formulas) can be entered. The current cell is identified in two ways. A reverse video rectangle called the **cell pointer** is displayed over the current cell, and the current cell address displays on the mode line at the top of the screen.
5. The area between the borders on the screen is called a **window**.
6. The three lines immediately above the window—mode line, input line, and menu line—are collectively called the **control panel**.
7. The **mode line** is the first line in the control panel. It indicates the current cell address and displays the mode of operation. If a value is already in the cell, the mode line also shows the type of entry and its contents.
8. The second line in the control panel is the **input line**. Depending on the mode of operation, it shows the characters you type as you enter data or edit cell contents; a menu of commands; or input prompts asking for additional command specifications.

9. The third line in the control panel is the **menu line**. It displays information about the menu item highlighted on the input line when 1-2-3 is in MENU mode.

10. The line at the bottom of the screen is the **status line**. It displays three items: the date and time of day as maintained by DOS and status indicators.

11. To move the cell pointer one cell at a time use the arrow keys found on the right side of the typewriter keys.

12. No matter where the cell pointer is on the worksheet, if you press the Home key, the cell pointer always moves to cell A1.

13. Three types of entries may be made in a cell: labels, numbers, and formulas.

14. A cell entry is a **label** if the first character is any character other than one that identifies it as a number or formula.

15. A cell entry is a **number** or a **formula** if the first character typed is one of the following: 0 1 2 3 4 5 6 7 8 9 (@ + – . # $.

16. A number or formula is also called a **value**.

17. You may use the **GOTO command** (function key F5) to move the cell pointer to any cell in the worksheet.

18. If a label begins with a letter or an apostrophe ('), it is positioned in the cell left-justified. If a label begins with a quotation mark ("), it is positioned right-justified. If a label begins with a circumflex (^), it is centered in the cell.

19. One of the most powerful features of 1-2-3 is the capability to assign a formula to a cell and calculate it automatically. The result of the calculation is displayed in the cell.

20. 1-2-3 uses the same order of operations as in algebra. Moving from left to right in a formula, the **order of operations** is as follows: all exponentiations (^) are completed first, then all multiplications (∗) and divisions (/), and finally all additions (+) and subtractions (–). Parentheses may be used to override the order of operations.

21. A **menu** is a list from which you can choose. To put 1-2-3 in **MENU mode**, press the **Slash key (/)**. To leave MENU mode, press the Esc key as many times as necessary.

22. The **edit cursor** shows where the next character will be placed on the input line. The **menu pointer** moves from command to command in the active menu.

23. If you get confused while making any kind of entry (command or data), press the **Esc key** to reset the current entry. When in doubt, press the Esc key.

24. To save a worksheet, enter the command **/File Save (/FS)** and the file name you intend to name the worksheet.

25. 1-2-3 automatically appends the file extension .WK1 (worksheet) to the file name.

26. The **screen image** is exactly what you see on the screen.

27. To print the screen image of the worksheet, make sure the printer is ready. Next, press the Print Screen key. After the worksheet has printed, eject the paper from the printer and carefully tear off the printed worksheet. A printed version of the worksheet is called a **hard copy**.

28. To edit the contents of a cell, press function key F2.

29. If the most recent entry into a cell is in error, use the UNDO command to erase it. You enter the UNDO command by holding down the Alt key and pressing the function key F4 (Alt-F4).

30. To erase the contents of a cell, move the cell pointer to the cell in question, enter the command **/Range Erase** (/RE), and press the Enter key.

31. To erase the entire worksheet, enter the command **/Worksheet Erase Yes (/WEY)**.

32. At any time while you are using 1-2-3, you may press function key F1 to gain access to the online help facility.

33. To exit 1-2-3 and return control to DOS, enter the command **/Quit (/Q)**. Press the Y key to confirm your exit. Before entering the Quit command, be sure that the DOS program COMMAND.COM is available to the system.

STUDENT ASSIGNMENTS

STUDENT ASSIGNMENT 1: True/False

Instructions: Circle T if the statement is true and F if the statement is false.

T F   1. With 1-2-3, each column is identified by a letter of the alphabet and each row by a number.

T F   2. One method of moving the worksheet cell pointer is by using the arrow keys.

T F   3. A cell entry that consists of just words or letters of the alphabet is called a formula.

T F   4. The current cell address on the mode line identifies the cell that the cell pointer is on in the worksheet.

T F   5. A cell is identified by specifying its cell address, the coordinates of the intersection of a column and a row.

T F   6. When 1-2-3 first begins execution, the column width is six characters.

T F   7. Numeric data entered into a worksheet is stored left-justified in a cell.

T F   8. The GOTO command moves the cell pointer directly to a designated cell.

T F   9. When text data is entered that contains more characters than the width of the column, an error message displays.

T F 10. The cell pointer is at C6. The formula +C4–C5 causes the value in cell C5 to be subtracted from the value in cell C4. The answer is displayed in cell C6.

T F 11. If a cell entry begins with a circumflex (^), the data is left-justified in the cell.

T F 12. To move the cell pointer from cell C1 to cell A2, press the Down Arrow key one time and the Left Arrow key one time.

T F 13. When you enter a formula in a cell, the formula is evaluated and the result is displayed in the same cell on the worksheet.

T F 14. The UNDO command erases the entire worksheet.

T F 15. Typing GOTO C1 causes the worksheet cell pointer to be positioned in cell C1.

STUDENT ASSIGNMENT 2: Multiple Choice

Instructions: Circle the correct response.

1. If the first character typed on the input line is the digit 5, the mode on the mode line changes from READY to _____ .
   a. VALUE
   b. LABEL
   c. MENU
   d. EDIT

2. In the border on the left side of the worksheet, each row is identified by a _____ .
   a. number
   b. letter
   c. pointer
   d. none of the above

3. To enter the UNDO command, hold down the Alt key and press _____ .
   a. function key F4
   b. function key F5
   c. function key F6
   d. function key F7

4. A cell is identified by a cell _____ .
   a. pointer
   b. address
   c. entry
   d. none of the above

5. Which one of the following best describes the function of the Backspace key?
   a. deletes the value in the current cell
   b. deletes the character on the input line under which the edit cursor is located
   c. deletes the character to the right of the edit cursor on the input line
   d. deletes the character to the left of the edit cursor on the input line

6. The command /Quit (/Q) is used to _____ .
   a. load a new worksheet
   b. save a worksheet on disk
   c. suspend work on the current worksheet and return control to the operating system
   d. make corrections in the current entry

Student Assignment 2 (continued)

7. Which one of the following should you press to *back out* of any command or entry on the input line?
   a. Esc key
   b. Alt key
   c. Ctrl key
   d. Delete key
8. Which one of the following should you press to put 1-2-3 in HELP mode?
   a. function key F1
   b. function key F2
   c. function key F3
   d. function key F5

STUDENT ASSIGNMENT 3: Understanding the Worksheet

Instructions: Answer the following questions.

1. In the following figure, a series of arrows points to the major components of a worksheet. Identify the various parts of the worksheet in the space provided in the figure.

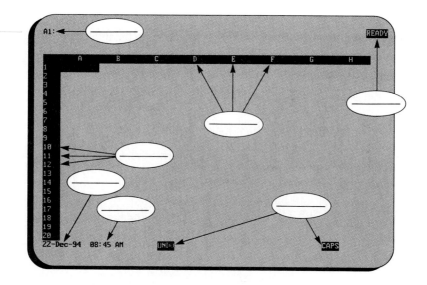

2. Explain the following entries that may be contained on the status line at the bottom of the screen.

   a. NUM _____
   _____

   b. 15:20 _____
   _____

   c. UNDO _____
   _____

   d. OVR _____
   _____

STUDENT ASSIGNMENT 4: Understanding 1-2-3 Commands

Instructions: Answer the following questions.

1. Indicate the value that will be assigned to cell C1 by the entry on the input line in the following figure. Assume that cell I23 contains the value 5 and cell I24 contains the value 6.

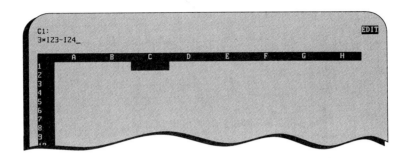

Value: _____

2. Which keystroke causes 1-2-3 to display the mode shown in the following figure?

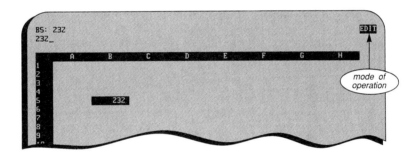

Keystroke: _____

3. Indicate the sequence of keystrokes for saving a worksheet that causes the display shown on the input line in the following figure. Assume that the first letter of each command is entered to issue the commands that cause the display.

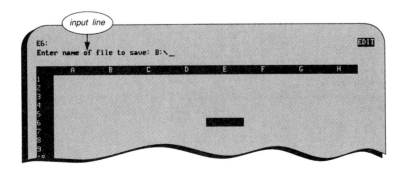

Keystroke sequence: _____

Student Assignment 4 (continued)

4. Use the following figure to answer the questions. Where is the cell pointer located in the worksheet? Which keystroke causes the display on the input line?

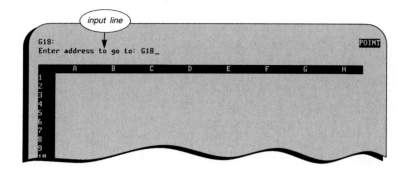

Cell pointer location: _____

Keystroke: _____

STUDENT ASSIGNMENT 5: Correcting Formulas in a Worksheet

Instructions: The worksheet illustrated in the following figure contains an error in the PROFIT row for January. Analyze the entries displayed on the worksheet. Explain the cause of the error and the method of correction in the space provided below.

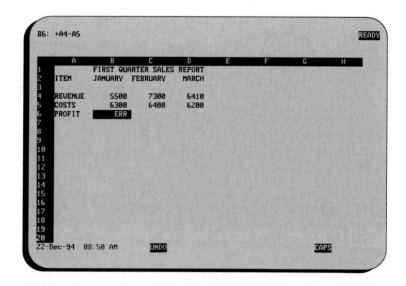

Cause of error: _____

_____

Method of correction: _____

_____

STUDENT ASSIGNMENT 6: Correcting Worksheet Entries

Instructions: The worksheet illustrated in the following figure contains errors in the PROFIT row for February (cell C6) and March (cell D6). Analyze the entries displayed on the worksheet. Explain the cause of the errors for the two months and the methods of correction in the space provided below.

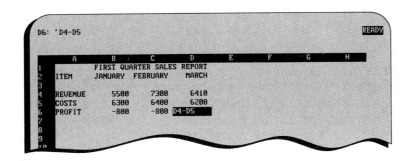

Cause of error in C6: _____

_____

Method of correction for C6: _____

_____

Cause of error in D6: _____

_____

Method of correction for D6: _____

_____

STUDENT ASSIGNMENT 7: Entering Formulas

Instructions: For each of the worksheets in this assignment, write the formula that accomplishes the specified task and manually compute the value assigned to the specified cell.

1. Use the following figure. Assign to cell A4 the sum of cell A2 and cell A3.

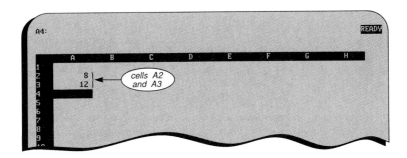

Formula: _____

Result assigned to cell A4: _____

Student Assignment 7 (continued)

2. Use the following figure. Assign to cell B5 the product of cells B2, B3, and B4, minus cell A5.

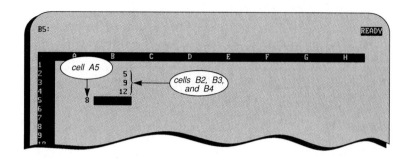

Formula: _____

Result assigned to cell B5: _____

3. Use the following figure. Assign to cell C3 five times the quotient of cell D2 divided by cell C2.

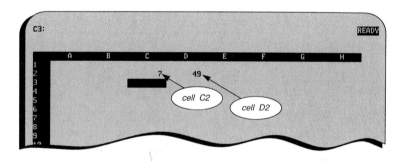

Formula: _____

Result assigned to cell C3: _____

4. Use the following figure. Assign to cell D5 the sum of cells D2 through D4 minus the product of cells C3 and C4.

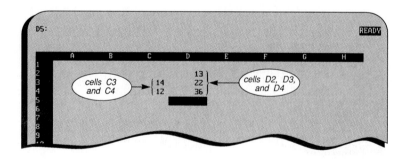

Formula: _____

Result assigned to cell D5: _____

STUDENT ASSIGNMENT 8: Building an Inventory Listing Worksheet

Instructions: Perform the following tasks using a personal computer.

1. Boot the computer.
2. Load 1-2-3 into main memory.
3. Build the worksheet illustrated in the following figure. The TOTAL line in row 9 contains the totals for Part A, Part B, and Part C for each of the plants (Chicago, San Jose, and Boston). For example, the total in cell B9 is the sum of the values in cells B5, B6, and B7.
4. Save the worksheet. Use the file name STUS1-8.
5. Print the screen image of the worksheet.

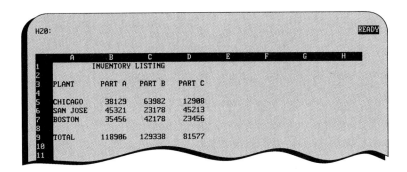

STUDENT ASSIGNMENT 9: Building a Yearly Business Expenses Comparison Worksheet

Instructions: Load 1-2-3 and perform the following tasks.

1. Build the worksheet illustrated in the following figure. Calculate the total expenses for THIS YEAR in column C and LAST YEAR in column E by adding the values in the cells representing the expenses.
2. Calculate the DIFFERENCE in column G by subtracting LAST YEAR expenses from THIS YEAR expenses.
3. Save the worksheet. Use the file name STUS1-9.
4. Print the screen image of the worksheet.

To total lengthy columns

@sum
(C5, C16)
enter
1C
copy enter
go to column
enter

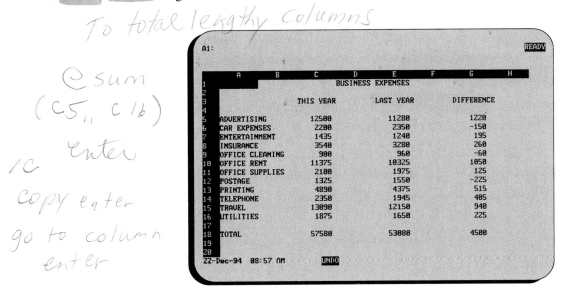

STUDENT ASSIGNMENT 10: Building a Semiannual Income and Expense Worksheet

Instructions: Load 1-2-3 and perform the following tasks.

1. Build the worksheet illustrated in the following figure. Calculate the total income in row 10 by adding the income for gas and oil, labor, and parts. Calculate the total expenses in row 17 by adding salaries, rent, and cost of goods. Calculate the net profit in row 19 by subtracting the total expenses from the total income.
2. Save the worksheet. Use the file name STUS1-10.
3. Print the screen image of the worksheet.

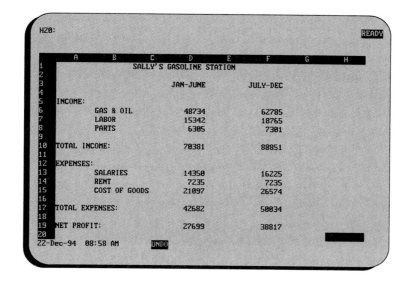

STUDENT ASSIGNMENT 11: Changing Data in the Semiannual Income and Expense Worksheet

Instructions: If you did not do Student Assignment 10, do it before you begin this assignment. With the worksheet in Student Assignment 10 stored on the disk, load 1-2-3 and perform the following tasks.

1. Retrieve the worksheet STUS1-10 you built in Student Assignment 10 from disk. Use the command /**File R**etrieve (/FR). When the list of worksheet names displays on the menu line, use the arrow keys to move the menu pointer to the worksheet name STUS1-10. Press the Enter key. The worksheet illustrated in Student Assignment 10 will display on the screen.
2. Make the changes to the worksheet described at the top of the next page in the table. Use the EDIT mode of 1-2-3. Recall that to use EDIT mode to change an entry in a cell, move the cell pointer to the cell and then press function key F2.

**List of Corrections to the Semiannual Income
and Expense Worksheet**

CELL	CURRENT CELL CONTENTS	CHANGE THE CELL CONTENTS TO
C1	SALLY'S GASOLINE STATION	SAL'S GAS STATION
D6	48734	48535
F6	62785	61523
D8	6305	63005
F8	7301	47523
D13	14350	22357
F13	16225	19876

As you edit the values in the cells containing numeric data, keep an eye on the total income (row 10), total expenses (row 17), and net profit (row 19) cells. The values in these cells are based on formulas that reference the cells you are editing. You will see that each time a new value is entered into a cell referenced by a formula, 1-2-3 automatically recalculates a new value for the formula. It then stores the new value in the cell assigned the formula. This automatic recalculation of formulas is one of the more powerful aspects of 1-2-3. After you have successfully made the changes listed in the table, the net profit for Jan–June in cell D19 should equal 76193 and the net profit for July–Dec should equal 74126.

3. Save the worksheet. Use the file name STUS1-12.
4. Print the screen image of the worksheet on the printer.

STUDENT ASSIGNMENT 12: Using the Online Help Facility

Instructions: Load 1-2-3 and perform the following tasks.

1. With 1-2-3 in READY mode, press function key F1. Print the screen image.
2. Select the topic "About 1-2-3 Help". Press the Enter key. Read and print the image of the screen.
3. Select the following help screens: Status Indicators; Control Panel; Mode Indicators; and Entering Data. Read and print the image of each help screen.
4. Press the Esc key to quit the online help facility.

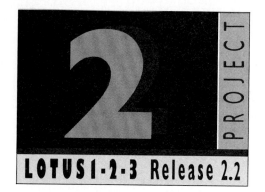

Formatting and Printing a Worksheet

OBJECTIVES

You will have mastered the material in this project when you can:

◆ Retrieve a worksheet from disk

◆ Increase the width of the columns in a worksheet

◆ Define a range of cells

◆ Format a worksheet

◆ Enter repeating characters into a cell using the Backslash key

◆ Copy one range of cells to another range of cells

◆ Add the contents of a range using the SUM function

◆ Determine a percentage

◆ Print a partial or complete worksheet without window borders

◆ Print the cell-formulas version of a worksheet

◆ Display the formulas assigned to cells, rather than their numeric results

The Sales Report worksheet we created in Project 1 contains the revenue, costs, and profit for each of the three months of the first quarter, but it is not presented in the most readable manner. For example, as you can see in Figure 2-1, the columns are too close together and the numbers are displayed as whole numbers, even though they are dollar figures.

In this project we will use the formatting capabilities of 1-2-3 to make the worksheet more presentable and easier to read. We will also add summary totals for the quarter, using formulas. As shown in Figure 2-2, the total revenue in cell B12 is the sum of the revenue values for January, February, and March. The total cost in cell B13 is the sum of the cost values for January, February, and March; and the total profit in cell B14 is the sum of the profit values for January, February, and March. The percent profit in cell B15 is determined by dividing the total profit by the total revenue. After the worksheet is complete, we will print it without the window borders.

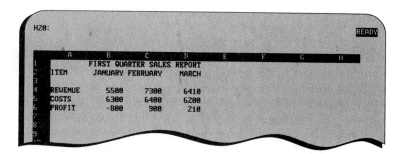

FIGURE 2-1   The worksheet we completed in Project 1.

RETRIEVING A WORKSHEET FROM DISK

◆   Recall that at the end of Project 1, the Save command was used to store the worksheet in Figure 2-1 on disk under the name PROJS-1.WK1. Since Project 2 involves making modifications to this stored worksheet, you can eliminate retyping the whole worksheet and save a lot of time by retrieving it from disk and placing it into main memory.

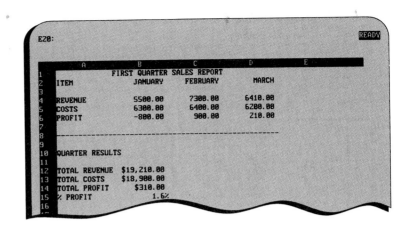

FIGURE 2-2
The worksheet we will
complete in Project 2.

After booting the computer and loading the 1-2-3 program, retrieve the worksheet PROJS-1 from the data disk. To retrieve the worksheet, enter the command /File Retrieve (/FR). First, press the Slash key (/) as illustrated in Figure 2-3. This causes 1-2-3 to display the Main menu on the input line at the top of the screen.

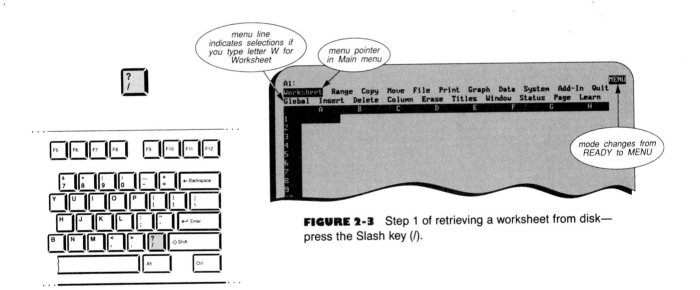

FIGURE 2-3 Step 1 of retrieving a worksheet from disk—press the Slash key (/).

Next, use the Right Arrow key to move the menu pointer to the word File. The result of this activity is shown in Figure 2-4. With the menu pointer on the word File, the File menu displays on the menu line, immediately below the Main menu. To select the File menu, press the Enter key or type the letter F.

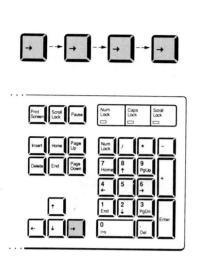

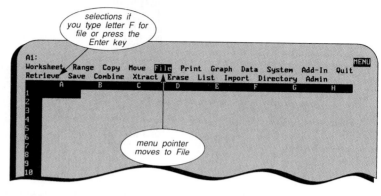

FIGURE 2-4 Step 2 of retrieving a worksheet from disk—use the arrow keys to move the menu pointer to the word File in the Main menu.

Let's press the Enter key. The menu pointer is now active in the File menu as illustrated in Figure 2-5. The Retrieve command is the first command in the list. The message on the menu line indicates the function of this command. With the menu pointer on the Retrieve command, type the letter R for Retrieve.

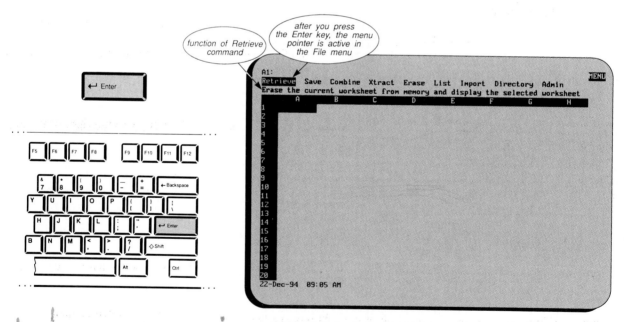

FIGURE 2-5 Step 3 of retrieving a worksheet from disk—press the Enter key to select the File command.

As illustrated in Figure 2-6, 1-2-3 displays on the menu line an alphabetized list of the file names on the default drive that have the extension .WK1. This helps you remember the names of the worksheets stored on the data disk. The list includes all the worksheets you were told to save in Project 1, including PROJS-1.WK1.

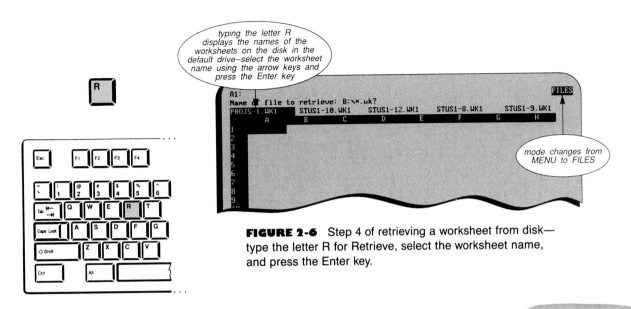

FIGURE 2-6 Step 4 of retrieving a worksheet from disk— type the letter R for Retrieve, select the worksheet name, and press the Enter key.

One way to select the worksheet you want to retrieve is to type PROJS-1 on the input line and press the Enter key. Better yet, because the menu pointer is on the file name PROJS-1.WK1 in the list in Figure 2-6, press the Enter key. This method saves keying time. While 1-2-3 is accessing the worksheet, the mode indicator in the upper right corner of the screen changes to WAIT and the status light flashes on the default drive. After the worksheet is retrieved, the screen appears as shown in Figure 2-1. According to Figure 2-2, all the new labels are in capitals. Therefore, before you modify the worksheet, press the Caps Lock key.

The tasks we want to complete in this project are to widen the columns, format the dollar amounts, and add the quarter results. The tasks may be accomplished in any sequence. Let's complete them in the following sequence:

1. Widen the columns from 9 characters to 13 characters to allow the quarter results titles and other numeric data to fit in the columns.
2. Change the numeric representations for the three months to dollars and cents—two digits to the right of the decimal place.
3. Determine the quarter results.
4. Change the percent profit to a number in percent.
5. Change the numeric representations of the quarter results to dollars and cents with a leading dollar sign.

CHANGING THE WIDTH OF THE COLUMNS

◆ When 1-2-3 first executes and the blank worksheet appears on the screen, all the columns have a default width of nine characters. You can change this default width to make the worksheet easier to read or to ensure that entries will display properly in the cells.

There are three ways to change the width of the columns in a worksheet. First, make a global change, which uniformly increases or decreases the width of all the columns in the worksheet. **Global** means the entire worksheet. Second, change the width of a series of adjacent columns. Third, make a change in the width of one column at a time. Let's use the first method and change the width of all the columns

Changing the Width of All the Columns

To change the width of all the columns, enter the command /Worksheet Global Column-Width (/WGC). When you press the Slash key, the Main menu displays at the top of the screen with the first command, Worksheet, highlighted as shown earlier in Figure 2-3. The Worksheet menu displays immediately below the Main menu. Notice that the first command in the Worksheet menu is Global. This command makes the changes to the entire worksheet. Type the letter W for Worksheet to move the menu pointer to the Worksheet menu, as shown in Figure 2-7.

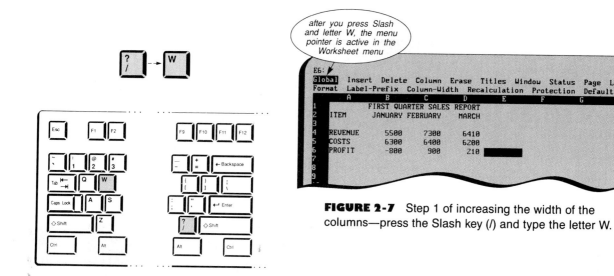

FIGURE 2-7 Step 1 of increasing the width of the columns—press the Slash key (/) and type the letter W.

Type the letter G for Global. This causes the Global menu to display on the input line and the global settings sheet to display in place of the worksheet. Press F6 if you want to view the worksheet, rather than the global settings sheet, when the Global menu is active. Press F6 again and the global settings sheet displays in place of the worksheet.

With the Global menu active, use the Right Arrow key to move the menu pointer to Column-Width. Now the menu line explains the purpose of the Column-Width command. This procedure is illustrated in Figure 2-8.

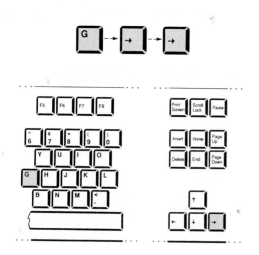

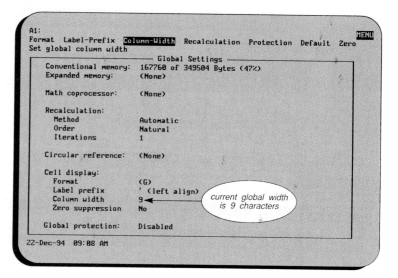

FIGURE 2-8 Step 2 of increasing the width of the columns—type the letter G and use the Right Arrow key to move the menu pointer to Column-Width in the Global menu.

Before you type the letter C for Column-Width, if you decided that you did not want to increase the width of the columns, how many times would you have to press the Esc key to *back out* of the MENU mode in Figure 2-8 and return to READY mode? If your answer is three, you're right—once for the Global command, once for the Worksheet command, and once for the Slash key (/).

Now type the letter C for Column-Width. The prompt message "Enter global column width (1..240): 9" displays on the input line at the top of the screen. This message is illustrated on the screen in Figure 2-9. The numbers 1–240 define the range of valid entries. The number 9 following the colon indicates the current global (default) column width.

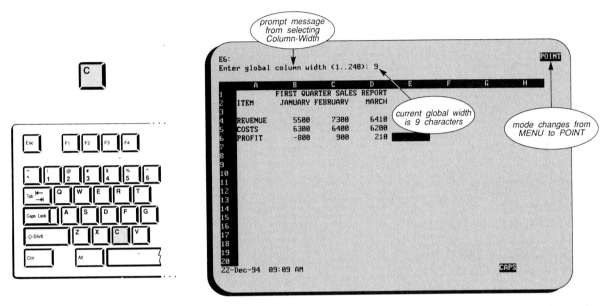

FIGURE 2-9 Step 3 of increasing the width of the columns—type the letter C for Column-Width.

Type the number 13 as shown in Figure 2-10, then press the Enter key. An alternative to typing the number 13 is to use the Right and Left Arrow keys to increase or decrease the number on the input line.

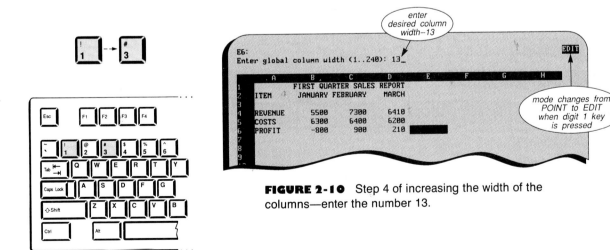

FIGURE 2-10 Step 4 of increasing the width of the columns—enter the number 13.

Figure 2-11 illustrates the worksheet with the new column width of 13 characters. Compare Figure 2-11 to Figure 2-1. Because the columns in Figure 2-11 are wider, the worksheet is easier to read. But because the columns are wider, fewer appear on the screen.

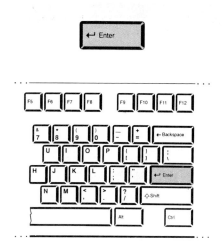

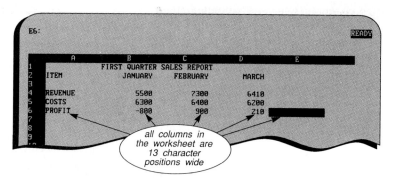

FIGURE 2-11 Step 5 of increasing the width of the columns—press the Enter key.

Changing the Width of a Series of Adjacent Columns

In Figures 2-7 through 2-11, the /Worksheet Global Column-Width (/WGC) command was used to uniformly change the width of all the columns. Since we were interested in changing only the width of columns A through E to 13 characters, we could have also used the command /Worksheet Column Column-Range Set-Width (/WCCS). This command works the same as the /Worksheet Global Column-Width (/WGC) command, except that you must enter the range of columns that will be affected by the change.

Changing the Width of One Column at a Time

You can change the width of one column at a time in the worksheet. Let's change the width of column A to 20 characters, while leaving the width of the other columns at 13 characters. To change the width of column A to 20 characters, do the following:

1. Press the Home key to move the cell pointer into column A.
2. Type the command /Worksheet Column Set-Width (/WCS). The Slash key (/) switches 1-2-3 to MENU mode. The letter W selects the Worksheet command. The letter C selects the command Column and the letter S selects the command Set-Width.
3. In response to the prompt message "Enter column width (1..240): 13" on the input line, type the number 20 and press the Enter key.

Now column A is 20 characters wide while the other columns in the worksheet are 13 characters wide. Let's change column A back to the default width of 13 characters. With the cell pointer in column A, enter the command /Worksheet Column Reset-Width (/WCR). This command changes column A back to the default width—13 characters. The UNDO command may also be used to reset the width of column A to the default width. You must be sure, however, that no other entry has been made into the worksheet, since the width was changed from 13 characters to 20 characters.

Use the GOTO command to move the cell pointer back to cell E6, where it was before the width of column A was set to 20 and then reset to 13.

DEFINING A RANGE

◆ Our next step is to format the monthly dollar amounts. The Format command requires you to specify the cells you want to format. For this reason, you need to understand the term *range* before using the Format command.

A **range** in 1-2-3 means one or more cells on which an operation can take place. A range may be a single cell, a series of adjacent cells in a row or column, or a rectangular group of adjacent cells. Hence, a range may consist of one cell or many cells. However, a range cannot be made up of cells that only run diagonally or are separated. Figure 2-12 illustrates several valid and invalid ranges of cells.

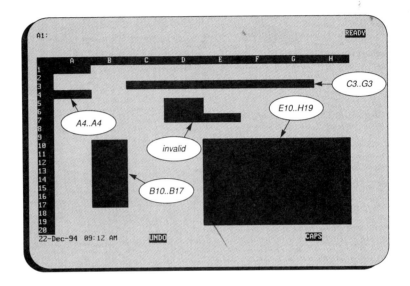

FIGURE 2-12
Valid and invalid ranges

When you are prompted by 1-2-3 to specify a range, you simply type the cell address for the first cell in the range, followed by a period (.), followed by the cell address for the last cell in the range. If a range defines a rectangular group of cells, any pair of diagonally opposite corner cells may be used to identify it. For example, the upper left cell and the lower right cell of the rectangular group of cells identify the range. Table 2-1 summarizes the ranges described in Figure 2-12.

TABLE 2-1 A Summary of the Ranges Specified in Figure 2-12

RANGE	COMMENT
A4..A4	The range is made up of one cell, A4.
C3..G3	The range is made up of five adjacent cells in row 3. The five cells are C3, D3, E3, F3, and G3.
B10..B17	The range is made up of eight adjacent cells in column B. The eight cells are B10, B11, B12, B13, B14, B15, B16, and B17.
E10..H19	The range is made up of a rectangular group of cells. The upper left cell (E10) and the lower right cell (H19) define the rectangle. The ranges H19..E10, H10..E19, and E19..H10 define the same range as E10..H19.

Now that you know how to define a range, we can move on to the next step in Project 2: formatting the numeric values in the worksheet.

FORMATTING NUMERIC VALUES

◆ The Format command is used to control the manner in which numeric values appear in the worksheet. As shown in Figure 2-2, we want to change the numeric values in the range B4 through D6 to display as dollars and cents with two digits to the right of the decimal point.

Invoking the Format Command

There are two ways to invoke the Format command. First, you can use the series of commands /**Worksheet Global Format** (/WGF) to format all the cells in the worksheet the same way. Second, you can use the commands /**Range Format** (/RF) to format just a particular range of cells. Since this project involves formatting a range rather than all the cells in the worksheet, type /RF to activate the menu pointer in the Format menu as shown in Figure 2-13. The Format menu on the input line lists the different ways to format a range. As indicated on the third line of the control panel, the first format type in the menu, Fixed, formats cells to a fixed number of decimal places. This is the format you want to use to display the monthly amounts to two decimal places. Type the letter F for Fixed.

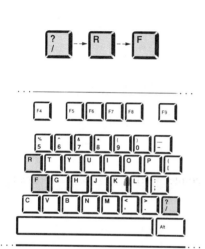

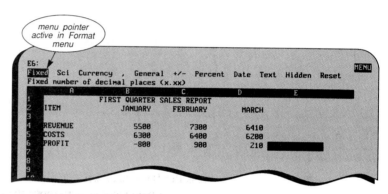

FIGURE 2-13 Step 1 of formatting a range of cells—press the Slash key (/) and type the letters R for Range and F for Format.

As shown in Figure 2-14, 1-2-3 displays the message "Enter number of decimal places (0..15): 2" on the input line at the top of the screen. Since most spreadsheet applications require two decimal positions, 1-2-3 displays "2" as the entry to save you time. Press the Enter key to enter two decimal positions.

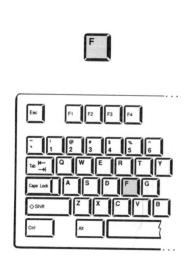

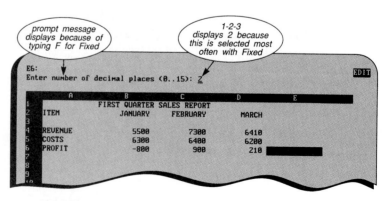

FIGURE 2-14 Step 2 of formatting a range of cells—type the letter F for Fixed and 1-2-3 displays a prompt message on the input line.

Next, 1-2-3 changes to POINT mode and displays the message "Enter range to format: E6..E6" (Figure 2-15). The range E6..E6 displays at the end of the input line because the cell pointer is at cell E6. Enter the range by typing B4.D6, or use the arrow keys to select the range. (Don't be concerned that 1-2-3 displays two periods between the cell address when you press the Period key once. It is the program's way of displaying a range.) Using the arrow keys to select a range is called **pointing.** Let's use the pointing method to select a range because it requires less effort.

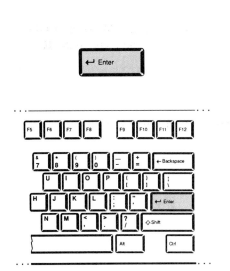

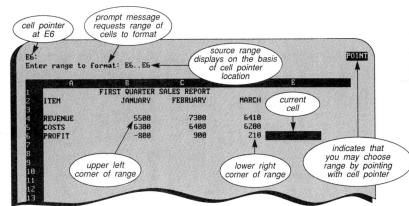

FIGURE 2-15 Step 3 of formatting a range of cells— press the Enter key to select two decimal places and 1-2-3 displays the prompt message on the input line, requesting the range to format.

Selecting a Range by Pointing

To select a range by pointing, first press the Backspace key (or Esc key) to change the default entry on the input line in Figure 2-15 from E6..E6 to E6. Next, use the arrow keys to move the cell pointer to B4, the upper left corner cell of the range you want. This procedure is shown in Figure 2-16.

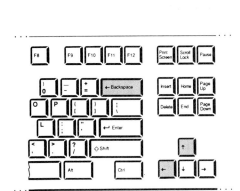

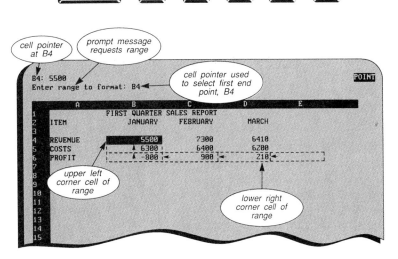

FIGURE 2-16 Step 4 of formatting a range of cells— press the Backspace key to unlock the first end point on the input line and use the arrow keys to select end point B4.

With the cell pointer at B4, press the Period key to *lock in*, or *anchor*, the first end point, B4. The B4 on the input line changes to B4..B4. Now use the arrow keys to move the cell pointer to cell D6, the lower right corner of the desired range. Press the Down Arrow key twice and the Right Arrow key twice. As the cell pointer moves, a reverse video rectangle forms over the range covered. The range on the input line changes from B4..B4 to B4..D6 (Figure 2-17).

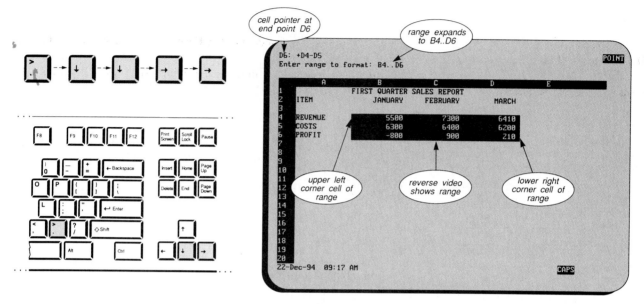

FIGURE 2-17   Step 5 of formatting a range of cells—press the Period key (.) to anchor the first end point and use the arrow keys to move the cell pointer to the opposite end point.

Press the Enter key. 1-2-3 immediately displays the monthly values in cells B4, C4, D4, B5, C5, D5, B6, C6, and D6 with two decimal places (dollars and cents). Everything else in the worksheet remains the same (Figure 2-18).

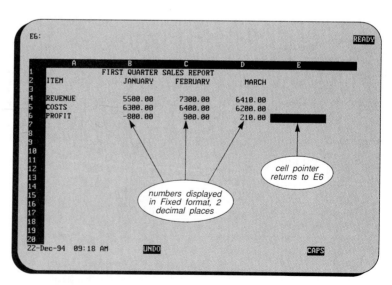

FIGURE 2-18   Step 6 of formatting a range of cells—press the Enter key and the numbers in the range B4..D6 display in Fixed format.

Don't forget that the UNDO command is available when 1-2-3 returns to READY mode after the worksheet is formatted. Thus, if you want to reset the worksheet to what it was before you formatted it, issue the UNDO command (Alt-F4).

We could have used three other ways to describe to 1-2-3 the rectangular group of cells B4..D6. Two other ways are B6..D4 and D4..B6. Can you identify the third way?

Summary of Format Commands

You can format numbers in cells in a variety of ways using the /Worksheet Global Format (/WGF) or /Range Format (/RF) command. Table 2-2 summarizes the various format options. You will find Table 2-2 helpful when you begin formatting your own worksheets. Also, remember that 1-2-3 rounds a number to the rightmost position if any digits are lost because of the format or number of decimal positions chosen.

TABLE 2-2 Format Types for Numeric Values in the Format Menu

MENU ITEM	DESCRIPTION
Fixed	Displays numbers to a specified number of decimal places. Negative values are displayed with a leading minus sign. Examples: 38; 0.912; –45.67.
Sci	Displays numbers in a form called *scientific notation*. The letter E stands for *times 10 to the power*. Examples: 3.7E + 01; –2.357E–30.
Currency	Displays numbers preceded by a dollar sign next to the leftmost digit, with a specified number of decimal places (0–15), and uses commas to group the integer portion of the number by thousands. Negative numbers display in parentheses. Examples: $1,234.56; $0.98; $23,934,876.15; ($48.34).
,	The , (comma) is the same as the Currency format, except the dollar sign does not display. Examples: 2,123.00; 5,456,023.34; (22,000).
General	This is the default format in which a number is stored when it is entered into a cell. Trailing zeros are suppressed and leading integer zeros display. Negative numbers display with a leading minus sign. Examples: 23.981; 0.563; 23401; –500.45.
+/–	Displays a single horizontal bar graph composed of plus (+) or minus (–) signs that indicate the sign of the number and the magnitude of the number. One plus or minus sign displays for each unit value. Only the integer portion of the number is used. Examples: + + + + + + for 6; ––– for –3.8.
Percent	Displays numbers in percent form. Examples: 34% for 0.34; .11% for 0.0011; –13.245% for –0.13245.
Date	Formats cells that contain a date or time.
Text	Displays formulas rather than their values. Numbers appear in General format. Examples: + B4–B5; 2*(F5 – G3).
Hidden	Prevents the display of the cell contents on the screen and when printed. To see what's in a hidden cell, move the pointer to that cell. The contents will display on the mode line.
Reset	Resets cells back to Global format.

Determining the Format Assigned to a Cell

You can determine the format assigned to a cell by the Range Format command by moving the cell pointer to that cell. The format displays on the mode line in the upper left corner of the screen, next to the cell address. In Figure 2-19, the cell pointer is at cell D6. Format F2 displays on the mode line in parentheses next to the cell address. F2 is an abbreviation for the format "Fixed, 2 decimal places." Recall that we assigned this format to cell D4 in Figures 2-13 through 2-18.

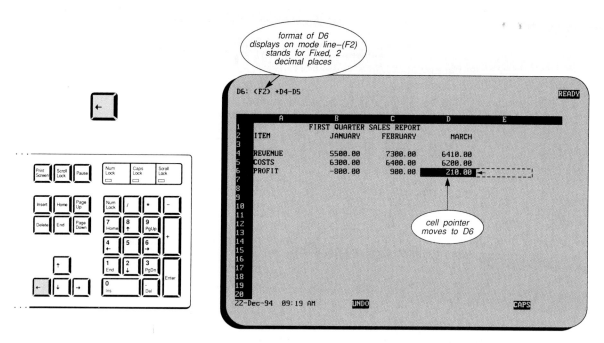

FIGURE 2-19 The format assigned to a cell displays on the mode line when the cell pointer is on the cell.

REPEATING CHARACTERS IN A CELL

In Figure 2-2, row 8 contains a dashed line. We will add the dashed line to the worksheet using repeating characters—characters that are repeated throughout a cell.

To enter the dashed line, move the cell pointer to cell A8 using the GOTO command. Recall that function key F5 invokes the GOTO command. Next, enter the cell address A8 and press the Enter key. The cell pointer immediately moves to cell A8 as shown in Figure 2-20.

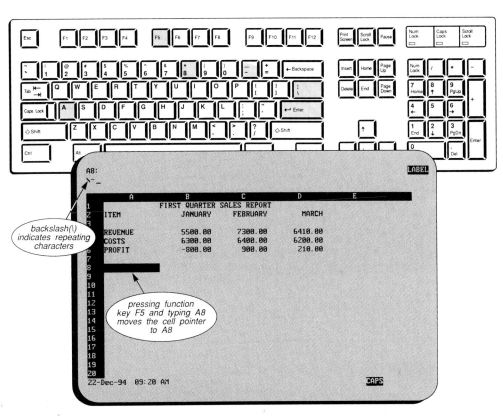

FIGURE 2-20 Moving the cell pointer to A8 and entering a repeating dash on the input line.

With the cell pointer at A8, press the Backslash key (\). The **Backslash key** signals 1-2-3 that the character or sequence of characters that follows it on the input line is to be repeated throughout the cell. Repeating the minus sign (–) creates the dashed line shown in Figure 2-2. Therefore, immediately after the Backslash key, press the Minus Sign key once as illustrated at the top of the screen in Figure 2-20.

To enter the repeating dash, press the Enter key. The dash repeats throughout cell A8 as shown in Figure 2-21. The Backslash key is not included as part of the cell entry. Like the quotation mark ("), circumflex (^), and apostrophe ('), the backslash (\) is used as the first character to tell 1-2-3 what to do with the characters that follow on the input line.

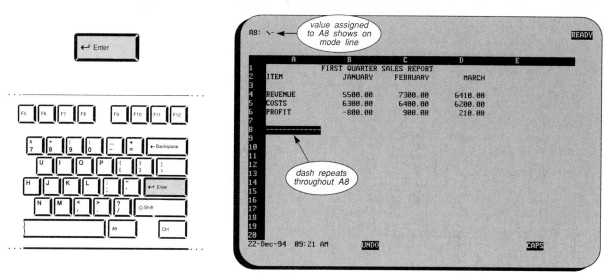

FIGURE 2-21 Press the Enter key to assign the repeating dash to cell A8.

We still need to extend the dashed line through cells B8, C8, and D8. We can move the cell pointer to each individual cell and make the same entry we made in cell A8, or we can use the Copy command. Let's use the Copy command.

REPLICATION—THE COPY COMMAND

The /Copy command (/C) is used to copy, or replicate, the contents of one group of cells to another group of cells. This command is one of the most useful because it can save you both time and keystrokes when you build a worksheet. We will use the Copy command to copy the dashes in cell A8 to cells B8 through D8. Press the Slash key (/) to place 1-2-3 in MENU mode. In the Main menu list, the Copy command is the third one. Type the letter C to invoke the Copy command.

Source Range

When you select the Copy command, the prompt message "Enter range to copy FROM: A8..A8" displays on the input line as shown in Figure 2-22. The **source range** is the range we want to copy. Since A8 is the cell to copy to B8 through D8, press the Enter key.

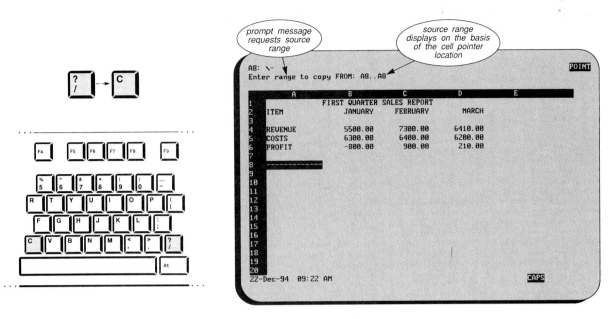

FIGURE 2-22 Step 1 of copying a range of cells—press the Slash key (/) and type the letter C for Copy.

Destination Range

After you press the Enter key, the prompt message "Enter range to copy TO: A8" displays on the input line as shown in Figure 2-23. The **destination range** is the range to which we want to copy the source range.

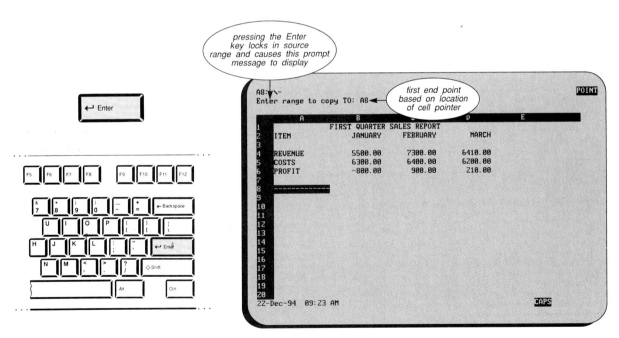

FIGURE 2-23 Step 2 of copying a range of cells—anchor the end points of the source range of cells to copy by pressing the Enter key.

Move the cell pointer to B8, the left end point of the range to copy to (Figure 2-24). Notice that following the prompt message on the input line, the cell address is now B8, the location of the cell pointer.

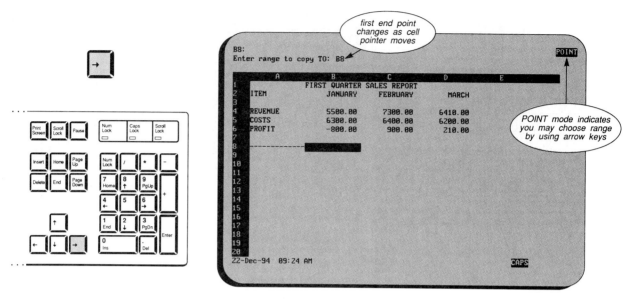

FIGURE 2-24 Step 3 of copying a range of cells—move the cell pointer to one of the end points of the destination range.

Press the Period key to anchor end point B8, and move the cell pointer to D8 as shown in Figure 2-25. Finally, press the Enter key to copy cell A8 to cells B8 through D8.

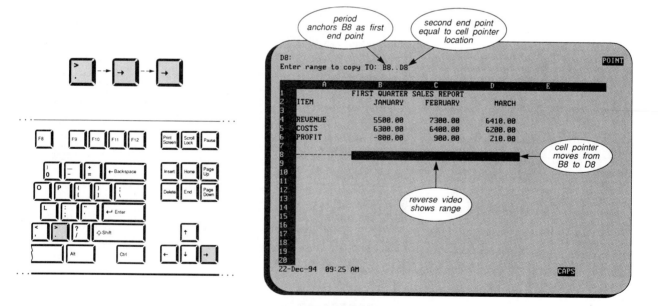

FIGURE 2-25 Step 4 of copying a range of cells—press the Period key, and move the cell pointer to the opposite end point of the destination range.

As illustrated in Figure 2-26, the dashed line is complete and the cell pointer is back at cell A8, where it was before you invoked the Copy command.

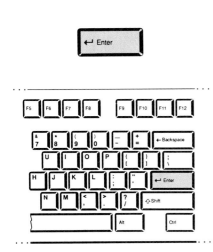

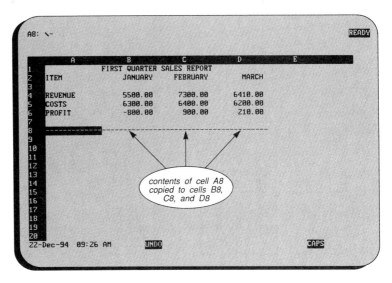

FIGURE 2-26 Step 5 of copying a range of cells—press the Enter key to anchor the end points of the destination range and complete the copy.

With the dashed line complete, move the cell pointer to A10 and begin entering the labels that identify the quarter results. First enter the label QUARTER RESULTS and press the Down Arrow key twice as shown in Figure 2-27.

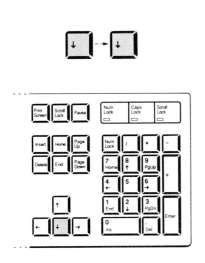

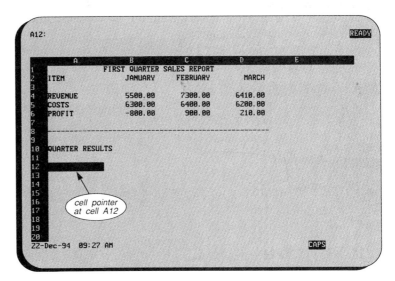

FIGURE 2-27 Step 1 of entering the total labels

Enter the remaining labels that identify the quarter results in cells A12 through A15 by using the Down Arrow key to enter each one. After you complete the label entries, the cell pointer ends up at cell A16 as illustrated in Figure 2-28. Use the GOTO command to move the cell pointer to cell B12, the location of the next entry.

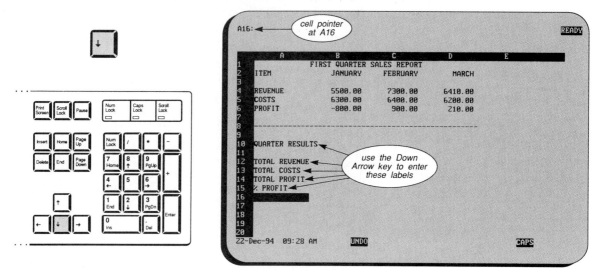

FIGURE 2-28 Step 2 of entering the total labels

SAVING AN INTERMEDIATE COPY OF THE WORKSHEET

◆ It's good practice to save intermediate copies of your worksheet. That way, if the computer loses power or you make a serious mistake, you can always retrieve the latest copy on disk. We recommend that you save an intermediate copy of the worksheet every 50 to 75 keystrokes. It makes sense to use the Save command often, because it saves keying time later if the unexpected happens.

Before we continue with Project 2, let's save the current worksheet as PROJS-2. Recall that to save the worksheet displayed on the screen you must do the following:

1. Enter the command /File Save (/FS).
2. In response to the prompt message on the input line, type the new file name, PROJS-2. As soon as you type the letter P in PROJS-2, the old file name, PROJS-1, disappears from the input line. File name PROJS-1 is on the input line because we retrieved it to begin this project, and 1-2-3 assumes we want to save the revised worksheet under the same name.
3. Press the Enter key.

After 1-2-3 completes the save, the worksheet remains on the screen. You can immediately continue with the next entry.

USING BUILT-IN FUNCTIONS

◆ 1-2-3 has many **built-in functions** that automatically handle calculations. These built-in functions save you a lot of time and effort because they eliminate the need to enter complex formulas. The first built-in function we will discuss is the SUM function, since it is one of the most widely used. For the remainder of the projects in this book, the term *function* will mean built-in function.

The SUM Function

In the worksheet for Project 2, the total revenue is calculated by adding the values in cells B4, C4, and D4. Whereas the calculation can be written in cell B12 as +B4+C4+D4, an easier and more general method to produce the same result is to use the SUM function. The **SUM function** adds the values in the specified range.

With the cell pointer at B12, enter @SUM(B4.D4) as illustrated on the input line at the top of the screen in Figure 2-29. Notice that the SUM function begins with the **at symbol** (@). Beginning an entry with the @ symbol indicates to 1-2-3 that the entry is a function.

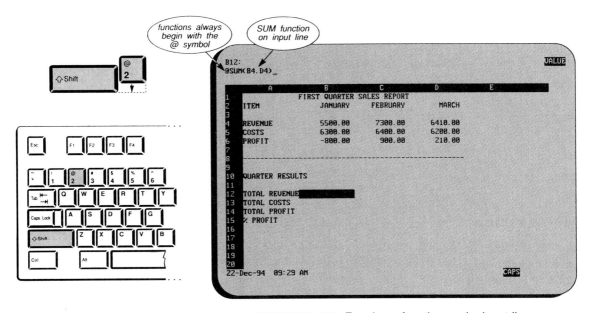

FIGURE 2-29 Entering a function on the input line

After the @ symbol, type the function name SUM (or sum) followed by a left parenthesis. Next, enter B4.D4, the range to be added. The range can be specified either by typing the beginning and ending cells or by using the pointing feature we described earlier. In this case, type the two end points of the range separated by a period (.). Finally, type the right parenthesis.

Press the Enter key as shown on the next page in Figure 2-30. As a result, 1-2-3 evaluates the sum of the entries in cells B4, C4, and D4 and displays the result in cell B12. Functions belong to the broader category called *formulas*. Therefore, 1-2-3 handles functions the same way it handles formulas—it evaluates the function and places a number in the cell. For example, in Figure 2-30, you can see on the mode line that the formula @SUM(B4..D4) is assigned to cell B12. However, the value 19210 displays in cell B12 of the worksheet. The value 19210 is the sum of the numbers in cells B4, C4, and D4.

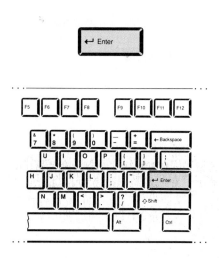

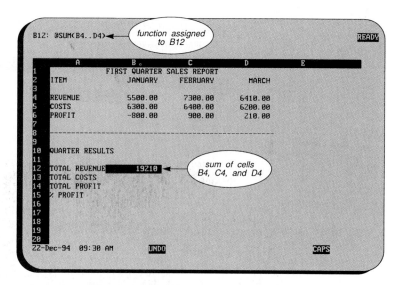

FIGURE 2-30 Press the Enter key to assign the function to B12. When a function is assigned to a cell, it is evaluated and the value displays in the cell.

Copying Functions

According to Figure 2-2, the two cells B13 and B14 require the identical function and similar ranges that we assigned to cell B12 in Figure 2-30. That is, cell B13 should contain the total costs for the quarter, or the sum of cells B5, C5, and D5. Cell B14 should contain the total profit for the quarter, or the sum of cells B6, C6, and D6. Table 2-3 illustrates the similarity between the entry in cell B12 and the entries required in cells B13 and B14.

TABLE 2-3 Three Function Entries for Cells B12, B13, and B14

CELL	FUNCTION ENTRIES
B12	@SUM(B4..D4)
B13	@SUM(B5..D5)
B14	@SUM(B6..D6)

There are two methods for entering the functions in cells B13 and B14. The first method involves moving the cell pointer to B13, entering the function @SUM(B5..D5), then moving the cell pointer to B14 and entering the function @SUM(B6..D6).

The second method, the one we recommend you use, involves the Copy command. That is, copy cell B12 to cells B13 and B14. In Table 2-3, however, the ranges do not agree exactly. Each cell below B12 has a range that is one row below the previous one. Fortunately, when the Copy command copies cell addresses, it adjusts them for the new position. This cell-address adjustment used by the Copy command is called relative addressing. In other words, after cell B12 is copied to cells B13 and B14, the contents of B13 and B14 are identical to the entries shown in Table 2-3.

Let's complete the copy from cell B12 to cells B13 and B14. With the cell pointer at B12 as shown in Figure 2-30, enter the command /Copy (/C). The prompt message "Enter range to copy FROM: B12..B12" displays on the input line as shown in Figure 2-31. Since B12 is the cell that we want to copy to cells B13 and B14, press Enter.

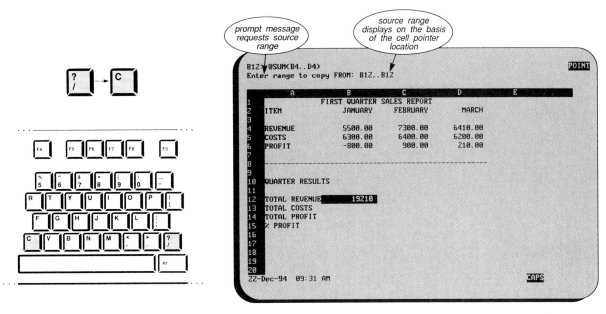

FIGURE 2-31 Step 1 of copying a function—press the Slash key (/) and type the letter C for Copy.

When you press the Enter key, the prompt message "Enter range to copy TO: B12" displays on the input line. This message is shown in Figure 2-32. Use the Down Arrow key to move the cell pointer to B13, the topmost end point of the destination range.

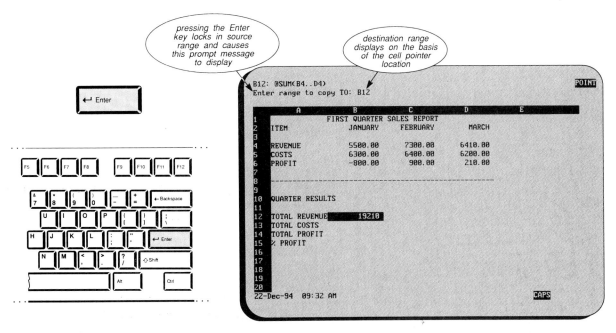

FIGURE 2-32 Step 2 of copying a function—anchor the end points of the source range of cells to copy by pressing the Enter key.

As shown in Figure 2-33, the cell address following the prompt message on the input line has changed from B12 to B13.

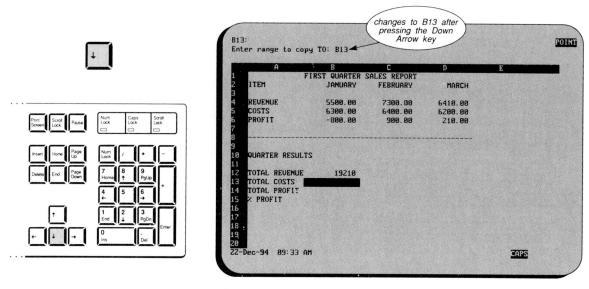

FIGURE 2-33 Step 3 of copying a function—move the cell pointer to one of the end points of the destination range.

Press the Period key to anchor the topmost end point, B13. Next, move the cell pointer to B14 as shown in Figure 2-34.

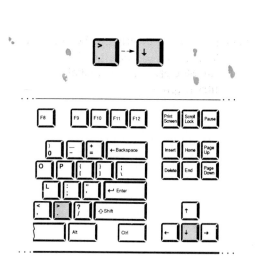

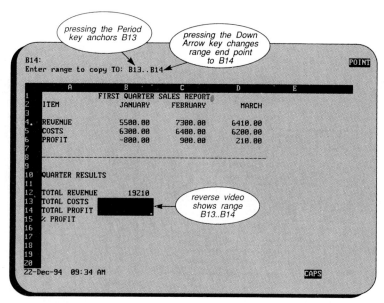

FIGURE 2-34 Step 4 of copying a function—move the cell pointer to the opposite end point of the destination range.

Finally, press the Enter key to copy the function in cell B12 to cells B13 and B14. As illustrated in Figure 2-35, cell B13 contains the total costs for the quarter and cell B14 contains the total profit for the quarter. The cell pointer remains at cell B12, where it was before invoking the Copy command.

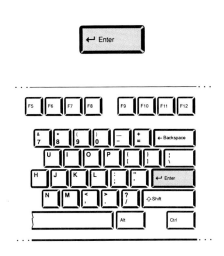

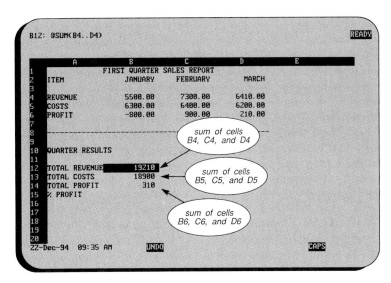

FIGURE 2-35 Step 5 of copying a function—press the Enter key to anchor the end points of the destination range and complete the copy.

Here again, you can undo the Copy command by entering the UNDO command (Alt-F4) after 1-2-3 completes the copy and returns to READY Mode.

DETERMINING A PERCENT VALUE

◆ According to Figure 2-2, the percent profit appears in cell B15. The percent profit is determined by assigning a formula that divides the total profit (cell B14) by the total revenue (cell B12). Recall that the Slash key (/) represents the operation of division, provided it is not the first key typed in READY mode and the entry is not a label.

Move the cell pointer to cell B15 and enter the formula +B14/B12 as shown on the input line in the top screen of Figure 2-36. Next, press the Enter key. 1-2-3 determines the quotient of +B14/B12 and stores the result, 0.0161374284, in cell B15. This is shown in the bottom screen of Figure 2-36.

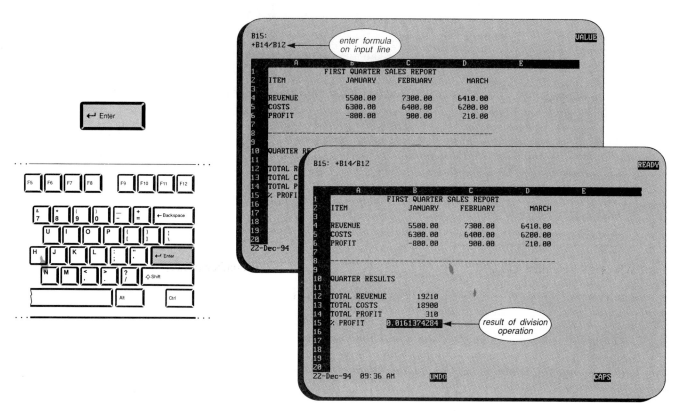

FIGURE 2-36 Entering a percentage

FORMATTING TO PERCENT AND CURRENCY

◆ Although the quarter totals displayed on the worksheet in Figure 2-36 are correct, they are not in an easy-to-read format. The dollar values are displayed as whole numbers and the percentage value is displayed as a decimal number carried out to ten places. In Figure 2-2, the dollar figures in the quarter results are displayed as dollars and cents with a leading dollar sign. Furthermore, the quotient in cell B15 is displayed as a percent with one decimal place. Let's complete the formatting for this project.

The Percentage Format

Since the cell pointer is at B15, first format the decimal value to a percentage value. With the pointer on cell B15, enter the command /**R**ange **F**ormat (/RF) as illustrated in Figure 2-37. With the menu pointer active in the Format menu, type the letter P to select the Percent format. Remember, you can also select the command Percent by moving the menu pointer to highlight the word Percent and pressing the Enter key.

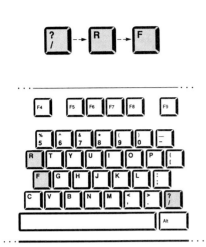

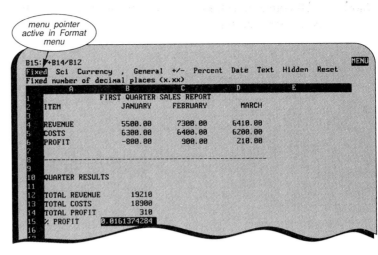

FIGURE 2-37 Step 1 of formatting Percent—press the Slash key (/), type the letter R for Range, and the letter F for Format.

When you type the letter P, 1-2-3 displays the prompt message "Enter number of decimal places (0..15): 2" on the input line. Type the number 1 for one decimal position. This procedure is shown in Figure 2-38.

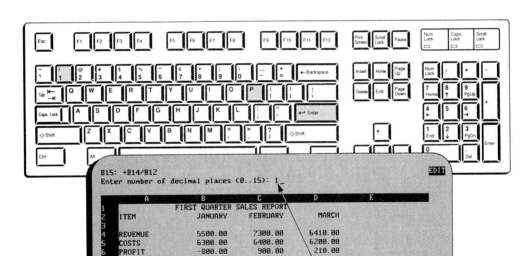

FIGURE 2-38 Step 2 of formatting Percent—type the letter P for Percent and the number 1 for decimal positions desired.

Next, press the Enter key. 1-2-3 displays the prompt message "Enter range to format: B15..B15" on the input line. Again press the Enter key, since we want to assign this format only to cell B15. The decimal number 0.0161374284, assigned to cell B15 by the formula +B14/B12, now displays as 1.6%. This result is shown in Figure 2-39.

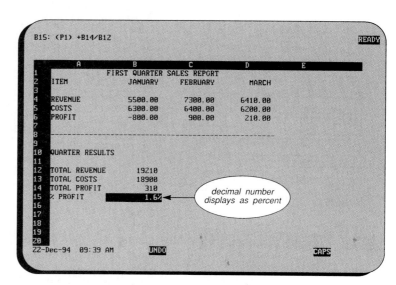

FIGURE 2-39   Step 3 of formatting Percent—press the Enter key, because the range of cells to be affected is only the cell where the cell pointer is located.

The Currency Format

The next step is to format the quarter results in cells B12, B13, and B14 to dollars and cents with a leading dollar sign. Scanning the list of available formats in Table 2-2 reveals that the Currency format is the one that displays monetary amounts with a leading dollar sign. Move the cell pointer to cell B12 and type the command /**R**ange **F**ormat **C**urrency (/RFC). This activity is shown in Figure 2-40.

Press the Enter key in response to the prompt message "Enter number of decimal places (0..15): 2" because the desired number of decimal positions is 2. As shown on the input line in Figure 2-41, 1-2-3 wants to know the range to assign the Currency format. Use the pointing method to enter the range.

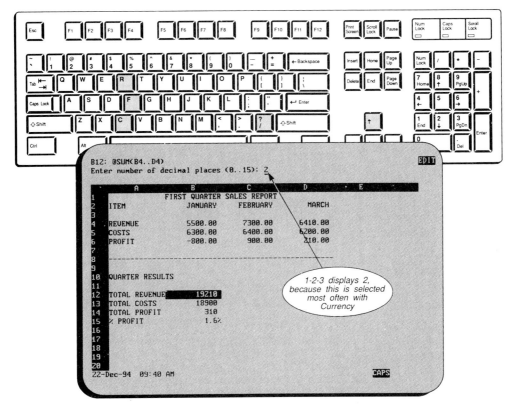

FIGURE 2-40 Step 1 of formatting Currency—move the cell pointer to one of the end points of the range of cells to be affected, press the Slash key (/), and type R for Range, F for Format, and C for Currency.

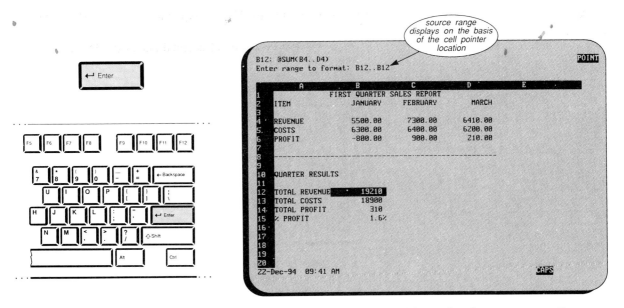

FIGURE 2-41 Step 2 of formatting Currency—press the Enter key. This sets decimal places to 2 and displays the prompt message on the input line.

The first cell address, B12, on the input line is correct. Therefore, move the cell pointer down to B14. As the cell pointer moves, 1-2-3 displays the range in reverse video. Also, the second cell address on the input line changes to agree with the location of the cell pointer. With the cell pointer on B14, the range we want to assign the Currency format is now correct (Figure 2-42).

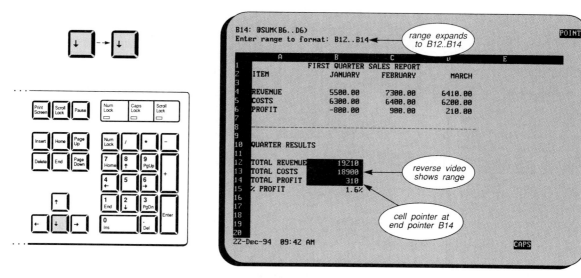

FIGURE 2-42 Step 3 of formatting Currency—use the arrow keys to select the range of cells to be affected.

Next, press the Enter key to assign the Currency format to the designated range in Figure 2-42, cells B12 through B14. Finally, press the Home key to move the cell pointer from cell B12 to cell A1 to prepare for the final step, printing the worksheet. Recall from Project 1 that regardless of where the cell pointer is in the worksheet, it immediately moves to cell A1 when you press the Home key. The complete worksheet is shown in Figure 2-43.

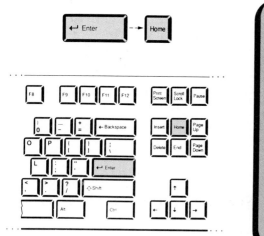
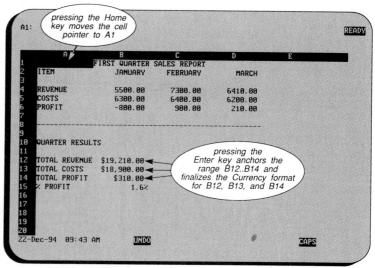

FIGURE 2-43 Step 4 of formatting Currency—press the Enter key to lock in the range B12..B14. The worksheet is complete. Press the Home key to move the cell pointer to A1.

SAVING THE WORKSHEET A SECOND TIME

◆ We already saved an intermediate version of the worksheet as PROJS-2. To save the worksheet again, do the following:

1. Enter the command /File Save (/FS).
2. Since we saved this worksheet earlier in the session, 1-2-3 assumes we want to save it under the same file name. Therefore, it displays the name PROJS-2.WK1 on the input line at the top of the screen as shown in the first screen in Figure 2-44. This saves keying time. Press the Enter key.
3. The menu at the top of the lower screen in Figure 2-44 gives three choices—Cancel, Replace, or Backup. Type the letter R for Replace. 1-2-3 replaces the worksheet we saved earlier on disk with the worksheet on the screen.

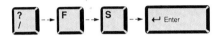

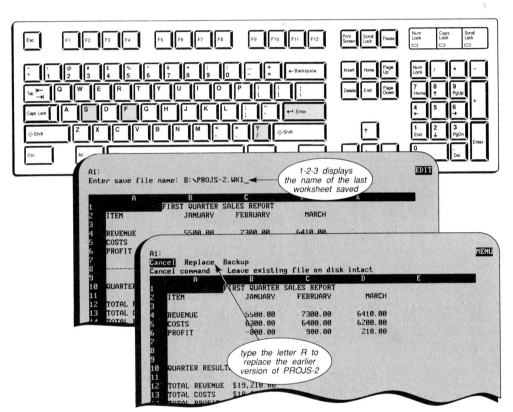

FIGURE 2-44 When a worksheet is saved a second time under the same file name, type the letter R to replace the previous version on disk.

If we type the letter C for Cancel, rather than R for Replace, the Save command is terminated, and 1-2-3 returns to READY mode. If we type the letter B for Backup, the worksheet on disk with the same name is saved under the file name PROJS-2.BAK, and the worksheet on the screen is saved under the name PROJS-2.WK1. A worksheet stored with the extension .BAK is referred to as a backup. Saving a backup copy of the worksheet is another form of protection against losing all your work.

PRINTING THE WORKSHEET

In Project 1 you printed the worksheet by pressing the Print Screen key. The printed report included the window borders as well as the control panel and indicator line. However, window borders clutter the report and make it more difficult to read. In this section, we will discuss how to print the worksheet without the window borders, how to print sections of the worksheet, and how to print the actual entries assigned to the cells in a worksheet.

The Print Printer Command

To print the worksheet without window borders, type the command **/Print Printer** (/PP). This activates the menu pointer in the Print menu at the top of the screen as shown in Figure 2-45. Below the Print menu, 1-2-3 displays the print settings sheet. Press F6 if you want to view the worksheet, rather than the print settings sheet, while the Print menu is active. Press F6 again to view the print settings sheet.

Since this is the first time this report is being printed using the Print command, you must enter the range to print. Type the letter R to select Range from the Print menu. The entire worksheet is in the range A1..D15. With the cell pointer at cell A1, press the Period key to anchor A1.

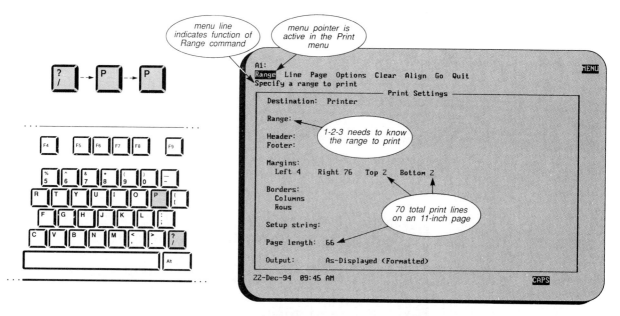

FIGURE 2-45 Step 1 of printing a worksheet using the Print command—press the Slash key (/) and type the letter P twice, once for Print and once for Printer.

Next, use the arrow keys to move the cell pointer to D15. As the cell pointer moves, the reverse video enlarges to encompass the entire range (Figure 2-46). Press the Enter key to anchor end point D15. The Print menu reappears as shown in Figure 2-47.

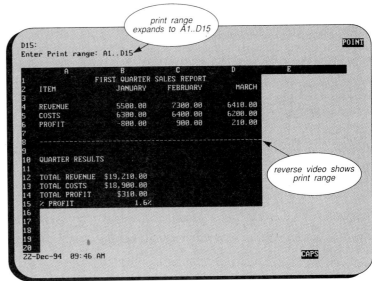

FIGURE 2-46 Step 2 of printing a worksheet using the Print command—type the letter R for Range, use the arrow keys to select the range, and press the Enter key.

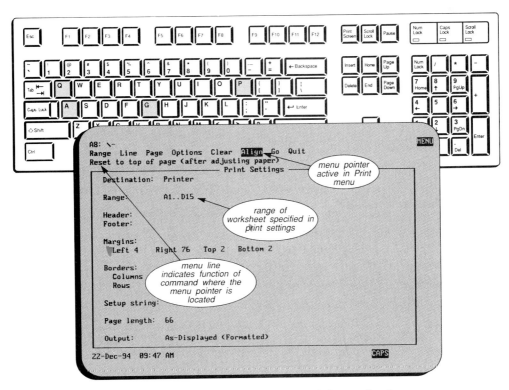

FIGURE 2-47 Step 3 of printing a worksheet using the Print command—type A for Align, G for Go, P for Page, and Q for Quit.

With the printer turned off, use the platen knob on the printer to align the perforated edge of the paper with the top of the print-head mechanism. Turn the printer on.

Type the letter A for Align, 1-2-3 has its own line counter. Invoking the Align command ensures that the program's line counter is the same as the printer's line counter; that is, that both counters are equal to zero after you turn the printer on and enter the Align command. If the two counters do not agree, the printed version of the worksheet may end up with a few inches of white space in the middle.

Next, type the letter G for Go. The printer immediately begins to print the worksheet. When the printer stops printing, type the letter P. Typing the letter P invokes the Page command, which causes the paper in the printer to move to the top of the next page. Carefully tear the paper just below the report at the perforated edge. The printed results are shown in Figure 2-48 ⟨a⟩.

Quitting the Print Command

The Print command is one of the few commands that does not immediately return 1-2-3 to READY mode when the command is finished executing. To return to READY mode after the Print command is complete, type the letter Q for Quit. This Quit command clears the menu from the control panel and returns 1-2-3 to READY mode with the worksheet displayed on the screen.

Printing a Section of the Worksheet

You may not always want to print the entire worksheet. Portions of the worksheet can be printed by entering the selected range in response to the Range command. Let's assume that you want to print only the quarter results as shown in Figure 2-48 ⟨b⟩. From Figure 2-43, you can see that the quarter results are in the range A10..B15.

To print the quarter results, enter the command /Print Printer (/PP) as shown in Figure 2-45. Next, type the letter R for Range. The screen in Figure 2-46 displays because 1-2-3 always remembers the last range entered for the Print command.

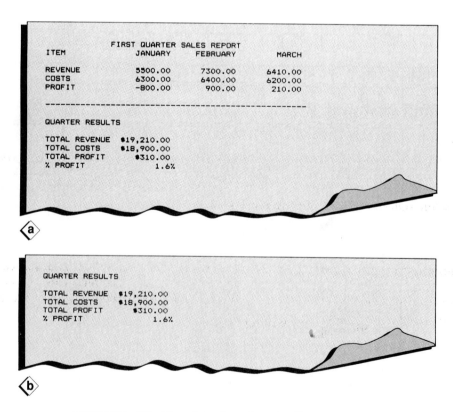

```
                    FIRST QUARTER SALES REPORT
        ITEM             JANUARY      FEBRUARY         MARCH

        REVENUE          5500.00      7300.00        6410.00
        COSTS            6300.00      6400.00        6200.00
        PROFIT           -800.00       900.00         210.00


        ------------------------------------------------------

        QUARTER RESULTS

        TOTAL REVENUE   $19,210.00
        TOTAL COSTS     $18,900.00
        TOTAL PROFIT       $310.00
        % PROFIT             1.6%
```
⟨a⟩

```
        QUARTER RESULTS

        TOTAL REVENUE   $19,210.00
        TOTAL COSTS     $18,900.00
        TOTAL PROFIT       $310.00
        % PROFIT             1.6%
```
⟨b⟩

FIGURE 2-48 Complete ⟨a⟩ and partial ⟨b⟩ printed versions of the worksheet.

To change the range, press the Backspace key to free the end points A1 and D15 on the input line. Use the arrow keys to move the cell pointer to A10. Press the Period key (.) to anchor the upper left end point of the range containing the quarter results. Move the cell pointer to B15. At this point, the screen appears as shown in Figure 2-49. Press the Enter key to anchor the lower right end point.

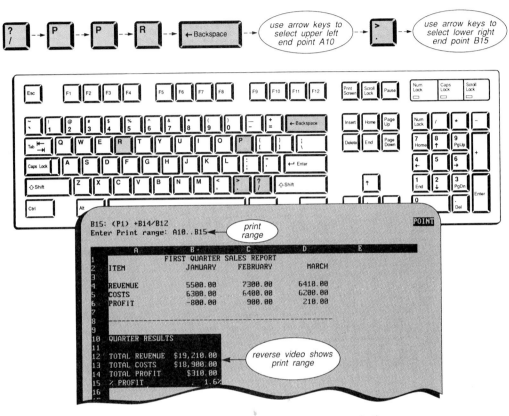

FIGURE 2-49 Printing a portion of the worksheet

Next, make sure the paper is aligned and the printer is ready. As described in Figure 2-47, type the letter A for Align and the letter G for Go to print the partial report. The partial report shown in Figure 2-48 ⟨b⟩ prints on the printer. When the report is complete, type the letter P to eject the paper from the printer. Finally, type the letter Q for Quit to complete the Print command. The Print menu disappears from the control panel, and 1-2-3 returns to READY mode with the worksheet displayed on the screen. At this point, if you enter the UNDO command (Alt-F4), 1-2-3 will reset the print settings to the ones shown in Figure 2-47.

Printing the Cell-Formulas Version of the Worksheet

Thus far, we have printed the worksheet exactly as it is on the screen. This is called the **as-displayed** version of the worksheet. Another variation that we print is called the cell-formulas version. The **cell-formulas** version prints what was assigned to the cells, rather than what's in the cells. It is useful for debugging a worksheet because the formulas and functions print out, rather than the numeric results.

Figure 2-50 illustrates the printed cell-formulas version of this worksheet. Each filled cell in the selected range is printed on a separate line. The cell address is printed in the left column, followed by any special formatting that was assigned to the cell, and the actual contents. The information displayed in the report is identical to the display on the mode line for the current cell.

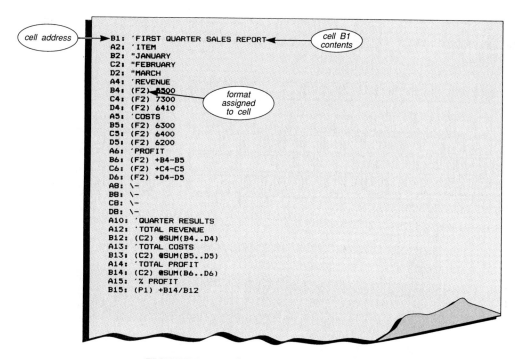

FIGURE 2-50 Cell-formulas version of the worksheet

To print the cell-formulas version of the worksheet, type the command **/P**rint **P**rinter **R**ange (/PPR). Enter the range A1..D15 and press the Enter key. With the menu pointer still active in the Print menu, enter the command **O**ptions **O**ther **C**ell-formulas **Q**uit **A**lign **G**o **P**age (OOCQAGP). 1-2-3 prints the cell-formulas version of Project 2 as shown in Figure 2-50.

Once the Print command option has been set to print the cell-formulas version, 1-2-3 will continue to print this variation each time you use the **/P**rint **P**rinter (/PP) command until you change the print option back to as-displayed. Therefore, after printing the cell-formulas version, but before quitting the Print command, enter the command **O**ptions **O**ther **A**s-displayed **Q**uit **Q**uit (OOAQQ). The last Quit in the chain of commands causes 1-2-3 to return to READY mode. The next time the Print command is used, 1-2-3 will print the as-displayed version. Another way to switch back to the as-displayed version is to use the UNDO command after the cell-formulas version is printed and after 1-2-3 has returned to READY mode.

Printing a Worksheet to a File

You can instruct 1-2-3 to transmit the printed version of a worksheet to a file. This can be useful if your printer is not functioning or if you prefer to print the worksheet at a later time. Use the command /Print File (/PF), rather than /Print Printer (/PP). When you enter the command /PF, 1-2-3 requests a file name. After you enter the file name, the Print menu in Figure 2-47 displays with the file name as the destination, rather than printer. From this point on, you can select commands from the Print menu as if you were printing the worksheet directly to the printer.

Later, after quitting 1-2-3, you can use the DOS command Type to display the worksheet on the screen or the DOS command Print to print the worksheet on the printer. The file extension .PRN, which stands for printer file, automatically appends to the file name you select.

Summary of Commands in the Print Menu

Table 2-4 summarizes the commands available in the Print menu.

TABLE 2-4   A Summary of Commands in the Print Menu

COMMAND	FUNCTION
Range	Allows you to specify what part of the worksheet is printed.
Line	Moves the paper in the printer one line.
Page	Advances the paper in the printer to the top of the next page on the basis of the program's page-length setting.
Options	Sets header, footer, margins, page length, borders, and special printer commands.
Clear	Sets Print command settings to their default and clears the current print-range setting.
Align	Resets the line counter for the printer.
Go	Starts printing the worksheet on the printer.
Quit	Returns 1-2-3 to READY mode.

DEBUGGING THE FORMULAS IN A WORKSHEET USING THE TEXT FORMAT

◆ **Debugging** is the process of finding and correcting errors in a worksheet. When formulas are assigned to the cells in a worksheet, the cell-formulas version is a handy tool for debugging it. Recall that the cell-formulas version shows the formulas associated with a worksheet (Figure 2-50). An alternative to printing the cell-formulas version of the worksheet is to format the worksheet to the Text type. This format allows you to see the formulas in the cells on the screen, instead of their numeric result. When the worksheet is formatted to the Text type, it is called the **text version**.

To view the text version of the worksheet, do the following:

1. Save the worksheet to disk so that you don't lose the formats currently assigned to the cells in the worksheet.
2. Enter the command /Range Format Text (/RFT) and enter the range A1..D15.

As shown in Figure 2-51, the formulas display in the cells instead of their numeric results. One problem with this procedure is that if a formula is longer than the width of the cell, a portion of it is hidden.

When you are finished viewing or printing the worksheet formatted to the Text type, retrieve from disk the original version of the worksheet—the one that contains the properly formatted cells.

Instead of saving the worksheet before changing the format to text, you can use the UNDO command (Alt-F4) after viewing the formulas in the cells and before making any new entries.

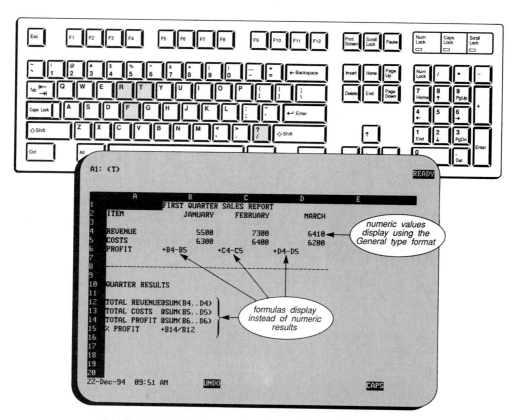

FIGURE 2-51 Display of the formulas in the cells instead of the numeric results. Use the command /Range Format Text (/RFT) and enter the range A1..D15.

PROJECT SUMMARY

In Project 2 you formatted the numeric values you entered in Project 1, added summaries, and formatted the summaries. Although this sequence of performing operations works well in many applications, it is not mandatory. For example, it may be more economical in terms of time and effort to enter portions of the data and then format it immediately, or it might be advisable to format the cells before entering the data into the worksheet. You will learn which sequence to choose as you gain experience with 1-2-3.

In Project 2 you learned how to load a worksheet, increase the size of columns, specify a range, copy cells, format a worksheet, and print a worksheet without window borders. All the activities that you learned for this project are summarized in the Quick Reference following the Appendix. The following is a summary of the keystroke sequence we used in Project 2.

SUMMARY OF KEYSTROKES — PROJECT 2

STEPS	KEY(S) PRESSED	RESULTS
1	/FR ↵	Retrieves PROJS-1 from disk.
2	Caps Lock	Sets Caps Lock on.
3	/WGC13↵	Sets column width to 13.
4	/RFF↵ Backspace ←←←↑↑.↓↓ →→↵	Sets monthly revenue, costs, and profit to a fixed format with two decimal places.
5	F5 A8↵	Moves the cell pointer to A8.
6	\-↵	Repeats dashes in cell A8.
7	/C↵→.→→↵	Copies dashes in cell A8 to cells B8, C8, and D8.
8	↓↓QUARTER RESULTS↓↓	Enters title.
9	TOTAL REVENUE↓	Enters title.
10	TOTAL COSTS↓	Enters title.
11	TOTAL PROFIT↓	Enters title.
12	% PROFIT↓	Enters title.
13	F5 B12↵	Moves the cell pointer to B12.
14	/FSPROJS-2↵	Saves worksheet as PROJS-2.
15	@SUM(B4.D4)↵	Enters SUM function for total revenue.
16	/C↵↓.↓↵	Copies SUM function from cell B12 to B13 and B14.
17	↓↓↓+B14/B12↵	Enters % profit formula.
18	/RFP1↵↵	Formats decimal number in cell B15 to percent.
19	↑↑↑/RFC↵↓↓↵	Formats the total revenue, costs, and profit to the Currency type.
20	Home	Moves the cell pointer to A1.
21	/FS↵R	Saves worksheet as PROJS-2.
22	/PPRA1.D15↵AGPQ	Prints the as-displayed version of the worksheet.
23	/PPRA10.B15↵AGPQ	Prints a portion of the worksheet.
24	/PPRA1.D15↵OOCQAGP	Prints the cell-formulas version of the worksheet.
25	OOAQQ	Changes the print option to as-displayed.
26	/RFTA1.D15↵	Formats the worksheet to the Text type.

The following list summarizes the material covered in Project 2.

1. To retrieve a worksheet from disk, enter the command /**F**ile **R**etrieve (/FR). Use the Left and Right Arrow keys to move the menu pointer in the alphabetized list on the menu line to the worksheet name you want to retrieve and then press the Enter key.
2. **Global** means the entire worksheet. To change the width of all the columns in the worksheet, type the command /**W**orksheet **G**lobal **C**olumn-Width (/WGC). Enter the desired column width (1–240) on the input line and press the Enter key.
3. To change the width of a range of columns, enter the command /**W**orksheet **C**olumn **C**olumn-Range **S**et-Width (/WCCS). Enter the range of columns and the desired column width. Press the Enter key to complete the command.
4. To change the width of a specific column in the worksheet, move the cell pointer to the column in question and type the command /**W**orksheet **C**olumn **S**et-Width (/WCS). Enter the new width and press the Enter key.

5. A **range** is one or more cells upon which you want to complete an operation. A range may be a single cell, a series of adjacent cells in a column or row, or a rectangular group of adjacent cells. A range cannot be made up of cells that only run diagonally or are separated.

6. To enter a range, type the cell address at one end point of the range, followed by a period (.) to anchor the first end point, followed by the cell address at the opposite end point of the range. If it is necessary to change the first end point after it is *anchored*, press the Backspace key.

7. If a range defines a rectangular group of cells, the two end points must be diagonally opposite corner cells of the rectangle.

8. To format a range, type the command /Range Format (/RF). Select the type of format you want to use from the menu. Enter the number of decimal places if required. Enter the range to be affected and press the Enter key.

9. To format the entire worksheet, type the command /Worksheet Global Format (/WGF). Follow the same steps described for formatting a range.

10. You can also enter a range by **pointing**. Pointing involves using the arrow keys to move the cell pointer to select the end points.

11. When you use pointing to select the range, use the Backspace key to *unlock* the end points of the range on the input line.

12. 1-2-3 displays the range with the end points separated by two periods (..), even though you enter only a single period (.) to anchor the first end point.

13. There are several ways to format numeric values using the /Worksheet Global Format (/WGF) or /Range Format (/RF) command.

14. Move the cell pointer to a cell to determine the format assigned to it. The format displays in parentheses next to the cell address on the mode line at the top of the screen.

15. To repeat a series of characters throughout a cell, begin the entry by typing the **Backslash key** (\).

16. To copy a range to another range, type the command /Copy (/C). Enter the **source range** and then the **destination range**.

17. It is good practice to save a worksheet to disk after every 50 to 75 keystrokes.

18. A **built-in function** automatically handles calculations.

19. The **SUM function** adds the contents of the range specified in parentheses.

20. All built-in functions begin with the @ **symbol**.

21. When you copy a function, the Copy command adjusts the range for the new position.

22. If the Slash key (/) is the first key pressed, 1-2-3 switches to MENU mode. If the Slash key follows any character in a nonlabel entry on the input line, it represents division.

23. When you save a worksheet the second time using the same file name, 1-2-3 requires that you type the letter R for Replace.

24. To print the **as-displayed** version of the worksheet without borders, type the command /Print Printer (/PP). If the range has not yet been established from a previous printout of the worksheet, you must enter the range to print. With the printer off, use the platen knob to align the perforated edge of the paper with the top of the print-head mechanism. Turn the printer on. Type the letter A for Align and the letter G for Go. After the worksheet is printed, type the letter P for Page. Carefully remove the printed version of the worksheet from the printer. Finally, type the letter Q for Quit.

25. To print a section of the worksheet, enter the command /Print Printer Range (/PPR). Use the Backspace key to *unlock* the range. Enter the desired range and continue with the steps just outlined.

26. To print the **cell-formulas** version of the worksheet, type the command /Print Printer Options Other Cell-formulas Quit Align Go Page (/PPOOCQAGP). It is important to change the print option back to as-displayed, so that future printouts will print the as-displayed version rather than the cell-formulas version. One way to change the printout back to as-displayed is to use the UNDO command after the cell-formulas version prints and 1-2-3 returns to READY mode.

27. To print the worksheet to a file, use the command /Print File (/PF). Later, after you have quit 1-2-3, you may use the DOS command Type to display the worksheet on the screen or the DOS command Print to print the worksheet on the printer.

28. To display formulas assigned to cells rather than their numeric result, assign the Text type format to the cells in the worksheet. When the worksheet is formatted to the Text type, it is called the **text version**.

STUDENT ASSIGNMENTS

STUDENT ASSIGNMENT 1: True/False

Instructions: Circle T if the statement is true or F if the statement is false.

T F   1. If you want to completely *back out* of the command /FR, press the Esc key once.
T F   2. The command /**W**orksheet **G**lobal **C**olumn-Width (/WGC) is used to set the width of all the columns in the worksheet.
T F   3. With the /**F**ile **R**etrieve (/FR) command, you are not required to type the name of the worksheet on the input line you want loaded into main memory.
T F   4. A range is made up of a minimum of two or more cells.
T F   5. When using the command /**R**ange **F**ormat (/RF), entire rows can be formatted; however, entire columns cannot be formatted.
T F   6. For a rectangular group of cells, you can enter the cell addresses of any two opposite corners to define the range.
T F   7. A range can be referenced by an entry such as B4..D6.
T F   8. With the format Currency, negative numbers display in parentheses.
T F   9. If you decide to use the point method when 1-2-3 requests a range, press the Backspace key to *unlock* the first end point, if necessary.
T F 10. If the Backslash key (\) is the first character typed on the input line, the characters that follow will repeat throughout the cell when you press the Enter key or one of the arrow keys.
T F 11. If the function @SUM(B4..D4) is assigned to cell A20, then A20 will be equal to the sum of the contents of cells B4 and D4.
T F 12. The command /**C**opy (/C) is used to copy the contents of a range of cells to another range of cells.
T F 13. The type of format assigned to a cell displays on the mode line at the top of the screen when the cell pointer is on the cell.
T F 14. When in POINT mode, anchor the first cell end point by moving the cell pointer to it and pressing the Period key.
T F 15. The Align command in the Print menu is used to align the decimal points in the selected range.
T F 16. If you save a worksheet a second time, you can use the same file name originally assigned to the worksheet.
T F 17. If the function @SUM(B4..B8) assigns a value of 10 to cell B9, and B9 is copied to C9, then C9 may or may not be equal to 10.
T F 18. It is possible to copy a single cell to a range of cells.

STUDENT ASSIGNMENT 2: Multiple Choice

Instructions: Circle the correct response.

1. Which one of the following is a valid entry for a range of cells?
   a. A1.A1
   b. B2,D2
   c. B2:D2
   d. both b and c
2. The format Comma (,) with two decimal places causes 5000 to display as _____.
   a. $5,000.00
   b. 5000.00
   c. 5,000.00
   d. $5000.00
3. Which one of the following instructs 1-2-3 to center characters in the current cell?
   a. circumflex (^)
   b. quotation mark (")
   c. apostrophe (')
   d. backslash (\)
4. Which of the following is the correct command for retrieving the worksheet PROJS-1.WK1 stored on the disk in the default drive?
   a. /FRPROJS-1 ↵
   b. /WRPROJS-1 ↵
   c. /CPROJS-1 ↵
   d. none of the above

Student Assignment 2 (continued)

5. When the command /Worksheet Global (/WG) is used, it means that _____ .
   a. only a single cell will be affected
   b. only a single column will be affected
   c. only a single row will be affected
   d. the entire worksheet will be affected
6. A listing on the printer of the worksheet as it displays on the screen is called the _____ version of the worksheet.
   a. cell-formulas
   b. as-displayed
   c. formatted
   d. content
7. Which one of the following causes the data in cells B4, C4, and D4 to be added together?
   a. @SUM(B4.D4)
   b. @ADD(B4.D4)
   c. @SUM(B4:D4)
   d. @SUM(B4 C4 D4)
8. Which one of the following correctly identifies the range of the rectangular group of cells with corner cells at B12, B20, E12, and E20?
   a. B12.E20
   b. B20.E12
   c. E20.B12
   d. all of the above

STUDENT ASSIGNMENT 3: Understanding Ranges

Instructions: List all the possible ranges for each of the designated areas in the following figure. For example, one range that identifies the first group of cells is A1..B3. There are three other ways to identify this first group of cells.

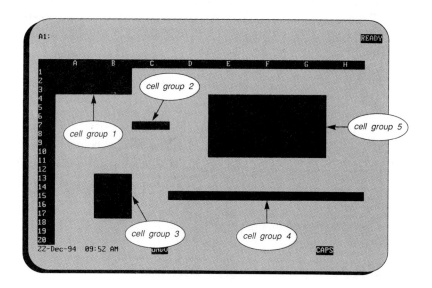

Cell group 1:   _A1..B3_   _____   _____   _____

Cell group 2:   _____

Cell group 3:   _____   _____

Cell group 4:   _____   _____

Cell group 5:   _____   _____   _____   _____

STUDENT ASSIGNMENT 4: Understanding Formats

Instructions: Using Table 2-2, fill in the *Results In* column of the following table. Assume that the column width of each cell is 10 characters. Use the character b to indicate positions containing the blank character. As examples, the first two problems in the table below are complete.

Determining the Value of a Number Based on a Given Format

PROBLEM	CELL CONTENTS	FORMAT TO	DECIMAL PLACES	RESULTS IN
1	25	Fixed	1	bbbbb25.0b
2	1.26	Currency	2	bbbb$1.26b
3	14.816	,(comma)	2	_____
4	−5281.42	Fixed	0	_____
5	123	Percent	2	_____
6	7	+/−	Not reqd.	_____
7	−3841.92	, (comma)	3	_____
8	72148.92	General	Not reqd.	_____
9	32	Percent	2	_____
10	.148	Fixed	2	_____
11	109234	Currency	0	_____
12	4.86	Scientific	1	_____
13	−1276	Currency	2	_____
14	51214.76	Scientific	0	_____
15	−5010.50	Currency	2	_____

STUDENT ASSIGNMENT 5: Correcting the Range in a Worksheet

Instructions: The worksheet illustrated in the following figure contains errors in cells B12 through B15. Analyze the entries displayed in the worksheet. Explain the cause of the errors and the method of correction in the space provided below.

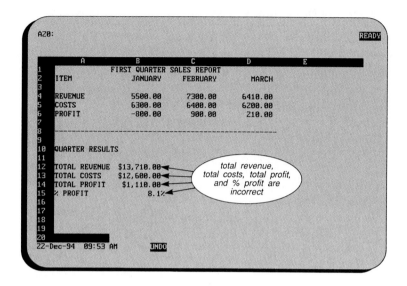

Cause of error: _____

_____

Method of correction for cell B12: _____

_____

Method of correction for cells B13, B14, and B15: _____

_____

_____

STUDENT ASSIGNMENT 6: Correcting Functions in a Worksheet

Instructions: The worksheet illustrated in the following figure contains invalid function entries in cells B12, B13, and B14. The invalid entries in these cells cause the diagnostic message ERR to display in cell B15. Analyze the entries displayed in the worksheet. Explain the cause of the errors and the method of correction in the space provided below.

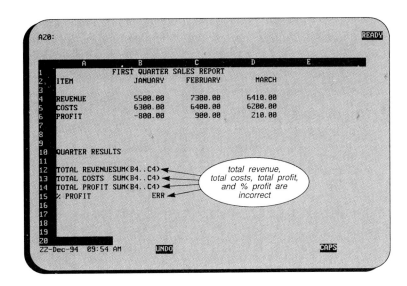

Cause of error: _____

_____

Method of correction for cell B12: _____

_____

Method of correction for cells B13, B14, and B15: _____

_____

_____

STUDENT ASSIGNMENT 7: Modifying an Inventory Worksheet

Instructions: Load 1-2-3 and perform the following tasks.

1. Load the worksheet that you created in Project 1, Student Assignment 8 (STUS1-8). This original worksheet is illustrated in the following figure ⟨a⟩.
2. Perform these modifications:
    a. Use the Comma (,) format with zero decimal places for the numbers in rows 5, 6, 7, and 9.
    b. Include the inventory total in the worksheet, as illustrated in the modified worksheet ⟨b⟩. The inventory total consists of a total for each plant (B15..B17). For example, the total for Chicago is the sum of cells B5 through D5. Separate the inventory total from the other values by a double line in row 11 (use the equal sign).
    c. Use the Comma (,) format with zero decimal places for the inventory totals.
3. Save the modified worksheet. Use the file name STUS2-7.
4. Print the entire worksheet on the printer using the /**Print Printer** (/PP) command.
5. Print only the inventory totals in the range A13..B19.
6. Print the worksheet after formatting all the cells to the Text type.

Handwritten annotation: /RFC enter 0 dec. move to 5-9 enter home

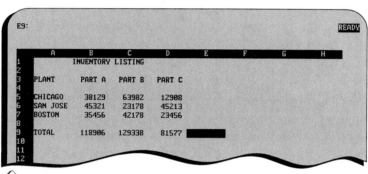

a. Original worksheet

Handwritten annotations at left: +B5+B5+D5 / @sum(B5..D5) / move to A16 / @sum(B6..D6)

Handwritten annotations at right: A1..D6 enter / Print screen

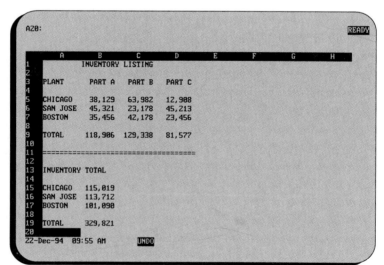

b. Modified worksheet

Handwritten annotation at bottom: /RFT enter range of all lines

STUDENT ASSIGNMENT 8: Building an Office Payroll
Comparison Worksheet

Instructions: Load 1-2-3 and perform the following tasks.

1. Build the worksheet illustrated in the following figure. Change the width of all the columns to 14 characters. The totals displayed in row 10 of the worksheet are the sum of the salaried personnel in column B and the hourly personnel in column C. The office totals by city (B15..B18) are the sum of the salaried personnel and the hourly personnel for each office. The total in B20 is the sum of the office totals.
2. Save the worksheet. Use the file name STUS2-8.
3. Print the as-displayed and cell-formulas versions of this worksheet.
4. Print the portion of the worksheet in the range A1..C10.

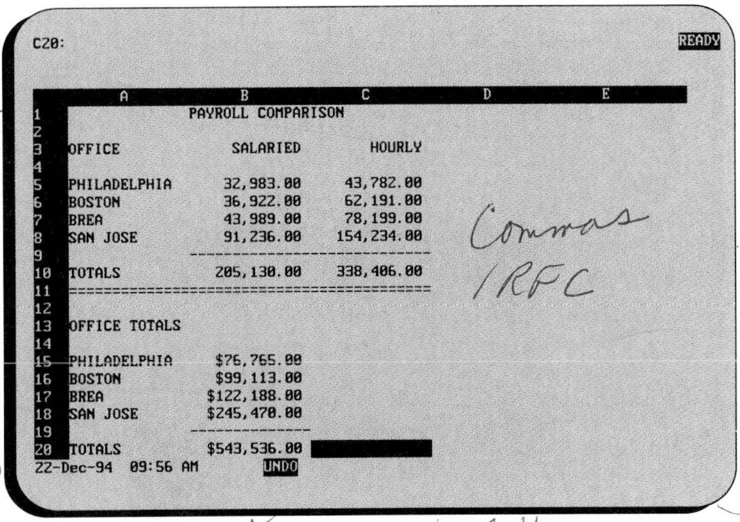

```
C20:                                                               READY

         A              B              C              D              E
1                  PAYROLL COMPARISON
2
3    OFFICE         SALARIED       HOURLY
4
5    PHILADELPHIA    32,983.00      43,782.00
6    BOSTON          36,922.00      62,191.00
7    BREA            43,989.00      78,199.00
8    SAN JOSE        91,236.00     154,234.00
9                   -----------    -----------
10   TOTALS         205,130.00     338,406.00
11   ================================================
12
13   OFFICE TOTALS
14
15   PHILADELPHIA   $76,765.00
16   BOSTON         $99,113.00
17   BREA          $122,188.00
18   SAN JOSE      $245,470.00
19                  -----------
20   TOTALS        $543,536.00    
22-Dec-94  09:56 AM          UNDO
```

(Handwritten annotations surrounding the figure:)

Dashes
F5 enter All enter key
with cursor on All
press \ key
hit = sign enter
Copy Dashes *

Adding
@sum (B5..B8) enter
" " (C5..C8) "
w/cursor on B15 /C
enter range from B15..B15 enter
enter range to copy to B15 \ arrow to B16
press . move to B17 . move to B.18

print screen — stay at A1
/PPR Backspace move cursor to A1..D9
move to C9 enter 6f

column width
/WGC
type # 14 enter

Adding
+B5+B6+B7+B8

Copy Row C
/C

Commas
/RFC

* /C
enter range to copy from A11..All enter
enter range to copy to A11
move cursor to B11
press . move to C11 enter

/RFT
A1..C20

STUDENT ASSIGNMENT 9: Building an Annual Expense Worksheet

Instructions: Load 1-2-3 and perform the following tasks.

1. Build the worksheet illustrated in the following figure. Change the width of all the columns to 15 character positions. The variances in column D of the worksheet are obtained by subtracting the actual expenses from the budgeted expenses. In the summary portion of the worksheet, the percentage of budget used (C17) is obtained by dividing the total actual amount (C15) by the total budgeted amount (C14).
2. Save the worksheet. Use the file name STUS2-9.
3. Print the as-displayed and cell-formulas versions of this worksheet.
4. Print the portion of the worksheet in the range A3..B8.
5. Print the worksheet after formatting all the cells to the Text type.

+C15/C14

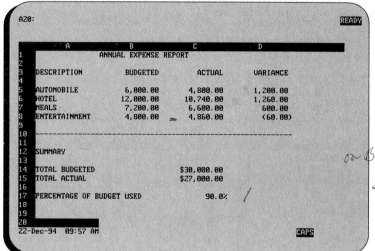

Division
C15 × C14 enter
on B15 / RFP enter
1 dec pls. enter
C17..C17 enter

STUDENT ASSIGNMENT 10: Changing Data in the Annual Expense Worksheet

Instructions: Load 1-2-3 and perform the following tasks.

1. Retrieve the worksheet STUS2-9 from disk. The worksheet is illustrated in the figure in Student Assignment 9.
2. Decrement each of the four values in the ACTUAL column by $360.00 until the percentage of budget used in C17 is as close as possible to 80%. All four values in column C must be decremented the same number of times. You should end up with a percentage of budget used in C17 equal to 80.4%.
3. After successfully modifying the worksheet, print it on the printer.
4. Save the modified worksheet. Use the file name STUS2-10.

+ C17/C18

STUDENT ASSIGNMENT 11: Building a Monthly Sales Analysis Worksheet

Instructions: Load 1-2-3 and perform the following tasks.

1. Build the worksheet illustrated in the following figure. Change the width of all the columns to 11 characters. Then change the width of column A to 14 positions. Center all the column headings using the circumflex (^). The net sales in column D of the worksheet is determined by subtracting the sales returns in column C from the sales amount in column B. The above/below quota amount in column F is obtained by subtracting the sales quota in column E from the net sales in column D. In the summary section of the worksheet, the totals for each group are obtained by adding the values for each salesperson. The percent of quota sold in cell C20 is obtained by dividing the total net sales amount in C17 by the total sales quota amount in C18.
2. Save the worksheet. Use the file name STUS2-11.
3. Print the as-displayed and cell-formulas versions of this worksheet.
4. Print the portion of the worksheet in the range A1..F9.
5. Print the worksheet after formatting all the cells to the Text type.

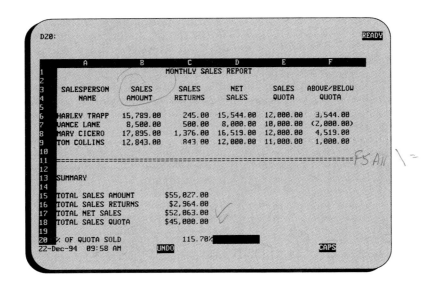

STUDENT ASSIGNMENT 12: Changing Data in the Monthly Sales Analysis Worksheet

Instructions: Load 1-2-3 and perform the following tasks.

1. Retrieve the worksheet STUS2-11 from disk. The worksheet is illustrated in the figure in Student Assignment 11.
2. Increment each of the four values in the sales quota column by $1,000.00 until the percent of quota sold in cell C20 is below, yet as close as possible to 100%. All four values in column E must be incremented the same number of times. The percent of quota sold in C20 should be equal to 98.23%.
3. Decrement each of the four values in the sales returns column by $100.00 until the percent of quota sold in cell C20 is below, yet as close as possible to 100%. All four values in column C must be decremented the same number of times. Your worksheet is correct when the percent of quota sold in C20 is equal to 99.74%.
4. After successfully modifying the worksheet, print it on the printer.
5. Save the modified worksheet. Use the file name STUS2-12.

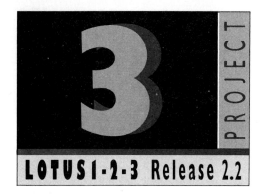

LOTUS 1-2-3 Release 2.2

Enhancing Your Worksheet

OBJECTIVES

You will have mastered the material in this project when you can:

◆ Display today's date and time in a worksheet using the NOW function

◆ Move a group of rows or columns to another area of the worksheet

◆ Insert and delete rows and columns

◆ Freeze the horizontal and vertical titles

◆ Enter percentage values using the percent sign (%)

◆ Copy absolute cell addresses

◆ Employ the pointing method to enter a range to be summed

◆ Print a worksheet in condensed mode

◆ Print selected nonadjacent columns

◆ Answer what-if questions

◆ Switch between manual and automatic recalculation of a worksheet

◆ Change the default settings

◆ Temporarily exit 1-2-3 and return control to DOS

◆ Produce presentation-quality printouts using the add-in program Allways

In the first two projects you learned to build, save, retrieve, format, copy, and print worksheets. In this project we continue to emphasize these topics and discuss some new ones. We especially want to examine the Copy command in greater detail. The capability to copy one range to another range is one of the most powerful features of 1-2-3.

The new topics in this project teach you to insert and delete rows and columns in a worksheet, move the contents of a range to another range, and use the add-in program Allways to produce presentation-quality printouts. In general, they make the job of creating, saving, and printing a worksheet easier.

Finally, this project illustrates using 1-2-3 to answer what-if questions, like *What if the marketing expenses decrease 3%—how would the decrease affect net income for the first quarter of the year?* This capability of quickly analyzing the effect of changing values in a worksheet is important in making business decisions. To illustrate answering what-if questions, we will prepare the quarterly budget report shown in Figure 3-1.

```
          A              B             C            D              E
 1  Quarterly Report - January through March                  12/22/94
 2  Prepared by SAS                                           10:01 AM
 3
 4
 5  ITEM             JANUARY      FEBRUARY        MARCH    QUARTER TOTAL
 6  ==================================================================
 7
 8  REVENUE
 9    Sales Revenue  232,897.95   432,989.76   765,998.61   1,431,886.32
10    Other Revenue    1,232.93     3,265.81     2,145.99       6,644.73
11
12    Total Revenue  234,130.88   436,255.57   768,144.60   1,438,531.05
13
14  EXPENSES
15    Manufacturing   88,969.73   165,777.12   291,894.95     546,641.80
16    Research        25,754.40    47,988.11    84,495.91     158,238.42
17    Marketing       37,460.94    69,800.89   122,903.14     230,164.97
18    Administrative  39,802.25    74,163.45   130,584.58     244,550.28
19    Fulfillment     18,730.47    34,900.45    61,451.57     115,082.48
20
21    Total Expenses 210,717.79   392,630.01   691,330.14   1,294,677.95
22
23  NET INCOME        23,413.09    43,625.56    76,814.46     143,853.10
24
25  Budget % Values
26
27    Manufacturing       38%
28    Research            11%
29    Marketing           16%
30    Administrative      17%
31    Fulfillment          8%
```

FIGURE 3-1 A printout of the worksheet we will build in Project 3.

The worksheet in Figure 3-1 contains a company's budgeted revenue and expenses for the quarterly period of January through March. In addition, this worksheet includes the quarter total for all revenues and budgeted expenses. The total revenues for each month and the quarter total in row 12 are determined by adding the corresponding sales revenue and other revenue.

Each of the budgeted expenses—manufacturing, research, marketing, administrative, and fulfillment—is determined by taking a percentage of the total revenue. The budget percent values located in rows 27 through 31 are as follows:

1. The manufacturing expense is 38% of the total revenue.
2. The research expense is 11% of the total revenue.
3. The marketing expense is 16% of the total revenue.
4. The administrative expense is 17% of the total revenue.
5. The fulfillment expense is 8% of the total revenue.

The total expenses for each month in row 21 of Figure 3-1 are determined by adding all the corresponding budgeted expenses together. The net income for each month in row 23 is determined by subtracting the corresponding total expenses from the total revenue. Finally, the quarter totals in the far right column are determined by summing the monthly values in each row.

Begin this project by booting the computer and loading 1-2-3. A few seconds after the copyright message displays, an empty worksheet appears on the screen. All the columns in the empty worksheet are nine characters wide. This default width is not enough to hold some of the larger numbers in the worksheet we plan to build. Therefore, let's change the width of the columns.

VARYING THE WIDTH OF THE COLUMNS

◆ In the worksheet shown in Figure 3-1, column A is 17 characters wide, columns B through D are 13 characters wide, and column E is 16 characters wide. You select a column width setting on the basis of the longest column entry and the general appearance of the worksheet. Change the widths of the columns in the following manner:

1. Enter the command /Worksheet Global Column-Width (/WGC) to change the width of all the columns to 13 characters. Change the number on the input line from 9 to 13 by pressing the Right Arrow key four times followed by the Enter key as shown in Figure 3-2. We can also enter the number 13 in response to the prompt message on the input line and press the Enter key. The Global command is used to change the width of all the cells in the worksheet to 13 characters because that is the desired width of most of the columns for this project.

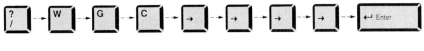

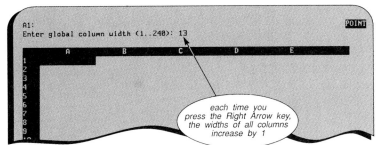

each time you press the Right Arrow key, the widths of all columns increase by 1

FIGURE 3-2 Using the command /WGC and the Right Arrow key to increase the width of all the columns in the worksheet to 13 characters

2. With the cell pointer at A1, enter the command /Worksheet Column Set-Width (/WCS) to change the width of column A to 17 characters. Again, press the Right Arrow key four times to change the number 13 to 17 on the input line. To complete the command, press the Enter key as shown in Figure 3-3. Notice on the top line of the control panel in Figure 3-3, next to the cell address, 1-2-3 displays the width of column A in brackets—[W17]. Anytime the cell pointer is in a column that has a width different from the global width, 1-2-3 displays it next to the cell address in the upper left corner of the screen.

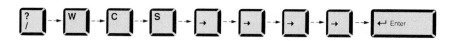

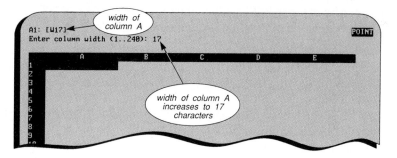

FIGURE 3-3

Using the command /WCS and the Right Arrow key to increase the width of column A to 17 characters

3. Move the cell pointer to E1 and enter the command /Worksheet Column Set-Width (/WCS) to change the width of column E to 16 characters. This is shown in Figure 3-4.

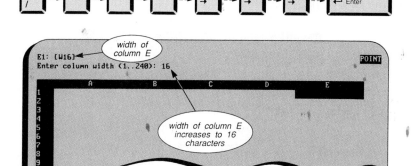

FIGURE 3-4

Using the command /WCS and the Right Arrow key to increase the width of column E to 16 characters

As we mentioned in Project 2, columns B, C, and D could have been set to 13 characters by using the command /Worksheet Column Column-Range Set-Width (/WCCS), rather than changing the width globally as shown in Figure 3-2. This command works the same as the /Worksheet Global Column-Width (/WGC), except that you must enter the range of columns involved in the change.

With the columns set to their designated widths, we can move on to the next step, formatting the worksheet globally.

FORMATTING THE WORKSHEET GLOBALLY

◆ In Project 2 we formatted the numbers after we entered the data. In some cases, especially when developing a large worksheet, you should consider issuing a global format before entering any data. This formats the numbers as you enter them, which makes them easier to read. The way to do this is to choose the format that is common to most of the cells. In choosing the format, don't count the empty cells or the ones with labels, because a numeric format does not affect them.

You can see from Figure 3-1 that, except for the budget percent values and the date and time, all the numbers appear as decimal numbers with two places of accuracy. These numbers also use the comma to group the integer portion by thousands. If you refer to Table 2-2 in Project 2, you will see that the required format corresponds to the Comma (,) type. Therefore, use this format for all the cells in the worksheet.

To invoke the global format command, enter the command /Worksheet Global Format (/WGF). This is shown in Figure 3-5.

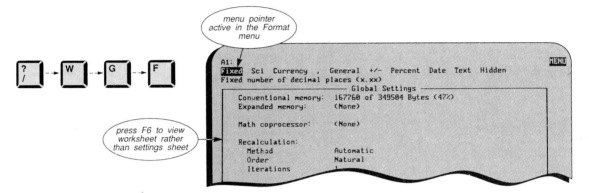

FIGURE 3-5 Step 1 of using the /WGF command to format all the cells in the worksheet to the Comma (,) type—press the Slash key (/) and type the letters W for Worksheet, G for Global, and F for Format.

With the menu pointer active in the Format menu, press the Comma key (,). The prompt message "Enter number of decimal places (0..15): 2" displays on the input line (Figure 3-6). Since we are working with dollars and cents, we want two decimal places to display, so press the Enter key.

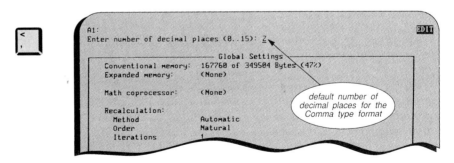

FIGURE 3-6 Step 2 of using the /WGF command to format all the cells in the worksheet to the Comma (,) type—press the Comma key (,).

The empty worksheet shown in Figure 3-7 displays. You can see that the columns are wider than nine characters. However, there is no indication of the Comma format assigned to all the cells. The format will appear as you enter data because 1-2-3 will automatically use the Comma format for any number entered into a cell.

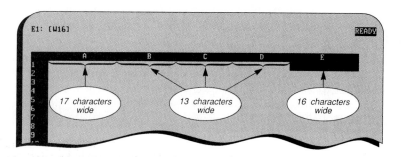

FIGURE 3-7
Step 3 of using the /WGF command to format all the cells in the worksheet to the Comma (,) type—press the Enter key.

DISPLAYING THE DATE AND TIME

With the column widths and the global format set, the next step is to enter the data into the worksheet. Enter the titles in cells A1 and A2 as you learned in Project 1. Cells E1 and E2 require today's date and time. Both values can be displayed by assigning each cell the NOW function.

The NOW Function

The **NOW function** uses the current DOS date and time that displays at the bottom of the screen to determine the number of days since December 31, 1899. It displays the value in the assigned cell as a decimal number. For this project assume that the DOS date is December 22, 1994 and the time is approximately 10:08 A.M..

To complete the time and date entries in the worksheet, move the cell pointer to E1 and enter the NOW function on the input line as illustrated in Figure 3-8.

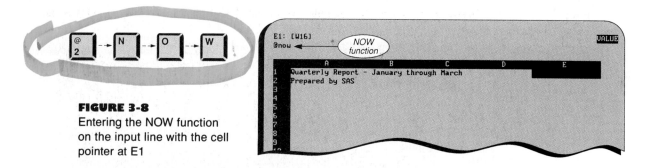

FIGURE 3-8
Entering the NOW function on the input line with the cell pointer at E1

Next, press the Down Arrow key and enter the same function in E2. Use the Up Arrow key to enter the function in E2. This places the cell pointer in E1 as shown in Figure 3-9. The value 34,690.42 in cells E1 and E2 represents the number of days since December 31, 1899. The integer portion of the number (34,690) represents the number of complete days, and the decimal portion (.42) represents the first 10 hours of December 22, 1994. Notice that the two entries are displayed in the Comma (,) format, the one assigned earlier to the entire worksheet. The next step is to format the date and time so they display in a more meaningful way.

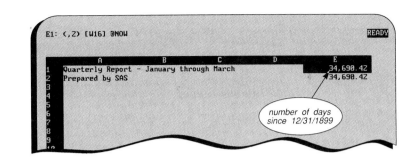

FIGURE 3-9
The NOW function assigned
to cells E1 and E2

Formatting the Date

In Figure 3-9, the cell pointer is at E1. To format the date, enter the command /Range Format Date (/RFD) as shown in Figure 3-10. With the menu pointer active in the Date menu, type the number 4 to select the fourth date format Long Intn'l (MM/DD/YY).

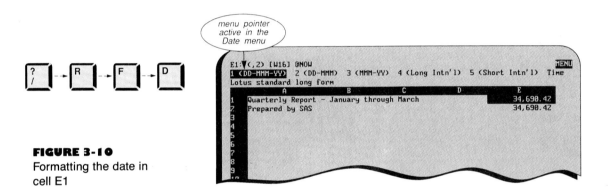

FIGURE 3-10
Formatting the date in
cell E1

1-2-3 responds by displaying the prompt message "Enter range to format: E1..E1" on the input line. E1 is the only cell we want to format, so press the Enter key. The date immediately changes in cell E1 to 12/22/94 as shown in Figure 3-11. Don't be concerned with trying to get the date in E1 to agree with 12/22/94. As long as the date in E1 represents the same day as the date on the status line at the bottom line of the screen, you have entered the NOW function correctly.

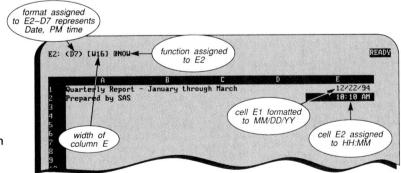

FIGURE 3-11
Date and time is displayed in
cells E1 and E2—10:10 AM
on December 22, 1994.

Formatting the Time

Move the cell pointer to E2. To format the time, enter the same command as for the date—**/R**ange **F**ormat **D**ate (/RFD). This is shown in Figure 3-10. With the menu pointer active in the Date menu, type the letter T for Time. The Time menu replaces the Date menu at the top of the screen. Select the second Time format (HH:MM AM/PM) by pressing the 2 key. Next, press the Enter key and the time in E2 displays as 10:10 AM (Figure 3-11). Here again, don't be concerned with trying to get the time in E2 to agree with 10:10 A.M.. The time in E2 should approximately agree with the time on the status line.

Updating the Time—Recalculation

The time displayed at the bottom of the screen updates every minute. However, the time displayed in a cell, as in E2, only updates when you enter a value into a cell in the worksheet. Any entry causes 1-2-3 to recalculate all the formulas and functions in the worksheet automatically.

If you are not entering values into the worksheet and want to instruct 1-2-3 to recalculate all formulas and functions, press function key F9. Pressing F9 updates the time as illustrated in Figure 3-12.

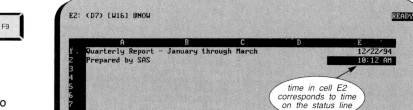

FIGURE 3-12
Press function key F9 to manually update the time in cell E2.

Date and Time Formats

Table 3-1 summarizes the date and time formats available in 1-2-3. Use this table to select formats when you want to display the date and time in a worksheet.

TABLE 3-1 Date and Time Formats
(Assume the DOS date is December 22, 1994 and the time is 3:12 PM)

FORMAT NUMBER	FORMAT TYPE	FORMAT CODE ON STATUS LINE	DATE OR TIME DISPLAYED
1	DD-MMM-YY	D1	22-Dec-94
2	DD-MMM	D2	22-Dec
3	MMM-YY	D3	Dec-94
4	Long Intn'l (MM/DD/YY)	D4	12/22/94
5	Short Intn'l (MM/DD)	D5	12/22
1	HH:MM:SS AM/PM	D6	3:12:00 PM
2	HH:MM AM/PM	D7	3:12 PM
3	Long Intn'l	D8	15:12:00
4	Short Intn'l	D9	15:12

ENTERING THE QUARTERLY BUDGET LABELS

◆ With the date and time formatted, we can enter the column headings, group titles, and row titles. Move the cell pointer to A5. Since the column headings consist of capital letters, press the Caps Lock key before entering them. Left-justify the first column heading and right-justify the rest. Recall that to left-justify a label, begin it with an apostrophe (') or a letter. For example, in A5 enter ITEM. To right-justify a label, begin the label with a quotation mark ("). For example, in B5, enter "JANUARY. The worksheet with the column headings is shown in Figure 3-13.

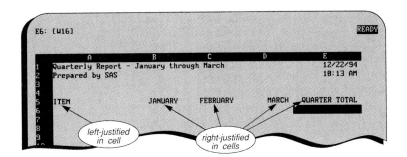

FIGURE 3-13
Column headings entered
into row 5

After completing the column headings, move the cell pointer to A6. Use the Backslash key (\) to repeat the equal sign (=) throughout cell A6. Next, use the command /Copy (/C) to copy the contents of cell A6 to cells B6 through E6. The result is a double-dashed line in row 6 as illustrated in Figure 3-14.

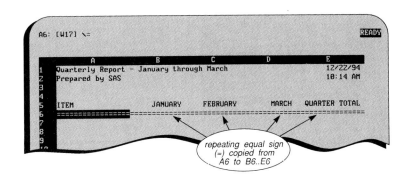

FIGURE 3-14
Column headings underlined

Once the column headings are complete, begin entering the group titles and row titles that are shown on the left side of Figure 3-1. All the labels are left-justified. The group subtitles are indented by two spaces to make the worksheet easier to read. Since most of the remaining labels are in lowercase letters, press the Caps Lock key to toggle off capital letters after entering the group title REVENUE in cell A8.

Do not enter the two subtitles Marketing and Administrative under the group title EXPENSES. We will add these subtitles shortly.

Figure 3-15 shows the group titles and row identifiers up to row 24. Notice in Figure 3-15 that with the cell pointer at A24, the window has moved down four rows, displaying rows 5 through 24 rather than rows 1 through 20. Once the cell pointer moves past row 20, the window begins to move down. The same applies when the cell pointer moves beyond the rightmost column on the screen.

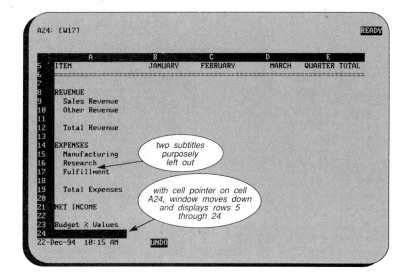

FIGURE 3-15
Group titles and subtitles
entered

INSERTING AND DELETING ROWS AND COLUMNS

◆ It is not unusual to forget to include rows or columns of data when building a worksheet, or to include too many rows or columns. 1-2-3 is forgiving. It has commands to insert or delete as many rows or columns as required. Furthermore, you can do this at any time, even after a worksheet is well under way.

The Insert Command

The command /**W**orksheet **I**nsert (/WI) is used to insert empty rows or columns anywhere in the worksheet. To make room for the new rows, 1-2-3 simply opens up the worksheet by *pushing down* the rows below the insertion point. If you are inserting columns, those to the right of the insertion point are *pushed* to the right. More importantly, if the *pushed* rows or columns include any formulas, 1-2-3 adjusts the cell references to the new locations.

Remember that the two subtitles Marketing and Administrative were purposely left out from the group title EXPENSES (Figure 3-15). Let's insert, that is, open up two blank rows in the worksheet so that we can add the two subtitles. According to Figure 3-1, the two subtitles belong immediately before Fulfillment in cell A17. Therefore, move the cell pointer to A17. To complete a row insert, always position the cell pointer on the first row you want *pushed* down. This is shown in Figure 3-16. For a row insert, the column location of the cell pointer is not important.

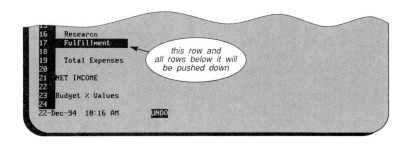

FIGURE 3-16
Step 1 of using the /WI command to insert rows—move the cell pointer to A17, the first row you want *pushed* down.

Enter the command /**Worksheet Insert** (/WI) as shown in Figure 3-17.

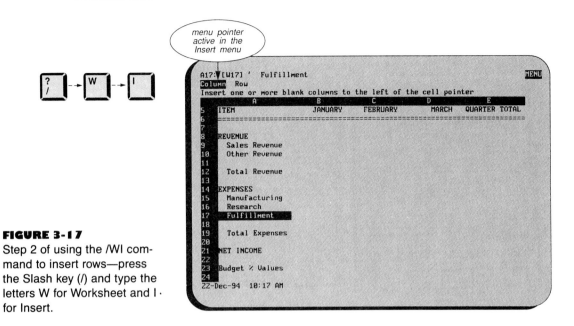

FIGURE 3-17

Step 2 of using the /WI command to insert rows—press the Slash key (/) and type the letters W for Worksheet and I · for Insert.

With the menu pointer active in the Insert menu, type the letter R for Row. 1-2-3 immediately responds on the input line at the top of the screen with the prompt message, "Enter row insert range: A17..A17". We want to add two new rows, A17 and A18. Therefore, use the Down Arrow key to increase the range on the input line from A17..A17 to A17..A18. This is illustrated in Figure 3-18.

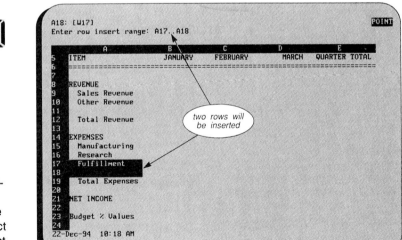

FIGURE 3-18

Step 3 of using the /WI command to insert rows—type the letter R for Row and use the Down Arrow key to select the number of rows you want to insert.

Press the Enter key and the worksheet *pushes down* all the rows beginning with row 17—the first row in the range A17..A18. This leaves rows 17 and 18 empty as shown in Figure 3-19.

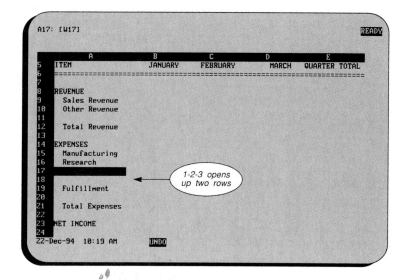

FIGURE 3-19
Step 4 of using the /WI command to insert rows—press the Enter key.

Enter the subtitle Marketing in cell A17 and the subtitle Administrative in cell A18 (Figure 3-20).

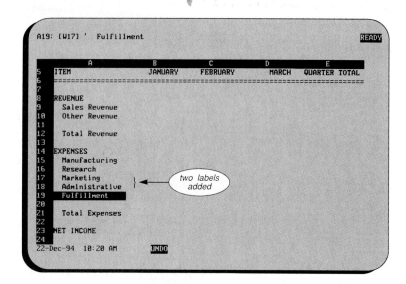

FIGURE 3-20
The two subtitles are inserted into the worksheet.

The Delete Command

You can delete unwanted rows or columns from a worksheet by using the command /Worksheet Delete (/WD). Let's delete rows 17 and 18 in Figure 3-20. After deleting these two rows, reinsert them using the command /Worksheet Insert (/WI).

With the cell pointer at cell A17, enter the command /**W**orksheet **D**elete (/WD). Next, type the letter R to instruct 1-2-3 to delete rows rather than columns. To delete columns you would type the letter C. When 1-2-3 requests the range to delete, press the Down Arrow key to change the range from A17..A17 to A17..A18. Press the Enter key. 1-2-3 immediately *closes up* the worksheet—rows 17 and 18 disappear. The worksheet appears as it did earlier in Figure 3-16. If you had decided to close up rows 17 and 18 immediately after inserting them, you could have used the UNDO command (Alt-F4), rather than the /WD command.

Be careful when you use the /**W**orksheet **D**elete (/WD) command. You do not want to delete rows or columns that are part of a range used in a formula or function elsewhere in the worksheet without carefully weighing the consequences. If any formula references a cell in a deleted row or column, 1-2-3 displays the diagnostic message "ERR" in the cell assigned the formula. ERR means that it was impossible for 1-2-3 to complete the computation.

Reinsert the two rows above row 17 and enter the row titles Marketing and Administrative before moving on. Follow the keystroke sequence we just described and shown in Figures 3-17 through 3-20.

COPYING CELLS WITH EQUAL SOURCE AND DESTINATION RANGES

The next step is to enter the subtitles in cells A27 through A31 (Figure 3-1). These subtitles are the same as the ones you entered earlier in cells A15 through A19. Therefore, you can use the Copy command to copy the contents of cells A15 through A19 to A27 through A31.

As shown in Figure 3-20, the cell pointer is at cell A19, one of the end points of the source range. Enter the command /**C**opy (/C). On the input line, the first end point of the source cell range (A19) is already anchored. Use the Up Arrow key to select the range A19..A15. Press the Enter key. Next, select the destination range by moving the cell pointer to A27 as shown in Figure 3-21.

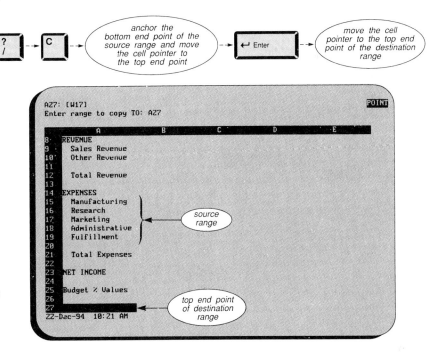

FIGURE 3-21
Step 1 of using the /C command to copy—press the Slash key (/), type the letter C for Copy, select the source range, press the Enter key, and move the cell pointer to A27.

Press the Enter key to conclude the Copy command (Figure 3-22). As shown in the figure, the source range (A15..A19) and the destination range (A27..A31) are identical.

FIGURE 3-22
Step 2 of using the /C command to copy—press the Enter key. The source range (A15..A19) is copied to the destination range (A27..A31).

Two important points to consider about copying the range A15..A19 are:

1. The source range was selected by entering A19..A15. Remember that the range A19..A15 is the same as A15..A19.
2. When both the source and destination ranges are the same size, it is not necessary to anchor the second end point of the destination range. 1-2-3 only needs to know the upper left end point, in this case A27. 1-2-3 copies the five cells in the source range beginning at cell A27. It always copies below the upper left end point of the destination range.

ENTERING NUMBERS WITH A PERCENT SIGN

◆ The five budget percent values begin in cell B27 and extend through cell B31. Use the arrow keys to move the cell pointer from its present location to B27. Rather than entering the percent value as a decimal number (.38), as we did in Project 2, enter it as a whole number followed immediately by a percent sign (%). 1-2-3 accepts the number (38%) as a percent and displays it in the cell using the global format assigned earlier to the worksheet. After you enter the five budget percent values, the worksheet appears as shown in Figure 3-23.

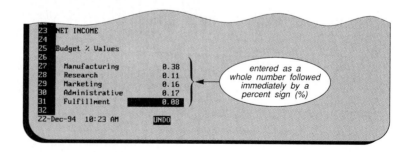

FIGURE 3-23
The five budget percent values in cells B27 through B31

To format the five budget percent values to the Percent format, enter the command /**R**ange **F**ormat **P**ercent (/RFP). When 1-2-3 displays the prompt message "Enter number of decimal places (0..15): 2" on the input line, type the digit zero and press the Enter key. The prompt message "Enter range to format: B31..B31" displays on the input line. Enter the range B31..B27. The first end point (B31) is anchored. Use the Up Arrow key to move the cell pointer to B27. The range on the input line now reads B31..B27. Press the Enter key. The five budget percent values display in percent form as shown in Figure 3-24.

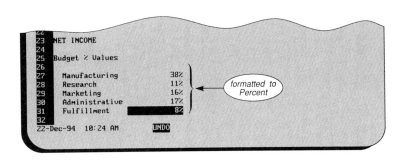

FIGURE 3-24
The five budget percent values in cells B27 through B31 formatted to the Percent type

FREEZING THE TITLES

◆ The worksheet for this project extends beyond the size of the window. When you move the cell pointer down or to the right, the column and row titles disappear off the screen. This makes it difficult to remember where to enter the data. To alleviate this problem, 1-2-3 allows you to **freeze the titles** so that they remain on the screen no matter where you move the cell pointer. The title and column headings in rows 1 through 6 are called the horizontal titles and the row titles in column A are called the vertical titles.

The Titles Command

To freeze the titles in this worksheet, press the Home key so that most of the titles are visible on the screen. Next, use the GOTO command to move the cell pointer to B7. The horizontal titles are just above cell B7 and the vertical titles are just to the left of cell B7. Enter the command /**W**orksheet **T**itles (/WT) as shown in Figure 3-25.

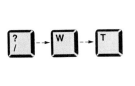

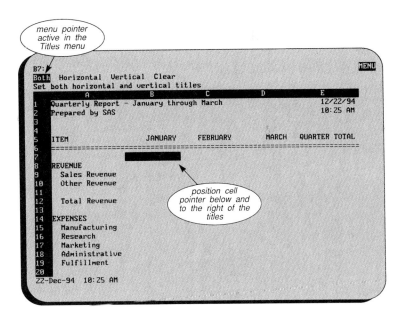

FIGURE 3-25
Step 1 of freezing both the horizontal and vertical titles—press the Slash key (/) and type the letters W for Worksheet and T for Titles.

With the menu pointer active in the Titles menu, type the letter B for Both. This keeps the titles visible regardless of where you move the cell pointer, as shown in Figure 3-26.

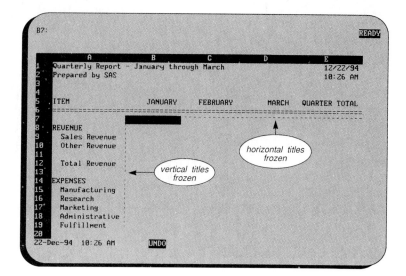

FIGURE 3-26
Step 2 of freezing both the horizontal and vertical titles—type the letter B to freeze both.

Unfreezing the Titles

Once you specify a title area, you cannot move the cell pointer into this area of the worksheet using the cursor movement keys. If you want to make a change to the titles after freezing them, you must **unfreeze** them. To unfreeze the titles, enter the command /Worksheet Titles Clear (/WTC). Once the titles are unfrozen, you can move the cell pointer anywhere on the worksheet, including the title area, to make your desired changes. To refreeze the titles, move the cell pointer to the cell (B7) just below the horizontal titles and just to the right of the vertical titles and enter the command /Worksheet Titles Both (/WTB).

Fig 3-1

MOVING THE CONTENTS OF CELLS

The command /Move (/M) moves the contents of a cell or range of cells to a different location in the worksheet. To illustrate the use of this command, let's make a mistake by entering the sales revenue (232897.95, 432989.76, and 765998.61) that belongs in cells B9 through E9 into cells B7 through E7—two rows above its location according to Figure 3-1. This type of error is common, especially when you're not careful about cell-pointer placement.

The sales revenues for January, February, and March are 232,897.95, 432,989.76, and 765,998.61. The quarter total in column E is the sum of the sales revenue for the three months. Enter the three numbers in cells B7, C7, and D7. Use the Right Arrow key after typing each number on the input line. With the cell pointer at E7, enter the function @SUM(B7..D7). 1-2-3 evaluates the function and stores the number 1,431,886.32 in E7 (232,897.95 + 432,989.76 + 765,998.61).

The values in cells C7, D7, and E7 are shown in Figure 3-27. Notice that with the cell pointer at F7, the row identifiers in column A display along with columns C, D, E, and F. However, column B does not display because the titles in column A are frozen.

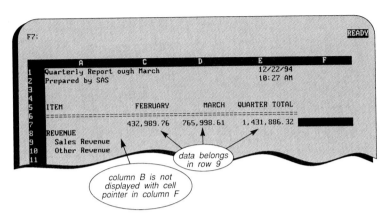

FIGURE 3-27 The sales revenue data entered into the wrong row

As we indicated earlier, the data entered in row 7 belongs in row 9. Let's correct the mistake and move the data from row 7 to row 9. With the cell pointer at F7, enter the command /Move (/M). 1-2-3 displays the message "Enter range to move FROM: F7..F7" on the input line. Press the Backspace key to *unlock* the first end point. Move the cell pointer to E7 and press the Period key. Next, move the cell pointer to B7. The range to be moved is shown in Figure 3-28. Press the Enter key to lock in the range to be moved.

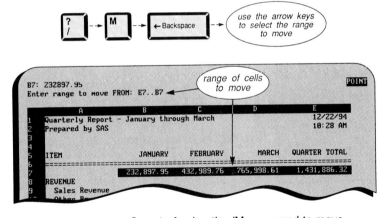

FIGURE 3-28 Step 1 of using the /M command to move data from one range to another—press the Slash key (/), type the letter M, and select the range of cells to move.

Next, 1-2-3 displays the message "Enter range to move TO: F7" on the input line. Move the cell pointer to E9. Press the Period key to anchor the first end point. Move the cell pointer to B9 as shown in Figure 3-29.

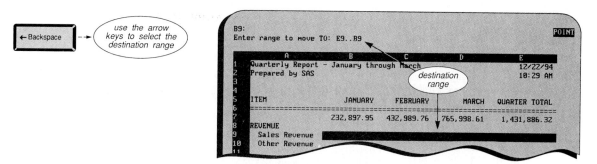

FIGURE 3-29 Step 2 of using the /M command to move data from one range to another—press the Enter key to lock in the range to move. Next, select the destination range.

To complete the command, press the Enter key and move the cell pointer to B10. Figure 3-30 illustrates the result of moving the contents of cells B7 through E7 to B9 through E9.

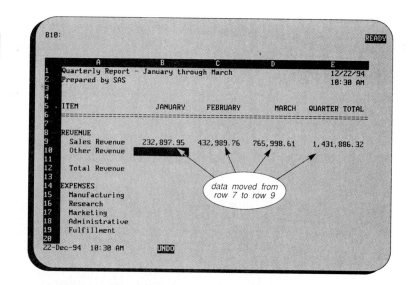

FIGURE 3-30 Step 3 of using the /M command to move data from one range to another—press the Enter key.

Some points to consider about the Move command are:

1. The Move and Copy commands are not the same. Where the Copy command copies one range to another, the Move command moves the contents of one range to another. Use the Move command to rearrange your worksheet. Use the Copy command to duplicate a range.
2. When you move a range containing a formula or function that references cell addresses, the referenced cell addresses are not changed relative to the new position, unless they refer to cells within the moved range. This was the case with the function in cell E7. Recall that we assigned the function @SUM(B7..D7) to cell E7. Following the Move command, the function assigned to cell E9 reads @SUM(B9..D9).
3. You can undo a Move command by entering the UNDO command, provided you do so prior to entering any other value or command.

DISPLAYING FORMULAS AND FUNCTIONS IN THE CELLS

◆ Enter the other revenue data in row 10 for January, February, and March (Figure 3-31). Leave the quarter total in column E alone for now. The monthly total revenue in row 12 is equal to the sum of the corresponding monthly revenues in rows 9 and 10. Therefore, assign cell B12 the function @SUM(B9..B10) as shown in Figure 3-31.

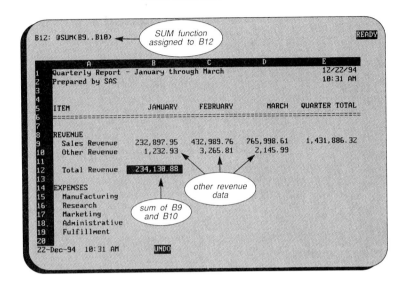

FIGURE 3-31
Other revenue and formula
for January total revenue
entered into worksheet

Use the /Copy (/C) command to copy the SUM function in cell B12 to cells C12 and D12. Remember, the Copy command adjusts the cell references in the function so that it adds the contents of the cells above the cell to which the SUM function is copied. Once the Copy command has been entered, 1-2-3 requests the source cell range and the destination cell range. In this case the source cell range is B12 and the destination cell range is C12..D12 (Figure 3-32).

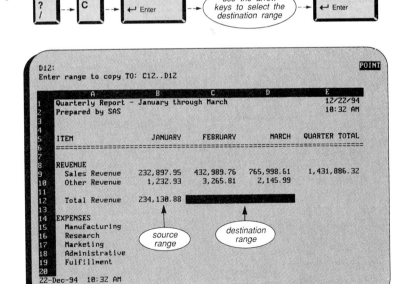

FIGURE 3-32
Using the /C command to
copy cell B12 to cells C12
and D12—press the Slash
key (/), type the letter C,
press the Enter key to select
the source range, use the
arrow keys to select the destination range, and press the
Enter key.

After you enter each range, press the Enter key. The result of the copy is shown in cells C12 and D12 in Figure 3-33. When entering or copying formulas, you might find it useful to view them in the cells, instead of their numeric result. Therefore, to illustrate what is actually copied, let's change the format from Comma (,) to Text for the range B9..E19 in the worksheet. Remember from Project 2 that the Text format instructs 1-2-3 to display the formula assigned to a cell, rather than the numeric result.

Enter the command /**R**ange **F**ormat **T**ext (/RFT). 1-2-3 responds with the prompt message "Enter range to format: B12..B12" on the input line. Enter the range B9..E19 as shown in Figure 3-33 and press the Enter key.

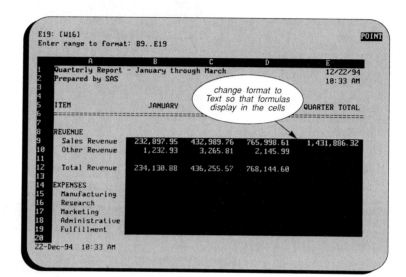

FIGURE 3-33

Step 1 of using the /RFT command to format cells B9..E19 to the Text type—press the Slash key (/), type the letters R for Range, F for Format, and T for Text, and select the range B9..E19.

The functions in the worksheet (cells E9, B12, C12, and D12) now display in their respective cells and the numeric entries display using the General type format. This is shown in Figure 3-34. Later, we will reassign the Comma (,) format to the range B9..E19.

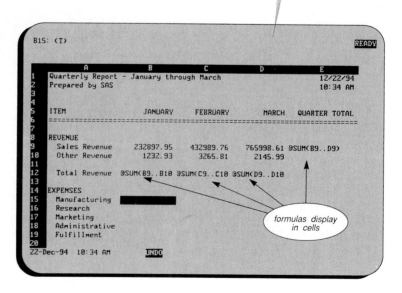

FIGURE 3-34

Step 2 of using the /RFT command to format cells B9..E19 to the Text type—press the Enter key.

ABSOLUTE VERSUS RELATIVE ADDRESSING

The next step is to determine the five monthly budgeted expenses in the rectangular group of cells B15 through D19. Each of these budgeted expenses is equal to the corresponding budgeted percent (cells B27 through B31) times the monthly total revenue (cells B12 through D12). The formulas for each of the cells in this range are similar. They differ in that the total revenue varies by the month (column) and the budgeted percent value varies by the type of expense (row).

Relative Addressing

We would like to be able to enter the formula +B27*B12 once in cell B15 (January budgeted manufacturing expense) and then copy this formula to the remaining cells in the rectangular group B15 through D19. However, we know that when a formula with relative addresses, like B27 and B12, is copied across a row or down a column, 1-2-3 automatically adjusts the cell references in the formula as it copies to reflect its new location.

Specifying cells in a formula using **relative addressing** has worked well in the previous examples of copying formulas, but it won't work here because the five budgeted percent values are all located in one column and the monthly total revenues are all located in one row. For example, if we copy +B27*B12 in cell B15 to cell C15, then cell C15 equals +C27*C12. This adjustment by the Copy command is because B27 and B12 are relative addresses. The C12 is okay, because it represents the total revenue for February, but cell C27 is blank. What we need here is for 1-2-3 to maintain cell B27 as it copies across the first row.

Absolute and Mixed Cell Addressing

1-2-3 has the capability to keep a cell, a column, or a row constant when it copies a formula or function by using a technique called **absolute addressing**. To specify an absolute address in a formula, add a dollar sign ($) to the beginning of the column name, row name, or both. For example, $B$27 is an absolute address and B27 is a relative address. Both reference the same cell. The difference shows when they are copied. A formula using $B$27 instructs 1-2-3 to use the same cell (B27) as it copies the formula to a new location. A formula using B27 instructs 1-2-3 to adjust the cell reference as it copies. Table 3-2 gives some additional examples of absolute addressing. A cell address with one dollar sign before either the column or the row is called a **mixed cell address**—one is relative, the other is absolute.

When you enter or edit a formula, you can use the function key F4 to cycle the cell address the edit cursor is on, or immediately to the right of, from relative to absolute to mixed.

TABLE 3-2 Absolute Addressing

CELL ADDRESS	MEANING
$A$22	Both column and row references remain the same when this cell address is copied.
A$22	The column reference changes when you copy this cell address to another column. The row reference does not change—it is absolute.
$A22	The row reference changes when you copy this cell address to another row. The column reference does not change—it is absolute.
A22	Both column and row references are relative. When copied to another row and column, both the row and column in the cell address are adjusted to reflect the new location.

Copying Formulas with Mixed Cell Addresses

With the cell pointer at B15, enter the formula $B27*B$12 as shown in Figure 3-35. Because B15 was in the range formatted to Text earlier, the formula displays in the cell, rather than the value. It is not necessary to enter the formula $B27*B$12 with a leading plus sign because, in this case, the $ indicates that the entry is a formula or a number. The cell reference $B27 (budgeted manufacturing % value) means that the row reference (27) changes when you copy it to a new row, but the column reference (B) remains constant through all columns in the destination range. The cell reference B$12 (January expenses) in the formula means that the column reference (B) changes when you copy it to a new column, but the row reference (12) remains constant through all rows in the destination range. Let's copy the formula $B27*B$12 in cell B15 to the rectangular group of cells B15 through D19.

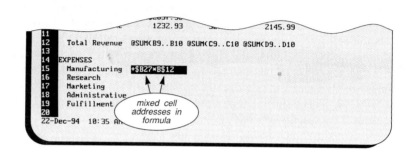

FIGURE 3-35
Formula with mixed cell addresses entered into cell B15

The cell pointer is located at B15 as shown in Figure 3-35. Enter the command /Copy (/C). When the prompt message "Enter range to copy FROM: B15..B15" displays on the input line, press the Enter key. When the message "Enter range to copy TO: B15" displays on the input line, use the arrow keys to select the range B15..D19. This is shown in Figure 3-36. Notice that cell B15 is copied on top of itself, because B15 is one of the end points of the destination range.

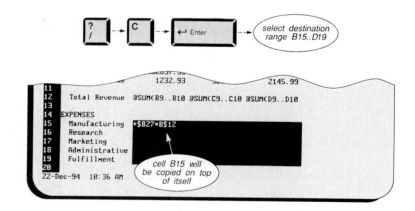

FIGURE 3-36
Step 1 of using the /C command to copy cell B15 to the range B15..D19—press the Slash key (/), type the letter C for Copy, press the Enter key, and select the destination range.

Press the Enter key. The Copy command copies the formula in cell B15 to the rectangular group of cells B15 through D19 as shown in Figure 3-37. Take a few minutes to study the formulas in Figure 3-37. You should begin to see the significance of mixed cell addressing. For example, every aspect of the five formulas in cells B15 through B19 is identical, except for the row in the first cell reference (budgeted % value). You can see in columns C and D, that the column in the second cell reference (monthly total revenue) changes based on the column in which the formula is located.

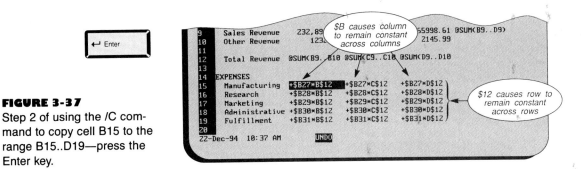

FIGURE 3-37
Step 2 of using the /C command to copy cell B15 to the range B15..D19—press the Enter key.

Switching from Text Format to the Global Comma Format

Let's change cells B9 through E19 from the Text format back to the Comma format, the one selected earlier as the global format. Recall that we switched the format of these cells from the global format (Comma) to Text so that we could view the formulas in the cells. To reset the format, move the cell pointer to the lower left end point (B19) of the range B19..E9. Enter the command /Range Format Reset (/RFR). When 1-2-3 requests the range, use the arrow keys to select the rectangular group of cells B19..E9. Press the Enter key. The format of the range B19..E9 is reset to the global format (Comma). The results of the formulas, rather than the formulas themselves, display in the cells (Figure 3-38).

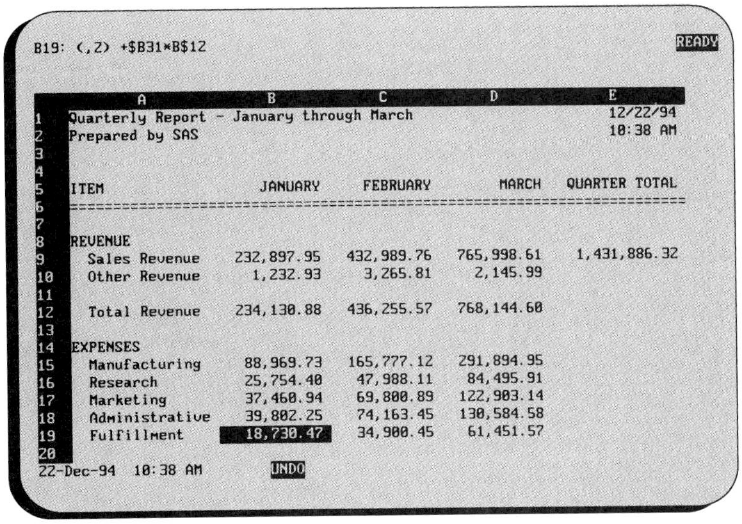

FIGURE 3-38
Range B9..E19 reformatted to the Comma (,) type

POINTING TO A RANGE OF CELLS TO SUM

◆   The total expenses for January (cell B21) are determined by adding the five monthly budgeted expenses in cells B15 through B19. The total expenses for February (C21) and March (D21) are found in the same way.

To sum the five monthly budgeted expenses for January, move the cell pointer to B21 and begin entering the SUM function. For this entry, let's apply the pointing method to enter the range to sum. Enter @sum(on the input line. Remember that function names can be entered in lowercase. After typing the open parenthesis, use the Up Arrow key to move the cell pointer to B15, the topmost end point of the range to sum. As the cell pointer moves upward, 1-2-3 changes the cell address following the open parenthesis on the input line. Move the cell pointer until it reaches B15 (Figure 3-39).

Press the Period key (.) to lock in the first end point of the range to sum. Next, use the Down Arrow key to move the cell pointer to B19 (Figure 3-40). To complete the entry, press the Close Parenthesis key and the Enter key.

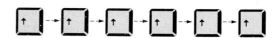

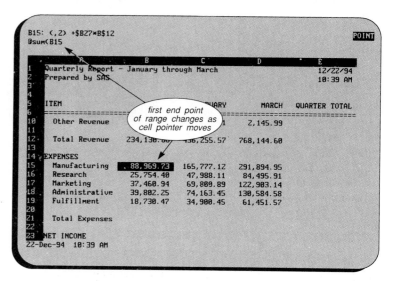

FIGURE 3-39 Step 1 of entering the SUM function using the pointing method—after the open parenthesis, use the arrow keys to select the first end point of the range.

FIGURE 3-40
Step 2 of entering the SUM function using the pointing method—press the Period key (.), use the arrow keys to select the second end point of the range, press the Close Parenthesis key, and press the Enter key.

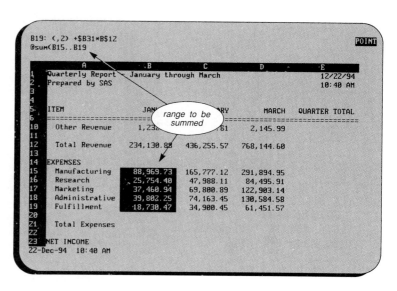

As shown in cell B21 of Figure 3-41, 1-2-3 displays the sum (210,717.79) of the five January budgeted expenses stored in cells B15 through B19.

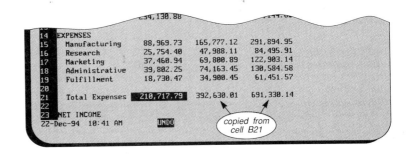

FIGURE 3-41
SUM function in cell B21
copied to cells C21 and D21

Pointing versus Entering a Range of Cells

The pointing method used to enter the range for the SUM function in cell B21 saves keying time. Anytime you need to enter a range, you may use the arrow keys to point to it. Alternatively, you may type the cell addresses. Once you begin typing a cell address, 1-2-3 is no longer in POINT mode.

Copying the Total Expenses and Net Income for Each Month

The next step in this project is to determine the total expenses in row 21 for February and March. To accomplish this task, copy the function in cell B21 to cells C21 and D21. Enter the command /Copy (/C). After entering the source range (B21), press the Enter key. Next, select the destination range (C21..D21) and press the Enter key. Figure 3-41 shows the result of copying cell B21 to cells C21 and D21.

You can now determine the net income for each month in row 23 by subtracting the total expenses for each month in row 21 from the total revenue for each month in row 12. Move the cell pointer to B23 and enter the formula +B12-B21. Copy this formula to cells C23 and D23. The result of entering the formula in cell B23 and copying it to C23 and D23 is shown in Figure 3-42.

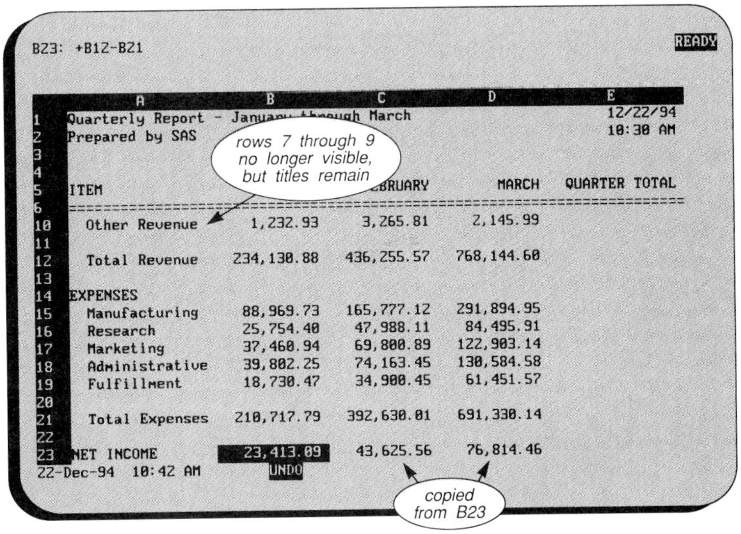

FIGURE 3-42
Formula in cell B23 copied to
cells C23 and D23

Summing Empty Cells and Labels

To complete the worksheet, determine the quarter totals in column E. Use the GOTO command to move the cell pointer to the quarter total in cell E9. Since cell E9 is not on the screen (Figure 3-42), the GOTO command causes the window to move so that cell E9 is positioned in the upper left corner, just below and to the right of the titles.

Recall that the quarter total for the sales revenue in cell E9 was determined earlier (Figure 3-30). The functions required for all the row entries (E10, E12, E15 through E19, E21, and E23) are identical to the function in cell E9. Therefore, let's copy the function in cell E9 to these cells.

Unfortunately, the cells in the destination range are not contiguous, that is, connected. For example, in the range E10 through E23, the function is not needed in E11, E13, E14, E20, and E22. We have three choices here: (1) use the Copy command several times and copy the function in E9 to E10, E12, E15 through E19, E21, and E23; (2) enter the function manually in each required cell; or (3) copy the function to the range E10 through E23. If we select the third method, we have to use the command /**R**ange **E**rase (/RE) to erase the function from E11, E13, E14, E20, and E22, the cells in which the function is not required. Let's use the third method.

With the cell pointer at E9, enter the command /**C**opy (/C). When 1-2-3 displays the prompt message "Enter range to copy FROM: E9..E9", press the Enter key. For the destination range, leave E9 anchored as the first end point and use the Down Arrow key to move the cell pointer to E23. This is shown in Figure 3-43.

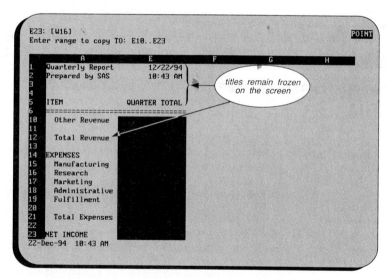

FIGURE 3-43 Step 1 of using the /C command to copy cell E9 to the range E9..E23—press the Slash key (/), type the letter C for Copy, press the Enter key, and select the destination range.

Press the Enter key and the function in cell E9 is copied to the cells in the range E9..E23 (Figure 3-44).

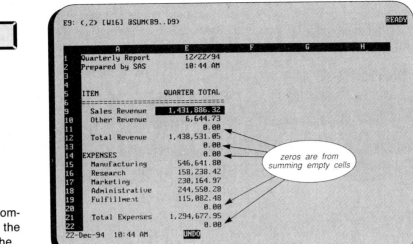

FIGURE 3-44

Step 2 of using the /C command to copy cell E9 to the range E9..E23—press the Enter key.

Notice the zeros in cells E11, E13, E14, E20, and E22. The formula in cell E11 reads @SUM(B11..D11). 1-2-3 considers empty cells and cells with labels to be equal to zero when they are referenced in a formula or function. Since cells B11, C11, and D11 are empty, the SUM function assigned to E11 produces the zero display. You need to erase the functions in the cells displaying zero. Recall from Project 1 that the command /Range Erase (/RE) erases the contents of a cell. Use this command to erase the zeros in cells E11, E13, E14, E20, and E22.

After the zeros in column E are erased, use the command /Worksheet Titles Clear (/WTC) to unfreeze the titles. Finally, press the Home key to move the cell pointer to A1. The worksheet is complete as shown in Figure 3-45.

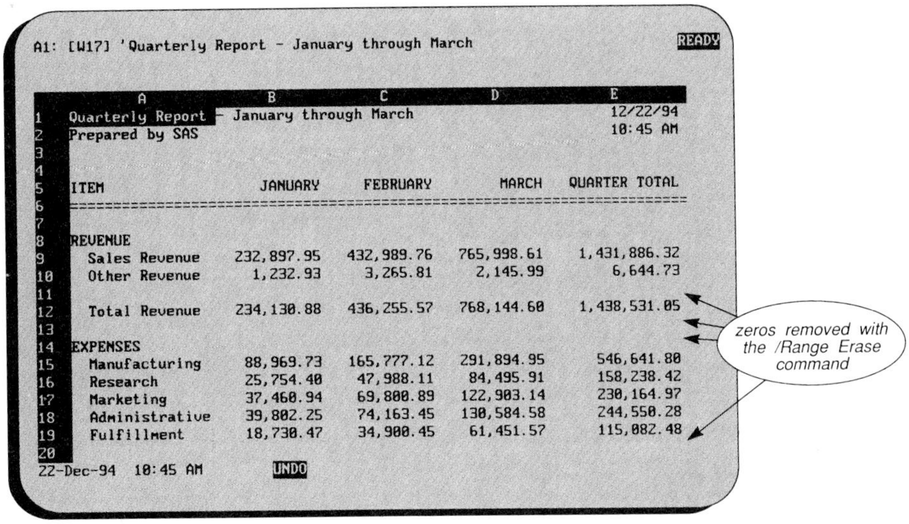

FIGURE 3-45

The completed worksheet

SAVING AND PRINTING THE WORKSHEET

◆ Save the worksheet on disk for later use. Use the command /**F**ile **S**ave (/FS) and the file name PROJS-3. As we discussed in Project 2, when you create a large worksheet such as this one, it is prudent to save the worksheet periodically—every 50 to 75 keystrokes. Then, if there should be an inadvertent loss of power to the computer or other unforeseen mishap, you will not lose the whole worksheet.

Printing the Worksheet

After you save the worksheet as PROJS-3, obtain a hard copy by printing the worksheet on the printer. Recall from Project 2, that to print the worksheet you use the command /**P**rint **P**rinter (/PP). This command activates the menu pointer in the Print menu and displays the printsheet settings (Figure 3-46). Type the letter R for Range. The cell pointer is at one end point of the range to print, A1. Use the arrow keys to move the cell pointer to E31. Press the Enter key to anchor the second end point.

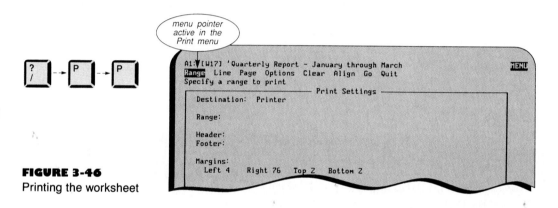

FIGURE 3-46
Printing the worksheet

Next, check the printer to be sure it is ready. Type the letter A for Align and the letter G for Go. The worksheet prints on the printer as shown in Figure 3-47. Finally, type the letter P for Page to move the paper through the printer so that you can tear the paper at the perforated edge below the printed version of the worksheet.

```
Quarterly Report - January through March                    12/22/94
Prepared by SAS                                             10:47 AM


ITEM              JANUARY       FEBRUARY        MARCH    QUARTER TOTAL
================================================================================

REVENUE
   Sales Revenue  232,897.95    432,989.76    765,998.61   1,431,886.32
   Other Revenue    1,232.93      3,265.81      2,145.99       6,644.73

   Total Revenue  234,130.88    436,255.57    768,144.60   1,438,531.05

EXPENSES
   Manufacturing   88,969.73    165,777.12    291,894.95     546,641.80
   Research         25,754.40     47,988.11     84,495.91     158,238.42
   Marketing        37,460.94     69,800.89    122,903.14     230,164.97
   Administrative   39,802.25     74,163.45    130,584.58     244,550.28
   Fulfillment      18,730.47     34,900.45     61,451.57     115,082.48

   Total Expenses 210,717.79    392,630.01    691,330.14   1,294,677.95

NET INCOME         23,413.09     43,625.56     76,814.46     143,853.10

Budget % Values

   Manufacturing      38%
   Research           11%
   Marketing          16%
   Administrative     17%
   Fulfillment         8%
```

FIGURE 3-47   The printed version of the worksheet in Project 3

Printing the Worksheet in Condensed Mode

If you have a graphics printer, you can print more than 80 characters per line by printing the worksheet in condensed mode. This mode can be helpful if the worksheet is wider than the screen. The **condensed mode** allows nearly twice as many characters to fit across the page. To print a worksheet in the condensed mode, do the following:

1. Enter the command /**P**rint **P**rinter **O**ptions **S**etup (/PPOS). Enter the code \015 and press the Enter key.
2. With the Printer Options menu at the top of the screen, enter the command **M**argins **R**ight. Type in a right margin of 132. Press the Enter key and type the letter Q to quit the Printer Options menu.
3. Select the range to print and follow the usual steps for printing the worksheet. The condensed printed version of the worksheet prints on the printer as shown in Figure 3-48.

```
Quarterly Report - January through March        12/22/94
Prepared by SAS                                 10:48 AM


ITEM             JANUARY    FEBRUARY     MARCH   QUARTER TOTAL
=============================================================

REVENUE
  Sales Revenue  232,897.95  432,989.76  765,998.61  1,431,886.32
  Other Revenue    1,232.93    3,265.81    2,145.99      6,644.73

  Total Revenue  234,130.88  436,255.57  768,144.60  1,438,531.05

EXPENSES
  Manufacturing   88,969.73  165,777.12  291,894.95    546,641.80
  Research        25,754.40   47,988.11   84,495.91    158,238.42
  Marketing       37,460.94   69,800.89  122,903.14    230,164.97
  Administrative  39,802.25   74,163.45  130,584.58    244,550.28
  Fulfillment     18,730.47   34,900.45   61,451.57    115,082.48

  Total Expenses 210,717.79  392,630.01  691,330.14  1,294,677.95

NET INCOME        23,413.09   43,625.56   76,814.46    143,853.10

Budget % Values

  Manufacturing       38%
  Research            11%
  Marketing           16%
  Administrative      17%
  Fulfillment          8%
```

FIGURE 3-48 A printout of the worksheet in the condensed mode

If the printer does not print in condensed mode, check the printer manual to be sure the current dip switch settings on the printer allow for it. You may have to change these settings. If you continue to experience problems, check the printer manual to be sure that code \015 instructs the printer to print in condensed mode. This code works for most printers.

To change 1-2-3 back to the normal print mode, do the following:

1. Enter the command /**P**rint **P**rinter **O**ptions **S**etup (/PPOS). Enter the code \018 and press the Enter key.
2. With the Printer Options menu at the top of the screen, enter the command Margins Right. Type in a right margin of 76. Press the Enter key and type the letter Q to quit the Printer Options menu.
3. With the menu pointer in the Print menu, follow the steps we outlined earlier for printing the worksheet in the normal mode.

Using Borders to Print Nonadjacent Columns

Up to this point, we have printed only columns that are side by side in the worksheet. Consider Figure 3-49. This partial printout is called a summary report, since only the row titles in column A and the corresponding totals in column E are printed.

We can print such a report through the use of the Borders command in the Printer Options menu. The Borders command prints specified columns to the left of the selected range or it prints specified rows above the selected range.

To print the summary report in Figure 3-49, do the following:

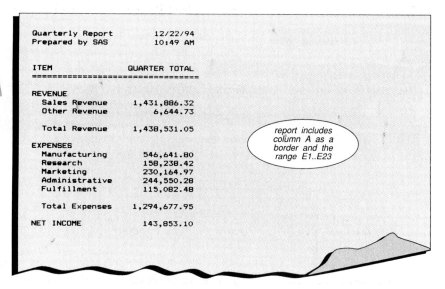

report includes column A as a border and the range E1..E23

FIGURE 3-49 A summary report made up of nonadjacent columns

1. Move the cell pointer to column A and enter the command /**P**rint **P**rinter Options **B**orders (/PPOB). Type C for Column and press the Enter key to select column A as the border. Type Q to quit the Printer Options menu.
2. With the Print menu at the top of the screen, select E1..E23 as the range to print.
3. Press A for Align and G for Go.

In Figure 3-49, column A prints as the border and column E prints because it was selected as the range to print. To clear column A as the border, select the Clear command in the Print menu. When the Clear menu displays at the top of the screen, type B for Borders.

Other Printer Options

There are other printer options that can enhance your worksheet. Table 3-3 summarizes the commands found in the **Printer Options** menu.

TABLE 3-3 A Summary of Commands in the Printer Options Menu

COMMAND	DEFAULT SETTING	FUNCTION
Header	none	Prints a line of text at the top of every page of the worksheet.
Footer	none	Prints a line of text at the bottom of every page of the worksheet.
Margins	Left 4 Right 76 Top 2 Bottom 2	Sets the margins.
Borders	none	Prints specified columns or rows on every page.
Setup	none	Sends commands to the printer, for example, to print the worksheet in condensed mode.
Pg-Length	66	Sets printed lines per page.
Other		Selects the As-Displayed or Cell-Formulas version to print.
Quit		Returns to the Print menu.

Many of the options you set with the /Print Printer Options (/PPO) command are saved with the worksheet and stay in effect when you retrieve it. Remember, if you change any of the printer options and you want the changes to stay with the worksheet, be sure to save the worksheet after you finish printing it. That way you won't have to change the options the next time you retrieve the worksheet.

If you use the command /Worksheet Erase (/WE) to clear the worksheet on the screen or restart 1-2-3, the printer options revert back to the default settings shown in Table 3.3.

WHAT-IF QUESTIONS

A powerful feature of 1-2-3 is the capability to answer **what-if questions**. Quick responses to these questions are invaluable when making business decisions. Using 1-2-3 to answer what-if questions is called performing **what-if analyses** or **sensitivity analyses**.

A what-if question for the worksheet in Project 3 might be, *What if the manufacturing budgeted percentage is decreased from 38% to 35%—how would this affect the total expenses and net income?* To answer questions like this, you need only change a single value in the worksheet. The recalculation feature of 1-2-3 answers the question immediately by displaying new values in any cells with formulas or functions that reference the changed cell.

Let's change the manufacturing budgeted percentage from 38% to 35% (Figure 3-50). Before the change, as shown in the top screen of Figure 3-50, the manufacturing budgeted percentage is 38%. After the change is made, the manufacturing budgeted percentage is 35%. When we make the change, all the formulas are immediately recalculated. This process generally requires less than one second, depending on how many calculations must be performed. As soon as the 35% replaces the 38% in cell B27, the new expenses and new net income values can be examined (bottom screen of Figure 3-50).

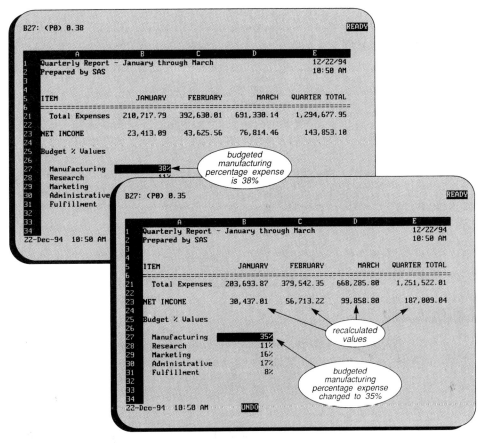

FIGURE 3-50 Using 1-2-3 to answer what-if questions by changing one value in the worksheet

By changing the value in B27 from 38% to 35%, the total January expenses decrease from 210,717.79 to 203,693.87, and the January net income increases from 23,413.09 to 30,437.01. The February and March figures change the same way. The quarter total expenses decrease from 1,294,677.95 to 1,251,522.01, and the quarter net income increases from 143,853.11 to 187,009.04. Thus, if the budgeted manufacturing expenses are reduced, it is clear that net income increases.

After the change, as shown in the bottom screen of Figure 3-51, you can change more than one percentage. Let's change all the percentages. The new calculations display immediately.

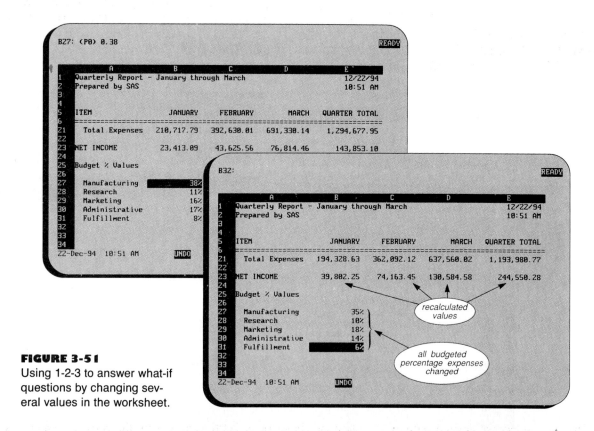

FIGURE 3-51
Using 1-2-3 to answer what-if questions by changing several values in the worksheet.

In Figure 3-51, we ask the question, *What if we change all the budgeted percent values to the following: Manufacturing (35%); Research (10%); Marketing (18%); Administrative (14%); Fulfillment (6%)—how would these changes affect the total expenses and the net income?* By merely changing the five values on the worksheet, all formulas are automatically recalculated to provide the answer to this question.

Manual versus Automatic Recalculation

Each time you enter a value in the worksheet, 1-2-3 automatically recalculates all formulas and functions in those cells that changed since the worksheet was last recalculated, and in the cells that depend on those cells. This feature is called **automatic recalculation**.

An alternative to automatic recalculation is manual recalculation. With **manual recalculation**, 1-2-3 only recalculates after you instruct it to. To change recalculation from automatic to manual, enter the command /Worksheet Global Recalculate (/WGR). With the menu pointer active in the Recalculate menu, type the letter M for Manual. Then recalculation of formulas takes place *only* after you press function key F9. To change back to automatic recalculation, use the same command but type the letter A for Automatic rather than M for Manual.

When you save a worksheet, the current recalculation mode is saved along with it. For an explanation of the other types of recalculation available with 1-2-3, enter the command /WGR and press function key F1. When you are finished with the online help facility, press the Esc key to return to your worksheet.

CHANGING THE WORKSHEET DEFAULT SETTINGS

1-2-3 comes with default settings. We have already discussed some of the more obvious ones—column width is nine characters, format is General, and recalculation of formulas is Automatic. Some of the default settings, like the format, can be changed for a range or for the entire worksheet. When you make a change to the entire worksheet using the command **/Worksheet Global (/WG)**, the change is saved with the worksheet when you issue the **/File Save (/FS)** command.

There is another group of default settings that affect all worksheets created or retrieved during the current session, until you quit 1-2-3. To view or change these settings, type the command **/Worksheet Global Default (/WGD)**. This command displays the Global Default menu and default settings sheet as shown in Figure 3-52. Then use the arrow keys or first letters of the commands in the Global Default menu to select features to change. Remember, when you are in MENU mode, you can display the worksheets, rather than the settings sheet, by pressing F6.

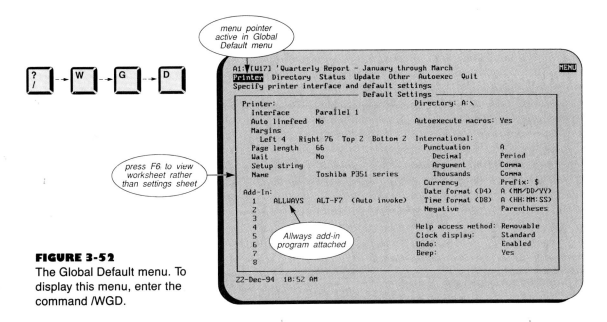

FIGURE 3-52
The Global Default menu. To display this menu, enter the command /WGD.

Once you select the desired settings, you have the choice of saving the changes for the current session or saving them permanently. To save the changes for the current session, type the letter Q to quit the Global Default menu. To save the changes permanently, type the letters U for Update and then Q for Quit. If you typed the letter U for Update, the new settings become the defaults for the current and future 1-2-3 sessions. Table 3-4 describes the features you can change by typing the command /WGD.

TABLE 3-4 A Summary of Commands in the Global Defaults Menu

COMMAND	FUNCTION
Printer	Specifies printer interface and default settings.
Directory	Changes the default directory.
Status	Displays default settings.
Update	Permanently changes default settings in configuration file.
Other	Changes international, help, add-in programs, and clock settings.
Autoexec	Instructs 1-2-3 whether to run autoexecute macros named \0 (zero).
QUIT	Quits Global Default menu.

INTERACTING WITH DOS

◆ Up to this point, we have used the File command to save and retrieve worksheets from disk. This command can also be used to carry out several other file management functions normally done at the DOS level. Table 3-5 summarizes the major file management commands available in 1-2-3.

TABLE 3-5 File Management Commands

COMMAND	FUNCTION	DUPLICATE DOS COMMAND
/FE	Erases a file from disk.	ERASE or DEL
/FL	Displays the names of the files of a particular type.	DIR
/FD	Changes the current directory to a new one.	CHDIR or CD

Other DOS commands and programs can be executed by placing 1-2-3 and your worksheet in a wait state. A **wait state** means that 1-2-3 has given up control to another program, like DOS, but still resides in main memory. To leave 1-2-3 temporarily, enter the command /System (/S). (If you do not have a fixed disk, place the DOS disk in the A drive before entering the /S command.)

You can use the System command to leave 1-2-3 to format a disk. Once the disk is formatted, you can return to 1-2-3 and the worksheet by typing the command Exit in response to the DOS prompt. One word of advice—save your worksheet before using the System command, especially if you plan to execute an external DOS command.

PRINTING THE WORKSHEET USING ALLWAYS

◆ Allways is a spreadsheet publishing add-in program that comes with Release 2.2 of 1-2-3. **Add-in** means the program is started while 1-2-3 is running. Allways allows you to produce presentation-quality printouts as shown in Figure 3-53.

To use Allways, you must be running 1-2-3 on a hard-disk or network system with at least 512K main memory. In addition, Allways must be attached, that is, available to 1-2-3 as an add-in program. To check if it is attached and ready to use, enter the command /Worksheet Global Default (/WGD). If Allways is attached, "ALLWAYS" displays in the add-in program list as shown in the lower left corner of the default settings sheet in Figure 3-52. The Alt-F7 that you see to the right of "ALLWAYS" in Figure 3-52 means that you can start this program while 1-2-3 is on the screen by pressing Alt-F7.

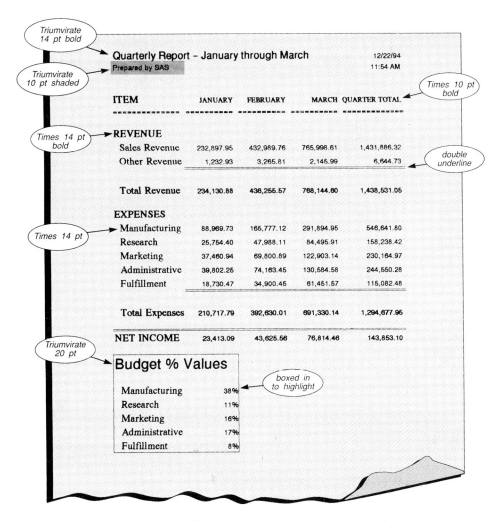

FIGURE 3-53 The worksheet in Project 3 printed using the spreadsheet publishing add-in program Allways

As shown in Figure 3-53, Allways allows you to improve the appearance of a report significantly. With Allways you can:

- Change the font (typeface and size)
- Boldface and underline text and numbers
- Adjust the height of rows and width of columns
- Shade cells
- Draw horizontal and vertical lines
- Outline a cell or range of cells
- Display the worksheet at 60% to 140% of its normal size
- Include a 1-2-3 graph in the same report as the worksheet (Project 5)
- Print in color if you have a color printer attached to your system

Another nice feature of Allways is that if you have a graphics monitor, you get a *What you see is what you get* (**Wysiwyg**) display on the screen that is nearly identical to what will print.

Starting and Quitting Allways

With 1-2-3 running, there are two ways to invoke Allways: (1) enter the command /**A**dd-In **I**nvoke (/AI) and select Allways; or (2) press Alt-F7. The latter method is available only if the F7 key was assigned the Allways program when it was initially attached to 1-2-3. Once control passes from 1-2-3 to Allways, the screen in Figure 3-54 appears. Notice that the characters in the worksheet display in graphics form, rather than text form, as they do in 1-2-3.

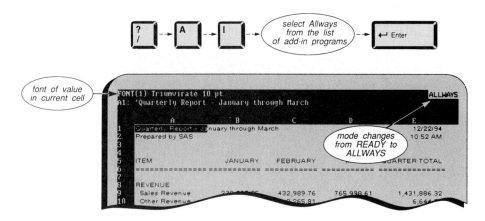

FIGURE 3-54   Project 3 displayed under Allways. To transfer control to Allways, enter the 1-2-3 command /**A**dd-In **I**nvoke (/AI). Select Allways from the list of add-in programs, and press the Enter key.

You would normally invoke Allways after you have completed the entries in the worksheet; but you can switch back and forth between Allways and 1-2-3 at any time.

There are three ways to quit Allways and return control to 1-2-3: (1) press the Esc key until 1-2-3 and the original worksheet reappear on the screen as shown in Figure 3-45; (2) enter the Allways command /**Q**uit (/Q); or (3) hold down the Alt key and press the function key assigned to Allways.

With the worksheet for Project 3 (Figure 3-45) on the screen, practice switching back and forth between 1-2-3 and Allways. As you move from 1-2-3 to Allways and back again to 1-2-3, the display on the screen switches between the one shown in Figure 3-45 (text display) and the one shown in Figure 3-54 (graphics display). Once you get a feel for how easy it is to transfer control between the two programs, switch to Allways to continue with this project.

The Allways Online Help Facility

To view Allways help screens, press the F1 key just as you do in 1-2-3. Allways displays a help screen that describes the activity you are currently performing in the program. For example, if you want information on the command /**L**ayout **O**ptions, enter /LO and press the F1 key.

The Allways Control Panel

The control panel in Allways is similar to the one in 1-2-3. The first line displays the format of the current cell: the font, color of data, boldface, underline, lines, or shading. The mode of operation also displays on the first line. The ALLWAYS mode means that you are in Allways (Figure 3-54). This mode is the same as READY mode in 1-2-3.

The second line of the control panel shows the address and contents of the current cell. As with 1-2-3, when you press the Slash key (/), the Main menu appears on the second line. If you press the Slash key in the middle of any command sequence, the Main menu will reappear. The third line in the control panel displays information about the menu item highlighted when Allways is in MENU mode.

The line at the bottom of the Allways screen displays the date, time, and status indicators, as does the line at the bottom of the 1-2-3 screen.

Type Styles and Cell Formats

When you initially enter Allways, all values in the cells are assigned the same font — Triumvirate 10 point (Figure 3-54). The **font** is a typeface (Triumvirate) of a particular size (10 point). A **point** is equal to 1/72 of an inch. Thus, 10 point is equal to about 1/7 of an inch. Figures 3-55 and 3-56 illustrate a variety of typefaces and point sizes.

Allways makes available two typefaces and four different point sizes for a total of eight different fonts. These eight *active* fonts can be changed as described in the 1-2-3 reference manual. The most important font is Font 1 — Triumvirate 10 point — because it is the one that is assigned to all the values in the worksheet when you first enter Allways.

This is Triumvirate
This is Times
This is Courier

FIGURE 3-55 Different typefaces

This is Times 10 point
This is Times 12 point
This is Times 14 point
This is Times 17 point
This is Times 20 point
This is Times 24 point

FIGURE 3-56 The Times typeface shown in different point sizes

Additional publishing terms with which you should be familiar are shading, bold, double underline, outlining a range of cells, and grid. **Shading** is the darkening of a range of cells and is useful for creating contrast (line 2 of Figure 3-53).

If a range of cells is **bold** or **boldface**, then the characters are darkened to make them stand out (line 1 of Figure 3-53). A **double underline** results in a double bar at the base of a range of cells. This is shown in Figure 3-53 below the row entitled Other Revenue.

You can request Allways to outline a range of cells. When we say a range **outlined**, we mean that a box has been drawn around it. The box highlights the range of cells as shown at the bottom of Figure 3-53.

Grid lines are dotted lines that surround each cell. The dotted lines run along the rows and columns of the worksheet. You can instruct Allways to display and print your worksheet with a grid by using the command **/L**ayout **O**ptions **G**rid (/LOG). You can also toggle the grid on and off by pressing Alt-G. With Project 3 on the screen, press Alt-G to create a grid on the worksheet. After the grid appears, press Alt-G again. The grid disappears. Since a grid is not called for in this project, make sure the grid is off before continuing.

Saving and Synchronizing Format Changes

To preserve the format changes made with Allways, return control to 1-2-3 and save the worksheet to disk. A separate Allways file with the same file name as the worksheet, but with an extension of .ALL, is saved along with the worksheet. The next time you load the worksheet and invoke Allways, the format changes will be the same as they were when you saved it earlier.

Allways automatically synchronizes the formats assigned to cells that are changed with 1-2-3. That is, after formatting with Allways, you can return to 1-2-3 and make any changes you want to the worksheet, such as moving cells, inserting columns or rows, or deleting columns or rows. Allways will automatically adjust the cell formats to agree with the most recent worksheet modifications.

Allways Main Menu

When you press the Slash key (/) in ALLWAYS mode, the Main menu displays. Table 3-6 summarizes the functions of these commands.

TABLE 3-6 A Summary of Commands in the Allways Main Menu

COMMAND	FUNCTION
Worksheet	Sets column widths, row heights, and page breaks.
Format	Changes font, boldface, underline, color, lines, or shading of a range of cells.
Graph	Inserts or deletes a graph from the current worksheet.
Layout	Changes page size, margins, headers, footers, prints borders, and grid lines.
Print	Prints worksheet on printer or file and configures printer.
Display	Enlarges or reduces worksheet display, displays worksheet in text or graphics, turns graphs on or off, and sets colors.
Special	Copy, move, or import formats. Justifies labels in a range.
Quit	Returns control to 1-2-3.

For the remainder of this project we will use Allways to format and print the worksheet so that it looks like Figure 3-53. Just as in 1-2-3, Allways allows you to make the format changes to the worksheet in any order you want. We will make the format changes in the following order:

1. Change A1 to Triumvirate 14-point font.
2. Change A5 and A8..31 to Times 14-point font.
3. Change A25 to Triumvirate 20-point font.
4. Shade A2.
5. Bold cells A1, A5..E5, A8, A12..E12, A14, A21..E21, and A23..E23.
6. Double underline B10..E10, B19..E19, and A22..E22.
7. Outline in the range A25..B31.
8. Change the width of column A from 17 to 18 characters.
9. Print the worksheet.
10. Preserve the format changes by returning to 1-2-3 and saving the worksheet.

Changing The Font

With the Allways program in control of the computer and the cell pointer at A1, change the font of the worksheet title. Enter the command /Format Font (/FF). The Slash key (/) instructs Allways to display the Main menu shown in the top screen of Figure 3-57. When you press the first F for Format, Allways displays the Format menu as shown in the middle screen of Figure 3-57. Typing the second letter F for Font, instructs Allways to display the Font menu. With the Font menu on the screen, highlight Triumvirate 14 point by pressing the Down Arrow key twice. This procedure is shown in the bottom screen of Figure 3-57.

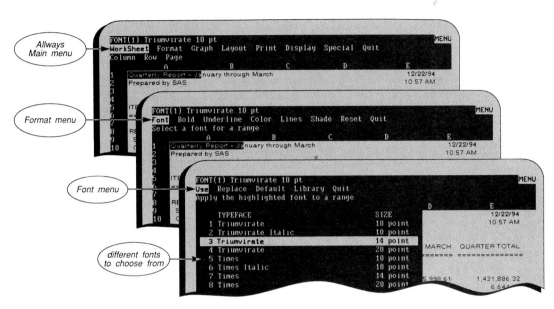

FIGURE 3-57 Step 1 of changing the font—press the Slash key (/), type the letter F for Format, type the letter F for Font, and use the Down Arrow key to select Triumvirate 14 point.

To assign the highlighted Triumvirate 14-point font to the worksheet title in A1, press the Enter key. Allways responds by prompting you to enter the range of cells to which the new font will be assigned. This procedure is shown in the top screen of Figure 3-58. Since we want to assign the font only to A1, press the Enter key. The contents of cell A1 display using the Triumvirate 14-point font as shown in the bottom screen of Figure 3-58.

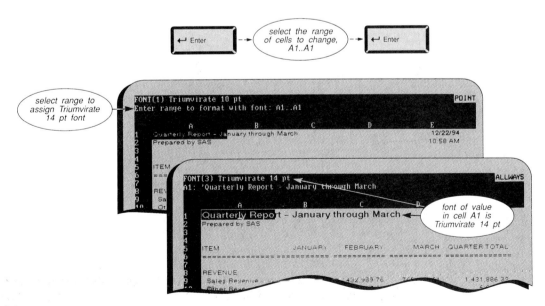

FIGURE 3-58 Step 2 of changing the font—press the Enter key to select Triumvirate 14 point and then press the Enter key again to select the range A1..A1.

Our next step is to change the font in cell A5 to Times 14 point. Move the cell pointer to A5 and enter the command /Format Font (/FF). Use the arrow keys to select Times 14 point from the Font menu (bottom screen of Figure 3-57) and press the Enter key. When Allways displays the prompt message "Enter range to format with font: A5..A5", press the Enter key. The characters in cell A5 display in Times 14-point font as shown in Figure 3-59.

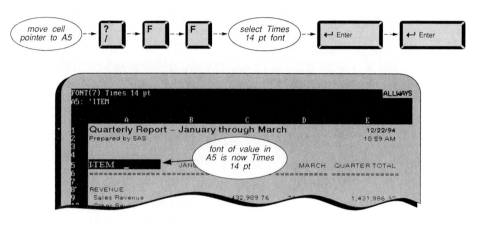

FIGURE 3-59 Triumvirate 10 point in cell A5 changed to Times 14 point. Use the command /Format Font (/FF).

Move the cell pointer to cell A8 to change the font in the range A8..A31 to Times 14 point. Enter the command /Format Font (/FF). The Font menu in the bottom screen of Figure 3-57 displays. Select Times 14 point and press the Enter key. When the prompt message "Enter range to format with font: A8..A8" displays on the second line, use the Down Arrow key to expand the range to A8..A31. Press the Enter key. Allways assigns Times 14-point font to the range A8..A31 as shown in Figure 3-60.

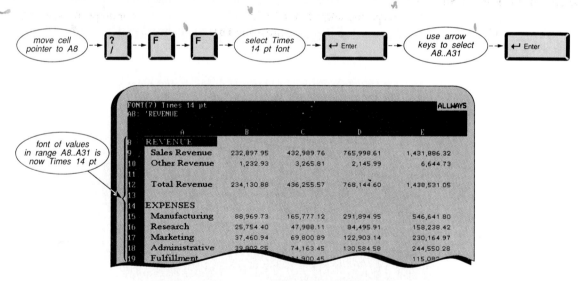

FIGURE 3-60 Triumvirate 10 point in range A8..A31 changed to Times 14 point

In Figure 3-53, the title Budget % Values shown in cell A25 is printed using Triumvirate 20-point font. Therefore, use the GOTO command to move the cell pointer from A8 to A25. Here again, enter the command /Format Font (/FF). When the Font menu shown in the bottom screen of Figure 3-57 displays, select Triumvirate 20-point font. Press the Enter key. Respond to the prompt message asking for the range by pressing the Enter key, as we want to assign the new font only to cell A25. The screen shown in Figure 3-61 displays.

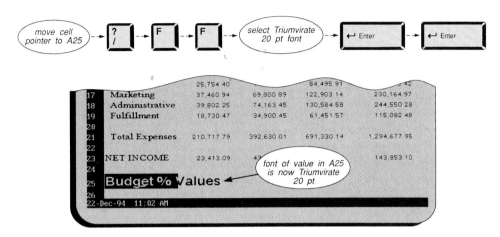

FIGURE 3-61 Times 14 point in cell A25 changed to Triumvirate 20 point

Shading Cells

In the top left corner of the formatted report in Figure 3-53, the label "Prepared by SAS" is shaded. This label is located in cell A2. To move the cell pointer from A25 to A2, press Home and then press the Down Arrow key. Next, enter the command /Format Shade (/FS). As shown in the top screen of Figure 3-62, the Shade menu has four options: Light, Dark, Solid, and Clear. Type the letter L for Light. Allways displays the prompt message "Enter range to shade: A2..A2". Since we want to shade only A2, press the Enter key. Allways shades A2 as shown in the bottom screen of Figure 3-62.

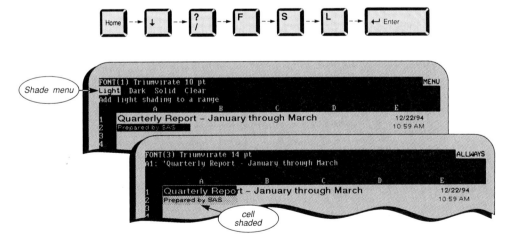

FIGURE 3-62 Shading a cell. Top screen shows Shade menu. Bottom screen shows cell A2 lightly shaded.

An alternative to using the command /Format Shade (/FS) to shade an individual cell is to position the cell pointer on the cell and press Alt-S. Each time you press this combination of keys, the shade changes from clear to light to dark to solid and back to clear. To use the Alt and S keys to shade a range of cells, first press the Period key (.) to anchor the cell pointer and use the arrow keys to highlight the range. With the range highlighted, enter Alt-S. To complete the command, press one of the arrow keys to move the highlight off the selected range.

Boldfacing Cells

The worksheet in Figure 3-53 calls for boldfacing a number of cells. Let's start by boldfacing the worksheet title in A1. Use the Up Arrow key to move the cell pointer to A1. Enter the command /Format **B**old **S**et (/FBS). Allways displays the prompt message "Enter range to bold: A1..A1". Press the Enter key. The worksheet title in cell A1 changes to bold as shown in Figure 3-63.

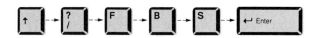

FIGURE 3-63
Boldfacing the title of the worksheet in A1 by using the command /Format **B**old **S**et (/FBS)

You can also bold an individual cell by positioning the cell pointer on the cell and pressing Alt-B. If you press this combination of keys again, Allways clears the boldface from the cell. Hence, Alt-B turns bold on or off in the current cell. Alt-B can also be used to bold a range of cells. Before you press the combination of keys, press the Period key to select the range. Once the range is highlighted, press Alt-B. To complete the command, press one of the arrow keys to move the highlight off the selected range.

Use Alt-B and the following steps to complete the boldfacing in this project.

1. Move the cell pointer to A5. Press the Period key. Use the Right Arrow key to highlight the range A5..E5. Press Alt-B.
2. Move the cell pointer to A8. Press Alt-B.
3. Move the cell pointer to A12. Press the Period key. Use the Right Arrow key to highlight the range A12..E12. Press Alt-B. Press the Down Arrow key one time.
4. Move the cell pointer to A14. Press Alt-B.
5. Move the cell pointer to A21. Press the Period key. Use the Right Arrow key to highlight the range A21..E21. Press Alt-B. Press the Down Arrow key one time.
6. Move the cell pointer to A23. Press the Period key. Use the Right Arrow key to highlight the range A23..E23. Press Alt-B. Press the Down Arrow key one time.

After completing step 6, the range A9..E23 displays as shown in Figure 3-64.

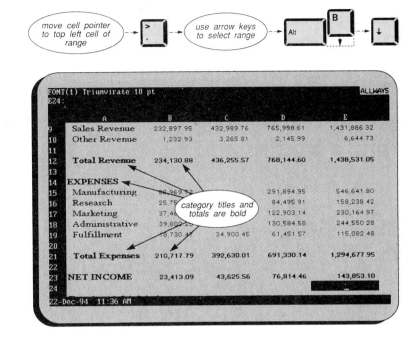

FIGURE 3-64
Boldfacing a range of cells.
Use the Period key (.) to
select the range, and then
press Alt-B.

Underlining Cells

As shown in Figure 3-53, the rows designated Other Revenue (cells B10..E10) and Fulfillment (cells B19..E19), and the empty cells A22..E22, are double underlined. Let's double underline the range B10..E10 first.

Use the GOTO command to move the cell pointer to B10. Enter the command /Format Underline (/FU). As shown in the top screen of Figure 3-65, the Underline menu has three options: Single, Double, and Clear. Type the letter D for Double. Allways displays the prompt message "Enter range to double underline: B10..B10". Use the Right Arrow key to highlight the range B10..E10. Press the Enter key. The range B10..E10 is double underlined as shown in the bottom screen of Figure 3-65.

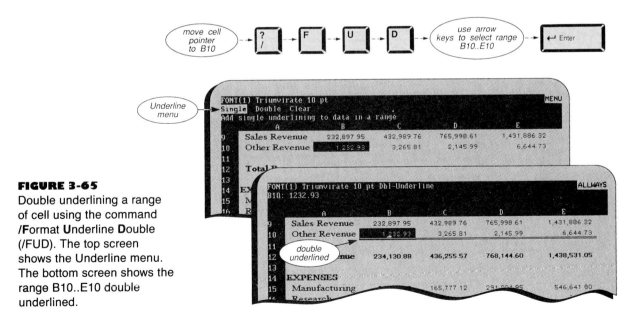

FIGURE 3-65
Double underlining a range
of cell using the command
/Format **U**nderline **D**ouble
(/FUD). The top screen
shows the Underline menu.
The bottom screen shows the
range B10..E10 double
underlined.

You can also use the Alt-U to underline an individual cell or range of cells. Each time you press Alt-U, the underlining changes from single to double to clear (no underline). To use Alt-U to underline a range of cells, first press the Period key to anchor the cell pointer; then use the arrow keys to highlight the range you want to underline. With the range highlighted, press Alt U. To complete the command, press any one of the arrow keys to move the highlight off the selected range.

Use Alt-U to complete the required double underlining as described in Figure 3-53. Issue the GOTO command to move the cell pointer to B19. Press the Period key to activate range selection. Use the Right Arrow key to highlight the range B19..E19. Press Alt-U twice. Press the Down Arrow key to move the highlight off the range B19..E19.

Next, issue the GOTO command to move the cell pointer to A22. Press the Period key. Use the Right Arrow key to highlight the range A22..E22. Press Alt-U twice. Press the Down Arrow key. The worksheet displays as shown in Figure 3-66.

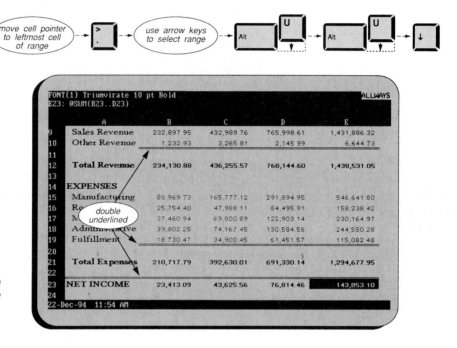

FIGURE 3-66
Double underlining a range of cells. Use the Period key (.) to select the range and then press Alt-U twice.

Outlining a Range of Cells

To outline the title Budget % Values at the bottom of the worksheet (Figure 3-53), use the GOTO command to move the cell pointer to A25. Enter the command /Format Lines Outline (/FLO). When Allways displays the prompt message "Enter range to outline: A25..A25", use the arrow keys to select the range A25..B31 as shown in the top screen of Figure 3-67. Press the Enter key. A box outlines the range A25..B31 as shown in the bottom screen of Figure 3-67. You can also outline a range of cells by first selecting the range using the Period key and then pressing Alt-L.

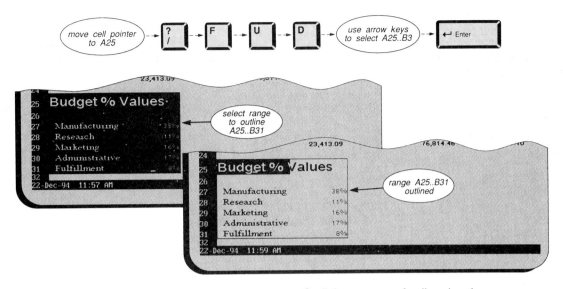

FIGURE 3-67 Outlining a range of cells using the command **/F**ormat **L**ines **O**utline (/FLO). The top screen shows the range selected. The bottom screen shows the range A25..B31 outlined.

In addition to outlining a range of cells, the **/F**ormat **L**ines (/FL) command can be used to draw vertical lines along the right or left edge of a range of cells or to draw horizontal lines along the top or bottom of a range of cells. You can also use /FL to draw a grid over a range of cells. For more information on drawing lines, enter **/F**ormat **L**ines (/FL), and press F1 to use the Allways online help facility.

Summary of Shortcut Keys for Invoking Commands

Shortcut keys allow you to execute a command sequence by holding down the Alt key and pressing a typewriter key. Table 3-7 summarizes the shortcut keys that invoke Allways commands. Use this table to speed the entry of your commands.

TABLE 3-7 Shortcut Keys for Invoking Allways Commands

KEYS	DESCRIPTION
Alt-B	Boldface (Set/Clear)
Alt-G	Grid lines (On/Off)
Alt-L	Lines (Outline/All/None)
Alt-S	Shade (Light/Dark/Solid/None)
Alt-U	Underline (Single/Double/None)
Alt-1	Set font 1
Alt-2	Set font 2
Alt-3	Set font 3
Alt-4	Set font 4
Alt-5	Set font 5
Alt-6	Set font 6
Alt-7	Set font 7
Alt-8	Set font 8

Changing the Widths of Columns and Heights of Rows Using Allways

When you use Allways to increase the point size in a range of cells, some characters may be truncated (chopped off) in those cells. You can overcome this problem by instructing Allways to increase the column width of the range of cells. Changing the column width in Allways does not affect the column width in 1-2-3.

Sometimes a value just fits into the cell, such as Total Expenses in cell A21 (Figure 3-68). In such cases, chances are that when the worksheet is sent to the printer, the last character will be partially or completely truncated. Therefore, we need to increase the width of column A from 17 characters to 18 characters.

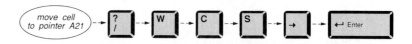

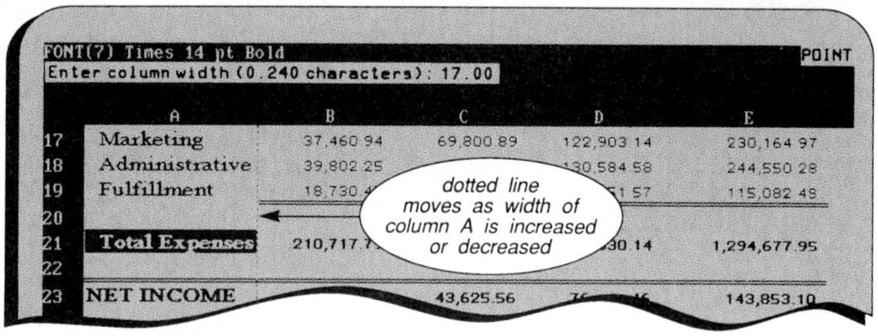

FIGURE 3-68
Increasing the width of column A. Use the command **/W**orksheet **C**olumn **S**et-Width (**/WCS**). Use the Right or Left Arrow key to increase or decrease the column width.

To change the width of column A, move the cell pointer to A21. (Actually, the cell pointer can be in any cell in column A.) Enter the command /Worksheet Column Set-Width (/WCS). The screen shown in Figure 3-68 appears. Notice the prompt message at the top of the screen and the vertical dotted line along the right edge of column A. Press the Right Arrow key to increase the width by 1, and the vertical line on the screen moves to the right to show the new column width. With the column width at 18.00, press the Enter key. Column A is now 18 characters wide. Press the Home key to move the cursor to A1. The completed worksheet is shown in Figure 3-69.

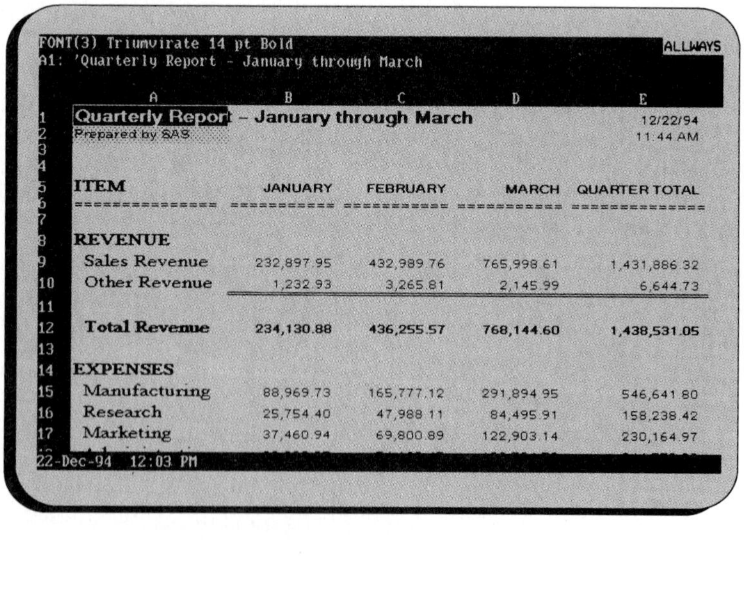

FIGURE 3-69
Format modifications to Project 3 completed

Consider one last point about the column width—as the prompt message indicates in Figure 3-68, Allways allows you to enter a column width to the nearest hundredths (two decimal places). You can type in the width you desire or you can increase or decrease the width by 1/10 of a character by holding down the Ctrl key and pressing the Right or Left Arrow key. Pressing the Right or Left Arrow key by itself increases or decreases the column width by 1 character.

Allways automatically adjusts the height of a row on the basis of the greatest point size assigned to the cells in the row. You can manually adjust the height of a row by moving the cell pointer into the row and entering the /Worksheet Row Set-Height (/WRS) command. You can also adjust the height of several adjacent rows by using the Period key to select the rows prior to issuing the /WRS command.

Printing the Worksheet

To print the worksheet using Allways, enter the command /**Print** (/P). This command activates the menu pointer in the Print menu (Figure 3-70). Type the letters R for Range and S for Set. Use the arrow keys to move the cell pointer to E31. Press the Enter key to anchor the second end point. The Print menu shown in Figure 3-70 reappears.

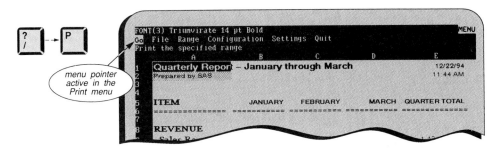

FIGURE 3-70 Printing the worksheet using Allways

Check to be sure the printer is ready. Type the letter G for Go. The worksheet prints on the printer as shown earlier in Figure 3-53. Move the paper through the printer so that you can tear the paper at the perforated edge below the printed version of the worksheet.

If the worksheet fails to print when you type the letter G for Go and you get an "Out of Memory" message on the status line at the bottom of the screen, return control to 1-2-3 and save the worksheet. After the worksheet is saved, return control to Allways and issue the print command again. If the worksheet still fails to print, use the command /**Worksheet Global Default Other Undo Disable** (/WGDOUD) to turn off the UNDO command and free up main memory. After disabling the UNDO command, issue the print command again.

One additional point about the Print command—once you establish a print range, Allways displays a dotted outline that defines the range whenever you switch from 1-2-3 to Allways.

Saving the Worksheet with Allways Format Changes

To preserve the format changes we have made to Project 3 using Allways, we need to save the worksheet to disk. To do this, return control to 1-2-3, and enter the command /**File Save Replace** (/FSR). 1-2-3 saves the worksheet as PROJS-3.WK1 and the corresponding Allways format changes as PROJS-3.ALL.

The Display Command

The **/D**isplay (/D) command in Allways allows you to control how the worksheet displays on the screen. Table 3-8 summarizes the functions of the commands in the Display menu.

TABLE 3-8   A Summary of Commands in the Allways Display Menu

COMMAND	FUNCTION
Colors	Sets color for background, foreground, and cell pointer.
Graphs	Turns the display of integrated graphs on or off. (Press F10 to issue this command.)
Mode	Switches display between text and graphics.
Quit	Quits Display menu and returns to ALLWAYS mode.
Zoom	Reduces or enlarges the display of the worksheet. (Use Alt-F4 to enlarge the worksheet. Press Alt-F4 repeatedly to enlarge the worksheet up to 140% of its normal size. Use F4 to reduce the size of the worksheet down to 60% of its normal size.)

The two screens in Figure 3-71 show the Project 3 worksheet reduced to 60% and enlarged to 140%.

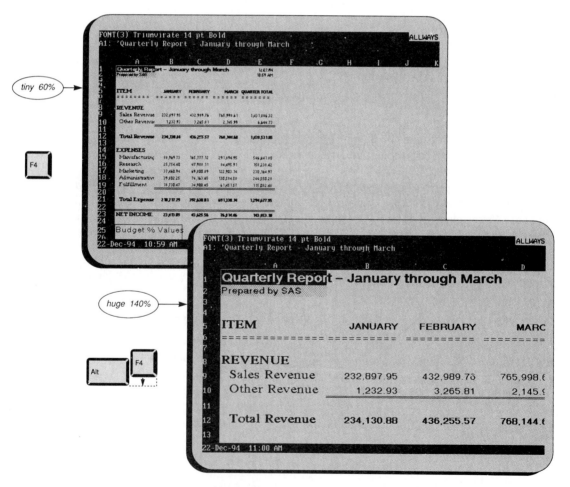

FIGURE 3-71   Minimizing and maximizing the display of the worksheet. Use the command **/D**isplay **Z**oom (/DZ) or use Alt-F4 to enlarge the display and F4 to reduce it.

PROJECT SUMMARY

In this project you learned a variety of ways to enhance a worksheet and simplify the steps of building, formatting, and printing large worksheets. You were introduced to the capabilities of 1-2-3 to answer what-if questions. Finally, you learned how to change the default settings, interact with DOS through 1-2-3, and produce presentation-quality printouts through Allways. All the activities that you learned for this project are summarized in the Quick Reference following the Appendix. The following is a summary of the keystroke sequence we used in Project 3.

SUMMARY OF KEYSTROKES — PROJECT 3

STEPS	KEY(S) PRESSED	RESULTS
1	/WGC → → → → ←	Sets width of all columns to 13.
2	/WCS17←	Sets width of column A to 17.
3	→ → → →/WCS16←	Sets width of column E to 16.
4	/WGF,←	Sets format of all columns to Comma (,).
5	← ← ← ←Quarterly Report - January through March↓	Enters report title in A1.
6	Prepared by SAS←	Enters author of worksheet in B1.
7	[F5] E1←@now↓	Enters @NOW function in E1.
8	@now↑	Enters @NOW function in E2.
9	/RFD4←	Formats date in E1.
10	↓/RFDT2←	Formats time in E2.
11	[F5] A5← [Caps Lock]	Moves cell pointer to A5 and engages Caps Lock.
12	ITEM→ "JANUARY →	Enters column titles in A5 and B5.
13	"FEBRUARY → "MARCH →	Enters column titles in C5 and D5.
14	"QUARTER TOTAL ←	Enters column title in E5.
15	[F5] A6←\ = ←	Underlines title in column A.
16	/C←.→.→ → → ←	Underlines titles in columns B through E.
17	↓↓REVENUE↓ [Caps Lock]	Enters group title in A8 and disengages Caps Lock.
18	' Sales Revenue↓' Other Revenue↓↓	Enters group subtitles in A9 and A10.
19	' Total Revenue↓↓	Enters group subtitle in A12.
20	EXPENSES↓' Manufacturing↓	Enters group title in A14 and group subtitle in A15.
21	' Research↓' Fulfillment↓↓	Enters group subtitles in A16 and A17.
22	' Total Expenses↓↓NET INCOME↓↓	Enters group subtitle in A19 and group title in A21.
23	Budget % Values↓	Enters group title in A23.
24	[F5] A17←	Moves cell pointer to A17.
25	/WIR↓ ←	Inserts two rows.
26	' Marketing↓' Administrative↓	Enters group subtitles in A18 and A19.
27	/CA15.A19←A27←	Copies group subtitles in A15..A19 to A27..A31.
28	[F5] B27←	Moves cell pointer to B27.
29	38%↓11%↓16%↓17%↓8%←	Enters budget % values in B27..B31.

(continued)

SUMMARY OF KEYSTROKES — PROJECT 3 (continued)

STEPS	KEY(S) PRESSED	RESULTS
30	/RFP0← ↑↑↑↑ ←	Sets format of B27..B31 to Percent.
31	[Home] [F5] B7 ←	Moves cell pointer to B7.
32	/WTB	Freezes row and column titles.
33	232897.95 → 432989.76 → 765998.61 →	Enters sales revenue in B7..D7.
34	@SUM(B7.D7) →	Sums sales revenue (B7..D7) in E7.
35	/M [Backspace] ←.← ← ← ←↓↓←.← ← ← ←	Moves sales revenue from B7..E7 to B9..E9.
36	↓↓↓← ← ← ←	Moves cell pointer to B10.
37	1232.93 → 3265.81 → 2145.99↓↓← ←	Enters other revenue in B10..D10 and moves cell pointer to B12.
38	@SUM(B9.B10) ←	Sums revenue (B9..D10) in B12.
39	/C← →.→ ←	Copies B12 to C12..D12.
40	/RFTB9.E19 ←	Sets format of B9..E19 to Text.
41	↓↓↓$B27*B$12 ←	Moves cell pointer to B15 and enters formula.
42	/C←.↓↓↓↓ → → ←	Copies B15 to B15..D19.
43	[F5] B19 ←/RF,←B19.E9 ←	Sets format of B19..E9 to Comma (,).
44	↓↓↓@SUM(↑↑↑↑↑↑.↓↓↓↓)←	Assigns the sum of B15..B19 to B21.
45	/C← →.→ ←	Copies B21 to C21..D21.
46	↓↓+B12−B21 ←	Assigns formula +B12−B21 to B23.
47	/C← →.→ ←	Copies B23 to C23..D23.
48	[F5] E9 ←	Moves cell pointer to E9.
49	/C←E9.E23 ←	Copies E9 to E9..E23.
50	↓↓/RE ←	Erases E11.
51	↓↓/RE↓ ←	Erases E13..E14.
52	↓↓↓↓↓↓↓/RE ←	Erases E20.
53	↓↓/RE ←	Erases E22.
54	/WTC [Home]	Clears titles and moves cell pointer to A1.
55	/FSPROJS-3 ←	Saves worksheet as PROJS-3.
56	/PPRA1.E31 ←	Sets A1..E31 as the print range.
57	AGPQ	Prints the worksheet.

SUMMARY OF KEYSTROKES — PROJECT 3   Using Allways

STEPS	KEY(S) PRESSED	RESULTS
1	/A|ALLWAYS ↵	Invokes ALLWAYS.
2	/FF↓↓ ↵ ↵	Assigns Triumvirate 14-point font to A1.
3	[F5] A5 ↵/FF↓↓↓↓↓↓ ↵ ↵	Assigns Times 14-point font to A5.
4	↓↓↓/FF↓↓↓↓↓↓ ↵A8.A31 ↵	Assigns Times 14-point font to A8..A31.
5	[F5] A25 ↵/FF↑↑↑ ↵ ↵	Assigns Triumvirate 14-point font to A25.
6	[Home]↓/FSL ↵	Shades A2.
7	↑/FBS ↵	Boldfaces A1.
8	[F5] A5 ↵.→ → → → [Alt-B] ↓	Boldfaces A5..E5.
9	[F5] A8 ↵ [Alt-B]	Boldfaces A8.
10	[F5] A12 ↵.→ → → → [Alt-B] ↓	Boldfaces A12..E12.
11	[F5] A14 ↵ [Alt-B]	Boldfaces A14.
12	[F5] A21 ↵.→ → → → [Alt-B] ↓	Boldfaces A21..E21.
13	[F5] A23 ↵.→ → → → [Alt-B] ↓	Boldfaces A23..E23.
14	[F5] B10 ↵/FUD→ → → → ↵	Draws double underline in B10..E10.
15	[F5] B19 ↵.→ → → → [Alt-U] [Alt-U] ↓	Draws double underline in B19..E19.
16	[F5] A22 ↵.→ → → → [Alt-U] [Alt-U] ↓	Draws double underline in A22..E22.
17	[F5] A25 ↵/FLO→ ↓↓↓↓↓↓ ↵	Boxes in A25..B31.
18	[F5] A21 ↵/WCS→ ↵ [Home]	Sets width of column A to 17.
19	/PRSA1.E31 ↵G	Prints the worksheet (A1.E31).
20	/Q	Quits ALLWAYS.
21	/FSR	Saves worksheet as PROJS-3.

The following list summarizes the material covered in Project 3.

1. After setting the column width for the entire worksheet, use the command /Worksheet Column Set-Width (/WCS) to set the width of individual columns requiring a different width.
2. Use the command /Worksheet Global Format (/WGF) to format all the cells in the worksheet to the same type.
3. To display the date and time as a decimal number, use the **NOW function**. The whole number portion is the number of complete days since December 31, 1899. The decimal portion represents today's time.
4. Use the command /Range Format Date (/RFD) to format today's date and time. Use Table 3-1 for a summary of the date and time formats.
5. The time stored in a cell is updated only after you make an entry into the worksheet or after you press function key F9.
6. To insert rows or columns into a worksheet, move the cell pointer to the point of insertion and enter the command /Worksheet Insert (/WI). Type the letter R to insert rows or the letter C to insert columns. Use the arrow keys to select how many rows or columns you want to insert.
7. To delete rows or columns from a worksheet, move the cell pointer to one of the end points of the range you want to delete. Enter the command /Worksheet Delete (/WD). Type the letter R to delete rows or the letter C to delete columns. Use the arrow keys to select how many rows or columns you want to delete.
8. Enter a percentage value in percent form by appending a percent sign (%) to the right of the number.
9. To **freeze the titles** so that they remain on the screen as you move the cell pointer around the worksheet, use the command /Worksheet Titles (/WT). You then have the choice of freezing vertical (row) titles, horizontal (column) titles, or both. Use the same command to **unfreeze** the titles.

10. To move a range to another range, use the command /**Move** (/M).

11. With the Copy command, a cell address with no dollar sign ($) is a **relative address**. A cell address with a dollar sign appended to the front of both the column name and row number is an **absolute address**. A cell address with a dollar sign added to the front of the column name or to the front of the row number is a **mixed cell address**.

12. When you enter a formula or function, you may use the arrow keys to point to the range.

13. It is valid to copy a cell to itself. This is necessary when you copy the end point of the destination range.

14. An empty cell or a cell with a label has a numeric value of zero.

15. Use the command /**Print Printer Option** (/PPO) to change the printer default settings.

16. **Condensed mode** allows nearly twice as many characters to fit across the page. Use the command /**Print Printer Options Setup** (/PPOS) to print a worksheet in the condensed mode.

17. The capability to answer **what-if questions** is a powerful and important feature of 1-2-3. Using 1-2-3 to answer what-if questions is called performing **what-if-analyses** or **sensitivity analyses**.

18. Once a worksheet is complete, you can enter new values into cells. Formulas and functions that reference the modified cells are immediately recalculated, thus giving new results. This feature is called **automatic recalculation**.

19. Use the command /**Worksheet Global Recalculation** (/WGR) to change from automatic to **manual recalculation**.

20. To change the default settings for the worksheet, use the command /**Worksheet Global Default** (/WGD).

21. Default settings changed with the command /WGD remain in force for the entire session, until you quit 1-2-3.

22. To permanently change the default settings, type the letter U for Update before quitting the Global Default menu.

23. The File command may be used to list the names of the files on disk, delete files, and change the current directory.

24. The System command allows you to temporarily place 1-2-3 in a **wait state** and return control to DOS. Once control returns to DOS, you may execute DOS commands. To return to 1-2-3, enter the command Exit.

25. Allways is a spreadsheet publishing add-in program that comes with Release 2.2 of 1-2-3. **Add-in** means the program is started while 1-2-3 is running.

26. There are two ways to invoke Allways: (1) enter the command /**Add-In Invoke** (/AI) and select Allways; or (2) hold down the Alt key and press F7. The latter method is available only if the F7 key was assigned the Allways program when it was initially attached to 1-2-3.

27. **Wysiwyg** stands for *What you see is what you get.*

28. The **font** is a typeface of a particular size. A **point** is equal to 1/72 of one inch.

29. To preserve the format changes made with Allways, return control to 1-2-3 and save the worksheet to disk.

30. To change the font of a cell or range of cells, enter the command /**Format Font** (/FF).

31. Shade a cell or range of cells by entering the command /**Format Shade** (/FS). The Shade menu has four options: Light, Dark, Solid, and Clear.

32. Bold a cell or range of cells by entering the command /**Format Bold Set** (/FBS).

33. To underline a cell or range of cells, enter the command /**Format Underline** (/FU). The Underline menu has three options: Single, Double, and Clear.

34. To outline a range of cells, enter the command /**Format Lines Outline** (/FLO).

35. **Shortcut keys** allow you to execute an Allways command sequence by holding down the Alt key and pressing a typewriter key. Some of the more important shortcut keys are: Alt-B for bold; Alt-S for shade; Alt-U for underline; and Alt-L for lines.

36. To use the shortcut keys on a range of cells, use the Period key to select the range and then press the shortcut key. To conclude the command, use one of the arrow keys to move the highlight off the range.

37. To change the column width in Allways, enter the command /**Worksheet Column Set-Width** (/WCS).

38. To change the height of rows, enter the /**Worksheet Row Set-Height** (/WRS) command.

39. To print the worksheet using Allways, enter the command /**Print** (/P). Select the range and then press G for Go.

40. The /**Display** (/D) command in Allways allows you to control how the worksheet displays on the screen.

STUDENT ASSIGNMENTS

STUDENT ASSIGNMENT 1: True/False

Instructions: Circle T if the statement is true and F if the statement is false.

T F   1. When you insert rows in a worksheet, 1-2-3 *pushes down* the current row and rows below the point of insertion to open up the worksheet.

T F   2. The /**W**orksheet **G**lobal **F**ormat (/WGF) command does not require that you enter a range in the worksheet to be affected.

T F   3. Use the NOW function to display the system date and time.

T F   4. To reset the format in a range to the global format, use the command /**R**ange **F**ormat **R**eset (/RFR).

T F   5. Labels, such as a name, are not affected by a global numeric format.

T F   6. Use the command /**W**orksheet **T**itles **C**lear (/WTC) to unfreeze the titles.

T F   7. When using the /**W**orksheet **T**itles (/WT) command, the title and column headings that run across the worksheet are called horizontal titles.

T F   8. The range B10..B15 is the same as B15..B10.

T F   9. A percentage value, like 5.3%, can not be entered exactly as 5.3% on the input line.

T F   10. When you start Allways, the default font is designated font 1 in the Font menu.

T F   11. If a cell within the range summed by the SUM function contains a label, 1-2-3 displays an error message.

T F   12. You can use the arrow keys to select the range for the SUM function.

T F   13. D23 is an absolute address and $D$23 is a relative address.

T F   14. When numbers are displayed using the Text format, they display right-justified in the cells.

T F   15. Use the /**M**ove (/M) command to move the contents of a cell or range of cells to a different location in the worksheet.

T F   16. The /**D**isplay (/D) command allows you to reduce the display of the worksheet to a maximum of 40% of its normal display.

T F   17. The format changes made with Allways are preserved as part of the .WK1 file when the worksheet is saved.

T F   18. To double underline a cell in Allways, move the cell pointer to the cell you want to double underline, and press Alt-U twice.

T F   19. ALLWAYS mode in Allways is similar to MENU mode in 1-2-3.

T F   20. Press Alt-B to boldface the current cell.

STUDENT ASSIGNMENT 2: Multiple Choice

Instructions: Circle the correct response.

1. Which one of the following commands is used to delete rows or columns from a worksheet?
   a. /**W**orksheet **U**nprotect (/WU)   c. /**W**orksheet **L**abel (/WL)
   b. /**W**orksheet **E**rase (/WE)   d. /**W**orksheet **D**elete (/WD)

2. Which one of the following is an absolute address?
   a. $B$45   b. !G!45   c. G45   d. #G#45

3. Which one of the following functions is used to display the time?
   a. TODAY   b. TIME   c. NOW   d. CLOCK

4. The command /**P**rint **P**rinter **O**ptions (/PPO) may be used to change _____ .
   a. the margins   c. from normal mode to condensed mode
   b. the page length   d. all of the above

5. The /**F**ile (/F) command can be used to _____ .
   a. format disks   c. erase worksheets from disk
   b. change the current directory   d. both b and c

Student Assignment 2 (continued)

6. If cell B14 is assigned the label TEN, then the function @SUM(B10.B14) in cell C25 considers B14 to be equal to _____ .
   a. 10   c. an undefined value
   b. 0   d. 3
7. The command /Move (/M) results in the same change to the worksheet as _____ .
   a. /Worksheet Erase (/WE)   c. /Worksheet Insert (/WI)
   b. /Copy (/C)   d. none of the above
8. The command /Worksheet Global Default (/WGD) can be used to _____ .
   a. display default settings   c. return control to DOS
   b. select a format for the worksheet   d. delete files
9. Which one of the following keys is used with Allways to select a range of cells before a shortcut key command is entered?
   a. Slash (/)   d. Circumflex (˜)
   b. Comma (,)   e. Number sign (#)
   c. Period (.)
10. Which of the following are the initial commands in the command sequence to instruct Allways to outline a range of cells?
    a. /Format Underline (/FU)
    b. /Format Font (/FF)
    c. /Format Display (/FD)
    d. /Format Lines (/FL)
    e. /Format Shade (/FS)

STUDENT ASSIGNMENT 3: Understanding Absolute, Mixed, and Relative Addressing

Instructions: Fill in the correct answers.

1. Write cell D15 as a relative address, absolute address, mixed address with the row varying, and mixed address with the column varying.

   Relative address: _____   Mixed, row varying: _____

   Absolute address: _____   Mixed, column varying: _____

2. In the following figure, write the formula for cell B8 that multiplies cell B1 times the sum of cells B4, B5, and B6. Write the formula so that when it is copied to cells C8 and D8, cell B1 remains absolute. Verify your formula by checking it with the values found in cells B8, C8, and D8 below.

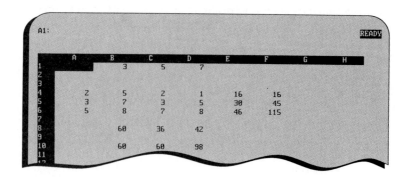

   Formula for cell B8: _____

3. In the figure at the bottom of page L144, write the formula for cell E4 that multiplies cell A4 times the sum of cells B4, C4, and D4. Write the formula so that when it is copied to cells E5 and E6, cell A4 remains absolute. Verify your formula by checking it with the values found in cells E4, E5, and E6.

   Formula for cell E4: _____

4. In the figure at the bottom of page L144, write the formula for cell B10 that multiplies cell B1 times the sum of cells B4, B5, and B6. Write the formula so that when it is copied to cells C10 and D10, 1-2-3 adjusts all the cell addresses according to the new location. Verify your formula by checking it with the values found in cells B10, C10, and D10.

   Formula for cell B10: _____

5. In the figure at the bottom of page L144, write the formula for cell F4 that multiplies cell A4 times the sum of cells B4, C4, and D4. Write the formula so that when it is copied to cells F5 and F6, 1-2-3 adjusts all the cell addresses according to the new location. Verify your formula by checking it with the values found in cells F4, F5, and F6.

   Formula for cell F4: _____

STUDENT ASSIGNMENT 4: Writing 1-2-3 Commands

Instructions: Write the 1-2-3 command to accomplish the task in each of the following problems. Write the command up to the point where you enter the range or type the letter Q to quit the command.

1. Move the range of cells A12..C15 to F14..H17. Assume the cell pointer is at A12.

   Command: _____

2. Return control to DOS temporarily.

   Command: _____

3. Insert three rows between rows 5 and 6. Assume the cell pointer is at A6.

   Command: _____

4. Freeze the vertical and horizontal titles. Assume that the cell pointer is immediately below and to the right of the titles.

   Command: _____

5. Delete columns A, B, and C. Assume the cell pointer is at A1.

   Command: _____

6. Switch control to the add-in program Allways.

   Command: _____

7. Change 1-2-3 from automatic to manual recalculation.

   Command: _____

8. Change to print in condensed mode with a right margin of 132.

   Command: _____

9. Change the left print margin to 1 and the right print margin to 79 for the current worksheet only.

   Command: _____

10. Set columns A and B as borders. Assume the cell pointer is at B1.

   Command: _____

Student Assignment 4 (continued)

11. Reset the format in the range A1..B10 to the global format. Assume the cell pointer is at A1.

    Command: _____

12. List the Allways command sequence for assigning bold to the range A10..E25 using the shortcut key.

    Command: _____

13. List the shortcut key commands to minimize and maximize the display of a worksheet using Allways.

    Command: Minimize _____   Maximize _____

STUDENT ASSIGNMENT 5: Correcting the Range in a Worksheet

Instructions: The worksheet illustrated in the following figure contains errors in cells C21 through E21. Analyze the entries displayed on the worksheet, especially the formula assigned to B21 and displayed at the top of the screen. Cell B21 was copied to C21..D21. Explain the cause of the errors and the method of correction in the space provided below.

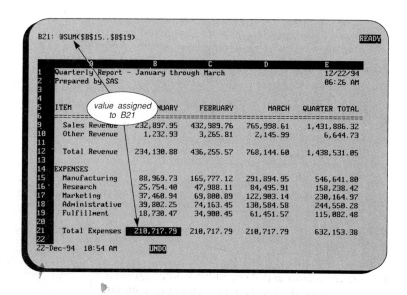

Cause of errors: _____

_____

Method of correction for cell B21: _____

_____

Method of correction for cells C21 through E21: _____

_____

_____

STUDENT ASSIGNMENT 6: Correcting Errors in a Worksheet

Instructions: The worksheet illustrated in the figure at the top of the next page contains errors in the range B15..E23. This worksheet contains the same formulas as the worksheet in Project 3. Analyze the entries displayed on the worksheet. Explain the cause of the errors and the method of correction in the space provided below. (Hint: Check the cells that are referenced in the range B15..E23.)

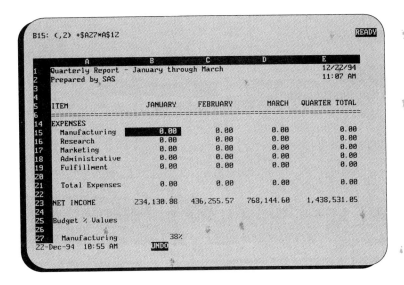

Cause of errors: _____

_____

Method of correction: _____ +B17 × B$9

_____

STUDENT ASSIGNMENT 7: Building a Projected Price Increase Worksheet

Instructions: Load 1-2-3 and perform the following tasks.

1. Build the worksheet illustrated in the following figure. Increase the width of columns B through E to 13 characters. Enter the title, column headings, model numbers in column A, and corresponding current prices in column B. The entries in the columns labeled 12.5% INCREASE, 16.25% INCREASE, and 21.5% INCREASE are determined from formulas. Multiply one plus the percent specified in the column heading by the current price. For example, assign C9 the formula 1.125*B9. To determine the total current price in cell B19, enter a formula that adds the products of the on-hand column and the corresponding current price. Copy this total formula in cell B19 to cells C19 through E19 to determine the totals in the remaining columns.

Insert Rows
Subtotals

Then Total

O/N do #3

Student Assignment 7 (continued)

2. Save the worksheet as STUS3-7.
3. Print the worksheet in the condensed mode. Reset 1-2-3 back to the normal print mode.
4. Print the cell-formulas version of the worksheet.
5. Print only the first 18 rows of the model number and current price columns.
6. Print the worksheet after formatting all the cells to the Text type.

STUDENT ASSIGNMENT 8: Building a Payroll Analysis Worksheet

Instructions: Load 1-2-3 and perform the following tasks.

1. Build the worksheet illustrated in the following figure. Change the global width to 13 characters. Change the width of column A to 19 characters. Enter the title, column headings, row titles, employee names in column A, and corresponding current hourly pay rate in column B. Use the NOW function to display the current date and time in cells E18 and E19. It is not necessary that the date and time in your worksheet agree with the date and time in the figure. Finally, enter the proposed percent increase in cell B15 and hours per week in cell B16.

Enter the following formulas once and copy them to complete the remainder of the worksheet:
  a. Cell C8—current weekly pay = hours per week × current hourly pay rate
  b. Cell D8—proposed hourly pay rate = current hourly pay rate × (1 + proposed percent increase in B15)
  c. Cell E8—proposed weekly pay = hours per week × proposed hourly pay rate
  Format the numbers in rows 8 through 12 to the Fixed type with two decimal places. Format the totals in rows 18 through 20 to the Currency type with two decimal places.
2. Save the worksheet as STUS3-8.
3. Print the worksheet in condensed mode. Reset 1-2-3 back to the normal print mode.
4. Print only the range A1..C13.

stus 3-8

5. Answer the following what-if questions. Print the worksheet for each question.
   3-8A
   a. What is the total proposed pay if the proposed percent increase is changed to 10%?
   b. What is the total proposed pay if the proposed percent increase is changed to 7.5%?
   3-8B
6. Use Allways to print the worksheet as shown in the figure below. Incorporate the following format changes:
   a. Change the font in B1 to Times 14 point.
   b. Change the font over the range A15..B20 to Times 10 point.
   c. Bold A1, A3..E5, and A15..B20.
   d. Shade dark E8..E12.
   e. Outline A15..B16.
   f. Double underline A20..B20.

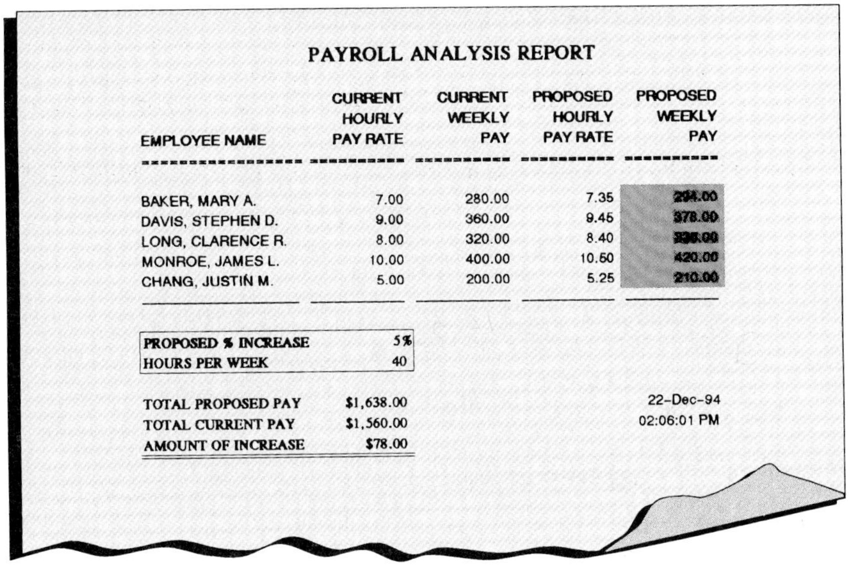

PAYROLL ANALYSIS REPORT

EMPLOYEE NAME	CURRENT HOURLY PAY RATE	CURRENT WEEKLY PAY	PROPOSED HOURLY PAY RATE	PROPOSED WEEKLY PAY
BAKER, MARY A.	7.00	280.00	7.35	294.00
DAVIS, STEPHEN D.	9.00	360.00	9.45	378.00
LONG, CLARENCE R.	8.00	320.00	8.40	336.00
MONROE, JAMES L.	10.00	400.00	10.50	420.00
CHANG, JUSTIN M.	5.00	200.00	5.25	210.00

PROPOSED % INCREASE	5%
HOURS PER WEEK	40

TOTAL PROPOSED PAY	$1,638.00	22–Dec–94
TOTAL CURRENT PAY	$1,560.00	02:06:01 PM
AMOUNT OF INCREASE	$78.00	

7. Save the worksheet with the Allways format characteristics as STUS3-8A.

STUDENT ASSIGNMENT 9: Building a Book Income Worksheet

Instructions: Load 1-2-3 and perform the following tasks.

1. Build the worksheet illustrated in the following figure. Set column A to a width of 18 characters and columns B through E to a width of 13 characters. The calculations for each author are determined as follows:

   a. The royalty in column C is the net sales of the book multiplied by the author's royalty percentage in cell B30 or B31.

   b. The manufacturing costs in column D are the net sales of the book multiplied by the manufacturing budgeted percent in cell B35.

   c. The net income in column E for each book is determined by subtracting the royalty and manufacturing costs from the net sales.

   d. The report totals in rows 25 and 26 are the sum of the individual book titles for each author.

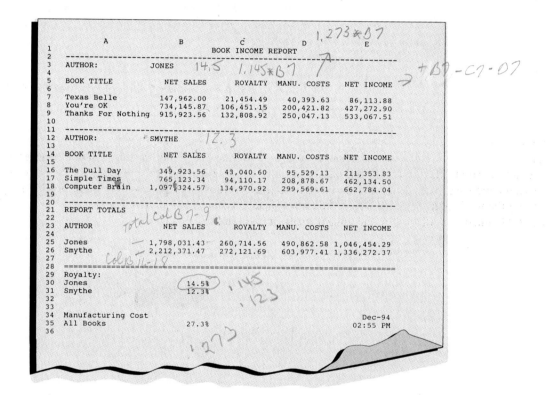

2. Save the worksheet. Use the file name STUS3-9.
3. Print the worksheet.
4. Print only the range A3..E9.
5. Print the worksheet after formatting all the cells to the Text type.

STUDENT ASSIGNMENT 10: Changing Manufacturing Costs and Royalty Rates in the Book Income Worksheet

Instructions: Load 1-2-3 and perform the following tasks.

1. Retrieve the worksheet STUS3-9 from disk. The worksheet is illustrated in the figure in Student Assignment 9.
2. Answer the following what-if questions. Print the worksheet for each question. Each question is independent of the others.
    a. If the manufacturing percentage cost in cell B35 is reduced from 27.3% to 25.7%, what is the net income from all of Jones's books?
    b. If Smythe's royalty percentage in cell B31 is changed from 12.3% to 15.8%, what would be the royalty amount for the book *Simple Times*?
    c. If Jones's royalty percentage in cell B30 is reduced from 14% to 13.5%, Smythe's royalty percentage is increased from 12.3% to 14.3%, and the manufacturing percentage costs are reduced from 27.3% to 24%, what would be the net incomes for Jones and Smythe?

STUDENT ASSIGNMENT 11: Building a Salary Budget Worksheet

Instructions: Load 1-2-3 and perform the following tasks.

1. Build the worksheet illustrated in the following figure. Change the width of all the columns in the worksheet to 15 characters. Then change the width of column A to 20 characters. Enter the title, column headings, row titles, date, time, and current salary for full- and part-time employees. Determine the projected salaries in column C by using the salary increase in cell B27 and the current salaries in column B. Determine the salaries by department by multiplying the total salaries in row 12 by the corresponding sales allocation percent value in the range B21..B24. Use the SUM function to determine the annual totals in column D.

```
              A               B             C              D
 1   SALARY BUDGET - CURRENT AND PROJECTED SALARIES      12/22/94
 2   PREPARED BY ACCOUNTING                              10:59 AM
 3
 4
 5                         CURRENT      PROJECTED
 6   SALARY TYPE           JAN - JUNE   JULY - DEC     ANNUAL TOTAL
 7   ===============================================================
 8
 9   FULL TIME             1,250,500.00  1,313,025.00   2,563,525.00
10   PART TIME               750,500.00    788,025.00   1,538,525.00
11
12   TOTAL SALARIES        2,001,000.00  2,101,050.00   4,102,050.00
13
14   SALARIES BY DEPARTMENT
15      Accounting           200,100.00    210,105.00     410,205.00
16      Production           600,300.00    630,315.00   1,230,615.00
17      Sales                500,250.00    525,262.50   1,025,512.50
18      Distribution         700,350.00    735,367.50   1,435,717.50
19
20   SALES ALLOCATION % VALUES
21      Accounting                10%
22      Production                30%
23      Sales                     25%
24      Distribution              35%
25
26
27   SALARY INCREASE %              5%
28
```

2. Save the worksheet using the file name STUS3-11.
3. Print the worksheet.
4. Print the portion of the worksheet in the range A14..D18.

Student Assignment 11 (continued)

5. Use Allways to print the worksheet as shown in the following figure. Incorporate these format changes:
   a. Bold A1, A5..D7, and A9..A27.
   b. Double underline B10..D10, A18..D18, A27..B27.
   c. Outline A20..B24.
   d. Shade dark D9..D10.
6. Minimize the display to 60%. Maximize the display to 140%.
7. Save the worksheet with the Allways format characteristics as STU3-11A.

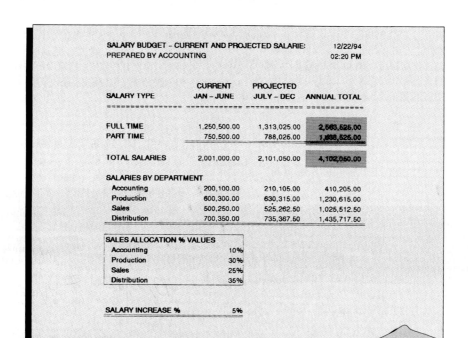

STUDENT ASSIGNMENT 12: Changing Sales Allocation Percent Values and Salary Increase Percent in the Salary Budget Worksheet

Instructions: Load 1-2-3 and perform the following tasks.

1. Retrieve the worksheet STUS3-11 from disk. The worksheet is shown in the first figure in Student Assignment 11.
2. Answer the following what-if questions. Print the worksheet for each question. Each question is independent of the other.
   a. If the four sales allocation percent values in the range B21..B24 are each decreased by 1% and the salary increase in cell B27 is changed from 5% to 4%, what are the annual totals in the Salary Budget worksheet?
   b. If the salary increase percent is cut in half, what would be the total projected salaries?

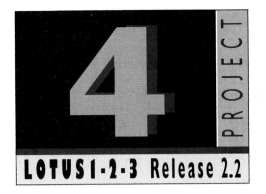

LOTUS 1-2-3 Release 2.2

Building a Worksheet with Functions and Macros

OBJECTIVES

You will have mastered the material in this project when you can:

◆ Assign a name to a range and refer to the range in a formula using the assigned name

◆ Apply the elementary statistical functions AVG, COUNT, MAX, MIN, STD, and VAR

◆ Determine the monthly payment of a loan using the financial function PMT

◆ Enter a series of numbers into a range using the Data Fill command

◆ Employ the IF function to enter one value or another in a cell on the basis of a condition

◆ Determine the present value of an annuity using the financial function PV

◆ Determine the future value of an investment using the financial function FV

◆ Build a data table to perform what-if analyses

◆ Store keystrokes as a macro and execute the macro

◆ Use the learn feature of 1-2-3 to enter macros into the worksheet

◆ Write program-like macros to automate your worksheet

◆ Divide the screen into multiple windows

◆ Protect and unprotect cells

In this project we will develop two worksheets, Project 4A and Project 4B. The worksheet for Project 4A, shown in Figure 4-1, is a grading report that displays a row of information for each student enrolled in DP 101. The student information includes a student identification number, three test scores, a test score total, and total percent correct. At the bottom of the worksheet is summary information for each test and all three tests grouped together. The summary includes the number of students that took the test, the highest and lowest test scores, the average test score, standard deviation, and variance. The standard deviation is a statistic used to measure the dispersion of test scores. The variance is used to make additional statistical inferences about the test scores.

```
DP 101                  Grading Report                 22-Dec-94

                   Test 1      Test 2      Test 3      Total    Percent
Student             139         142         150         431     Correct
================================================================
1035                121         127         142         390      90.5
1074                114         113         132         359      83.3
1265                 79          97         101         277      64.3
1345                 85         106          95         286      66.4
1392                127         124         120         371      86.1
3167                101         120         109         330      76.6
3382                110         104         120         334      77.5
3597                 92         104         100         296      68.7
4126                105         100          96         301      69.8
5619                125         135         143         403      93.5
7561                112         130         123         365      84.7
----------------------------------------------------------------
Count                11          11          11          11
Lowest Grade         79          97          95         277
Highest Grade       127         135         143         403
Average Grade     106.5       114.5       116.5       337.5
Std Deviation      15.2        12.6        16.8        41.4
Variance          230.2       159.0       282.8      1711.2
```

FIGURE 4-1 The grading report we will build in Project 4A.

L153

Project 4B has three parts. The first part is shown in Figure 4-2. This worksheet determines the monthly payment and an amortization table for a car loan. An amortization table shows the beginning and ending balances and the amount of payment that applies to the principal and interest for each period. This type of worksheet can be very useful if you are planning to take out a loan and want to see the effects of increasing the down payment, changing the interest rate, or changing the length of time it takes to pay off the loan.

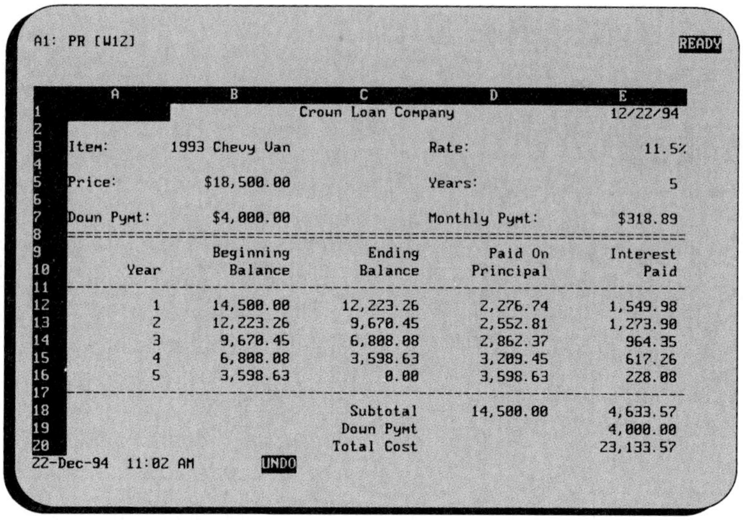
A1: PR [W12] READY

	A	B	C	D	E
1			Crown Loan Company		12/22/94
2					
3	Item:	1993 Chevy Van		Rate:	11.5%
4					
5	Price:	$18,500.00		Years:	5
6					
7	Down Pymt:	$4,000.00		Monthly Pymt:	$318.89
8	==========	==========	==========	==========	==========
9		Beginning	Ending	Paid On	Interest
10	Year	Balance	Balance	Principal	Paid
11	----------	----------	----------	----------	----------
12	1	14,500.00	12,223.26	2,276.74	1,549.98
13	2	12,223.26	9,670.45	2,552.81	1,273.90
14	3	9,670.45	6,808.08	2,862.37	964.35
15	4	6,808.08	3,598.63	3,209.45	617.26
16	5	3,598.63	0.00	3,598.63	228.08
17	----------	----------	----------	----------	----------
18			Subtotal	14,500.00	4,633.57
19			Down Pymt		4,000.00
20			Total Cost		23,133.57

22-Dec-94 11:02 AM UNDO

FIGURE 4-2
The monthly payment and amortization table we will build for the Crown Loan Company in Part 1 of Project 4B.

The second part of this worksheet is shown in Figure 4-3. Here we use a data table to analyze the effect of different interest rates on the monthly payment and total amount paid for the car loan. A data table is an area of the worksheet set up to contain answers to what-if questions. By using a data table you can automate your what-if questions and organize the answers returned by 1-2-3 into a table. For example, the data table in Figure 4-3 displays the monthly payments and total cost of the loan for interest rates varing between 8.5% and 15% in increments of 0.5%.

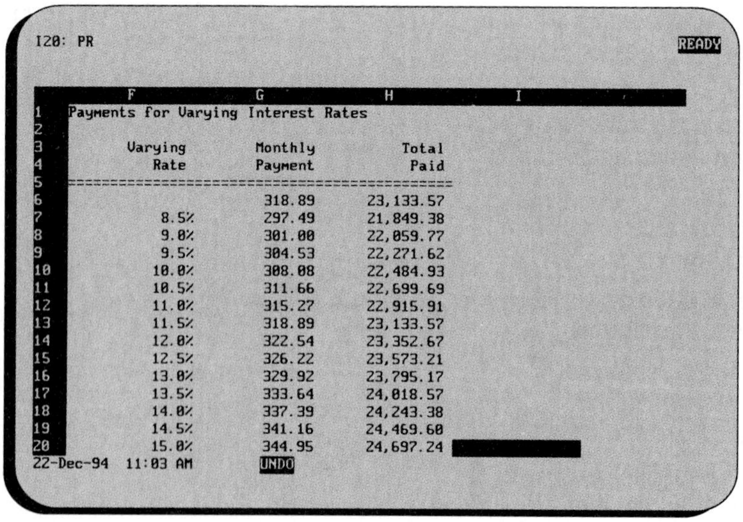
I20: PR READY

	F	G	H	I
1	Payments for Varying Interest Rates			
2				
3	Varying	Monthly	Total	
4	Rate	Payment	Paid	
5	==========	==========	==========	
6		318.89	23,133.57	
7	8.5%	297.49	21,849.38	
8	9.0%	301.00	22,059.77	
9	9.5%	304.53	22,271.62	
10	10.0%	308.08	22,484.93	
11	10.5%	311.66	22,699.69	
12	11.0%	315.27	22,915.91	
13	11.5%	318.89	23,133.57	
14	12.0%	322.54	23,352.67	
15	12.5%	326.22	23,573.21	
16	13.0%	329.92	23,795.17	
17	13.5%	333.64	24,018.57	
18	14.0%	337.39	24,243.38	
19	14.5%	341.16	24,469.60	
20	15.0%	344.95	24,697.24	

22-Dec-94 11:03 AM UNDO

FIGURE 4-3
The data table we will build for the Crown Loan Company in Part 2 of Project 4B.

The third part of Project 4B involves writing the four macros shown in Figure 4-4. A macro is a series of keystrokes or instructions that are stored in a cell or a range of cells associated with that particular worksheet. They are executed by pressing only two keys: the Alt key and the single letter macro name. Macros save you time and effort. For example, they allow you to store a complex sequence of commands in a cell. Later you can execute the macro (stored commands) as often as you want by simply typing its name.

```
                   A            B            C            D                     E
            22              Crown Loan Company Worksheet Macros
            23
            24    Macro                    Macro Name    Function
            25    ============             ==========    ==================================
            26    /FS~R                    \S            Saves worksheet
            27
            28    /PPAGPQ                  \P            Prints worksheet
            29
            30    /PPOOCQAGOOAQPQ          \C            Prints cell-formulas version
            31
            32
            33    {HOME}                   \D            Accept loan information
            34    {GOTO}B3~/RE~                          --Clear cell B3
            35    {DOWN}{DOWN}/RE~                       --Clear cell B5
            36    {DOWN}{DOWN}/RE~                       --Clear cell B7
            37    {GOTO}E3~/RE~                          --Clear cell E3
            38    {DOWN}{DOWN}/RE~                       --Clear cell E5
            39    {HOME}                                 --Move to cell A1
            40    /XLPurchase Item:~B3~                  --Accept item
            41    /XNPurchase Price:~B5~                 --Accept price
            42    /XNDown Payment:~B7~                   --Accept down payment
            43    /XNInterest Rate in %:~E3~             --Accept interest rate
            44    /XNTime in Years:~E5~                  --Accept time in years
            45    {HOME}                                 --Move to cell A1
            46    /XQ                                    --End of macro
            47
```

FIGURE 4-4   The four macros we will build for the Crown Loan Company in Part 3 of Project 4B.

When executed, the macro in cell A26 of Figure 4-4 saves the worksheet. The one in cell A28 prints the worksheet on the basis of the previously defined range. The macro in cell A30 prints the cell-formulas version of the worksheet on the basis of the previously defined range. The multicell macro in the range A33..A46 is a type of computer program. When it executes, it automatically clears the cells containing the loan information in Figure 4-2, requests new loan data on the input line, and displays the new loan information.

PROJECT 4A — ANALYZING STUDENT TEST SCORES

◆ Begin Project 4A with an empty worksheet and the cell pointer at A1, the home position. The first step is to change the widths of the columns in the worksheet. Set the width of column A to 13 characters, so that the row identifier "Std Deviation" fits in cell A22 (Figure 4-1). Change the width of the rest of the columns in the worksheet from 9 to 11 characters so that all the student information fits across the screen. To change the columns to the desired widths, do the following:

1. Enter the command /**W**orksheet **G**lobal **C**olumn-Width (/WGC). Change the default width on the input line from 9 to 11 and press the Enter key.
2. With the cell pointer at A1, enter the command /**W**orksheet **C**olumn **S**et-Width (/WCS). Change the number 11 on the input line to 13 and press the Enter key.

If you reverse steps 1 and 2, the results will still be the same. That is, you can change the width of column A first and then change the width of the rest of the columns. The command /WGC affects only those columns that were not previously changed by the /WCS command.

The next step is to add the titles and student data to the worksheet. Enter the course number, worksheet title, date, column headings, maximum possible points for each test, student number, test scores, and summary identifiers as specified in Figure 4-1. Follow the first 20 steps in the Summary of Keystrokes—Project 4A at the end of this project. The first 20 rows display as shown in Figure 4-5.

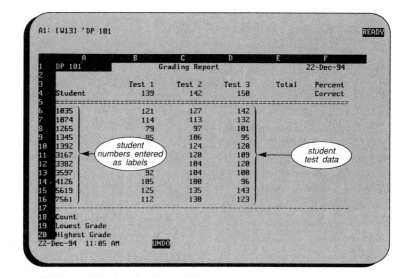

FIGURE 4-5
Labels and student data are entered into the grading report.

With the student data in the worksheet, the totals and summaries can be determined. Let's start with the maximum number of points for all three tests in cell E4. Use the GOTO command to move the cell pointer from cell A1 to cell E4 and enter the function @SUM(B4..D4). The range B4..D4 contains the maximum possible points for each test.

The SUM function in cell E4 is the same one required in the range E6..E16 to determine the total number of points received by each student. Hence, use the Copy command to copy cell E4 to the range E6..E16. With the cell pointer at E4, enter the command /Copy (/C), press the Enter key to lock in the source range, and use the Down Arrow key and Period key to select the destination range E6..E16. Press the Enter key. The total number of points received by each student displays in the range E6..E16 (Figure 4-6).

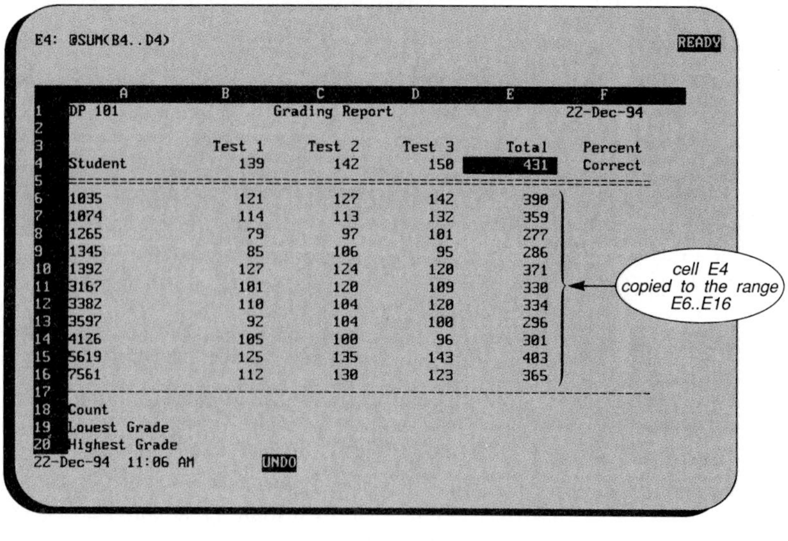

FIGURE 4-6
Student test totals are entered into column E of the grading report.

Once the total number of points received by each student is part of the worksheet, the total percent correct in column F can be determined. Move the cell pointer to F6 and enter the formula +E6/$E$4*100. The numerator in this formula, cell E6, is equal to the total number of points for the first student. The denominator, cell E4, is equal to the maximum number of points for the three tests. Multiplying the quotient +E6/$E$4 by 100 converts the ratio to a percent value. This procedure is used to display a percent value rather than formatting it in the Percent type because the column heading already indicates that the values in column E are in percent. Recall that the Percent type adds a percent sign (%) to the right side of the number.

Copy cell F6 to the range F7..F16. Notice that the dollar sign ($) character in the denominator of the formula in cell E6 makes cell E4 an absolute cell address. Therefore, when the formula in cell F6 is copied, the relative address E6 in the numerator changes based on the new location and the absolute address $E$4 in the denominator stays the same.

Format the percent correct in column F to the Fixed type with one decimal place. Enter the command /**R**ange **F**ormat **F**ixed (/RFF). Select one decimal position and press the Enter key. Enter the range F6..F16 and press the Enter key. The worksheet with each student's percent correct formatted to the Fixed type with one decimal place is illustrated in Figure 4-7.

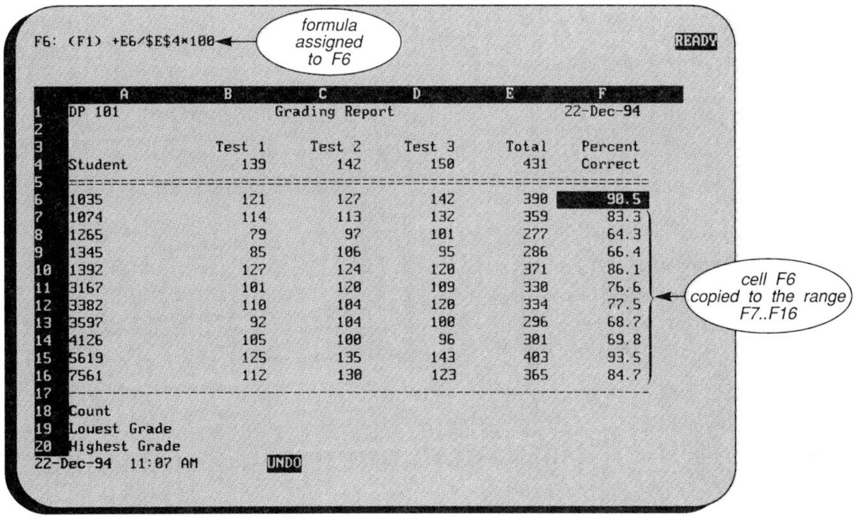

FIGURE 4-7
Total percent correct for each student is formatted to the Fixed type with one decimal position.

The next step is to determine the summaries in rows 18 through 23. To make the job of entering these summaries easier, we need to discuss range names.

Assigning a Name to a Range of Cells

One of the problems with using a range is remembering the end points that define it. The problem becomes more difficult as worksheets grow in size and the same range is referred to repeatedly. This is the situation in the summary rows at the bottom of the grading report. For example, each summary item for Test 1 in cells B18 through B23 reference the same range, B6..B16. To make it easier to refer to the range, 1-2-3 allows you to assign a name to it. You may then use the name to reference the range, rather than the cell addresses of the end points. A range name can consist of up to 15 characters. Let's assign the name TEST1 to the range B6..B16.

Move the cell pointer to B6, one of the end points of the range B6..B16. Enter the command /**R**ange **N**ame (/RN). With the menu pointer active in the Range Name menu (Figure 4-8), type the letter C for Create.

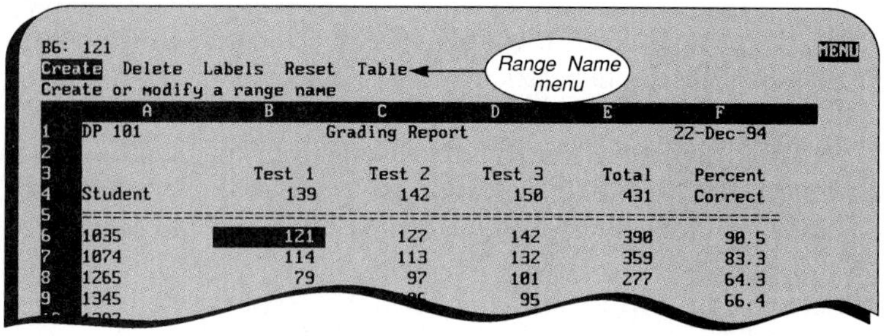

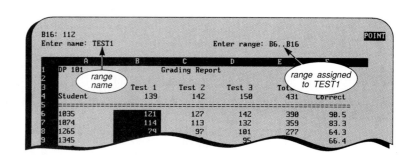

FIGURE 4-8
The display after entering the command /**R**ange **N**ame (/RN)

1-2-3 responds with the prompt message "Enter name:" on the input line (Figure 4-9). Enter the name TEST1 and press the Enter key. The prompt message "Enter range: B6..B6" immediately displays on the input line. Use the arrow keys to select the range B6..B16 as shown in Figure 4-9. Press the Enter key. The range name TEST1 can now be used in place of B6..B16.

FIGURE 4-9
Range name TEST1 assigned to the range B6..B16

As shown in the Range Name menu in Figure 4-8, there are several Range Name commands. These commands are summarized in Table 4-1. When 1-2-3 is in POINT mode, you can display a list of all the range names associated with the current worksheet by pressing function key F3.

TABLE 4-1 A Summary of Commands in the Range Name Menu

COMMAND	FUNCTION
Create	Assigns a name to a range. The name can be no longer than 15 characters.
Delete	Deletes the specified range name.
Labels	Assigns the label in the current cell as a name to the cell above, below, to the right, or to the left of the current cell.
Reset	Deletes range names associated with the worksheet.
Table	Places an alphabetized list of range names in the worksheet beginning at the upper left corner cell of the specified range.

Statistical Functions — AVG, COUNT, MIN, MAX, STD, and VAR

1-2-3 has several statistical functions that return values that are handy for evaluating a group of numbers, like the test scores in the grading report. The statistical functions are summarized in Table 4-2.

TABLE 4-2 Statistical Functions

FUNCTION	FUNCTION VALUE
AVG(R)	Returns the average of the numbers in range R by summing the nonempty cells and dividing by the number of nonempty cells. Labels are treated as zeros.
COUNT(R)	Returns the number of cells that are not empty in range R.
MAX(R)	Returns the largest number in range R.
MIN(R)	Returns the smallest number in range R.
STD(R)	Returns the standard deviation of the numbers in range R.
SUM(R)	Returns the sum of the numbers in range R.
VAR(R)	Returns the variance of the numbers in range R.

In the grading report, cell B18 displays the number of students that received a grade for Test 1. This value can be obtained by using the COUNT function. With the cell pointer at B18, enter the function @COUNT(TEST1). 1-2-3 immediately displays the value 11—the number of students that received a grade for Test 1. This is shown in Figure 4-10. Remember, the range name TEST1 is equal to the range B6..B16.

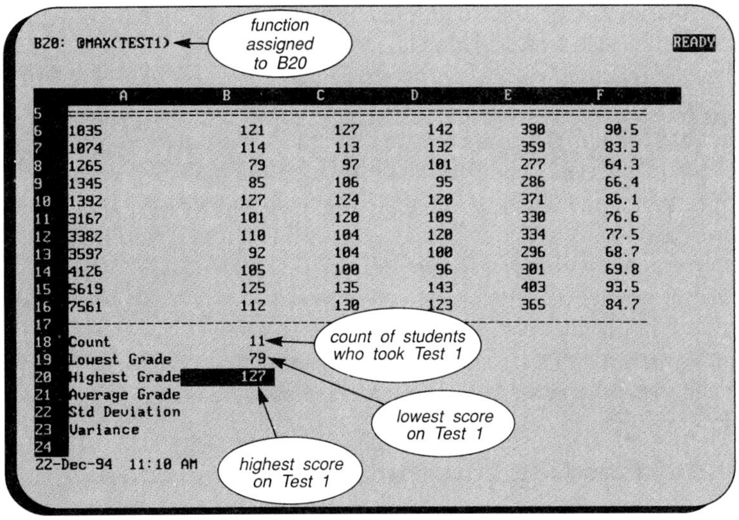

FIGURE 4-10
COUNT, MIN, and MAX functions entered into the grading report for Test 1

In cells B19 and B20, the grading report contains the lowest score and the highest score received on Test 1. Student 1265 received the lowest score—79. Student 1392 received the highest score—127. To display the lowest score obtained on Test 1, enter the function @MIN(TEST1) in cell B19. To display the highest score, enter the function @MAX(TEST1) in cell B20. The results of entering these functions are shown in cells B19 and B20 in Figure 4-10.

The next step is to determine the average of the scores received on Test 1. Enter the function @AVG(TEST1) in cell B21. As illustrated in Figure 4-11, the average score for Test 1 in cell B21 is 106.454545. 1-2-3 arrives at this value by summing the scores for Test 1 and dividing by the number of nonempty cells in the range B6..B16.

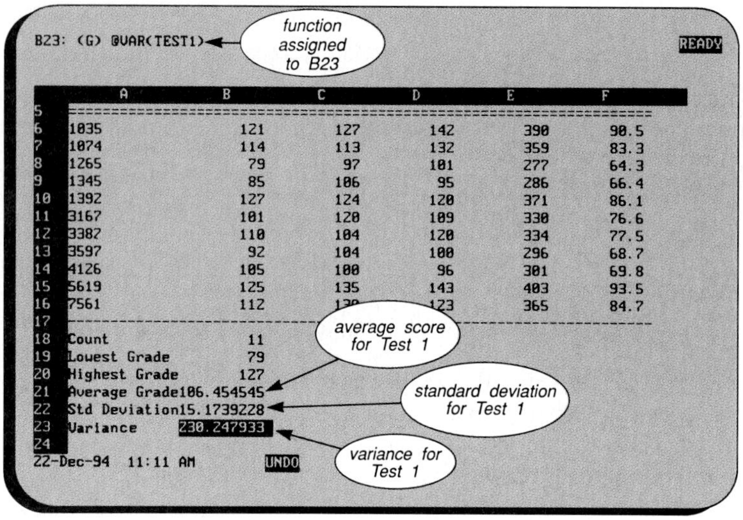

FIGURE 4-11
AVG, STD, and VAR functions entered into the grading report for Test 1

The last two summary lines require the use of the functions STD and VAR. As indicated in Table 4-2, the STD function returns the standard deviation and the VAR function returns the variance. To complete the summary lines for Test 1, enter the functions @STD(TEST1) in cell B22 and @VAR(TEST1) in cell B23. The results are shown in Figure 4-11.

The same six functions that are used to summarize the results for Test 1 are required for Test 2, Test 3, and the sum of the test scores for each student in column E. With the cell pointer at B23, enter the command /**C**opy (/C). Copy the source range B23..B18 to the destination range C23..E18.

As the functions in column B are copied to the new locations in columns C, D, and E, 1-2-3 adjusts the range TEST1 (B6..B16) to C6..C16 for Test 2, D6..D16 for Test 3, and E6..E16 for the sum of the test scores in column E.

To complete the worksheet, format the last three rows in the worksheet to the Fixed type with one decimal place. With the cell pointer at B23, enter the command /**R**ange **F**ormat **F**ixed (/RFF). In response to the prompt message "Enter number of decimal places (0..15): 2" on the input line, type the number 1 and press the Enter key. Next, 1-2-3 displays the prompt message "Enter range to format: B23..B23". Use the arrow keys to select the range B23..E21 and press the Enter key. The complete grading report is shown in Figure 4-1.

Saving and Printing the Worksheet

To save the grading report worksheet to disk, enter the command /**F**ile **S**ave (/FS). In response to the prompt message on the input line, enter the file name PROJS-4A, and press the Enter key.

Perform these steps to obtain a printed version of the worksheet.

1. Make sure the printer is ready.
2. Press the Home key to move the cell pointer to A1.
3. Enter the command /**P**rint **P**rinter **R**ange (/PPR) and select the range A1..F23.
4. Type the letters A for Align and G for Go.
5. After the worksheet prints on the printer, type the letter P for Page. Recall that the Page command moves the paper through the printer to the top of the next page.
6. Type the letter Q to quit the /PP command and carefully remove the grading report from the printer.

Erasing the Worksheet from Main Memory

After saving and printing the grading report, erase it from main memory so that you can begin Project 4B. Recall from Project 1, that to erase the current worksheet, enter the command /Worksheet Erase (/WE). Finally, type the letter Y for Yes. 1-2-3 responds by clearing all the cells in the worksheet and changing all the settings to their default values.

PROJECT 4B — DETERMINING THE MONTHLY PAYMENT FOR A CAR LOAN

The car loan payment worksheet is shown in Figures 4-2, 4-3, and 4-4. It is by far the most complex worksheet undertaken thus far. For this reason, we will use the divide and conquer strategy to build it. This strategy involves completing a section of the worksheet and testing it before moving on to the next section. Let's divide the worksheet into five sections:

1. Determine the monthly payment on a five-year loan for a 1993 Chevy Van with a sticker price of $18,500.00, down payment of $4,000.00, at an interest rate of 11.5%—range A1..E7 in Figure 4-2.
2. Display the amortization schedule—range A8..E20 in Figure 4-2.
3. Generate the data table—range F1..H20 in Figure 4-3.
4. Create the simple macros—range A22..E30 in Figure 4-4.
5. Create the multicell macro—range A33..E46 in Figure 4-4.

The first step in determining the car loan payment is to change the column widths. Set the width of column A to 12 characters and set the global width of the columns in the worksheet to 15 characters. Change the widths of the columns as follows:

1. With the cell pointer at A1, enter the command /Worksheet Column Set-Width (/WCS) to change the width of column A to 12 characters.
2. Enter the command /Worksheet Global Column-Width (/WGC). Change the default value 9 on the input line to 15 and press the Enter key.

With the column widths set, enter the worksheet title, the date, the six cell titles, and the five data items in the range A1..E7 (Figure 4-12). Assign cell E1 the NOW function.

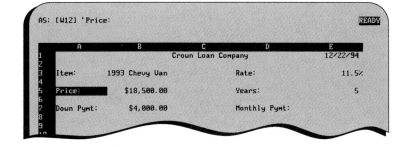

FIGURE 4-12
Labels and data entered into the Crown Loan Company worksheet

Use the command /Range Format (/RF) to change the format of the cells assigned numeric data in the range A1..E7 as follows:

1. Cell E1 to the Long Intn'l (MM/DD/YY) type.
2. Cells B5, B7, and E7 to the Currency type with two decimal positions.
3. Cell E3 to the Percent type with one decimal position.

The formatted worksheet with the cell pointer at A5 is shown in Figure 4-12.

Assigning a Label Name to an Adjacent Cell

In Project 4A we used the command **/R**ange **N**ame **C**reate (/RNC) to assign the name TEST1 to the range B6..B16. Later, when we built the summary lines, we used the name TEST1 several times in functions to reference the range B6..B16, because the name TEST1 is easier to remember than the range B6..B16. Another advantage of using range names is that they make it easier to remember what the range represents in the worksheet. This is especially helpful when you are working with complex formulas or functions.

The function for determining the monthly payment in cell E7 uses the purchase price (B5), down payment (B7), rate (E3), and years (E5). Let's name each of these cells. In this case, we'll use a second technique for assigning names to the individual cells. Rather than typing in a new name for each cell, use the adjacent cell title—the label located immediately to the left of each cell you want to name. For example, use the label Price: in cell A5 to name cell B5.

With the cell pointer at A5, enter the command **/R**ange **N**ame **L**abel (/RNL). By entering the command Label, you instruct 1-2-3 to use a label in the worksheet as the name, rather than to create a new name. With the menu pointer active in the Range Name Label menu (Figure 4-13), type the letter R for Right. This command allows you to assign any adjacent cell to the label name. Typing the letter R tells 1-2-3 to assign the cell to the right of the label name.

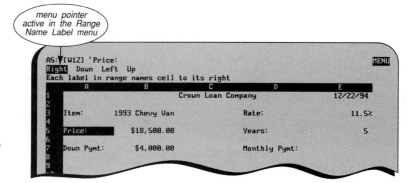

FIGURE 4-13

Display after entering the command **/R**ange **N**ame **L**abel (/RNL)

Next, 1-2-3 requests that the range containing the labels that you want to assign to the cells to the right. Use the Down Arrow key to select the range A5..A7. Press the Enter key. You can now use the name Price: to refer to cell B5 and Down Pymt: to refer to cell B7.

Name cells E3, E5, and E7 in a similar fashion. Move the cell pointer to D3. Enter the command **/R**ange **N**ame **L**abel (/RNL). Type the letter R for Right, select the range D3..D7, and press the Enter key. You can now use Rate: to refer to cell E3, Years: to refer to cell E5, and Monthly Pymt: to refer to cell E7.

Three points to remember about the /RNL command are: first, if a label in a cell is subsequently changed, the old label remains the name of the range; second, numbers cannot be used as range names; and third, 1-2-3 uses only the first 15 characters of the label as the name.

Determining the Loan Payment — PMT

1-2-3 has several financial functions that save you from writing out long, complicated formulas. One of the most important of these is the PMT function. This function determines the payment of a loan on the basis of the amount of the loan (principal), the interest rate (interest), and the length of time required to pay back the loan (term). If the term is in months, the PMT function returns the monthly payment. The general form of the PMT function is:

@PMT(principal,interest,term)

To display the monthly payment of the car loan in cell E7, move the cell pointer to E7 and enter the function:

```
@PMT($Price:-$Down Pymt:,$Rate:/12,12*$Years:)
```

The first argument ($Price:–$Down Pymt:) is the principal. The second argument ($Rate:/12) is the interest rate charged by the Crown Loan Company compounded monthly. The third argument (12*$Years:) is the number of months required to pay back the loan. As illustrated in cell E7 of Figure 4-14, it will cost $318.89 per month for 5 years to purchase the 1993 Chevy Van with a sticker price of $18,500.00, down payment of $4,000.00, at an annual interest rate of 11.5%.

Notice that we preceded all the names in the function arguments with a dollar sign ($). We do this because the function will be copied to another part of the worksheet later, and we want the cell references to remain the same.

Remember, 1-2-3 automatically recalculates the formula in E7 when a new entry is made into a cell referenced in the formula assigned to E7. If you change the purchase price, the amount of the down payment, the interest rate, the number of years, or any combination of these, 1-2-3 immediately adjusts the monthly payment displayed in cell E7.

The Data Fill Feature

The next step is to add the amortization table in cells A8..E16 (Figure 4-2). Enter the double underline in row 8, the column headings in rows 9 and 10, and the single underline in row 11 as shown in Figure 4-15.

In the range A12..A16, the series of numbers 1 though 5 represent the years. You can enter these numbers one at a time or you can use the Data Fill command. The **Data Fill command** allows you to quickly enter a series of numbers into a range using a specified increment or decrement. In this case, the series of numbers in the range A12..A16 that begins with 1, increments by 1, and ends with 5.

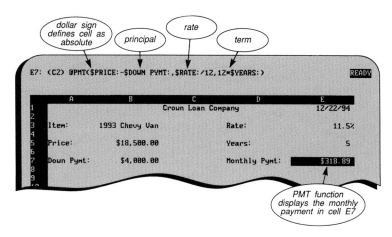

FIGURE 4-14 The PMT function entered into cell E7

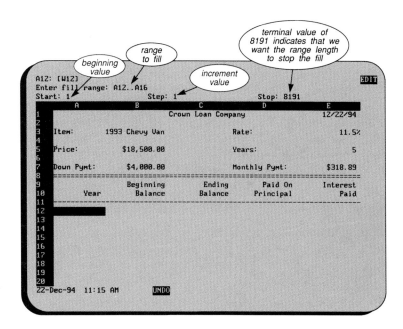

FIGURE 4-15 The display due to entering the command / Data Fill (/DF)

With the cell pointer at A12, enter the command /**D**ata **F**ill (/DF). In response to the prompt message "Enter Fill range: A12" on the input line, press the Period key to anchor the first end point, A12. Use the Down Arrow key to move the cell pointer to the second end point (A16) and press the Enter key. Next, 1-2-3 requests the start, increment, and stop values. In response to the prompt messages on the input line, enter a start value of 1, an increment value of 1, and a stop value of 8191. The length of the range (five cells) will terminate the Data Fill command before it reaches the stop value 8191. The entries are shown at the top of the screen in Figure 4-15.

Press the Enter key and the range A12..A16 is filled with the series of numbers 1 through 5 (Figure 4-16).

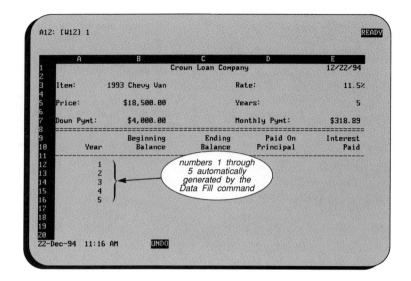

FIGURE 4-16
The display after using the
Data Fill command

Move the cell pointer to B12 and enter the beginning balance for year 1. This value is equal to the amount of the loan, which is +Price:−Down Pymt: or +B5−B7.

Before you enter any more values in the amortization table, format cells B12 through E20 to the Comma (,) type with two decimal positions. The Comma (,) type with two decimal positions displays the numbers in the form of dollars and cents. Although labels will be part of the range (B12..E20), recall that a numeric format is used only if a numeric value is stored in the cell. Enter the command /Range Format , (/RF,). Press the Enter key to select two decimal positions. Enter the range B12..E20 and press the Enter key.

Determining the Yearly Ending Balance — PV

Another important financial function is the PV function. This function returns the present value of an annuity. An annuity is a series of fixed payments made at the end of each of a fixed number of terms at a fixed interest rate. This function can be used to determine how much the borrower of the car loan still owes at the end of each year (C12..C16).

The general form of the PV function is:

@PV(payment,interest,term)

Use this function to determine the ending balance after the first year (C12) by using a term equal to the number of months the borrower must still make payments. For example, if the loan is for five years (60 months, therefore 60 payments), as it is in Figure 4-16, then the borrower still owes 48 payments after the first year. After the second year, the number of payments remaining is 36, and so on.

The entry for cell C12 that determines the ending balance is:

@PV($Monthly Pymt:,$Rate:/12,12*($Years:−A12))

The first argument, $Monthly Pymt:, refers to cell E7, the monthly payment. The second argument, $Rate:/12, refers to the interest rate in cell E3. The third argument, 12*($Years:−A12), indicates the number of monthly payments that still must be made—48 after the first year. Notice that each name in the three arguments of the PV function for cell C12 is preceded by a dollar sign ($). This tells 1-2-3 to treat these cell references as absolute. That is, when 1-2-3 copies the PV function in cell C12 to cells C13 through C16, the cell references in the arguments will not be adjusted.

Making Decisions — The IF Function

If you assign the PV function just described to cell C12 and copy it to cells C13 through C16, the ending balances for each year of a five-year loan will display properly as illustrated in Figure 4-2. If the loan is for a period of time less than five years, the ending balances displayed for the years beyond the time the loan is due are invalid. For example, if a loan is taken out for three years, the ending balance for years four and five in the amortization table should be zero. However, the PV function will display negative values even though the loan has already been paid off.

What is needed is a way to assign the PV function to the range C12..C16 as long as the corresponding year in the range A12..A16 is less than or equal to the number of years in cell E5, which contains the number of years of the loan. If the corresponding year in column A is greater than the number of years in cell E5, cells C12 through C16 must be assigned the value zero. 1-2-3 has a function that can handle this type of decision making. It is called the IF function.

The IF function is useful when the value you want assigned to a cell is dependent on a condition. A **condition** is made up of two expressions and a relation. Each **expression** may be a cell, a number, a label, a function, or a formula.

The general form of the IF function is:

@IF(condition,true,false)

The argument **true** is the value you want to assign to the cell when the condition is true. The argument **false** is the value you want to assign to the cell when the condition is false. For example, assume @IF(A1 = A2,C3 + D4,C3–D4) is assigned to cell B12. If the value assigned to A1 is equal to the value assigned to A2, then the sum of the values in C3 and D4 is assigned to B12. If the value assigned to A1 does not equal the value assigned to A2, then B12 is assigned the difference between the values in C3 and D4.

Valid relations and examples of their use in IF functions are shown in Table 4-3.

TABLE 4-3 Valid Relational Operators and Their Use in Conditions

RELATIONAL OPERATOR	MEANING	EXAMPLE
=	Equal to	@IF(A5 = B7,A22–A3,G5^E3)
<	Less than	@IF(E12/D5 < 6,A15,B13–5)
>	Greater than	@IF(@SUM(A1..A5) > 100,1,0)
< =	Less than or equal to	@IF(A12 < = $YEARS,A4*D5,1)
> =	Greater than or equal to	@IF(@NOW > = 30000,H15,J12)
< >	Not equal to	@IF(5 < >F6,"Valid","Invalid")

The logical operators NOT, AND, and OR also may be used to write a **compound condition**—two or more conditions in the same IF function. A summary of the logical operators is given in Table 4-4. Multiple logical operators in the same compound condition are evaluated from left to right.

TABLE 4-4 Valid Logical Operators and Their Use in Conditions

LOGICAL OPERATOR	MEANING	EXAMPLE
#NOT#	The compound condition is true if, and only if, the simple condition is false.	@IF(#NOT#($A$2 = A6),2,4)
#AND#	The compound condition is true if, and only if, both simple conditions are true.	@IF($J6 = R$4#AND#G5–S2 > D2, D4*D6,T3/D2)
#OR#	The compound condition is true if, and only if, either simple condition is true or both simple conditions are true.	@IF(A1 > $PRINCIPAL#OR#B7 = E4, "Contact","OK")

By using the IF function, you can assign the PV function or zero as the ending balance to cells C12 through C16. In cell C12 enter the IF function:

@IF(A12<=$Years:,@PV($Monthly Pymt:,$Rate:/12,12*($Years:-A12)),0)

condition	*true task*	*false task*

If the condition A12< = $Years: is true, then 1-2-3 assigns C12 the PV function. If the condition is false, then 1-2-3 assigns C12 the value zero.

Use the command /Copy (/C) to copy cell C12 to the range C13..C16. The results of this copy are shown in Figure 4-17.

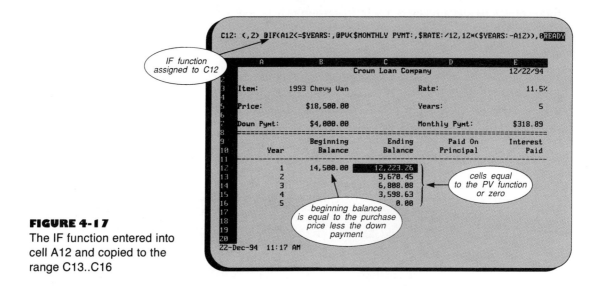

FIGURE 4-17
The IF function entered into cell A12 and copied to the range C13..C16

Let's go back now and complete the entries in the beginning balance column, cells B13 through B16. The beginning balance in B13 is equal to the ending balance in cell C12. Therefore, enter +C12 in cell B13 and copy this cell to B14 through B16. The beginning balance for each year in cells B12 through B16 displays as shown in Figure 4-18.

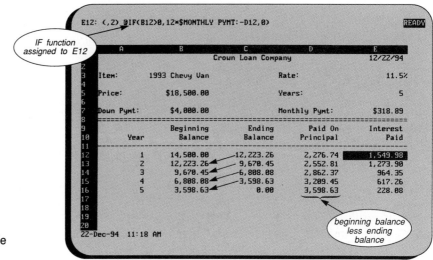

FIGURE 4-18
The amortization table filled in

The total amount paid on the principal each year in column D is determined by subtracting the ending balance from the beginning balance. Enter the formula +B12-C12 in cell D12. Copy cell D12 to cells D13 through D16 (Figure 4-18).

The total amount of interest paid each year by the borrower to the lender in column E is equal to 12 times the monthly payment in cell E7 less the amount paid on the principal. Here again, use the IF function because the loan may be for less than five years. Interest is paid in any year in which the beginning balance is greater than zero. Therefore, in cell E12, enter the IF function @IF(B12>0,12*$Monthly Pymt:-D12,0). Copy cell E12 to cells E13 through E16. The interest paid each year for a loan of $14,500.00 at 11.5% for 5 years is shown in column E of the worksheet in Figure 4-18.

To complete the amortization table, add the single underline in row 17 and the labels that identify the totals in cells C18 through C20. In cell D18, enter the function @SUM(D12..D16). This agrees with the original amount of the loan, $14,500.00. In cell E18, enter the function @SUM(E12..E16). Cell E18 displays the total interest paid for the loan, $4,633.57. In cell E19, enter the name +Down Pymt:. Cell E19 displays $4,000.00, the amount in cell B7. Finally, in cell E20, enter the formula +D18+E18+E19. Cell E20 displays the total cost of the 1993 Chevy Van (Figure 4-19).

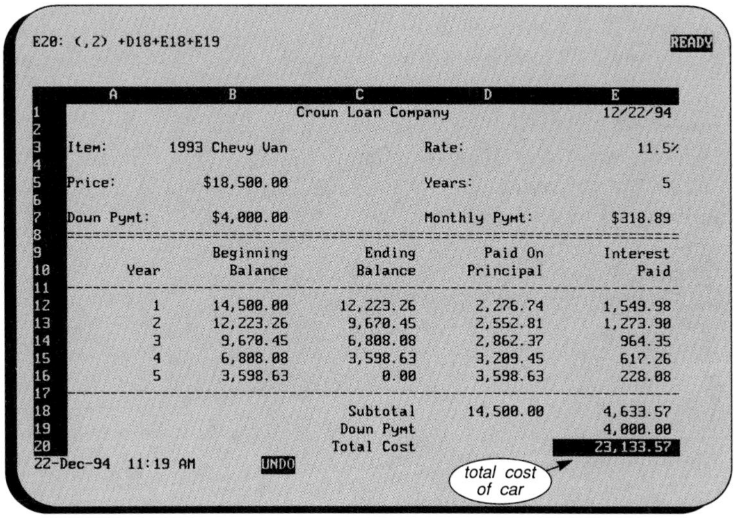

FIGURE 4-19
Part 1 of Project 4B complete

```
E20: (,2) +D18+E18+E19                                              READY

        A              B              C              D              E
1                              Crown Loan Company             12/22/94
2
3  Item:        1993 Chevy Van             Rate:                11.5%
4
5  Price:       $18,500.00                 Years:                  5
6
7  Down Pymt:    $4,000.00                 Monthly Pymt:      $318.89
8  =================================================================
9                 Beginning      Ending       Paid On      Interest
10       Year      Balance       Balance      Principal       Paid
11 ----------------------------------------------------------------
12        1      14,500.00     12,223.26     2,276.74      1,549.98
13        2      12,223.26      9,670.45     2,552.81      1,273.90
14        3       9,670.45      6,808.08     2,862.37        964.35
15        4       6,808.08      3,598.63     3,209.45        617.26
16        5       3,598.63          0.00     3,598.63        228.08
17 ----------------------------------------------------------------
18                             Subtotal     14,500.00      4,633.57
19                             Down Pymt                   4,000.00
20                             Total Cost                 23,133.57
   22-Dec-94  11:19 AM      UNDO                   total cost
                                                   of car
```

With the amortization table complete, try various combinations of loan data to evaluate the what-if capabilities of 1-2-3. If you change the purchase price (B5), down payment (B7), interest rate (E3), term (E5) or any combination of these values, 1-2-3 will immediately change the monthly payment and the numbers in the amortization table.

Saving the Worksheet

Before continuing with Project 4B, save the worksheet as PROJS-4B. Enter the command /File Save (/FS). Enter the file name PROJS-4B and press the Enter key. The worksheet is saved on the default drive.

Using a Data Table to Answer What-If Questions

The next step is to build the data table at the right side of the amortization table (Figure 4-3). A **data table** has one purpose—it organizes the answers to what-if questions into a table. We have already seen that if a value is changed in a cell referenced elsewhere in a formula, 1-2-3 immediately recalculates and stores the new value in the cell assigned the formula. You may want to compare the results of the formula for several different values, but it would be unwieldy to write down or remember all the answers to the what-if questions. This is where a data table comes in handy.

Data tables are built in an unused area of the worksheet. You may vary one or two values and display the results of the specified formulas in table form. Figure 4-20 illustrates the makeup of a data table.

In Project 4B, the data table shows the impact of changing interest rates on the monthly payment and the total cost of the loan. The interest rates range from 8.5% to 15% in increments of 0.5%. Therefore, in this data table we are varying one value, the interest rate (E3). We are interested in its impact on two formulas: the monthly payment (E7) and the total cost (E20).

To construct the data table, enter the headings in the range F1..H5 as described in Figure 4-3. Next, move the cell pointer to F7 and use the command /**D**ata **F**ill (/DF) to enter the varying interest rates. Select the range F7..F20. Use a start value of 8.5%, an increment value of 0.5%, and a stop value of 8191. After you press the Enter key, the range F7..F20 contains the varying interest rates. Format the interest rates to the Percent type with one decimal position (Figure 4-21).

In cell G6 enter +E7, the cell with the monthly payment formula. In cell H6 enter +E20, the cell with the total cost of the loan formula. Format the range G6..H20 to the Comma (,) type with two decimal positions. Move the cell pointer to F6. The range F1..H20 of the worksheet is shown in Figure 4-21.

This cell must be empty	Formula-1	Formula-2	. . .	Formula-k
Value-1				
Value-2	1-2-3 places results of formulas here on the basis of the values in the left-hand column.			
Value-3				
Value-4				
Value-n				

ⓐ **Data table with one value varying**

Assign formula to this cell	Value-2a	Value-2b	. . .	Value-2k
Value-1a				
Value-1b	1-2-3 places results of the formula in the upper left corner cell here on the basis of the two corresponding values.			
Value-1c				
Value-1d				
Value-1n				

ⓑ **Data table with two values varying**

FIGURE 4-20 General forms of a data table with one value varying ⓐ and two values varying ⓑ.

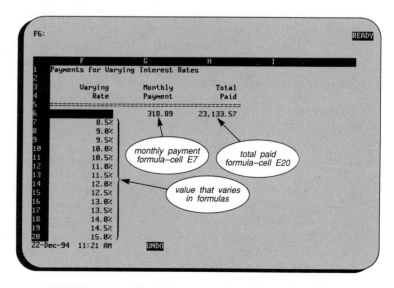

FIGURE 4-21 Monthly payment formula, total paid formula, and varying interest rates entered into the worksheet in preparation for applying a data table in the range F6..H20.

To define the data table, enter the command /**D**ata **T**able **1** (/DT1). 1-2-3 responds by displaying the prompt message "Enter Table range: F6" on the input line. Press the Period key to anchor F6 as one of the end points. Use the arrow keys to move the cell pointer to H20 and press the Enter key. (The data table itself does not include the headings above F6.) 1-2-3 responds with the prompt message "Enter Input cell 1: F6" on the input line. The **input cell** is defined as the cell in the worksheet that contains the value you want to vary. For this data table, vary the interest rate in cell E3 (also called Rate:). Therefore, enter the name `Rate:` in response to the prompt message on the input line and press the Enter key.

The data table, in the range F6..H20, immediately fills with monthly payments and total loan costs for the corresponding varying interest rates, as shown in Figure 4-22.

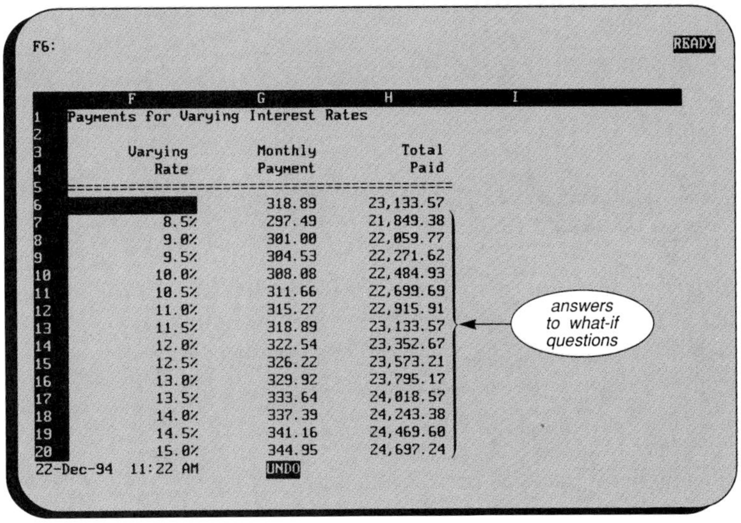
F6: READY

Payments for Varying Interest Rates

	Varying Rate	Monthly Payment	Total Paid
6		318.89	23,133.57
7	8.5%	297.49	21,849.38
8	9.0%	301.00	22,059.77
9	9.5%	304.53	22,271.62
10	10.0%	308.08	22,484.93
11	10.5%	311.66	22,699.69
12	11.0%	315.27	22,915.91
13	11.5%	318.89	23,133.57
14	12.0%	322.54	23,352.67
15	12.5%	326.22	23,573.21
16	13.0%	329.92	23,795.17
17	13.5%	333.64	24,018.57
18	14.0%	337.39	24,243.38
19	14.5%	341.16	24,469.60
20	15.0%	344.95	24,697.24

22-Dec-94 11:22 AM UNDO

FIGURE 4-22
Data table in the range F6..H20 is filled with answers to what-if questions regarding varying interest rates.

Look over the table. Notice how it allows you to compare the monthly payments and total loan costs for different interest rates. For example, at 10%, the monthly payment on the loan of $14,500.00 for 5 years is $308.08. At 10.5%, the monthly payment is $311.66 for the same loan. The two numbers at the top of the table, in cells G6 and H6, are the same as the monthly payment and total cost displayed in cells E7 and E20.

Some important points to remember about data tables are:

1. You can have only one active data table in a worksheet. If you want to move or establish a new data table, use the command /**D**ata **T**able **R**eset (/DTR) to deactivate the current data table.
2. For a data table with one varying value, the cell in the upper left corner of the table (F6) must be empty. With two values varying, assign the formula you want to analyze to the upper left corner cell of the table (Figure 4-20 (b)).
3. If you change any value in a cell referenced by the formula that is part of the data table but does not vary in the data table, you must press function key F8 to instruct 1-2-3 to recalculate the data table values.

MACROS

◆ A **macro** is a series of keystrokes entered into a cell or a range of cells. The macro is assigned a name using the command /**R**ange **N**ame **C**reate (/RNC). Later, when you enter the macro name, the keystrokes stored in the cell or range of cells execute one after another, as if you entered each keystroke manually at the keyboard. A macro can be as simple as the series of keystrokes required to save a worksheet or as complex as a sophisticated computer program.

Whether simple or complex, macros save time and help remove the drudgery associated with building and using a worksheet. You should consider using a macro when you find yourself repeatedly typing the same keystrokes; when the series of keystrokes required is difficult to remember; or if you want to automate the use of the worksheet.

Designing a Simple Macro

In Project 2 we suggested that you save your worksheet every 50 to 75 keystrokes. If you follow this suggestion, you will be frequently entering the series of keystrokes shown in Table 4-5. This is an excellent example of how a macro can save you time and effort.

TABLE 4-5 Series of Keystrokes for Saving a Worksheet Under the Same File Name

KEYSTROKE	PURPOSE
/	Switches 1-2-3 to MENU mode.
F	Selects File command.
S	Selects Save command.
↵	Saves worksheet under the same file name.
R	Replaces the worksheet on disk.

One of the keystrokes in Table 4-5 is the Enter key(↵). In a macro, we use the **tilde character** (˜) to represent the Enter key. Therefore, /FS˜R represents the series of keystrokes in Table 4-5.

After determining the makeup of the macro, the next step is to move the cell pointer to a cell in an unused area of the worksheet. According to Figure 4-4, the macros for this project are to be placed below the amortization table. Hence, use the GOTO command and move the cell pointer to A22.

Documenting Macros

We recommend that all macros be documented, even the simple ones. **Documenting** a macro means writing a comment off to the side of the cell or range containing the macro. The comment explains the purpose of the macro, and if it is complex, how it works. To document this macro, as well as the other macros in this worksheet, first enter the macro title and column headings in cells A22 through E25 (Figure 4-23).

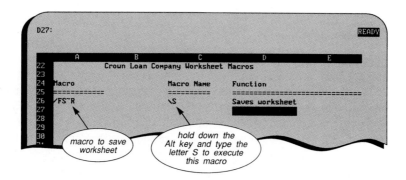

FIGURE 4-23 The macro \S is entered into cell A26 and documented in cells C26 and D26.

Entering and Naming a Macro

Move the cell pointer to A26 and enter the macro '/FS~R. It is important that you begin the macro with an apostrophe or one of the other characters that defines the entry as a label (^, "). If you don't begin the macro with an apostrophe, 1-2-3 immediately switches to MENU mode because the Slash key (/) is the first character entered.

With the macro in cell A26, enter the command **/R**ange **N**ame **C**reate (/RNC) and assign the macro name \S to cell A26. A macro name can consist of up to 15 characters. It is to your advantage, however, to use a name made up of only two characters in which the first character is the backslash (\) and the second character is a letter. In this way you can invoke the macro by holding down the Alt key and pressing the second letter in the macro name. Complete the documentation in cells C26 and D26. Figure 4-23 illustrates the \S macro in cell A26 and the corresponding documentation.

The macro name \0 (zero) has special meaning to 1-2-3. If you name a macro \0, then 1-2-3 automatically executes the macro whenever you first load the worksheet from disk into main memory.

Invoking a Macro

After entering the macro '/FS~R in cell A26 and naming it \S, execute it by pressing Alt-S. 1-2-3 automatically executes the series of keystrokes in cell A26 and saves the worksheet. The \S macro is part of the worksheet that is saved. Hence, the macro will be available the next time you load the worksheet into main memory.

An alternative method of executing macros is to press Alt-F3. Alt-F3 displays a menu of range names at the top of the screen. Select the macro name, in this case, \S, from the menu, and press the Enter key. 1-2-3 immediately executes the \S macro. This second method of invoking a macro *must be used* to execute macros whose names are longer than two characters or begin with a character other than the backslash (\).

Adding More Macros to the Worksheet

When 1-2-3 executes a macro, it starts at the specified cell. After executing the keystrokes in this cell, it inspects the adjacent cells. First it checks the cell below, then the cell to the right. If they are empty, the macro terminates. If they are not empty, 1-2-3 considers the nonempty cell to be part of the macro and executes its contents. Hence, 1-2-3 is finished executing a macro when the cells below and to the right are empty. It is for this reason that when you add additional macros to a worksheet, make sure that there is at least one empty cell between each macro.

With this rule in mind, enter the macro /PPAGPQ in cell A28 and /PPOOCQAGOOAQPQ in cell A30. Also enter the corresponding documentation in cells C28 through D30 (Figure 4-24). Use the command **/R**ange **N**ame **C**reate (/RNC) and assign the names \P to cell A28 and \C to cell A30.

FIGURE 4-24
The macros \P and \C are entered into cells A28 and A30 and documented in the range C28..D30.

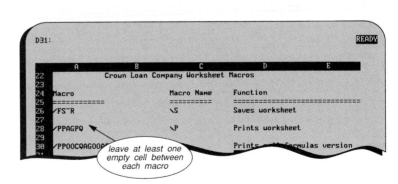

The \P macro in cell A28 prints the worksheet on the basis of the previous printer range setting. It also ejects the paper in the printer and quits the Print command. Build a print macro like this one when you expect to print the worksheet often. To prepare to execute the \P macro, use the **/P**rint **P**rinter **R**ange (/PPR) command to set the range to A1..E20. Invoke the \S macro again to save the print range permanently.

Now, imagine you are the loan officer for the Crown Loan Company. A customer comes in and requests information on the 1993 Chevy Van we discussed earlier. With the monthly payment and the amortization table on the screen, you can print a copy of the loan information and give it to the customer. First, make sure the printer is ready. Next, hold down the Alt key and press the letter P. The monthly payment and amortization table shown in Figure 4-19 prints on the printer.

The \C macro in cell A30 prints the cell-formulas version of the worksheet according to the previously defined printer range. After printing the as-displayed version of the range A1..E20, hold down the Alt key and type the letter C. This invokes the \C macro. Notice that after the printer is done printing the cell-formulas version, the macro resets the print setting to the as-displayed version.

Creating Macros Using the Learn Feature of 1-2-3

1-2-3 has a macro learn feature that automatically records your keystrokes and allows you to test the command sequence at the same time. You enter the keystrokes, such as /PPAGPQ, and 1-2-3 saves the command sequence in a specified cell as a macro. To illustrate the learn feature, let's erase the macro /PPAGPQ in cell A28 by using the command /**R**ange **E**rase (/RE). With cell A28 blank, do the following:

1. Enter the command/**W**orksheet **L**earn **R**ange (/WLR). Specify the range A28..A28.
2. Turn on the learn feature by pressing Alt-F5. The LEARN status indicator displays at the bottom of the screen to inform you that the learn feature is active.
3. Enter the command /PPAGPQ. 1-2-3 carries out the command sequence and prints the range A1..E20 on the printer. (Recall that the range A1..E20 was established earlier.) More importantly, 1-2-3 records the command sequence.
4. Turn off the learn feature by pressing Alt-F5.
5. Press F9 to recalculate the worksheet.

After step 5, the command sequence entered in step 3 is assigned to cell A28. If you hadn't already assigned the name \P to A28, then after step 5 you would name the macro by using the /**R**ange **N**ame **C**reate (/RNC) command.

Guarding Against Macro Catastrophes

Take care when you apply macros to a worksheet. If you enter the wrong letter, forget the tilde (˜) when it's required, place macros in adjacent cells, or transpose characters in a macro, serious damage in the form of lost data can occur. For this reason we recommend you save the worksheet before executing a macro for the first time.

You should also use **STEP mode** of 1-2-3 to test the macro. STEP mode allows you to watch 1-2-3 execute the macro keystroke by keystroke just as if you entered the keystrokes one at a time at the keyboard. Let's execute the \S macro again using STEP mode. To place 1-2-3 in STEP mode, hold down the Alt key and press function key F2. The indicator "STEP" appears on the status line at the bottom of the screen. Next, invoke the \S macro by holding down the Alt key and pressing the S key. With STEP mode active, 1-2-3 displays two items at the bottom of the screen on the left side of the status line: the cell address of the macro being executed and the contents of that cell. Also, the keystroke that corresponds to the command being executed within the macro is highlighted. Now press any key on the keyboard to execute the next keystroke in the macro.

If you encounter an error while in STEP mode, terminate the macro by holding down the Ctrl key and pressing the Break key. Next, press the Esc or Enter key and the macro terminates execution. Edit the macro and execute it once again using STEP mode. Continue in this fashion until the macro is doing exactly what you intend it to do. To quit STEP mode, press Alt-F2. This process of finding and correcting errors in a macro is called debugging.

Macro Commands and Macro Words

The final step in Project 4B is to enter the macro that extends from cell A33 through A46. Before entering this macro, we need to discuss macro commands and macro words. **Macro commands** are used to write programs that can guide you or another user of the worksheet through complex tasks such as accepting data into various cells. Some of the macro commands are listed in Table 4-6. Notice that each macro command is enclosed in curly braces { }. For a complete list of the macro commands, press function key F1 and go to the Help Index of the online help facility. Select the title Macro Command Index from the Help Index. Select subroutine. Press the Enter key to scroll through the macros. Press the Esc key to return to the worksheet.

TABLE 4-6 Frequently Used Macro Commands

COMMAND	EXAMPLE	EXPLANATION
{BRANCH location}	{BRANCH TALL}	Transfers macro control to the macro command with the label TALL.
{GETLABEL prompt,location}	{GETLABEL "Purchase Item: ",B3}	Displays the prompt message "Purchase Item:" followed by a space on the input line, accepts a label, and assigns it to B3.
{GETNUMBER prompt,location}	{GETNUMBER "Purchase Price: ",B5}	Displays the prompt message "Purchase Price:" followed by a space on the input line, accepts a number, and assigns it to B5.
{IF condition}	{IF B10<=40} {BRANCH SHORT}	If cell B10 has a value less than or equal to 40, then macro control transfers to the macro command with the label SHORT, else macro control passes to the cell below.
{QUIT}	{QUIT}	Ends the execution of a macro.
{RETURN}	{RETURN}	Returns control to the command following the corresponding subroutine call.
{subroutine}	{BONUS}	Executes the macro beginning at BONUS. Saves the location of the macro command following {BONUS} for the corresponding {RETURN}.

Macro words are used to handle special circumstances in a macro, like moving the cell pointer from one cell to another. Except for the tilde (˜), which represents the Enter key, all macro words are enclosed in curly braces { }. The frequently used words are listed in Table 4-7. For a complete list of the macro words, load 1-2-3, press function key F1, and select Macro Key Names from the Help Index. After reading or printing the screens, press the Esc key to return to the worksheet.

TABLE 4-7 Frequently Used Macro Words That Represent Special Keys on the Keyboard

CATEGORY	MACRO WORD
Cell pointer	{UP} {DOWN} {RIGHT} {LEFT} {PGUP} {PGDN} {HOME} {END} {BACKSPACE}
Function keys	{EDIT} {NAME} {ABS} {GOTO} {WINDOW} {QUERY} {TABLE} {CALC} {GRAPH}
Special keys	{ESC} {DEL} {INS} {MENU}
Enter key	˜
Interaction	{?}

The cell pointer movement macro words in Table 4-7 move the pointer, as if you pressed the key named within the curly braces. The function key macro words operate the same as pressing one of the function keys. The macro word {?} makes the macro pause and wait for keyboard input from the user. For example, the macro /FR{?} ˜ may be used to retrieve a worksheet from disk. The macro word {?} following /FR tells the macro to pause and wait for the user to select a file name. When you press the Enter key after entering the file name, the macro resumes execution and accepts the name entered on the input line.

Interactive Macros

The macro defined in cells A33 through A46 in Figure 4-4 automates the entry of the loan data in cells B3, B5, B7, E3, and E5. The instructions in cells A34 through A39 clear the cells that contain the loan data. The instructions in cells A40 through A44 prompt the user to enter the loan data. Each {GETLABEL} and {GETNUMBER} command displays a prompt message and halts the execution of the macro until the user responds by entering a value on the input line. {QUIT} in cell A46 terminates the macro.

Enter the macro and documentation in the range A33..D46 as shown in Figure 4-4. Use the command /**R**ange **N**ame **C**reate (/RNC) and assign cell A33 the macro name \D. It is not necessary to assign the range A33..A46 to the macro name \D, since a macro executes downward until it comes across an empty cell. Invoke the \D macro and reenter the loan data for the 1993 Chevy Van shown in Figure 4-19. In a step-by-step fashion, Table 4-8 explains how the \D macro works. Use Table 4-8 to step through the macro activity when you execute it.

TABLE 4-8 Step-by-Step Explanation of the \D Macro in the Range A33..A46

STEP	CELL	ENTRY	FUNCTION
1	A33	{HOME}	Moves the cell pointer to A1.
2	A34	{GOTO}B3˜/RE˜	Moves the cell pointer to B3 and erases the contents.
3	A35	{DOWN}{DOWN}/RE˜	Moves the cell pointer to B5 and erases the contents.
4	A36	{DOWN}{DOWN}/RE˜	Moves the cell pointer to B7 and erases the contents.
5	A37	{GOTO}E3˜/RE˜	Moves the cell pointer to E3 and erases the contents.
6	A38	{DOWN}{DOWN}/RE˜	Moves the cell pointer to E5 and erases the contents.
7	A39	{HOME}	Moves the cell pointer to A1.
8	A40	{GETLABEL "Purchase Item: ",B3} ˜	Accepts the purchase item (1993 Chevy Van) and assigns it to cell B3.
9	A41	{GETNUMBER "Purchase Price: ",B5} ˜	Accepts the purchase price (18500) and assigns it to cell B5.
10	A42	{GETNUMBER "Down Payment : ",B7} ˜	Accepts the down payment (4000) and assigns it to cell B7.
11	A43	{GETNUMBER "Interest Rate in %: ",E3} ˜	Accepts the interest rate (11.5) and assigns it to cell E3.
12	A44	{GETNUMBER "Time in Years: ",E5} ˜	Accepts the time (5) and assigns it to cell E5.
13	A45	{HOME}	Moves the cell pointer to A1.
14	A46	{QUIT}	Quits the macro.

WINDOWS

◆ When you have a large worksheet like the one in Project 4B, it is helpful to view two parts of the worksheet at one time. 1-2-3 lets you divide the screen into two horizontal windows or two vertical windows. For example, by dividing the screen into two horizontal windows, you can view the \D macro in cells A33..A46 and the cells (A1..E7) that are affected by this macro at the same time.

To show two windows, press the Home key and use the arrow keys to move the cell pointer to A8. Enter the command /**W**orksheet **W**indow **H**orizontal (/WWH). The rows above row 8 display in the top window and rows 8 through 19 display in the lower window.

Immediately after a window split, the cell pointer is active in the window above or to the right of the split. You can move the cell pointer from window to window by pressing function key F6. Press function key F6 and use the Page Down and Down Arrow keys to move the cell pointer to A44. As shown in Figure 4-25, the top window shows the cells that are modified by the \D macro in the lower window.

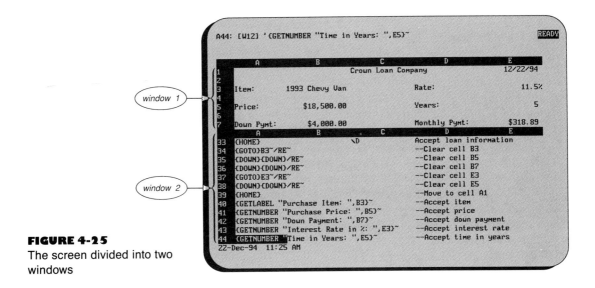

FIGURE 4-25
The screen divided into two windows

Press function key F6 to move the cell pointer to the top window. Execute the \D macro a second time. Step through the macro in the lower window and watch the cells change in the top window.

It is important to understand that the entire worksheet is available through any window. If you make a change to a cell in one window, the change will show up in any other window. Table 4-9 summarizes the window commands available when you enter the command /**W**orksheet **W**indow (/WW).

TABLE 4-9 A Summary of Commands in the Worksheet Window Menu

COMMAND	FUNCTION
Horizontal	Splits the screen from side to side.
Vertical	Splits the screen from top to bottom.
Sync	Causes windows that are aligned horizontally or vertically to scroll together.
Unsync	Causes each window to scroll independently.
Clear	Returns the screen to a single window.

Synchronizing Windows

If you look closely at the two windows in Figure 4-25, you'll notice that they are synchronized, that is, the same column letters are aligned in both windows. The windows scroll together. You can unsynchronize the windows so that they scroll independent of one another. To unsynchronize the windows, enter the command /Worksheet Window Unsync (/WWU). To synchronize the windows after unsynchronizing them, enter the command /Worksheet Window Sync (/WWS).

Clearing the Windows

To return to the normal worksheet display with one window, enter the command /Worksheet Window Clear (/WWC). This command switches the screen from two windows back to one window.

CELL PROTECTION

◆ Cells are either protected or unprotected. When you create a new worksheet, all cells are unprotected. **Unprotected cells** are cells whose values may be changed at any time, but **protected cells** cannot be changed. If a cell is protected and the user attempts to change its value, the computer beeps and 1-2-3 displays the error message "Protected cell" on the status line at the bottom of the screen.

Once the worksheet has been fully tested and displays the correct results, you should protect the cells that you don't want changed by mistake. You should protect cells that contain information that will not change or is unlikely to change, cells that contain macros, and cells whose values are determined by formulas. In the case of Project 4B, we want to protect all the cells in the worksheet except for B3, B5, B7, E3, E5, and the data table in the range F6..H20.

The first step in protecting cells is to protect all the cells in the worksheet. Once all the cells are protected, you can be selective and *unprotect* those that you want to change. To protect all the cells in the worksheet, enter the command /Worksheet Global Protection Enable (/WGPE). Next, move the cell pointer to B3. Enter the command /Range Unprotect (/RU). Press the Enter key when 1-2-3 requests the range to unprotect. Do the same for cells B5, B7, E3, and E5. Finally, move the cell pointer to F6 and unprotect the range F6..H20, which contains the data table information.

You can check whether a cell is unprotected by moving the cell pointer to the cell in question. The letter U displays on the mode line at the top of the screen if the cell is unprotected. The letters PR display if the cell is protected. If you mistakenly unprotect the wrong cell, you may protect it by using the command /Range Protect (/RP). This command is meaningless unless global protection has been enabled (turned on).

If for some reason you need to modify the cells that are in a protected area, such as the macros, disable (turn off) global protection by using the command /Worksheet Global Protection Disable (/WGPD). Once you are finished modifying the cells, enable (turn on) global protection. The worksheet will be protected exactly as it was before you disabled (turned off) global protection.

Saving and Printing the Worksheet

To save the Crown Loan Company worksheet to disk with the cells protected, invoke the \S macro by holding down the Alt key and pressing the S key. To obtain a printed version of the worksheet,

1. Enter the command /Print Printer Range (/PPR) and select the range A1..H46.
2. Type the letter Q to quit the Print menu.
3. Invoke the \P macro by holding down the Alt key and typing the letter P.

1-2-3 prints the three parts of the worksheet on multiple pages. After the printer stops, carefully remove the Crown Loan Company worksheet from the printer. The complete worksheet is shown in Figures 4-2, 4-3, and 4-4.

OBTAINING A SUMMARY OF ALL THE 1-2-3 FUNCTIONS

◆ 1-2-3 has over 100 useful functions. We have discussed those most widely used. You may find the others to be useful in certain situations. For a complete listing and description of the functions available, load 1-2-3 and press function key F1. Select the title @Function Index. Press the Up Arrow key once when the @Function Index displays. Select @Function by Categories at the bottom of the screen. Print the screen for each category of functions by pressing the Print Screen key. After you are finished, press the Esc key to return to the worksheet.

PROJECT SUMMARY

In Project 4 we developed two worksheets. Project 4A introduced you to statistical functions and range names. Project 4B taught you how to use the IF, PMT, and PV functions, the data fill feature, data tables, and macros. You also learned how to protect cells in the worksheet and how to use multiple windows to see different parts of the worksheet at the same time. All the activities that you learned for this project are summarized in the Quick Reference following the Appendix. The following is a summary of the keystroke sequence we used in Projects 4A and 4B.

SUMMARY OF KEYSTROKES — PROJECT 4A

STEPS	KEY(S) PRESSED	RESULTS
1	/WGC → → ←	Sets width of all columns to 11.
2	/WCS → → ←	Sets width of column A to 13.
3	DP 101 → → Grading Report → → →	Enters report title in row 1.
4	@NOW ←/RFD1 ←	Enters NOW function in F1 and formats F1 to Date 1.
5	F5 B3 ← "Test 1 → "Test 2 → "Test 3 → "Total → "Percent ←	Enters column titles in row 3.
6	F5 A4 ← Student → 139 → 142 → 150 → → "Correct ←	Enters column titles and total test points in row 4.
7	F5 A5 ← \ = ←/C ← . → → → → → → ←	Underlines column titles.
8	↓ '1035 → 121 → 127 → 142 ←	Enters student 1035 ID and test scores.
9	F5 A7 ← '1074 → 114 → 113 → 132 ←	Enters student 1074 ID and test scores.
10	F5 A8 ← '1265 → 79 → 97 → 101 ←	Enters student 1265 ID and test scores.
11	F5 A9 ← '1345 → 85 → 106 → 95 ←	Enters student 1345 ID and test scores.
12	F5 A10 ← '1392 → 127 → 124 → 120 ←	Enters student 1392 ID and test scores.
13	F5 A11 ← '3167 → 101 → 120 → 109 ←	Enters student 3167 ID and test scores.
14	F5 A12 ← '3382 → 110 → 104 → 120 ←	Enters student 3382 ID and test scores.
15	F5 A13 ← '3597 → 92 → 104 → 100 ←	Enters student 3597 ID and test scores.
16	F5 A14 ← '4126 → 105 → 100 → 96 ←	Enters student 4126 ID and test scores.
17	F5 A15 ← '5619 → 125 → 135 → 143 ←	Enters student 5619 ID and test scores.
18	F5 A16 ← '7561 → 112 → 130 → 123 ←	Enters student 7561 ID and test scores.

(continued)

SUMMARY OF KEYSTROKES — PROJECT 4A (continued)

STEPS	KEY(S) PRESSED	RESULTS
19	[F5] A17↵\-↵/C↵.→→→→→↵	Underlines students' test scores in A6..F16.
20	↓Count↓Lowest Grade↓Highest Grade↓Average Score↓Std Deviation↓Variance↵ [Home]	Enters row titles in column A below students' scores and moves cell pointer to A1.
21	[F5] E4↵@SUM(B4.D4)↵	Sums total test scores (B4..D4) in E4.
22	/C↵E6.E16↵	Copies E4 to E6..E16.
23	[F5] F6↵+E6/$E$4*100↵	Assigns formula +E6/$E$4*100 to F6.
24	/C↵F6.F16↵	Copies F6 to F6..F16.
25	/RFF1↵F6.F16↵	Sets format of F6..F16 to Fixed.
26	[F5] B6↵/RNCTEST1↵B6.B16↵	Assigns the range name TEST1 to B6..B16.
27	[F5] B18↵@COUNT(TEST1)↓@MIN(TEST1)↓@MAX(TEST1)↓	Assigns @COUNT(TEST1), @MIN(TEST1), and @MAX(TEST1) to B18, B19, and B20.
28	@AVG(TEST1)↓@STD(TEST1)↓@VAR(TEST1)↵	Assigns @AVG(TEST1), @STD(TEST1), and @VAR(TEST1) to B21, B22, and B23.
29	/CB18.B23↵C18.E23↵	Copies B18..B23 to C18..E23.
30	/RFF1↵↑↑→→→→↵	Sets format of B21..E23 to Fixed.
31	/FSPROJS-4A↵	Saves worksheet as PROJS-4A.
32	[Home] /PPRA1.F23↵	Sets A1..F23 as the print range.
33	AGPQ	Prints the worksheet.
34	/WEY	Erases the worksheet.

SUMMARY OF KEYSTROKES — PROJECT 4B

STEPS	KEY(S) PRESSED	RESULTS
1	/WCS12↵	Sets width of column A to 12.
2	/WGC15↵	Sets global width to 15.
3	→→Crown Loan Company→→	Enters report title in C1.
4	@NOW↵/RFD4↵	Enters NOW function in E1 and formats E1 to Date 4.
5	[F5] A3↵Item:↓↓Price:↓↓Down Pymt:↵	Enters row titles in A3, A5, and A7.
6	[F5] D3↵Rate:↓↓Years:↓↓Monthly Pymt:↵	Enters row titles in D3, D5, and D7.
7	[F5] B3↵'1993 Chevy Van↓↓18500↓↓4000↵/RFC.↑↑↵	Enters loan data in B3, B5, and B7. Sets format of B5 and B7 to Comma (,).
8	[F5] E3↵11.5%↵/RFP1↵↵↓↓5↓↓/RFC↵↵	Enters loan data in E3, E5, and E7. Sets format of E3 to Percent. Sets format of E7 to Comma (,).
9	[F5] A5↵/RNLR.↓↓↵	Assigns label names in A5..A7 to B5..B7.
10	[F5] D3↵/RNLR.↓↓↓↓↵	Assigns label names in D3..A7 to E3..E7.
11	[F5] E7↵@PMT($Price:-$Down Pymt:,$Rate:/12,$Years:*12)↵	Assigns PMT function to E7.
12	[F5] A8↵\=↵/C↵.→→→→→↵	Underlines loan information in A1..E7.
13	[F5] B9↵"Beginning→"Ending→"Paid On→"Interest↓	Enters column titles in row 9.

SUMMARY OF KEYSTROKES — PROJECT 4B (continued)

STEPS	KEY(S) PRESSED	RESULTS
14	"Paid← "Principal ← "Balance← "Balance← "Year↓	Enters column titles in row 10.
15	\-←/C←.→ → → → ←	Underlines column titles in A9..E10.
16	↓/DF.↓↓↓↓←1←←	Generates numbers 1 through 5 in A12..A16.
17	→+Price:-Down Pymt:←	Assigns beginning balance to B12.
18	/RF,←B12.E20←	Sets format of B12..E20 to Comma (,).
19	→@IF(A12<=$YEARS:,@PV($Monthly Pymt:, $Rate:/12,12*($Years:-A12)),0)←	Assigns ending balance to C12.
20	/C←.↓↓↓↓←	Copies C12 to C12..C16.
21	↓←+C12←/C←.↓↓↓←	Assigns C12 to B13 and copies B13 to B13..B16.
22	(F5) D12←+B12-C12←/C←.↓↓↓↓←	Assigns +B12-C12 to D12 and copies D12 to D12..D16.
23	→@IF(B12>0,12*$Monthly Pymt:-D12,0) ←/C←.↓↓↓↓←	Assigns interest paid to E12 and copies E12 to E12..E16.
24	(F5) A17←\-←/C←.→ → → → ←	Underlines amortization table tin A9..E17.
25	(F5) C18←"Subtotal↓"Down Pymt↓ "Total Cost←	Enters row titles to C18..C20.
26	(F5) D18←@SUM(D12.D16)→	Assigns sum of D12..D16 to D18.
27	@SUM(E12.E16)↓	Assigns sum of E12..E16 to E18.
28	+Down Pymt:↓	Assigns down payment to E19.
29	+D18+E18+E19←	Assigns total cost of car to E20.
30	/FSPROJS-4B←	Saves worksheet as PROJS-4B.
31	(F5) F1←Payments for Varying Interest Rates↓↓	Enters data table title in F1.
32	"Varying→ "Monthly→ "Total↓	Enters data table column titles in F3..H3.
33	"Paid← "Payment ← "Rate↓	Enters data table column titles in F4..H4.
34	\=→\=→\=↓	Underlines data table column titles in F3..H4.
35	(F5) F7←/DFF7.F20←8.5%←0.5%←←	Generates numbers .085 to .15 in increments of .05 in the range F7..F20.
36	/RFP1←F7.F20←	Sets format of F7..F20 to Percent.
37	↑→+E7→+E20←	Assigns monthly payment in E7 to G6 and total amount paid in E20 to H6.
38	/RF,←G6.H20←	Sets format of G6..H20 to Comma (,).
39	/DT1H6.F20←Rate:←	Defines G6..H20 as data table 1 with the rate in E3 (Rate:) varying.
40	(F5) A22←→Crown Loan Company Worksheet Macros←	Enters title of area in worksheet where macros will be defined.
41	(F5) A24←Macro→ →Macro Name→Function↓	Enters macro column titles in A24..D24.
42	\=→\=←←=========←←\=↓	Underlines macro column titles in A24..D24.
43	'/FS~R→ →'\S→Saves worksheet under same name←	Enters save worksheet macro, name of macro, and documentation in A26, C26, and D26.
44	←←←/RNC\S←←	Names macro in A26 \S.
45	(Alt-S)	Executes \S macro to save worksheet.

(continued)

SUMMARY OF KEYSTROKES — PROJECT 4B (continued)

STEPS	KEY(S) PRESSED	RESULTS
46	↓↓'/PPAGPQ→→'\P→Prints worksheet↵	Enters print worksheet macro, name of macro, and documentation in A28, C28, and D28.
47	←←←/RNC\P↵↵	Names macro in A28 \P.
48	↓↓'/PPOOCQAGOOAQPQ→→'\C→Prints cell-formulas version↵	Enters print cell-formulas macro, name of macro, and documentation in A30, C30, and D30.
49	←←←/RNC\c↵↵	Names macro in A30 \C.
50	/PPRA1.E20↵Q	Sets A1..E20 as the print range.
51	[Alt-P]	Executes \P macro to print worksheet.
52	[Alt-C]	Executes \C macro to print cell-formulas version of worksheet.
53	↓↓↓{HOME}→→'\D→Accept loan information↵	Enters step 1 of macro, name of macro, and documentation in A33, C33, and D33.
54	←←←/RNC\D↵↵	Names macro beginning in A33 \D.
55	↓{GOTO}B3~/RE~→→→'--Clear cell B3↵	Enters step 2 of macro and documentation in A34 and D34.
56	[F5] A35↵{DOWN}{DOWN}/RE~→→→ '--Clear cell B5↵	Enters step 3 of macro and documentation in A35 and D35.
57	[F5] A36↵/CA35↵A36↵→→→'--Clear cell B7↵	Enters step 4 of macro and documentation of A36 and D36.
58	[F5] A37↵{GOTO}E3~/RE~→→→'--Clear cell E3↵	Enters step 5 of macro and documentation of A37 and D37.
59	[F5] A38↵{DOWN}{DOWN}/RE~→→→ '--Clear cell E5↵	Enters step 6 of macro and documentation of A38 and D38.
60	[F5] A39↵{HOME}→→→'--Move to cell A1↵	Enters step 7 of macro and documentation of A39 and D39.
61	[F5] A40↵{GETLABEL "Purchase Item: ",B3}~ →→→'--Accept purchase item↵	Enters step 8 of macro and documentation of A40 and D40.
62	[F5] A41↵{GETNUMBER "Purchase Price: ", B5}~→→→'--Accept purchase price↵	Enters step 9 of macro and documentation of A41 and D41.
63	[F5] A42↵{GETNUMBER "Down Payment: ",B7}~ →→→'--Accept down payment↵	Enters step 10 of macro and documentation of A42 and D42.
64	[F5] A43↵{GETNUMBER "Interest Rate in %: ", E3}~→→→'--Accept interest rate↵	Enters step 11 of macro and documentation of A43 and D43.
65	[F5] A44↵{GETNUMBER "Time in Years: ",E5}~ →→→'--Accept time in years↵	Enters step 12 of macro and documentation of A44 and D44.
66	[F5] A45↵{HOME}→→→'--Move to cell A1↵	Enters step 13 of macro and documentation of A45 and D45.
67	[F5] A46↵{QUIT}→→→'--End of macro↵	Enters step 14 of macro and documentation of A46 and D46.
68	[Alt-D] 1993 Chevy Van↵18500↵4000↵ 11.5%↵5↵	Executes \D macro and enters requested loan information.
69	/WGPE	Enables cell protection.
70	→↓↓/RU↵	Unprotects B3.
71	↓↓/RU↵	Unprotects B5.
72	↓↓/RU↵	Unprotects B7.

SUMMARY OF KEYSTROKES — PROJECT 4B (continued)

STEPS	KEY(S) PRESSED	RESULTS
73	[F5] E3 ↵ /RU ↵	Unprotects E3.
74	↓↓/RU ↵	Unprotects E5.
75	[F5] F6 ↵ /RUF6.H20 ↵ [Home]	Unprotects data table in F6..H20.
76	[Alt-S]	Executes \S macro to save worksheet.
77	/PPRA1.H46 ↵ Q	Sets A1..H46 as the print range.
78	[Alt-P]	Executes \P macro to print worksheet.

The following list summarizes the material covered in Project 4.

1. If you intend to reference a range repeatedly, assign a name to it. To name a range, use the command /**R**ange Name Create (/RNC).
2. The Range Name command allows you to create range names, delete range names, assign labels as range names, clear all range names, and insert the list of range names in the worksheet. Refer to Table 4-1.
3. Several statistical functions in 1-2-3 are AVG, COUNT, MAX, MIN, STD, and VAR. Refer to Table 4-2.
4. The command /**R**ange Name Label (/RNL) allows you to assign a label in a cell as the name of the cell immediately above, below, to the right, or to the left.
5. The PMT function determines the payment of a loan on the basis of the amount of the loan (principal), the interest rate (interest), and the length of time required to pay back the loan (term). The general form of the PMT function is @PMT(principal,interest,term).
6. The command /**D**ata Fill (/DF) allows you to quickly enter a series of numbers into a range using a specified increment or decrement.
7. The PV function can be used to return the amount the borrower still owes at the end of a period at any time during the life of a loan. The general form of the PV function is @PV(payment,interest,term).
8. The general form of the IF function is @IF(condition,true,false). When the IF function is assigned to a cell, the value displayed will depend on the condition. If the condition is **true**, the cell is assigned the true value. If the condition is **false**, the cell is assigned the false value.
9. A **condition** is made up of two expressions and a relation. Each **expression** may be a number, label (in quotation marks), function, or formula. Refer to Table 4-3 for a list of the valid relations.
10. The true and false values in an IF function may be a number, label (in quotation marks), function, or formula.
11. A **compound condition** is one that includes a logical operator like #AND#, #OR#, and #NOT#. Refer to Table 4-4 for examples. Multiple logical operators in the same compound condition are evaluated from left to right.
12. A **data table** is used to automate asking what-if questions and organize the values returned by 1-2-3.
13. A data table may have one value or two varying values. The **input cell** is defined as the cell in the worksheet that contains the value to vary.
14. A **macro** is a series of keystrokes entered into a cell or range of cells. The macro is assigned a name using the command /**R**ange Name Create (/RNC).
15. A macro name can consist of 15 characters. Execute a macro by pressing Alt-F3. Select the desired macro from the list displayed.
16. If the macro name is two characters long with the first character the backslash (\) and the second character a letter, then you can execute the macro by holding down the Alt key and pressing the key that corresponds to the second letter in the macro name. If you name a macro \0 (zero), then 1-2-3 automatically executes the macro whenever the worksheet is first loaded from disk into main memory.
17. If you have more than one macro associated with a worksheet, each macro should be separated by an empty cell.
18. The **tilde character** (˜) is used to represent the Enter key in a macro.
19. All macros should be documented. **Documenting** a macro means writing a comment off to the side of the cell or range containing the macro.
20. Use the learn feature of 1-2-3 to enter and test macros at the same time.

21. A poorly designed macro can damage a worksheet. Before you execute a new macro, save the worksheet. To test a macro, place 1-2-3 in **STEP mode**, hold down the Alt key, and press function key F2. When you are finished testing the macro, hold down the Alt key and press function key F2 to toggle STEP mode off.

22. If you encounter an error in a macro while in STEP mode, hold down the Ctrl key and press the Break key to stop the macro followed by the Esc or Enter key.

23. **Macro commands** are used to write programs. Refer to Table 4-6.

24. **Macro words** represent special keys, like the pointer movement and function keys. Refer to Table 4-7.

25. 1-2-3 allows you to divide the screen into two windows for viewing different parts of the worksheet at the same time. Use the command /**Worksheet Window** (/WW). Refer to Table 4-9.

26. **Unprotected cells** are cells whose values may be changed at any time, but **protected cells** cannot be changed.

27. To protect cells in a worksheet that you do not want the user to change, enter the command /**Worksheet Global Protection Enable** (/WGPE). Once all the cells in the worksheet are protected, use the command /**Range Unprotect** (/RU) to unprotect the cells you want the user to be able to change. If you unprotect the wrong cell, use the command /**Range Protect** (/RP) to protect it.

28. To correct the values in protected cells, enter the command /**Worksheet Global Protection Disable** (/WGPD). After the cells are corrected, enable (turn on) global protection. 1-2-3 remembers the cells you unprotected earlier.

STUDENT ASSIGNMENTS

STUDENT ASSIGNMENT 1: True/False

Instructions: Circle T if the statement is true and F if the statement is false.

T   F   1. If there are seven cells in range R and five of the cells each have a value of 5 and two of the cells are empty, then the function @AVG(R) returns a value of 5.

T   F   2. A data table allows you to automate what-if questions.

T   F   3. You may assign a single cell a name using the /**Range Name Create** (/RNC) command.

T   F   4. The @MIN(R) function returns the smallest number in the range R.

T   F   5. To fill a range from top to bottom with the sequence of numbers 1, 2, 3, 4, and 5, use the /**Data Fill** (/DF) command with a start value of 5, a step value of 1, and a stop value of 1.

T   F   6. The command /**Worksheet Erase** (/WE) may be used to erase the contents of the cells in the worksheet.

T   F   7. The PMT function may be used to determine the monthly payment on a loan.

T   F   8. The command /**Range Name Label** (/RNL) is used to name a cell that contains a label.

T   F   9. The learn feature of 1-2-3 is used to enter macros.

T   F   10. You may vary one, two, or three values in a data table.

T   F   11. 1-2-3 recalculates the values in a data table when you press function key F8.

T   F   12. To invoke a macro, hold down one of the Shift keys and type the letter that names the macro.

T   F   13. The logical operator #OR# requires both conditions to be true for the compound condition to be true.

T   F   14. The IF function is used to assign one value or another to a cell on the basis of a condition that may be true or false.

T   F   15. The macro commands allow you to write programs.

T   F   16. The /**Worksheet Window** (/WW) command allows you to divide the screen into two windows.

T   F   17. To protect cells in the worksheet, global protection must be disabled (turned off).

T   F   18. Each macro should be separated by at least one empty cell.

T   F   19. STEP mode is used to enter a macro into a cell.

T   F   20. To name a macro, use the /**Range Name Create** (/RNC) command.

STUDENT ASSIGNMENT 2: Multiple Choice

Instructions: Circle the correct response.

1. Which one of the following functions is used to assign one value or another value to a cell on the basis of a condition?
   a. IF b. FALSE c. CHOOSE d. TRUE
2. Which one of the following functions returns the payment on a loan?
   a. PMT b. TERM c. PV d. RATE
3. Which one of the following functions returns the average of the numbers in a range?
   a. MAX b. COUNT c. AVG d. MIN
4. Which one of the following allows you to assign a name to one or more adjacent cells?
   a. /**R**ange Name Label (/RNL)   c. /**R**ange Name Create (/RNC)
   b. /**W**orksheet Name Create (/WNC)   d. /**R**ange Name Table (/RNT)
5. Which one of the following relations is used to represent not equal to?
   a. < > b. > c. < d. none of these
6. Which one of the following is used to instruct 1-2-3 to terminate the Data Fill command?
   a. the last cell in the selected range terminates the command
   b. the STOP parameter terminates the command
   c. either a or b can terminate the command
   d. none of the above
7. Which one of the following characters represents the Enter key in a macro?
   a. backslash (\) b. curly braces ({ }) c. circumflex (^) d. tilde (~)
8. Which one of the following turns the learn feature of 1-2-3 on and off?
   a. Alt-F9 b. Alt-F5 c. Alt-F7 d. Alt-F2

STUDENT ASSIGNMENT 3: Understanding Functions

Instructions: Enter the correct answers.

1. Write a function that will determine the monthly payment on a loan of $75,000, over a period of 20 years, at an interest rate of 8.4% compounded monthly.

   Function: _____

2. Write a function that will display the largest value in the range F1..F13.

   Function: _____

3. Write a function that will find the average of the nonempty cells in the range C18..F18.

   Function: _____

4. Write a function that will count the nonempty cells in the range C12..C43.

   Function: _____

5. When there are multiple logical operators in a compound condition, 1-2-3 determines the truth value of each simple condition. It then evaluates the logical operators left to right. Determine the truth value of the compound conditions below, given the following cell values: E1 = 500 F1 = 500 G1 = 2 H1 = 50 I1 = 40
   a. E1<400#OR#G1 = 1   Truth value: _____
   b. F1<300#AND#I1<50#OR#G1 = 2   Truth value: _____
   c. #NOT#(F1>600)#OR#G1 = 0#AND#I1 = 40 Truth value: _____
   d. E1 + F1 = 800#AND#H1*4/10 = 30   Truth value: _____

Student Assignment 3 (continued)

6. The cell pointer is at F15. Write a function that assigns the value zero or 1 to cell F15. Assign zero to cell F15 if the value in cell B3 is greater than the value in cell C12, else assign 1 to cell F15.

   Function: _____

7. The cell pointer is at F15. Write a function that assigns the value Credit OK or Credit Not OK to cell F15. Assign the label Credit OK if the value in cell A1 is not equal to the value in cell B1 or the value of cell C12 is less than 500. If both conditions are false, assign the label Credit Not OK.

   Function: _____

STUDENT ASSIGNMENT 4: Understanding Macros

Instructions: Enter the correct answers.

1. Describe the function of each of the following macros.
   a. /FS˜R/QY

      Function of macro: _____

   b. /RE˜

      Function of macro: _____

   c. /RFC2˜{?}˜

      Function of macro: _____

   d. /C˜{?}˜

      Function of macro: _____

   e. /PPOML2˜MR78˜Q

      Function of macro: _____

   f. /PPR{?}˜AGPQ

      Function of macro: _____

   g. {DOWN}{DOWN}/RE˜

      Function of macro: _____

   h. /DF{?}˜1˜2˜˜

      Function of macro: _____

2. Describe the function of each of the following macro commands and macro words.

a. tilde (˜)   Function: _____   g. {UP}   Function: _____

b. curly braces ({})   Function: _____   h. {QUIT}   Function: _____

c. {GETNUMBER}   Function: _____   i. {IF}   Function: _____

d. {?}   Function: _____   j. Alt-F2   Function: _____

e. {HOME}   Function: _____   k. Alt-F3   Function: _____

f. {GOTO}   Function: _____   l. Alt-F5   Function: _____

STUDENT ASSIGNMENT 5: Using the Data Fill Command

Instructions: Enter the worksheet illustrated in the following figure. The worksheet is a multiplication table. Change the global width of the columns to 6 characters. Use the Data Fill command twice, once to enter the numbers 1 to 18 in column A, and once to enter the numbers 2 to 22 by 2 in row 1. Enter the formula $A3*B$1 in cell B3. Copy the formula to the range B3..L20. Save the worksheet as STUS4-5. Print the as-displayed version of the worksheet. Format all the cells in the worksheet to the Text type and print the worksheet.

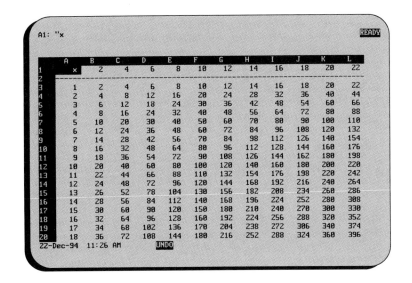

STUDENT ASSIGNMENT 6: Using the Data Table Command

Instructions: Create the worksheets as described in Parts 1 and 2.

Part 1: The worksheet illustrated in the following figure contains a data table with one value (time) varying. At the top of the worksheet, the PMT function is used to determine the monthly mortgage payment for a loan of $100,000.00 at 9.5% annual interest for 30 years. The data table indicates the monthly payment for the same loan for different terms (10 years, 15 years, 20 years).

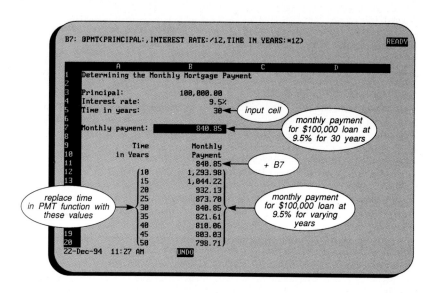

Do the following to create the worksheet in the figure:

a. Increase the global column width to 17.

b. Format the entire worksheet to the Comma (,) type with two decimal places.

c. Enter the labels and numeric values in the range A1 through B5 and in cell A7. Format cell B4 to the Percent type with one decimal position. Format cell B5 to the Fixed type with zero decimal positions.

d. Use the Range Name Label command to assign the labels in cells A3 through A7 to B3 through B7.

e. Assign the PMT function shown on the input line in the previous figure to cell B7.

f. Enter the labels in the range A9..B10.

g. Use the Data Fill command to enter the multiples of five shown in the range A12..A20. Format A12..A20 to the Fixed type with zero decimal positions.

h. Assign cell B11 the formula +B7.

i. Use the command /Data Table 1 (/DT1) to create a data table in the range A11..B20. Use B5 (time in years) as the input cell.

j. After the data table displays, save the worksheet using the file name STUS4-6A.

k. Print the worksheet.

l. Select and enter several other sets of numbers into cells B3, B4, and B5. When necessary, use function key F8 to reset the data table.

Part 2: The worksheet illustrated in the following figure contains a data table with two values varying. It also uses the FV function in cell B7 to determine the future value of a fund. The FV function tells you how much money you will have in a fund if you pay a fixed payment and earn a fixed interest rate over a period of time.

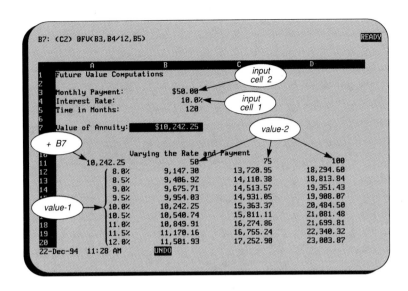

The data table describes the future values for varying interest rates and varying monthly payments. For example, if you invest $75.00 per month instead of $50.00 per month and if the interest rate is 11.5%, then you will have $16,755.24 rather than $10,242.25 at the end of 10 years.

Do the following to create the worksheet in the previous figure:

a. Increase the global column width to 17.

b. Enter the labels and numeric values in the range A1 through B5 and in cell A7.

c. Assign the FV function @FV(B3,B4/12,B5) to cell B7 to determine the future value of a fund in which you invest $50.00 per month at 10% interest, compounded monthly, for 10 years (120 months).

d. Use the Data Fill command to build the percent values in the range A12..A20. Assign +B7 to cell A11.

e. With the cell pointer at A11, enter the command /**D**ata **T**able **2** (/DT2). Enter the data table range A11..D20.

f. Enter an input cell-1 value of B4 and an input cell-2 value of B3. Press the Enter key. The data table should fill as shown in the previous figure.

g. Format the worksheet according to the figure.

h. Save the worksheet using the file name STUS4-6B.

i. Print the worksheet.

j. Try several different investment combinations in cells B3, B4, and B5. Use function key F8 to instruct 1-2-3 to recalculate the data table if you change the value in cell B5.

STUDENT ASSIGNMENT 7: Building a Biweekly Payroll Worksheet

Instructions: Load 1-2-3 and perform the following tasks.

1. Build the worksheet illustrated in the following figure. For each employee, use these formulas to determine the gross pay in column E, federal tax in column F, state tax in column G, and net pay in column H:
   a. If Hours $\leq$ 80, then Gross Pay = Rate $*$ Hours, otherwise Gross Pay = Rate $*$ Hours + 0.5 $*$ Rate $*$ (Hours – 80).
   b. If (Gross Pay – Dependents $*$ 38.46) > 0, then Federal Tax = 20% $*$ (Gross Pay – Dependents $*$ 38.46), otherwise Federal Tax = 0.
   c. State Tax = 3.2% $*$ Gross Pay.
   d. Net Pay = Gross Pay – (Federal Tax + State Tax).

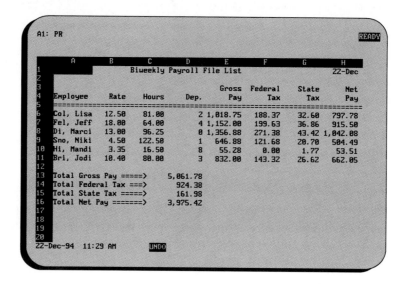

2. Use the Range Name Create command to name cells B6, C6, and D6 so that you can use the variable names described in step 1 when you enter the formulas in cells E6, F6, G6, and H6.
3. Protect all the cells in the worksheet except those in the range C6..C11. Try to enter values into the protected cells.
4. Save the worksheet as STUS4-7.
5. Print the worksheet.
6. Print the cell-formulas version of the worksheet.
7. Print the worksheet after formatting all the cells to the Text type.
8. Retrieve STUS4-7. Increase the number of hours worked for each employee by 7.5 hours. Print the as-displayed version of the worksheet with the new values.

STUDENT ASSIGNMENT 8: Building a Future Value Worksheet

Instructions: Load 1-2-3 and perform the following tasks.

1. Build the worksheet illustrated in the following figure. Set column A to a width of 16 characters and the rest of the columns to a width of 14 characters. Use the Range Name Label command to name B3, B5, E3, and E5. Use the label to the right of each cell in the figure as the label name. Determine the future value in cell E5 from the function @FV($Monthly Pymt:, $Rate:/12,12*$Time:). The FV function tells you how much money you will have in a fund if you pay a fixed payment and earn a fixed interest rate over a period of time. Enter the following data: monthly payment, 250; rate of interest, 9%; time in years, 10. Print the range A1..E19.

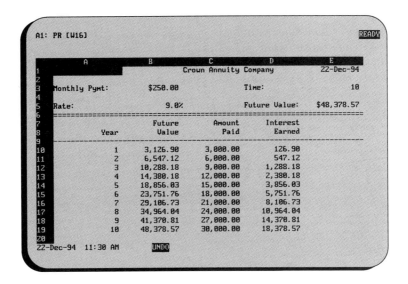

Determine the values in the table in rows 10 through 19 as follows:

a. Use the Data Fill command to create the series of numbers in the range A10..A19.
b. Assign the function @IF(A10< = $Time:,@FV($Monthly Pymt:,$Rate:/12,12*A10),0) to B10 and copy B10 to B11..B19.
c. Assign the function @IF(A10< = $Time:,12*A10*$Monthly Pymt:,0) to C10 and copy C10 to C11..C19.
d. Assign the formula +B10–C10 to D10 and copy D10 to D11..D19.
e. Format the cells in the worksheet as shown in the figure.

2. Enable cell protection. Unprotect B3, B5, and E3.
3. Save the worksheet. Use the file name STUS4-8.
4. Determine the future value for the following: monthly payment, 500; rate of interest, 11.5%; time in years, 10. For this data, the future value is equal to $111,701.61.
5. Print the worksheet with the future value for the data described in step 4.
6. Print only the range A1..E5 with the future value for the data described in step 4.

STUDENT ASSIGNMENT 9: Building a Data Table for the Future Value Worksheet

Instructions: Load 1-2-3 and perform the following tasks.

1. Load STUS4-8, the future value worksheet, which you created in Student Assignment 8. This worksheet is illustrated in the figure in Student Assignment 8. Determine the future value for the following: monthly payment, 1200; rate of interest, 10%; time in years, 7.
2. Do the following to create the data table shown in the following figure.
   a. Disable cell protection.
   b. Use the Data Fill command to enter the series of numbers 6.5% to 12.5% in increments of 0.5% in the range F8..F20.
   c. Assign +E5 (future value) to cell G7.
   d. Assign the formula +Future Value:−Time:∗12∗Monthly Pymt: to cell H7.
   e. Use the command /**D**ata **T**able **1** (/DT1) to establish the range F7..H20 as a data table.
   f. Enter an input cell value of B5, the interest rate.
   g. Format the data table as shown in the figure.
   h. Enable cell protection. Unprotect the range F7..H20.

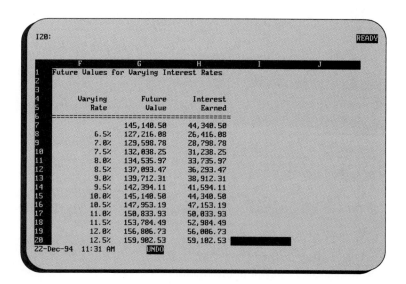

3. Save the worksheet using the file name STUS4-9.
4. Print the complete worksheet (A1..H20) with the future value for the data described in step 1.

STUDENT ASSIGNMENT 10: Building Macros for the Future Value Worksheet

Instructions: Load 1-2-3 and perform the following tasks.

1. Load STUS4-9, the future value worksheet, which was created in Student Assignments 8 and 9. This worksheet is illustrated in the figures in Student Assignments 8 and 9.
2. Enter the three macros shown in the following figure.

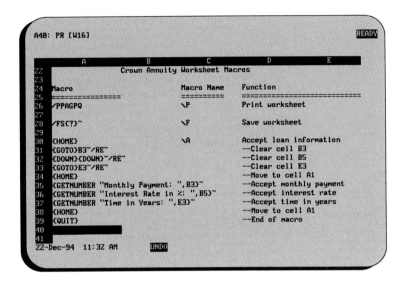

3. Change the printer range to A1..E19.
4. Use STEP mode to test each macro. For the \F macro in cell A28, use the file name STUS4-10. For the \A macro (A30..A39), use the following data: monthly payment, 350; rate of interest, 8%; time in years, 7. For this data, the future value equals $39,239.66.
5. Enable cell protection for the worksheet.
6. Press function key F8 to recalculate the data table.
7. Use the \F command to save the worksheet a second time.
8. Print the complete worksheet (A1..H39) with the future value for the data described in step 4.

STUDENT ASSIGNMENT 11: Building Macros for the Biweekly Payroll Worksheet

Instructions: Load 1-2-3 and perform the following tasks.

1. Load STUS4-7, the weekly payroll worksheet, which was created in Student Assignment 7. This worksheet is illustrated in the figure in Student Assignment 7.
2. Disable cell protection and add macros that will do the following:
   a. Save the worksheet under the file name entered by the user (\S).
   b. Print the range A1..H16 (\P).
   c. Erase the current hours worked and accept the new hours worked (\A).
3. Enable cell protection for the worksheet.
4. Use STEP mode to test each macro. For the save macro, use the file name STUS4-11. For the accept hours worked macro, enter the following hours worked: Col, Lisa—78.5; Fel, Jeff—84.5; Di, Marci—120; Sno, Niki—80; Hi, Mandi—80; Bri, Jodi—132.5.
5. Use the save macro to save the worksheet a second time. Use the file name STUS4-11.
6. Print the worksheet (A1..H16) for the data described in step 4.
7. Print the macros entered in step 2.

Graphing with 1-2-3 and Allways

LOTUS 1-2-3 Release 2.2

OBJECTIVES

You will have mastered the material in this project when you can:

◆ Create a pie chart
◆ Create a line graph
◆ Create a multiple-line graph
◆ Create a scatter graph
◆ Create a simple bar graph
◆ Create a side-by-side bar graph
◆ Create a stack-bar graph
◆ Create an XY graph
◆ Assign multiple graphs to the same worksheet
◆ Dress up a graph by adding titles and legends
◆ Save a graph as a PIC file
◆ Save a worksheet with the graph settings
◆ Print a graph
◆ View the current graph and graphs saved on disk
◆ Use Allways to place a graph alongside the data in a worksheet

As we have seen in the previous four projects, a worksheet is a powerful tool for analyzing data. Sometimes, however, the message you are trying to convey gets lost in the rows and columns of numbers. This is where the graphics capability of 1-2-3 becomes useful. With only a little effort, you can have 1-2-3 create, display, and print a graph of the data in your worksheet and get your message across in a dramatic pictorial fashion. With the Graph command, you can select a pie chart, a line graph, a variety of bar graphs, an XY graph, or a scatter graph. We will study these types of graphs in this project.

We will use the year-end sales analysis worksheet shown in Figure 5-1 to illustrate all the graphs except the XY graph. The worksheet in Figure 5-1 includes the quarter sales for each of six cities in which King's Computer Outlet has a store. Total sales for each quarter and the year are displayed in row 13. The total sales for each of the six cities are displayed in column F.

Before going any further, let's build the worksheet shown in Figure 5-1. As a guide, follow the first 23 steps in the list of keystrokes given in the Project Summary section at the end of this project.

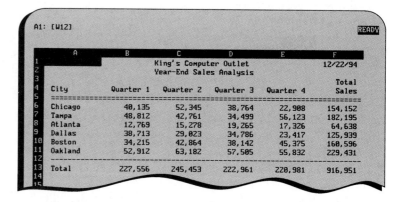

FIGURE 5-1 The year-end sales analysis report we will use to illustrate graphing with 1-2-3.

THE GRAPH COMMAND

◆ With the worksheet in Figure 5-1 in main memory, the first step in drawing a graph is to enter the command /Graph (/G). The Graph menu and the graph settings sheet display as shown in Figure 5-2.

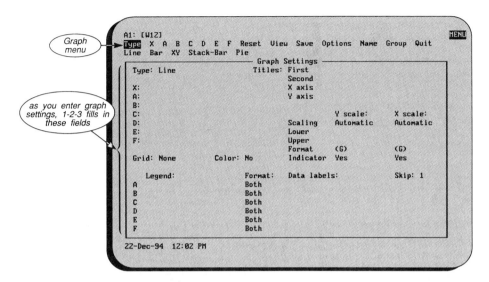

FIGURE 5-2 The Graph menu of 1-2-3—enter the command /Graph (/G).

The functions of the commands listed in the Graph menu are described in Table 5-1.

TABLE 5-1 A Summary of Commands in the Graph Menu

COMMAND	FUNCTION
Type	Allows you to select the type of graph you want to display—Line, Bar, XY, Stack-bar, Pie.
X	Defines a range of labels for the X axis for a line or bar graph. Defines a range of labels to describe each piece of a pie chart. In an XY graph the X range is assigned the X coordinates.
ABCDEF	Allows you to define up to six Y-axis data ranges. For example, in a multiple-line graph each data range is represented by a line.
Reset	Clears the current graph specifications.
View	Displays the current graph.
Save	Saves the current graph to disk. 1-2-3 automatically adds the extension .PIC to the graph file.
Options	Allows you to define titles or labels for the X and Y axes and for the top of the graph.
Name	Allows you to save a set of graph settings by name. In this way you can have several different graphs associated with the same worksheet.
Group	Allows you to define multiple graph data ranges when the ranges are located in consecutive columns or rows.
Quit	Quits the Graph command.

PIE CHARTS

◆ A **pie chart** is used to show how 100% of an amount is divided. Let's create the pie chart in Figure 5-3. This pie chart shows the percentage of total annual sales for each of the six cities where King's Computer Outlet has a store.

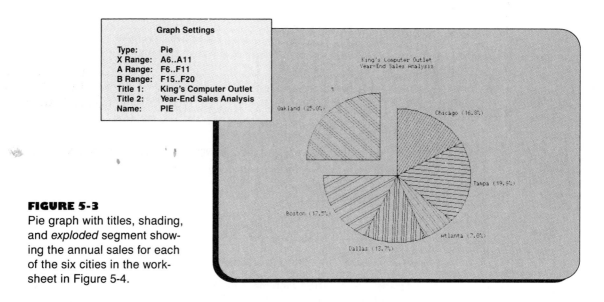

Graph Settings

Type:	Pie
X Range:	A6..A11
A Range:	F6..F11
B Range:	F15..F20
Title 1:	King's Computer Outlet
Title 2:	Year-End Sales Analysis
Name:	PIE

FIGURE 5-3
Pie graph with titles, shading, and *exploded* segment showing the annual sales for each of the six cities in the worksheet in Figure 5-4.

The total annual sales for each of the six stores are in the range F6..F11 of the worksheet in Figure 5-4.

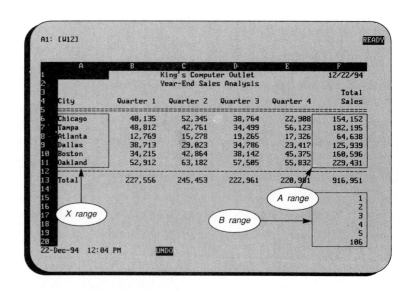

FIGURE 5-4
Ranges specified in the worksheet for the pie graph in Figure 5-3

To create any graph using 1-2-3, you need to enter the type of graph, the ranges in the worksheet to graph, graph titles, and graph options. Collectively, these are called the **graph settings** and they display on the graph settings sheet when the Graph menu is active. Remember, function key F6 toggles the display between the graph settings sheet and the worksheet when the Graph menu is active.

With the Graph menu on the screen (Figure 5-2), enter the command **T**ype **P**ie (TP). This command tells 1-2-3 to create a pie chart as the current graph. The **current graph** is the one that displays when you enter the command /**G**raph **V**iew (/GV).

Selecting the A Range

After typing the letter P for Pie, the menu pointer returns to the Graph menu, (Figure 5-2). For a pie chart, you can select only one data range to graph, and it must be assigned as the A range. As shown in Figure 5-4, assign the annual sales for each city (F6..F11) as the A range. Type the letter A. 1-2-3 responds by displaying the prompt message "Enter first data range: A1" on the input line. Enter the range F6..F11 and press the Enter key.

Selecting the X Range

The X range is used to identify each *slice*, or segment, of the pie. You must select a range that can identify the cells in the A range. Since the A range is equal to the annual sales for each of the six cities, select the names of the cities (A6..A11) to identify each segment of the pie. With the menu pointer in the Graph menu, type the letter X. 1-2-3 responds by displaying the prompt message "Enter x-axis range: A1" on the input line. Enter the range A6..A11 and press the Enter key.

After defining the A range and X range, 1-2-3 has enough information to draw a *primitive* pie chart, one that shows the characteristics assigned thus far. With the menu pointer in the Graph menu, type the letter V for View and the primitive pie chart in Figure 5-5 displays on the screen. After viewing it, press any key on the keyboard to redisplay the Graph menu and graph settings. Once a range has been assigned you may view the pie chart at any time and make changes if you feel the pie chart is not being drawn the way you want it.

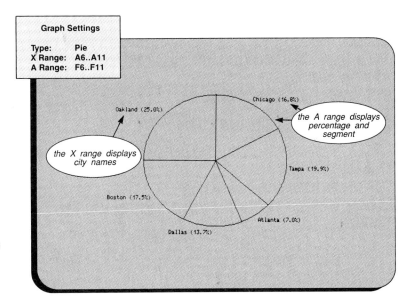

FIGURE 5-5
Primitive pie chart with no titles or shading. It shows the proportion of annual sales contributed by each city in the form of a *slice of the pie.*

It is the A range that causes the pie in Figure 5-5 to be divided into segments. Each segment is proportionate to the annual sales for each city. The A range is also responsible for the percentage value displayed within parentheses outside each segment. The city names outside each segment of the pie are the labels assigned as the X range.

In certain instances, you may want to assign the same group of cells to both the A and X ranges. When both ranges are assigned the same group of cells, the values in the A range that determine the size of each segment of the pie are also used to identify (label) each segment.

Selecting the B Range

The B range is used to enhance the pie chart and make it more presentable and easier to read. Through the use of the B range, you can create segment shading and *explode* a pie chart. An **exploded pie chart** is one in which one or more segments are offset or slightly removed from the main portion of the pie so that they stand out (Figure 5-3).

The B range is usually set up off to the side or below the worksheet. To shade and explode the pie chart in Figure 5-5 so that it looks more like Figure 5-3, you need to choose six adjacent cells for the B range, one for each pie segment. In each cell, enter a code number between 0 and 7. Each code represents a different type of shading. A code of zero instructs 1-2-3 to leave the corresponding segment of the pie chart unshaded.

Let's use the range F15..F20 to enter the code numbers. The first of the six cells, F15, will refer to the first entry in the A range, Chicago. The last of the six cells will refer to the last entry in the A range, Oakland.

To enter the shading codes, first quit the Graph menu by typing the letter Q. Use function key F5 to move the cell pointer to F15. Enter the shading codes 1 through 5 in the range F15..F19. To explode one or more segments of the pie chart, add 100 to the shading values. Explode the segment representing Oakland by entering the number 106, rather than 6, in cell F20. The six shading codes are shown in the range F15..F20 in Figure 5-4.

Select the range F15..F20 by entering the command /Graph **B** (/GB). Enter the range F15..F20 and press the Enter key. Type the letter V to view the pie chart. The pie chart (without titles) displays as shown earlier in Figure 5-3. Except for the graph titles, the pie chart is complete. After viewing the pie chart, press any key to redisplay the Graph menu and graph settings.

Adding a Title to the Pie Chart

To add graph titles above the pie chart, type the letter O for Options. This causes the Graph Options menu to display at the top of the screen. With the Graph Options menu on the screen, type the letter T for Titles. We are allowed two title lines—First Line and Second Line—up to 39 characters each. Type the letter F for First Line. Enter the title `King's Computer Outlet` and press the Enter key. Type the letters T for Titles and S for Second Line. Enter the second line of the title `Year-End Sales Analysis` and press the Enter key.

To quit the Graph Options menu, type the letter Q for Quit. 1-2-3 returns to the Graph menu. The graph settings for the pie chart are complete as shown in Figure 5-6. Type the letter V for View and 1-2-3 displays the pie chart with titles as shown earlier in Figure 5-3. To terminate the View command, press any key on the keyboard and the Graph menu redisplays on the screen.

If the title you plan to use for a graph is identical to one in the worksheet, you can press the Backslash (\) key followed by the cell address in place of the title. For example, you could have entered \C1 for the first title and \C2 for the second title, since the titles are identical to the worksheet titles in cells C1 and C2 (Figure 5-4).

Naming the Pie Chart

With the menu pointer in the Graph menu and the pie chart complete, the next step is to name the graph settings. That way you can develop a new graph from the same worksheet and still have the pie chart settings stored away to view and modify at a later time. To assign a name to the graph settings, type the letter N for Name. The Graph Name menu displays at the top of the screen as shown in Figure 5-6. Type the letter C for Create. 1-2-3 displays the prompt message "Enter graph name:" on the input line. Enter the name `PIE` for pie chart and press the Enter key. After assigning the name, 1-2-3 returns control to the Graph menu.

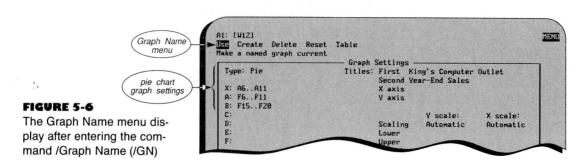

FIGURE 5-6

The Graph Name menu display after entering the command /Graph Name (/GN)

The graph settings shown in Figure 5-6 are now stored under the name PIE. Graph names, like PIE, can be up to 15 characters long and should be as descriptive as possible. Table 5-2 summarizes the commands available in the Graph Name menu.

TABLE 5-2 A Summary of Commands in the Graph Name Menu

COMMAND	FUNCTION
Use	Lists the directory of graph names associated with the current worksheet. Assigns the selected named set of graph settings as the current graph and displays the graph.
Create	Saves the current graph settings as a part of the worksheet so that another graph can be built. This command does not save the graph settings to disk.
Delete	Deletes the named set of graph settings.
Reset	Deletes all graph names and their settings.
Table	Creates a table of named graphs in the worksheet.

The Effect of What-If Analyses on the Pie Chart

Once you have assigned the pie chart settings to the worksheet, any values changed in the worksheet will show up in the pie chart the next time it is drawn. For example, quit the Graph menu and change the sales amount for Quarter 1 for Chicago in cell B6 from 40,135 to 45,550. Press the F10 key to view the pie chart. When the worksheet is displayed on the screen, it is quicker to press the F10 key to display the current graph than it is to enter the command /GV. Compare the displayed pie chart to the one in Figure 5-3. Notice that the segments representing all six cities have changed because of the change in the first quarter sales for Chicago. After viewing the pie chart, press any key on the keyboard to return to the worksheet. Before continuing with this project, change the sales amount for Chicago in cell B6 back to 40,135.

Saving the Worksheet with the Pie Chart Graph Settings

When you assign a name, like PIE, to the current set of graph settings using the /GNC command, they are not saved to disk. To save the named graph settings, you must save the worksheet itself using the File Save command. When the /FS command is used, both the current graph settings and any named graph settings are saved with the worksheet. To complete the save, first type the letter Q to quit the Graph menu. When the worksheet reappears on the screen, enter the command /File Save (/FS). When the file name PROJS-5A appears on the input line, press the Enter key. Finally, type the letter R for Replace.

Later, when you retrieve the worksheet, the pie chart settings will be available and you can display or print the pie chart at any time. If you retrieve the worksheet and decide to change any of the pie chart settings, you must save the worksheet again or the latest changes will be lost.

Printing the Pie Chart

Printing a graph is a three-step process: first, save the graph to disk using the command /Graph Save (/GS); second, quit 1-2-3; and third, load the PrintGraph program (PGRAPH) into main memory and print the graph. The Print-Graph program allows you to print graphs that have been saved with the /Graph Save (/GS) command.

Let's print the pie chart by following the three steps we just described. With 1-2-3 in READY mode, enter the command /Graph Save (/GS). In response to the prompt message on the input line, enter the file name PIE-5A and press the Enter key. The pie chart (not the worksheet) is saved to disk under the name PIE-5A with an extension of .PIC (picture). We call a graph file, like PIE-5A.PIC, a **PIC file**. With a snapshot of the graph saved, quit the Graph menu and quit 1-2-3.

Next, load the PrintGraph program into main memory. If you have a computer with a fixed disk, then at the DOS prompt enter PGRAPH and press the Enter key. If you have a computer with no fixed disk, replace the 1-2-3 system disk in the A drive with the PrintGraph disk and make sure the disk with PIE-5A.PIC is in the B drive. At the DOS prompt, enter PGRAPH and press the Enter key. After several seconds the PrintGraph menu displays on the screen (Figure 5-7).

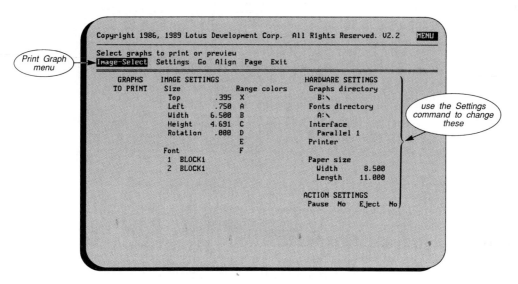

FIGURE 5-7   The PrintGraph menu

Table 5-3 describes the commands available in the PrintGraph menu.

TABLE 5-3   A Summary of Commands in the PrintGraph Menu

COMMAND	FUNCTION
Image-Select	Allows you to specify the graph to print.
Settings	Lets you set the default drive; adjust the size of the graph; select colors, fonts, and the hardware.
Go	Starts printing the graph.
Align	Resets the PrintGraph line counter.
Page	Ejects the paper in the printer to the top of the next page.
Exit	Ends the PrintGraph session.

With the PrintGraph menu on the screen, type the letter I for Image-Select. PrintGraph displays the Image-Select menu (Figure 5-8). This menu includes a list of all the PIC files on the default drive. Use the Up Arrow and Down Arrow keys to highlight the one to print. In our case, there is only one PIC file and it is highlighted. Press the Enter key to select PIE-5A. The PrintGraph menu shown in Figure 5-7 redisplays on the screen.

Check the printer to be sure it is in READY mode. Type the letters A for Align and G for Go. The pie chart prints on the printer. Type the letter P for Page to advance the paper to the top of the next page. If the graph fails to print properly, refer to the section entitled Solving PrintGraph Problems in the Lotus 1-2-3 Release 2.2 reference manual.

To the right of the list of PIC files in the Image-Select menu in Figure 5-8 are instructions explaining how to select a graph from the list. The Spacebar is used to mark or unmark the highlighted graph in the list. A graph name that is marked has a number sign (#) displayed to the left of the name. All marked graph names print when you use the Go command in the PrintGraph menu. Hence, when you print a second graph, you should unmark the previous one or it will print also.

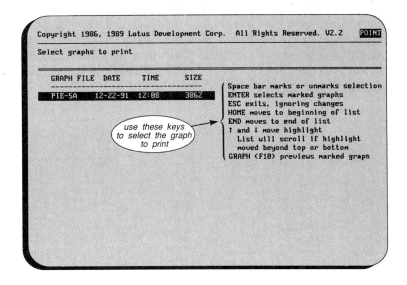

FIGURE 5-8
The Image-Select menu

The GRAPH key is the function key F10. You can press this key to display the highlighted graph on the screen. When you are finished viewing the graph, press any key to return to the Image-Select menu.

To quit PrintGraph, type the letters E for Exit and Y for Yes to confirm your exit from the PrintGraph program. At the DOS prompt, type 123 to reenter the spreadsheet program.

LINE GRAPHS

Line graphs are used to show changes in data over time. For example, a line graph can show pictorially whether sales increased or decreased during quarters of the year. The lines are drawn on X and Y axes. You can have from one to six lines in the graph. Each line represents a different data range in the worksheet. We will create two line graphs, one with a single data range and another with six data ranges.

First, we will create a line graph with a single data range that shows the trend of the total sales for the four quarters (Figure 5-9). Begin by resetting the current graph settings associated with PROJS-5A. That is, clear the pie chart—the current graph—to begin the line graph because the settings are different.

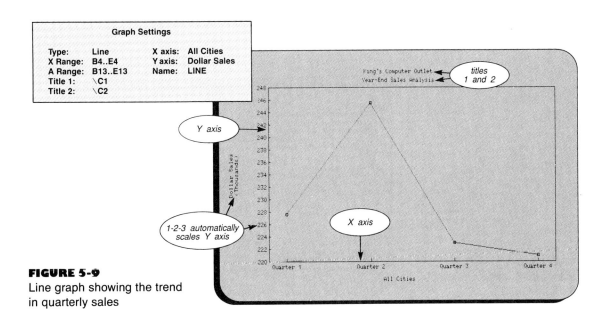

FIGURE 5-9
Line graph showing the trend
in quarterly sales

With the Graph menu on the screen, type the letter R for Reset. The Graph Reset menu displays at the top of the screen as shown in Figure 5-10. The graph settings can be reset on an individual basis (X, A, B, C, D, E, F) or for the entire graph (Graph). In this case, reset all the graph settings. With the menu pointer in the Graph Reset menu, type the letter G for Graph. The pie chart settings disappear from the screen since it is no longer the current graph. Remember, however, that the pie chart settings are stored under the name PIE and can be accessed at any time using the /Graph Name Use (/GNU) command (Table 5-2).

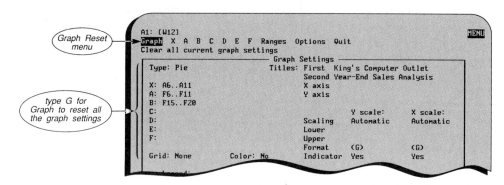

FIGURE 5-10   The Graph Reset menu—enter the command /Graph Reset (/GR).

The menu pointer returns to the Graph menu after erasing the pie chart settings. We can now proceed to build the line graph in Figure 5-9. There are four steps involved:

1. With the Graph menu on the screen, enter the command Type Line (TL).
2. Define the X range—the cells that contain the desired labels for the X axis.
3. Define the A range—the cells that include the values that the line graph will represent.
4. Enter the title of the line graph and titles for the X and Y axes.

Selecting the X Range

With the menu pointer in the Graph menu, type the letter X and assign the range B4..E4 as the X range. As shown in Figure 5-11, cells B4 through E4 contain the labels Quarter 1, Quarter 2, Quarter 3, and Quarter 4. These labels display along the X axis in the line graph (Figure 5-9).

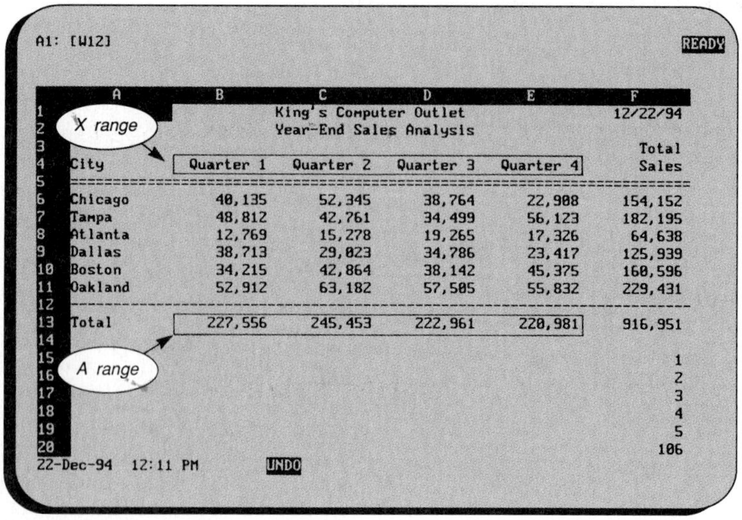

FIGURE 5-11

Range settings for line graph in Figure 5-9

Selecting the A Range

The next step is to select the A range. Assign to the A range the cells that include the values to graph. This is also called the Y-axis data range. With the menu pointer in the Graph menu, type the letter A and enter the range B13..E13. The A range is shown in the worksheet in Figure 5-11.

Adding Titles to the Line Graph

You can add three different titles to the line graph: (1) line graph title (you are allowed two of these); (2) X-axis title; (3) Y-axis title. Let's add the same line graph titles used for the pie chart. To add these titles, type the letter O for Options while the Graph menu is on the screen. The Graph Options menu shown in Figure 5-12 displays. Type the letters T for Titles and F for First. Enter \C1 and press the Enter key. \C1 instructs 1-2-3 to use the label assigned to cell C1 in the worksheet as the first title. Next, type the letters T and S to enter the second title. Enter \C2 and press the Enter key. The label in cell C2 serves as the second title.

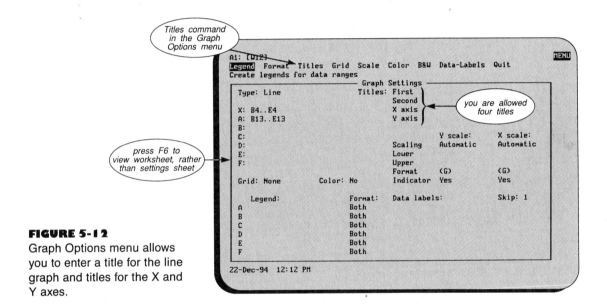

FIGURE 5-12
Graph Options menu allows you to enter a title for the line graph and titles for the X and Y axes.

Enter the X-axis title by typing the letters T and X and the label All Cities. Press the Enter key. Enter the Y-axis title by typing the letters T and Y and the label Dollar Sales. Press the Enter key. Finally, type the letter Q to quit the Graph Options menu.

Viewing the Line Graph

With the menu pointer in the Graph menu, type the letter V for View. The line graph previously shown in Figure 5-9 displays. Notice that 1-2-3 automatically scales the numeric labels along the Y axis on the basis of the numbers in the A range. The small squares that the line graph passes through represent the points whose coordinates are the corresponding values in the X and A ranges.

You can see from Figure 5-9 that the line graph is useful for showing a trend. The line graph clearly shows that sales for King's Computer Outlet increased significantly during the second quarter and then fell sharply in the third quarter. Finally, there was a slight drop in sales during the fourth quarter. Here again, if we change any numeric values in the worksheet, the line graph will show the latest values the next time we invoke the View command. After viewing the graph, press any key to redisplay the Graph menu.

Naming the Line Graph

With the line graph complete and the menu pointer active in the Graph menu, type the letters N for Name and C for Create. When 1-2-3 requests the graph name, enter the name LINE and press the Enter key. The line graph settings are stored under the name LINE.

Saving and Printing the Line Graph

To save the named graph settings (LINE) with the worksheet to disk, type the letter Q to quit the Graph menu. Enter the command /File Save (/FS). Press the Enter key when the file name PROJS-5A appears on the input line. Type the letter R for Replace to rewrite the file to disk. Now there are two sets of graph settings associated with PROJS-5A— PIE and LINE. The line graph continues to be the current graph.

Make a hard copy of the line graph in the same manner we described for the pie chart. That is, with the menu pointer in the Graph menu, type the letter S for Save and name the graph LINE-5A. Quit the Graph menu and quit 1-2-3. At the DOS prompt, enter PGRAPH. When the PrintGraph menu displays, type the letter I for Image-Select and select the PIC file LINE-5A. Turn the printer on, type A for Align, G for Go, and P for Page. When the printing activity is complete, quit PrintGraph, load 1-2-3, and retrieve PROJS-5A.

Multiple-Line Graphs

1-2-3 allows up to six Y-axis data ranges (A–F) and the range of corresponding labels (X) to be assigned to a line graph. When more than one data range is assigned to a line graph, it is called a **multiple-line graph**. The multiple-line graph in Figure 5-13 includes six lines, each representing the four quarterly sales for one of the six cities in the worksheet. Multiple-line graphs like this one are used not only to show trends, but also to compare one range of data to another.

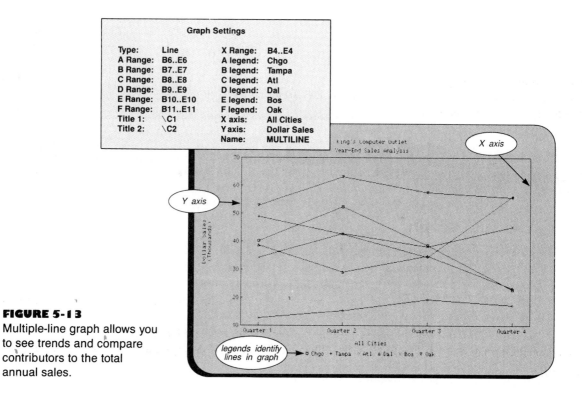

FIGURE 5-13
Multiple-line graph allows you to see trends and compare contributors to the total annual sales.

The multiple-line graph in Figure 5-13 uses the same titles, X range, and graph type as the line graph in Figure 5-9, the current graph associated with the worksheet. Therefore, rather than resetting the current graph settings, modify them.

Selecting the Data Ranges One at a Time

With the menu pointer active in the Graph menu, assign to the six data ranges A through F the quarterly sales of the six cities shown in Figure 5-14. Type the letter A for the A range. Enter the range B6..E6 and press the Enter key. Follow the same procedure for the other five ranges—assign the B range B7..E7, the C range B8..E8, the D range B9..E9, the E range B10..E10, and the F range B11..E11.

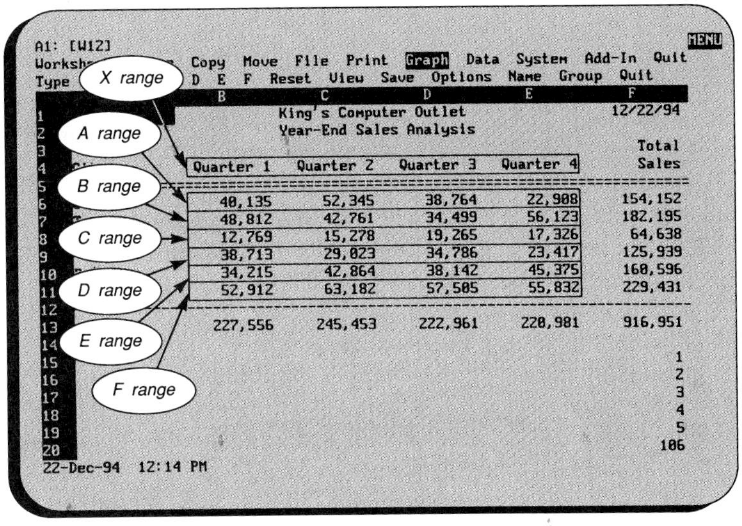

FIGURE 5-14
Multiple-line graph range settings

Selecting the Data Ranges as a Group

If the majority of the data ranges are in adjacent rows or adjacent columns, you can use the Group command in the Graph menu (Figure 5-2) to select all the data ranges at once, rather than one by one. In Figure 5-14, the data ranges A through F are in adjacent rows, and the X range is separated from the rest of the data ranges by row 5. Let's use the Group command to assign the range B5..E11 to X through F, and then let's change the X range to B4..E4.

With the Graph menu active, type the letter G for Group. 1-2-3 responds by prompting you to enter the range. Enter B5..E11 and press the Enter key. 1-2-3 then asks if the selected range should be assigned by columns or rows to the data ranges. Since Figure 5-14 shows that the data ranges are in rows, type the letter R. 1-2-3 responds by assigning X range B5..E5, A range B6..E6, B range B7..E7, C range B8..E8, D range B9..E9, E range B10..E10, and F range B11..E11. To complete the selection, change the X range. With the Graph menu still on the screen, type the letter X. Change the X range to B4..E4.

This alternative method for selecting the data ranges saves time because you can assign all the data ranges with two commands instead of seven.

Assigning Legends to the Data Ranges

Before quiting the Graph menu, enter legends that help identify each of the six lines that are drawn in the multiple-line graph. Without legends, the multiple-line graph is useless because you cannot identify the lines in the graph.

To enter the legend that identifies the A range, type the letters O for Options, L for Legend, and A for A range. From Figure 5-14 you can determine that the A range was assigned the quarterly sales for Chicago (B6..E6). Therefore, enter the label Chgo in response to the prompt message "Enter legend for A range:" on the input line. Assign the abbreviated city names as the legends for the B through F ranges as described at the top of Figure 5-13.

Viewing the Multiple-Line Graph

Next, type the letter V for View and the multiple-line graph illustrated in Figure 5-13 displays on the screen. The six lines in the graph show the trend in quarterly sales for each of the six cities. The graph also allows us to compare the sales for the six cities. To identify the line that represents a particular city, scan the legends at the bottom of the graph in Figure 5-13. Before each abbreviated city name is a special character called a symbol, like the square for Chicago. The line that passes through the square in the graph represents Chicago's four quarterly sales. After viewing the multiple-line graph, press any key to return control to the Graph menu.

Naming the Multiple-Line Graph

To assign a name to the multiple-line graph specifications, type the letters N for Name and C for Create. When 1-2-3 requests the graph name, enter the name MULTLINE and press the Enter key. The multiple-line graph settings are stored under the name MULTLINE.

There are now three graphs associated with the worksheet—PIE, LINE, and MULTLINE. However, there is only one current graph. At this point, the current graph is the multiple-line graph because it was the last one created.

Saving and Printing the Multiple-Line Graph

Type Q to quit the Graph menu. The worksheet in Figure 5-1 reappears on the screen. Save the worksheet. This ensures that the graph settings under the name MULTLINE are saved with the worksheet on disk. Enter the command /File Save (/FS). When the file name PROJS-5A appears on the input line, press the Enter key. Type the letter R to replace the old version of PROJS-5A with the new one.

After saving the worksheet, enter the command /Graph Save (/GS) to save the multiple-line graph as a PIC file using the name MLINE-5A. Quit the graph menu and quit 1-2-3. At the DOS prompt enter PGRAPH. Follow the steps for printing a graph outlined earlier.

Scatter Graphs

A **scatter graph** displays the points (symbols) in a graph without any connecting lines. Sometimes a scatter graph is better able to illustrate what a multiple-line graph is attempting to show. To create the scatter graph shown in Figure 5-15, you need only instruct 1-2-3 not to connect the symbols with lines in the multiple-line graph. Remember, the multiple-line graph is still the current graph.

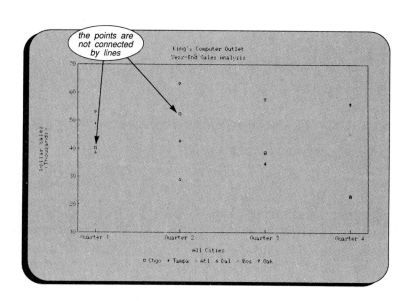

FIGURE 5-15
The scatter graph is an alternative to the multiple-line graph.

Changing the Multiple-Line Graph to a Scatter Graph   With the Graph menu on the screen, type the letters O for Options, F for Format, and G for Graph. The default setting for the Format Graph command is Both. This means that both lines and symbols are displayed for the current multiple-line graph. Change this to Symbols so that only the symbols are displayed. Type the letter S for Symbols. Finally, type the letter Q twice, once to quit the Format section of the Graph Options menu and once to quit the Graph Options menu.

Viewing the Scatter Graph   Type the letter V and the original multiple-line graph (Figure 5-13) displays as a scatter graph (Figure 5-15). Here again, the symbols are identified by the legends displayed below the scatter graph. Press any key to redisplay the Graph menu.

Naming, Saving, and Printing the Scatter Graph   To assign a name to the scatter graph settings, type the letters N for Name and C for Create. When 1-2-3 requests the graph name, enter the name SCATTER and press the Enter key. Type the letter Q to quit the Graph menu and save the worksheet to disk using the File Save command. Now there are four graphs associated with the worksheet—PIE, LINE, MULTLINE, and SCATTER.

To print the scatter graph, first save it as a PIC file using the /Graph Save (/GS) command and the file name SCAT-5A. Next, quit 1-2-3 and use PGRAPH to print the PIC file SCAT-5A.

BAR GRAPHS

The **bar graph** is the most popular business graphic. It is used to show trends and comparisons. The bar graph is similar to a line graph, except that a bar rather than a point on a line represents the Y-axis value for each X-axis value. Unlike the line graph that shows a continuous transition from one point to the next, the bar graph emphasizes the magnitude of the value it represents.

We will discuss three types of bar graphs: simple bar graphs, side-by-side bar graphs, and stack-bar graphs. The following examples change the preceding line graphs to bar graphs. The range settings, titles, and legends remain the same.

Simple Bar Graphs

A **simple bar graph** has a single bar for each value in the X range. The graph settings for a bar graph are similar to those for a line graph. Let's create the bar graph in Figure 5-16. It is a bar graph of the same data used earlier for the line graph shown in Figure 5-9. Recall that the line graph showed the trend in total sales for the four quarters.

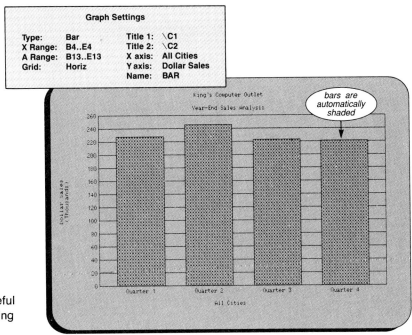

FIGURE 5-16
A simple bar chart is useful for comparing and showing trends.

Using a Named Graph   The first step in creating the bar graph is to assign the line graph settings stored under the graph name LINE as the current graph. Therefore, with the Graph menu on the screen, type the letters N for Name and U for Use. 1-2-3 displays an alphabetized list of all the graph names associated with the worksheet PROJS-5A—LINE, MULTLINE, PIE, and SCATTER. With the menu pointer on the name LINE, press the Enter key. The line graph shown earlier in Figure 5-9 immediately displays on the screen. Press any key on the keyboard and the Graph menu reappears. The graph settings for the line graph (LINE) now represent the current graph.

Changing the Line Graph to a Bar Graph   With the Graph menu on the screen, type the letters T for Type and B for Bar. The current graph is now a bar graph, rather than a line graph. To improve the appearance of the bar graph and make it easier to read, add a horizontal grid. Type the letter O for Options. With the Graph Options menu displayed, type the letters G for Grid and H for Horizontal. Quit the Graph Options menu by typing the letter Q for Quit.

Viewing the Simple Bar Graph   Type the letter V for View. The simple bar graph shown in Figure 5-16 displays on the screen. Notice that it gives a more static view of the total sales for each quarter as compared to the line graph in Figure 5-9. The horizontal grid in the simple bar graph makes it easier to recognize the magnitude of the bars that are not adjacent to the Y axis. When you are finished viewing the graph, press any key on the keyboard. The Graph menu reappears on the screen.

Naming, Saving, and Printing the Simple Bar Graph   To name the simple bar graph, type the letters N for Name and C for Create. Enter the graph name BAR and press the Enter key. Type the letter Q to quit the Graph menu. Use the command /File Save (/FS) to save the worksheet to disk. Press the Enter key when the file name PROJS-5A appears on the input line. Next, press the letter R to replace PROJS-5A on disk with the latest version. Now there are five graphs associated with the worksheet—PIE, LINE, MULTLINE, SCATTER, and BAR.

Save the simple bar graph as a PIC file by entering the command /Graph Save (/GS). When 1-2-3 requests a file name, enter BAR-5A and press the Enter key. Use PrintGraph to print the bar graph.

Side-by-Side Bar Graphs

Like a line graph, a bar graph can have from one to six independent bars (data ranges) for each value in the X range. When a bar graph has more than one bar per X value, we call it a **side-by-side bar graph** (Figure 5-17). This type of graph is primarily used to compare data. For example, you might want to compare the sales in each quarter for Oakland to the sales of the rest of the cities.

Using a Named Graph   To create a side-by-side bar graph, let's assign the graph name MULTLINE as the current graph. With the menu pointer in the Graph menu, type the letters N for Name and U for Use. When the list of named graphs display on the screen, select the name MULTLINE and press the Enter key. The multiple-line graph displays on the screen and is assigned to the worksheet as the current graph. Press any key to redisplay the Graph menu.

Changing the Multiple-Line Graph to a Side-by-Side Bar Graph   Change the current graph from a multiple-line graph to a side-by-side bar graph by typing the letters T for Type and B for Bar. All the other graph settings (A–F ranges, titles, and legends) remain the same. Add the horizontal grid, as we did earlier with the simple bar graph, by typing the letters O for Options, G for Grid, and H for Horizontal. Quit the Graph Options menu by typing the letter Q.

Viewing the Side-by-Side Bar Graph   Type the letter V for View. The side-by-side bar graph shown in Figure 5-17 displays on the screen. The different shading that you see for each bar (data range) is automatically done by 1-2-3. The legends below the graph indicate which shaded bar corresponds to which city. Compare Figure 5-17 to Figure 5-13. The side-by-side bar graph is much easier to interpret than the multiple-line graph. For example, it is clear that Oakland had the greatest sales during the first three quarters. For the fourth quarter, Oakland had about the same sales as Tampa. After viewing the graph, press any key to redisplay the Graph menu.

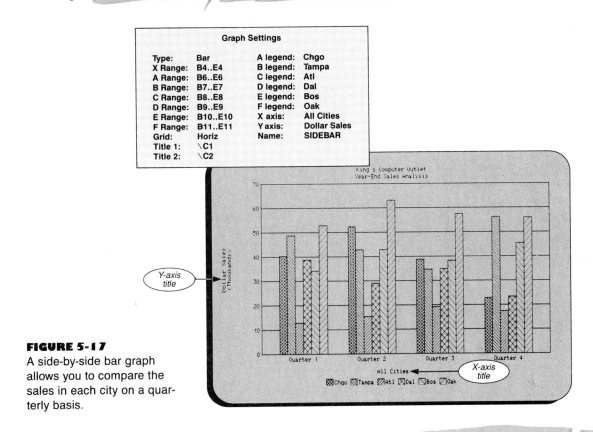

FIGURE 5-17
A side-by-side bar graph allows you to compare the sales in each city on a quarterly basis.

Naming, Saving, and Printing the Side-by-Side Bar Graph   With the Graph menu on the screen, type the letters N for Name and C for Create to name the side-by-side bar graph. Enter the graph name SIDEBAR and press the Enter key. Next, type the letter Q to quit the Graph menu.

   Use the command /File Save (/FS) to save the worksheet to disk. Press the Enter key when the file name PROJS-5A appears on the input line. Finally, type the letter R for Replace. Now there are six graphs associated with the worksheet—PIE, LINE, MULTLINE, SCATTER, BAR, and SIDEBAR.

   With the worksheet on the screen, enter the command /Graph Save (/GS) to save the side-by-side bar graph as a PIC file. Use the file name MBAR-5A. Quit 1-2-3 and load PrintGraph into main memory. Type the letter I for Image-Select and highlight MBAR-5A. Press the Enter key and the PrintGraph menu redisplays. Type the letters A for Align and G for Go. The side-by-side bar graph shown in Figure 5-17 prints on the printer.

Stack-Bar Graphs

One of the problems with the side-by-side bar graph in Figure 5-17 is that it does not show the combined total sales for the six cities for any quarter. An alternative graph to consider is the stack-bar graph. A **stack-bar graph** has a single bar for every value in the X range (Figure 5-18). Each bar is made up of shaded segments. Each segment or piece of the total bar represents an element (city) as a distinct contributor. Together, the stacked segments make up a single bar that shows the cumulative amount (total quarterly sales) of all elements for each value in the X range (quarter).

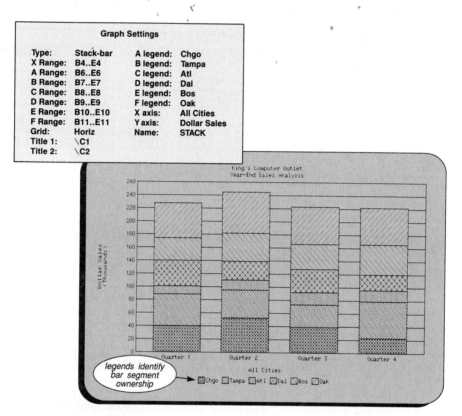

FIGURE 5-18   A stack-bar graph allows you to compare the sales in each city on a quarterly basis. It also shows the total sales for each quarter.

Changing the Side-by-Side Bar Graph to a Stack-Bar Graph   The side-by-side bar graph is still the current graph associated with the worksheet. Therefore, let's modify it to display the stack-bar graph shown in Figure 5-18. With the Graph menu on the screen, enter the command **Type Stack-bar (TS)**. This command changes the side-by-side bar graph (Figure 5-17) to a stack-bar graph (Figure 5-18). All the other side-by-side bar graph settings (A–F ranges, titles, horizontal grid, and legends) remain the same for the stack-bar graph.

Viewing the Stack-Bar Graph   Type the letter V for View. The stack-bar graph shown in Figure 5-18 displays on the screen. Compare Figure 5-18 to Figure 5-17. Notice how the stack-bar graph shows both the quarterly contributions of each city and the total sales for each quarter. The stack-bar graph is an effective way of showing trends and contributions from all segments, while still showing a total for each quarter.

Naming, Saving, and Printing the Stack-Bar Graph   With the stack-bar graph still on the screen, press any key to redisplay the Graph menu. Type the letters N for Name and C for Create to name the stack-bar graph. Enter the graph name STACK and press the Enter key. Quit the Graph menu by typing the letter Q.

Save the worksheet to disk. Enter the command /File Save (/FS). Press the Enter key when the file name PROJS-5A appears on the input line. Press the letter R for Replace. Now there are seven graphs associated with the worksheet—PIE, LINE, MULTLINE, SCATTER, BAR, SIDEBAR, and STACK.

Save the stack-bar graph as a PIC file by entering the command /Graph Save (/GS). Use the file name SBAR-5A. Finally, use PrintGraph to print the stack-bar graph.

ADDITIONAL GRAPH OPTIONS

◆   Three graph options that we did not cover in this project are the Data-Labels, Scale, and Color/B&W commands.

Data-Labels

Data-labels are used to explicitly label a bar or a point in a graph. Select the actual values in the range that the bar or point represents. 1-2-3 then positions the labels near the corresponding points or bars in the graph (Figure 5-19).

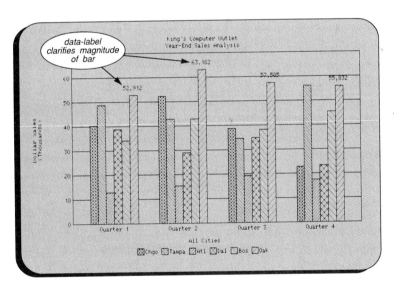

FIGURE 5-19 Data-labels are useful for clarifying and emphasizing various segments of the graph.

To illustrate the use of data-labels, make the SIDEBAR graph settings the current graph by entering the command /Graph Name Use (/GNU). When the alphabetized list of named graphs display on the screen (Figure 5-20), use the Down Arrow key to select SIDEBAR and press the Enter key. 1-2-3 immediately displays the side-by-side bar graph shown in Figure 5-17. Press any key on the keyboard and the Graph menu reappears on the screen.

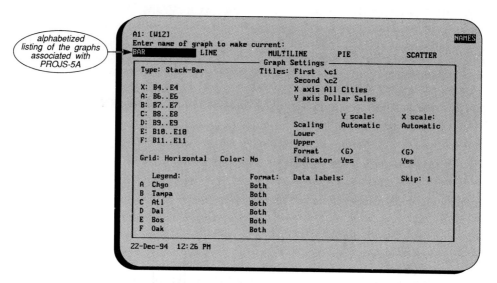

alphabetized listing of the graphs associated with PROJS-5A

FIGURE 5-20 Directory of named graphs associated with the worksheet PROJS-5A—enter the command /Graph Name Use (/GNU).

Let's emphasize the four bars in Figure 5-17 that represent the quarterly sales for Oakland by displaying the actual quarterly sales above each corresponding bar. Enter the command Options Data-Labels (OD). This command causes the Data-Labels menu to display.

Type the letter F to select the F range because it was assigned the range representing the four quarterly sales for Oakland. The worksheet reappears on the screen and 1-2-3 responds with the prompt message "Enter data label for F range data: A1". Type the range B11..E11 and press the Enter key. The range B11..E11 contains the four quarterly sales for Oakland. Therefore, select the same range for the F data-label that was selected earlier for the F range.

After you press the Enter key, 1-2-3 prompts you to enter the desired position of the data-labels in the graph. A response to this prompt is only possible for line and XY graphs. For simple and side-by-side bar graphs, 1-2-3 automatically positions data-labels above each bar. Hence, press the Enter key. Next, type the letter Q twice, once to quit the Data-Labels section of the Graph Options menu and once to quit the Graph Options menu. Finally, type the letter V for View. The modified side-by-side bar graph in Figure 5-19 displays on the screen. Notice how the data-labels above the four bars representing Oakland emphasize and clarify them in the graph.

Press any key to redisplay the Graph menu. Type the letter Q to quit the Graph menu. The worksheet shown earlier in Figure 5-1 reappears on the screen.

Scale Command

When you build a graph, 1-2-3 automatically adjusts the graph to include all points in each data range. The Scale command in the Graph Options menu may be used to override 1-2-3 and manually set the scale on the X or Y axis or both. This command may also be used to specify the display of labels on the X axis and to format the numbers that mark the X and Y axes.

Color/B&W Commands

If your monitor can display colors, the Color command in the Graph Options menu causes bars, lines, and symbols to display in contrasting colors. Alternatively, the B&W command causes the bar and stack-bar graphs to have cross-hatched patterns. The Color and B&W commands are mutually exclusive.

XY GRAPHS

◆ XY graphs differ from the graphs we have discussed thus far. Rather than graphing the magnitude of a value at a fixed point on the X axis, an **XY graph** plots points of the form (x,y), where x is the X-axis coordinate and y is the Y-axis coordinate. Adjacent points are connected by a line to form the graph (Figure 5-21). The XY graph is the type of graph used to plot mathematical functions.

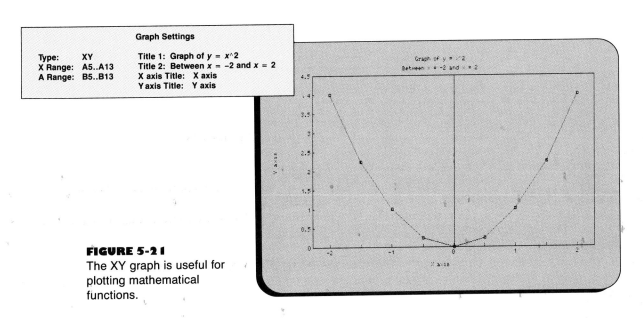

FIGURE 5-21
The XY graph is useful for plotting mathematical functions.

In an XY graph, both the X and Y axes are automatically scaled relative to the low and high values, so that all (x,y) points display and the graph fits on the screen. You can switch to manual scaling and scale either the X or Y axis yourself by using the Scale command in the Graph Options menu.

To illustrate an XY graph, we will use the worksheet in Figure 5-22. As the title indicates, this worksheet includes a table of x and y coordinates for the function $y = x^2$. The x coordinates are in the range A5..A13. They begin at –2 and end at 2 in increments of 0.5. The x coordinates are formed in the worksheet by using the Data Fill command. The y coordinates are determined by assigning the formula +A5^2 to cell B5 and then copying B5 to the range B6..B13. Enter the worksheet in Figure 5-22 by following the first six steps in the Summary of Keystrokes—PROJS-5B in the Project Summary at the end of this project.

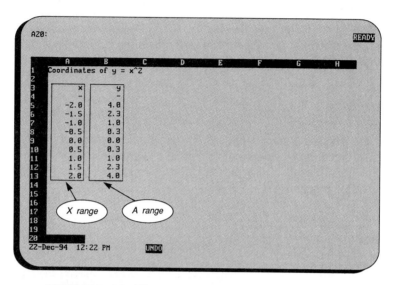

FIGURE 5-22   The worksheet we will use to plot the function $y = x^2$.

To plot the function $y = x^2$ in the form of an XY graph, enter the command **/Graph Type XY** (/GTX). Next, type the letter X to define the X range. Assign the X range the x coordinates (cells A5 through A13). Type the letter A to define the A range. Assign the A range the y coordinates (cells B5 through B13).

To complete the XY graph, let's enhance it using the Graph Options menu. Enter Graph of y = x^2 on the first line of the title and enter Between x = -2 and x = 2 on the second line. Enter the X-axis label X axis and the Y-axis label Y axis. Type the letter Q to quit the Graph Options menu.

With the menu pointer in the Graph menu, type the letter V for View. The XY graph shown in Figure 5-21 displays on the screen. To return to the Graph menu after viewing the graph, press any key on the keyboard.

Quit the Graph menu and save the worksheet shown in Figure 5-22 as PROJS-5B. Print the XY graph in Figure 5-21 by saving it as a PIC file using the file name XYGRAPH.PIC. Finally, quit 1-2-3 and use PrintGraph to print the XY graph.

ADDING A GRAPH TO THE WORKSHEET USING ALLWAYS

In the previous sections we printed the graph independent of the worksheet by using PrintGraph. In this section we will demonstrate how to use the add-in program Allways to place a graph alongside the data in a worksheet, and how to print the graph and data in the same report. Allways allows you to add up to 20 graphs in a worksheet and you can place them wherever you like. Once a graph is part of the worksheet, you can enhance its appearance by resizing it, shading its background, changing the graph title to a larger font, or drawing a box around the graph. To illustrate how to add a graph to the worksheet, we will place the graph of $y = x^2$ next to the table of coordinates in the worksheet as shown in Figure 5-23.

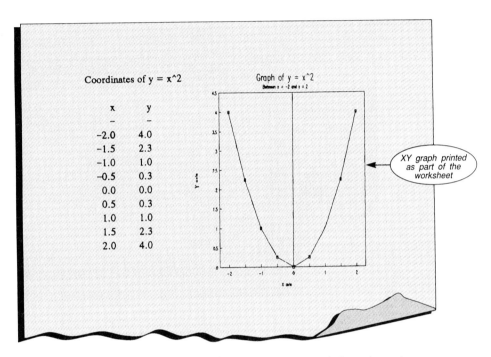

FIGURE 5-23   The XY graph is included in the worksheet through the use of the Allways command **/G**raph **A**dd (/GA).

Starting Allways

With the worksheet in Figure 5-22 on the screen and the XY graph saved under the name XYGRAPH.PIC, enter the command **/A**dd-In **I**nvoke (/AI). Select the add-in program Allways and press the Enter key. The worksheet with the table of coordinates shown earlier in Figure 5-21 displays on the screen in graphics form, rather than in text form.

Adding the Graph to the Worksheet

Enter the Allways command /Graph (/G). The Graph menu displays as shown in the top screen of Figure 5-24. Type the letter A for Add. Allways displays a list of the PIC files on the default drive. Select XYGRAPH and press the Enter key. Allways prompts you to enter the range of cells where you want the graph to appear in the worksheet. Enter the range D1..H13 and press the Enter key. Allways responds by crosshatching the range to indicate where the graph will display (bottom screen of Figure 5-24).

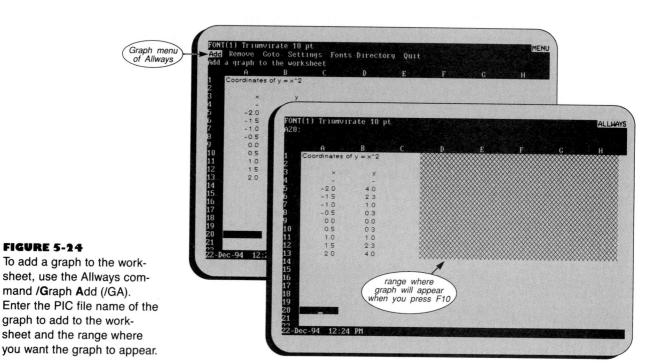

FIGURE 5-24

To add a graph to the worksheet, use the Allways command /Graph Add (/GA). Enter the PIC file name of the graph to add to the worksheet and the range where you want the graph to appear.

Press the F10 key to display the graph (Figure 5-25), rather than the crosshatched design. The F10 key serves as a toggle key. Press it once and the graph appears in the specified range. Press it again and the crosshatched design appears in place of the graph. The advantage of displaying the crosshatched design in the range is that Allways redisplays the worksheet faster when you are enhancing it because Allways does not have to continually redraw the graph.

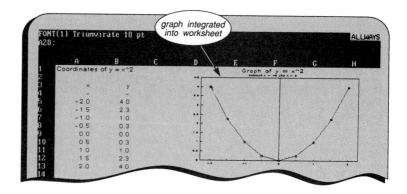

FIGURE 5-25

Press the F10 key to display the XYGRAPH.PIC graph in the specified range of the worksheet.

Compare the graph in Figure 5-25 to the one in Figure 5-21. Notice that Allways automatically sizes the graph in Figure 5-25 so that it fits in the specified range.

Before printing the worksheet, let's change the table of coordinates font to Times 14 point and resize the graph.

Changing the Font

Press the Home key to move the cell pointer to A1. Enter the Allways command /**F**ormat **F**ont (/FF). Select Times 14 point from the menu of fonts. Press the Enter key. Next, select the entire table of coordinates (A1..B13) and press the Enter key. The table of coordinates display in Times 14-point font as shown in Figure 5-26.

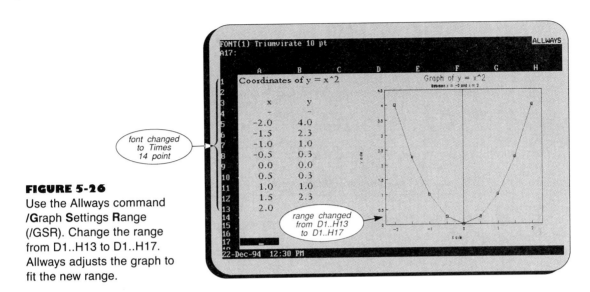

FIGURE 5-26
Use the Allways command /**G**raph **S**ettings **R**ange (/GSR). Change the range from D1..H13 to D1..H17. Allways adjusts the graph to fit the new range.

Resizing the Graph

Once the graph displays in the worksheet, you can resize it by increasing or decreasing the graph range. Enter the command /**G**raph **S**ettings (/GS). Allways prompts you to enter the name of the graph you want to adjust. Select XYGRAPH from the list. Next, type the letter R for Range. Allways highlights the old range (D1..H13) and prompts you to enter the new range. Enter the range D1..H17 and press the Enter key. Finally, type the letter Q to return to ALLWAYS mode. Allways immediately adjusts the graph to fit the new range as shown in Figure 5-26. Compare Figure 5-26 to Figure 5-25 and notice the difference in the graph sizes.

Printing the Worksheet with the Graph

To print the worksheet (table of coordinates and graph), enter the Allways command /**P**rint **R**ange **S**et (/PRS). Select the range A1..H17 and press the Enter key. Check to be sure the printer is ready. Type the letter G for Go. The worksheet containing both the table of coordinates and the graph prints on the printer as shown earlier in Figure 5-23.

If an "Out of Memory" message appears on the status line at the bottom of the screen, return control to 1-2-3 and save the worksheet. After the worksheet is saved, return control to Allways and issue the print command again. If the worksheet still fails to print, return control to 1-2-3 and enter the command /**W**orksheet **G**lobal **D**efault **O**ther **U**ndo **D**isable (/WGDOUD) to disable the UNDO command. After disabling the UNDO command, return control to Allways and issue the print command again.

Saving the Worksheet

To preserve the graph in the worksheet, use 1-2-3 to save it to disk. Use the Allways command /**Q**uit (/Q). Enter the 1-2-3 command /**F**ile **S**ave **R**eplace (/FSR). 1-2-3 saves the worksheet as PROJS-5B.WK1 and the corresponding Allways format changes as PROJS-5B.ALL.

The next time the worksheet is loaded into main memory and displayed using Allways, the graph will appear as part of the worksheet.

The Graph Commands

To add or modify a graph in a worksheet, enter the Allways command /**G**raph (/G). The Graph menu shown in the top screen of Figure 5-24 displays. Table 5-4 summarizes the function of each of the commands in the Graph menu.

TABLE 5-4 A Summary of Commands in the Allways Graph Menu

COMMAND	FUNCTION
Add	Adds a graph to the worksheet.
Remove	Erases a graph from the worksheet.
Goto	Moves the cell pointer to the specified graph.
Settings	Specifies fonts, scaling, colors, margins, and graph replacement.
Fonts-Directory	Defines the directory where the graph fonts are located.
Quit	Quits the Graph command.

The command /**G**raph **S**ettings (/GS) displays the Graph Settings menu. This menu is primarily used to enhance the appearance of the graph in the worksheet. Table 5-5 summarizes the commands available in the Graph Settings menu.

TABLE 5-5 A Summary of Commands in the Allways Graph Settings Menu

COMMAND	FUNCTION
PIC-File	Replaces a graph in the worksheet with another graph.
Fonts	Sets fonts for text in graphs.
Scale	Sets the scaling factor for fonts.
Colors	Sets colors for the graph data ranges.
Range	Resizes the graph or moves it to another area of the worksheet.
Margins	Sets margins for the graph.
Default	Restores the default graph settings.
Quit	Returns control to ALLWAYS mode.

PROJECT SUMMARY

In this project we created several graphs. All the activities that you learned for the projects are summarized in the Quick Reference following the Appendix. The following is a summary of the keystroke sequence we used in Project 5.

SUMMARY OF KEYSTROKES — PROJS-5A
(Figure 5-1 and Associated Graphs)

STEPS	KEY(S) PRESSED	RESULTS
1	/WGC12↵ (Build worksheet)	Sets width of all columns to 12.
2	→ →King's Computer Outlet↓	Enters line 1 of report title in row 1.
3	Year-End Sales Analysis→ → →↑	Enters line 2 of report title in row 2.
4	@NOW↵	Enters @NOW function in F1.
5	/RFD4↵	Formats F1 to Date 4.
6	↓↓"Total↵	Enters line 1 of column headings in F3.
7	[F5] A4↵City→"Quarter 1→"Quarter 2→	Enters first part of line 2 of column headings in row 4.
8	"Quarter 3→"Quarter 4→"Sales↵	Enters second part of line 2 of column headings in row 4.
9	[F5] A5↵\=↵/C↵.→ → → → →↵	Underlines column titles.
10	↓Chicago→40135→52345→38764→22908↵	Enters Chicago sales in row 6.
11	[F5] A7↵Tampa→48812→42761→34499→56123↵	Enters Tampa sales in row 7.
12	[F5] A8↵Atlanta→12769→15278→19265→17326↵	Enters Atlanta sales in row 8.
13	[F5] A9↵Dallas→38713→29023→34786→23417↵	Enters Dallas sales in row 9.
14	[F5] A10↵Boston→34215→42864→38142→45375↵	Enters Boston sales in row 10.
15	[F5] A11↵Oakland→52912→63182→57505→55832↵	Enters Oakland sales in row 11.
16	[F5] A12↵\-↵/C↵.→ → → → →↵	Underlines sales.
17	[F5] F6↵@SUM(B6.E6)↵	Sums B6..E6 in F6.
18	/C↵.↓↓↓↓↓↵	Copies F6 to F6..F11.
19	[F5] A13↵Total→	Enters row title in A13.
20	@SUM(B6.B11)↵	Sums B6..B11 in B13.
21	/C↵.→ → → → →↵	Copies B13 to B13..F13.
22	/RF,0↵B6.F13↵ [HOME]	Sets format of B6..F13 to Comma (,) and moves cursor to A1.
23	/FSPROJS-5A↵	Saves worksheet as PROJS-5A.
24	/GTP (Build pie chart)	Selects pie chart.
25	AF6.F11↵	Defines A range as F6..F11.
26	XA6.A11↵Q	Defines X range as A6..A11 and quits Graph command.
27	[F5] F15↵1↓2↓3↓4↓5↓106↵	Enters values in F15..F20 to crosshatch and explode pie chart.
28	/GBF15.F20↵	Defines B range as F15..F20.
29	OTFKing's Computer Outlet↵	Enters first title line to pie chart.
30	TSYear-End Sales Analysis↵Q	Enters second title line to pie chart.
31	V	Views pie chart.
32	↵NCPIE↵Q	Assigns pie chart characteristics to the graph name PIE and quits Graph command.
33	/FS↵R	Saves worksheet with PIE as PROJS-5A.

(continued)

SUMMARY OF KEYSTROKES — PROJS-5A (continued)
(Figure 5-1 and Associated Graphs)

STEPS	KEY(S) PRESSED		RESULTS
34	/GS		Initiates saving a snapshot image of the pie graph.
35	PIE-5A↵		Enters PIC file name PIE-5A.PIC.
36	RG	(Build line graph)	Resets current graph settings.
37	TL		Selects line graph.
38	XB4.E4↵		Defines X range as B4..E4.
39	AB13.E13↵		Defines A range as B13..E13.
40	OTF\C1↵TS\C2↵		Enters first and second title lines to line graph.
41	TXAll Cities↵TYDollar Sales↵Q		Enters x-axis and y-axis titles to line graph.
42	V		Views line graph.
43	↵NCLINE↵Q		Assigns line graph characteristics to the graph name LINE and quits Graph command.
44	/FS↵R		Saves worksheet with PIE and LINE as PROJS-5A.
45	/GSLINE-5A↵		Saves a snapshot image of the line graph as LINE-5A.PIC.
46	AB6.E6↵	(Build multiple-line graph)	Changes A range to B6..E6.
47	BB7.E7↵		Defines B range as B7..E7.
48	CB8.E8↵		Defines C range as B8..E8.
49	DB9.E9↵		Defines D range as B9..E9.
50	EB10.E10↵		Defines E range as B10..E10.
51	FB11.E11↵		Defines F range as B11..E11.
52	OLAChgo↵LBTampa↵LCAtl↵		Defines A, B, and C legends.
53	LDDal↵LEBos↵LFOak↵Q		Defines D, E, and F legends.
54	V		Views multiple-line graphs.
55	↵NCMULTLINE↵Q		Assigns multiple-line graph characteristics to the graph name MULTLINE and quits Graph command.
56	/FS↵R		Saves worksheet with PIE, LINE, and MULTLINE as PROJS-5A.
57	/GSMLINE-5A↵		Saves a snapshot image of the multiple-line graph as MLINE-5A.PIC.
58	OFGSQQ	(Build scatter graph)	Changes multiple-line graph to scatter graph.
59	V		Views scatter graph.

SUMMARY OF KEYSTROKES — PROJS-5A (continued)
(Figure 5-1 and Associated Graphs)

STEPS	KEY(S) PRESSED		RESULTS
60	←NCscatter←Q		Assigns scatter graph characteristics to the graph name SCATTER and quits Graph command.
61	/FS←R		Saves worksheet with PIE, LINE, MULTLINE, and SCATTER as PROJS-5A.
62	/GSscat-5a ←		Saves a snapshot image of the multiple-line graph as SCAT5A.PIC.
63	NU→ ←	(Build simple bar graph)	Selects LINE graph characteristics.
64	←TB		Selects bar graph.
65	OGHQ		Selects horizontal grid.
66	V		Views bar graph.
67	←NCBAR←Q		Assigns bar graph characteristics to the graph name BAR and quits Graph command.
68	/FS←R		Saves worksheet with PIE, LINE, MULTLINE, SCATTER, and BAR as PROJS-5A.
69	/GSbar-5a ←		Saves a snapshot image of the multiple-line graph as BAR-5A.PIC.
70	NUmultline ←	(Build side-by-side bar graph)	Selects MULTLINE graph characteristics.
71	←TB		Selects bar graph.
72	OGHQ		Selects horizontal grid.
73	V		Views side-by-side bar graph.
74	←NCsidebar ←Q		Assigns side-by-side bar graph characteristics to the graph name SIDEBAR and quits Graph command.
75	/FS←R		Saves worksheet with PIE, LINE, MULTLINE, SCATTER, BAR, and SIDEBAR as PROJS-5A.
76	/GSmbar-5a ←		Saves a snapshot image of the side-by-side bar graph as MBAR-5A.PIC.
77	TS	(Build stack-bar graph)	Selects stack-bar graph.
78	V		Views stack-bar graph.
79	←NCstack←Q		Assigns stack-bar graph characteristics to the graph name STACK and quits Graph command.
80	/FS←R		Saves worksheet with PIE, LINE, MULTLINE, SCATTER, BAR, SIDE-BAR, and STACK as PROJS-5A.
81	/GSsbar-5a ←		Saves a snapshot image of the stack-bar graph as SBAR-5A.PIC.

SUMMARY OF KEYSTROKES — PROJS-5B
(Figures 5-21 through 5-26)

STEPS	KEY(S) PRESSED	RESULTS
1	/WEY	Erases current worksheet.
2	Coordinates of y = x^2↓↓	Enters table title in A1.
3	"x→"y↓"-←"-↓	Enters column titles in A3..B4.
4	/DFA5.A13←-2←0.5←←	Generates numbers –2 through 2 in A5..A13.
5	→+A5^2←/C←B6.B13←	Enters +A5^2 in B5 and copies B5 to B6..B13.
6	/RFF1←A5.B13←	Formats A5..B13 to Fixed.
7	/GTX (Start XY graph)	Selects XY chart.
8	XA5.A13←	Defines X range as A5..A13.
9	AB5.B13←	Defines A range as B5..B13.
10	OTFGraph of y = x^2←	Enters first title line to XY graph.
11	TSBetween x = -2 and x = 2←	Enters second title line to XY graph.
12	TXX axis←	Enters x-axis title to XY graph.
13	TYY axis←Q	Enters y-axis to XY graph.
14	V	Views XY graph.
15	←Q/FSPROJS-5B←	Quits Graph command and saves worksheet with XY graph characteristics as PROJS-5B.
16	/GSXYGRAPH←Q	Saves a snapshot image of the XY graph as XYGRAPH.PIC.
17	/AIALLWAYS←	Invokes ALLWAYS.
18	/GAXYGRAPH←D1.H13←Q F10	Adds XY graph to worksheet in range D1..H13. Quits Graph command and displays XY graph rather than crosshatched design.
19	/FF↓↓↓↓↓↓←A1.B13←	Enters Times 14-point font to A1..B13.
20	/GS←RD1.H17←Q	Resizes the XY graph using the range D1..H17.
21	/PRSA1.H17←G	Prints the worksheet with the XY graph.
22	/Q	Returns control to 1-2-3.
23	/FSR	Saves the worksheet with the Allways settings as PROJS-5B.
24	/Q	Returns control to DOS.

The following list summarizes the material covered in Project 5.

1. 1-2-3 allows you to create, display, and print a graph of the data in your worksheet and get your message across in a dramatic pictorial fashion.
2. The first step in drawing a graph is to enter the command **/Graph (/G)**. This command activates the menu pointer in the Graph menu.
3. A **pie chart** is used to show how 100% of an amount is divided.
4. With a pie chart, you are allowed only three ranges. The A range specifies the data that is used to segment the pie. The X range is assigned the range of labels that identify the segments. The B range is used to shade and explode segments of the pie chart.
5. The type of graph, the ranges in the worksheet to graph, graph titles, and graph options are called the **graph settings**. They display on the graph settings sheet when the Graph menu is active.
6. The **current graph** is the one that displays when you enter the command **/Graph View (/GV)**.
7. An **exploded pie chart** is one in which one or more segments are offset or slightly removed from the main portion of the pie so that they stand out.

8. Through the Graph Options menu, you can assign two title lines of 39 characters each to identify the graph. Except on the pie chart, you may also add titles up to 39 characters each for the X axis and Y axis. Titles may be entered by keying in the title or by keying in a cell address preceded by a backslash (\\).

9. When numbers are changed in a worksheet, the current graph will reflect the changes the next time it is displayed.

10. The command /Graph Name Create (/GNC) can be used to store the current graph settings under a name. This allows you to have more than one set of graph settings associated with a worksheet. To assign a named set of graph settings as the current graph, use the command /Graph Name Use (/GNU).

11. To save any named graph settings to disk, you must save the worksheet. Use the /File Save (/FS) command.

12. The command /Graph Reset (/GR) allows you to reset all the current graph settings or any individual ones.

13. Printing a graph is a three-step process: first, save the graph to disk as a PIC file; second, quit 1-2-3; and third, use the PrintGraph program (PGRAPH) to print the graph. A **PIC file** is a snapshot of the graph saved.

14. **Line graphs** are used to show trends. You can have from one to six lines drawn in the graph. Each line represents a different data range (A through F) in the worksheet.

15. In a line graph, assign the labels for the X axis to the X range and assign the data ranges to the A through F ranges.

16. When more than one line is assigned to a line graph, it is called a **multiple-line graph**. Multiple-line graphs are used to show trends and comparisons.

17. The Group command in the Graph menu allows you to assign multiple data ranges when the ranges are located in consecutive rows or columns.

18. To identify the lines in a multiple-line graph, use the Legends command in the Graph Options menu.

19. A **scatter graph** displays the points in a graph without any connecting lines.

20 To create a scatter graph, follow the steps for a multiple-line graph. Next, through the Graph Options menu, use the Format Graph Symbols command to draw the symbols and delete the connecting lines.

21. A **bar graph** is used to show trends and comparisons.

22. A **simple bar graph** has a single bar (A range) for each value in the X range.

23. To add a horizontal grid to a graph, display the Graph Options menu and type the letters G for Grid and H for Horizontal.

24. A **side-by-side bar graph** is used to compare multiple data ranges. A side-by-side bar graph may have up to six bars per X-range value.

25. A **stack-bar** graph shows one bar per X-range value. However, the bar shows both the sum of the parts and the individual contributors.

26. Data-labels are used to explicitly label a bar or point in a graph. You may label any of the six data ranges A through F.

27. 1-2-3 automatically scales the Y axis for bar and line graphs and the X and Y axes for XY graphs. If you prefer to set the scales manually, use the Scale command in the Graph Options menu.

28. The Color and B&W commands in the Graph Options menu are used to display graphs in color or in black and white.

29. **XY graphs** are used to plot mathematical functions. In an XY graph the X range is assigned the X-axis values and the A range is assigned the Y-axis values.

30. The add-in program Allways allows you to place a graph alongside the data in a worksheet and to print the graph and data in the same report.

31. Allways allows you to add up to 20 graphs to a worksheet.

32. To add a graph to the worksheet, first use the 1-2-3 command /Graph Save (/GS) to save the graph as a PIC file. Next, use the Allways command /Graph Add (/GA) to add the graph to the worksheet.

33. Once the graph is part of the worksheet, use the F10 key to toggle between displaying the graph and the cross-hatched design in the range.

34. To resize the graph in the worksheet, use the command /Graph Settings Range (/GSR).

STUDENT ASSIGNMENTS

STUDENT ASSIGNMENT 1: True/False

Instructions: Circle T if the statement is true and F if the statement is false.

T F   1. The PrintGraph program is used to print WK1 files.
T F   2. A PIC file contains a worksheet.
T F   3. The Save command in the Graph Options menu saves a snapshot of the current graph.
T F   4. A line graph is used to show a trend.
T F   5. A line graph can have at most from one to four lines.
T F   6. To store the graph settings assigned to a worksheet under a name, save the worksheet using the Save command in the Graph menu.
T F   7. A pie chart can have from one to six data ranges.
T F   8. The X range is used to shade the segments of a pie chart.
T F   9. Data-labels are used to clarify a bar or a point in a graph.
T F   10. Legends are used to identify the bars and lines in a graph.
T F   11. If the title for a graph is the same as a label in a cell of the corresponding worksheet, enter the cell address preceded by a backslash (\) for the title.
T F   12. Multiple-line graphs are used to show trends and comparisons.
T F   13. The XY command in the Graph Type menu is used to display a bar graph.
T F   14. 1-2-3 automatically scales the axes in a graph unless you use the Scale command in the Graph Options menu.
T F   15. A stack-bar graph differs from a side-by-side bar graph in that it shows the combined total of the contributors.
T F   16. Side-by-side bar graphs are used to compare data ranges for the same period.
T F   17. A scatter graph shows a random sample of points in the graph.
T F   18. Once a graph is part of a worksheet, it can be moved to another range, resized, or deleted from the worksheet.
T F   19. The Reset command in the Graph Options menu allows you to reset individual graph specifications, like the ranges A through F.
T F   20. A graph must be saved as a PIC file before it can be added to the worksheet using the add-in program Allways.

STUDENT ASSIGNMENT 2: Multiple Choice

Instructions: Circle the correct response.

1. A side-by-side bar graph can have up to _____ bars per value in the X range.
   a. 3   b. 5   c. 6   d. 8
2. A line graph is used to show _____ .
   a. how 100% of an amount is divided   c. how two or more data ranges compare
   b. trends   d. none of these
3. Which of the following ranges are meaningless for a pie chart?
   a. X   b. A   c. B   d. C through F
4. Which of the following types of graphs can you draw with 1-2-3?
   a. line   b. bar   c. pie   d. XY   e. all of these
5. Which one of the following commands in the Graph menu displays the current graph?
   a. View   b. Type   c. Save   d. both a and b
6. In a stack-bar graph each bar shows _____ .
   a. the total amount for a label in the X range   c. none of these
   b. the contribution of each participant   d. both a and b

7. To explode a segment of a pie chart, add _____ to the corresponding cell in the _____ range.
   a. 100, C   b. 10, B   c. 1000, A   d. none of these
8. Data-labels are used to _____ .
   a. assign a title to the graph
   b. define which bar or line belongs to which data range
   c. clarify points and bars in a graph
   d. scale the X and Y axes

STUDENT ASSIGNMENT 3: Understanding Graph Commands

Instructions: Describe the function of each of the following 1-2-3 commands.

a. /G   _____
b. /GRG   _____
c. /GNU   _____
d. /GO   _____
e. /GTB   _____
f. /GTP   _____
g. /GOTF _____
h. /GRXQ _____

i. /GS   _____
j. /GV   _____
k. /GQ   _____
l. /GND   _____
m. /GTS   _____
n. /GNC   _____
o. /GOL   _____
p. /GG   _____

STUDENT ASSIGNMENT 4: Understanding the Graph Options

Instructions: Describe the purpose of the following titled sections in the Graph Options menu.

a. DATA-LABELS

   Purpose: _____

b. TITLES

   Purpose: _____

c. LEGEND

   Purpose: _____

d. SCALE

   Purpose: _____

e. FORMAT

   Purpose: _____

f. GRID

   Purpose: _____

g. COLOR

   Purpose: _____

h. B&W

   Purpose: _____

i. QUIT

   Purpose: _____

STUDENT ASSIGNMENT 5: Drawing a Pie Chart

Instructions: Load 1-2-3. Retrieve the worksheet PROJS-2 built in Project 2 (Figure 2-2).

Draw a pie chart that shows the revenue contribution for each month to the total quarterly revenue in the first quarter sales report. The pie chart should resemble the one shown in the following figure. Use these graph settings:

Type = Pie
X range = B2..D2
A range = B4..D4
B range = E4..E6
   (explode the March revenue)
Title 1 = \B1
Title 2 = TOTAL REVENUE

   Save the worksheet with the graph settings as STUS5-5. Save the graph as STUSP5-5.PIC. Use PrintGraph to print the pie chart.

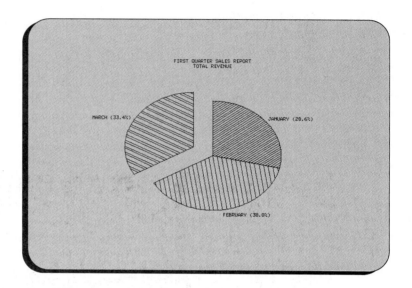

STUDENT ASSIGNMENT 6: Drawing a Multiple-Line Graph and a Side-by-Side Bar Graph

Instructions: Load 1-2-3. Retrieve the worksheet PROJS-2 built in Project 2 (Figure 2-2). Draw a multiple-line graph and a side-by-side bar graph that show the trends in the revenue, costs, and profit of the first quarter sales report. Use Allways to add graphs to the worksheet and enhance the worksheet's appearance.

Part 1: Draw the multiple-line graph. This graph should resemble the one shown in the following figure. Use these graph settings, and name the multiple-line graph MULTLINE. Save the multiple-line graph as STUSM5-6.PIC. Save the worksheet as STUS5-6. Use PrintGraph to print the multiple-line graph.

Type = Line
X range = B2..D2
A range = B4..D4
B range = B5..D5
C range = B6..D6
Title 1 = \B1
Y-axis title = Dollars
A legend = \A4
B legend = \A5
C legend = \A6

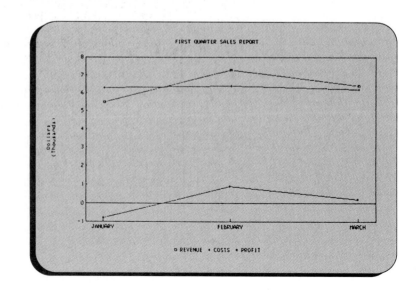

Part 2: Draw a side-by-side bar graph to show the same trends for the first quarter. This graph should resemble the one shown in the following figure. Use the same graph settings given above for the multiple-line graph, and name the graph SIDEBAR. For the side-by-side bar graph, change the Type to Bar. Save the side-by-side bar graph as STUSS5-6.PIC. Save the worksheet as STUS5-6. Use Print-Graph to print the side-by-side bar graph.

Part 3: Add the multiple-line graph and side-by-side graph to the worksheet STUS5-6 as shown in the figure below and to the right. Use Allways to modify the worksheet in the following ways:

1. Increase the width of column A to 15 characters.
2. Change the report title in cell B1 and the totals title in cell A10 to Times 14-point font.
3. Add the multiple-line graph in the range A17..C34.
4. Add the side-by-side graph in the range D17..F34.
5. Print the range A1..F34.

   Return control to 1-2-3 and save the worksheet as STUS5-6.

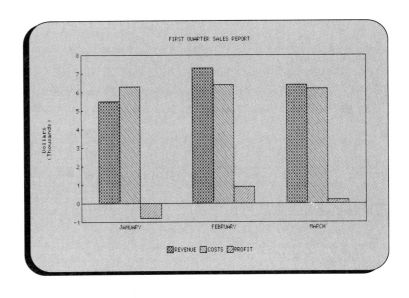

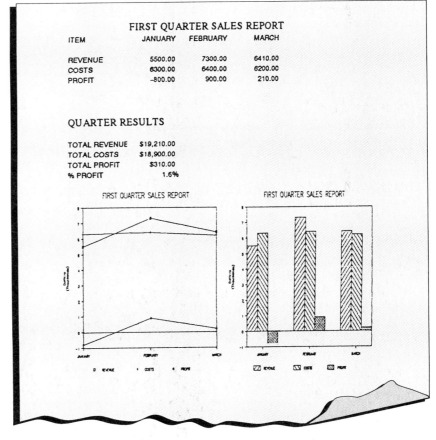

STUDENT ASSIGNMENT 7: Drawing a Stack-Bar Graph

Instructions: Load 1-2-3. Retrieve the worksheet STUS3-11 built in Student Assignment 11 of Project 3.

Draw a stack-bar graph that shows the individual contributions of each expense category and the total estimated expenses for each of the three months. The stack-bar graph should resemble the one shown in the following figure. Use these graph settings:

Type = Stack-bar
X range = B6..C6
A range = B15..C15
B range = B16..C16
C range = B17..C17
D range = B18..C18
Title 1 = Current and Projected Salaries

Y-axis title = Dollars
A legend = Accounting
B legend = Production
C legend = Sales
D legend = Distribution
Grid = Horizontal

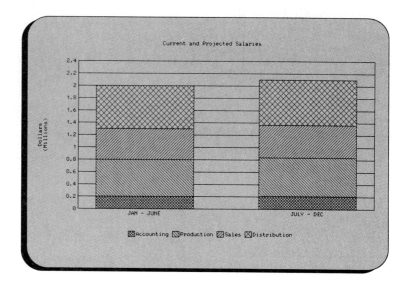

Save the worksheet with the stack-bar graph settings as STUS5-7. Save the stack-bar graph as STUSS5-7.PIC. Use PrintGraph to print the stack-bar graph.

STUDENT ASSIGNMENT 8: Building a Table of Coordinates and Drawing the Corresponding XY Graph

Instructions: Load 1-2-3. Complete Parts 1 and 2 below.

Part 1: Build the table of coordinates for the function $y = 2x^3 + 6x^2 - 18x + 6$ shown on the next page in the top screen of the figure and draw the corresponding XY graph shown on the next page in the bottom screen of the figure.
   For the worksheet, use the Data Fill command to build the column of X coordinates in the range A5..A19. Start with –5, increment by 0.5, and stop at 8191. Assign to B5 the formula 2*A6^3 + 6*A6^2–18*A6 + 6. Copy B5 to the range B6..B19. Format the range A5..B19 to the Fixed type with 1 decimal position. For the XY graph in the figure, use these graph settings:

Type = XY
X range = A5..A19
A range = B5..B19
Title 1 = Graph of y = 2x^3 + 6x^2 – 18x + 6
X-axis title = X axis
Y-axis title = Y axis

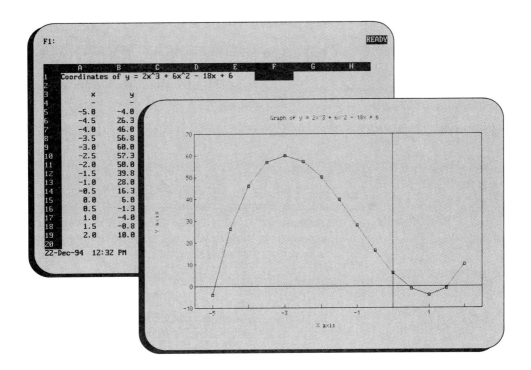

Save the worksheet with XY graph settings as STUS5-8. Save the graph as STUSX5-8.PIC. Use PrintGraph to print the XY graph.

Part 2: Add the XY graph in the bottom screen of the previous figure to the worksheet STUS5-8 as shown in the figure below. Use Allways to modify the worksheet in the following ways:

1. Change the report title in A1 to Times 14-point font.
2. Add the XY graph in the range D3..H20.
3. Print the range A1..H20.

Return control to 1-2-3 and save the worksheet as STUS5-8.

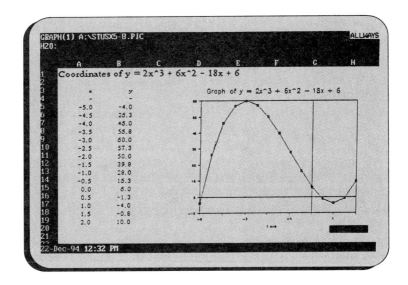

Sorting and Querying a Worksheet Database

LOTUS 1-2-3 Release 2.2

OBJECTIVES

You will have mastered the material in this project when you can:

◆ Define the terms database, DBMS, field, field name, and record

◆ Differentiate between records in ascending and descending sequence

◆ Sort a database on the basis of a primary key

◆ Sort a database on the basis of both primary and secondary keys

◆ Establish criteria for selecting records in a database

◆ Find records in a database that match specified criteria

◆ Extract records from a database that match specified criteria

◆ Apply the database functions to generate information about the database

◆ Utilize the lookup functions to select values from a list or a table

◆ Search for strings in the worksheet

◆ Replace strings in the worksheet

In this project we will discuss some of the database capabilities of 1-2-3. A **database** is an organized collection of data. For example, a telephone book, a grade book, and a list of company employees are databases. In these cases, the data related to a person is called a **record**, and the data items that make up a record are called **fields**. In a telephone book database, the fields are name, address, and telephone number.

A worksheet's row and column structure can easily be used to organize and store a database (Figure 6-1). Each row of a worksheet can be used to store a record and each column can store a field. Additionally, a row of column headings at the top of the worksheet can be used as **field names** to identify each field.

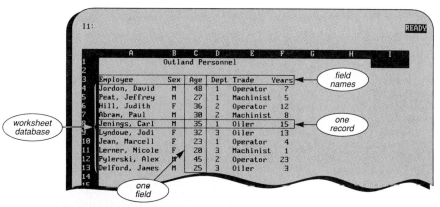

FIGURE 6-1 The worksheet database we will use to illustrate the database capabilities of 1-2-3.

A **database management system (DBMS)** is a software package that is used to create a database and store, access, sort, and make additions, deletions, and changes to that database. Although somewhat limited by the number of records that can be stored, 1-2-3 is capable of carrying out many of the DBMS functions. We have already used 1-2-3 as a database management system when we built, formatted, and enhanced our worksheets in the earlier projects.

In this project we will focus on the two functions of a DBMS that we have not yet discussed—sorting and accessing records. We also discuss the special database and table lookup functions and the Search command available with 1-2-3. For the remainder of this project, the term *database* will mean *worksheet database*.

The database for this project is illustrated in Figure 6-1. It consists of 10 personnel records. Each record represents an employee for the Outland Company. The names, columns, types, and sizes of the fields are described in Table 6-1. Since the database is visible on the screen, it is important that it be readable. Therefore, most of the field sizes (column widths) in Table 6-1 are determined from the column headings (field names) and not the maximum length of the data as is the case with most database management systems. For example, column E represents the Trade field, which has a width of nine characters because the longest trade designation is machinist (nine characters). Column F, which represents the years of seniority, is five characters wide because the field name Years is five letters long. The column headings in the row immediately above the first record (row 3) play an important role in the database commands issued to 1-2-3.

TABLE 6-1 Field Descriptions for the Outland Personnel Database

FIELD NAME	COLUMN	TYPE OF DATA	SIZE
Employee	A	Label	16
Sex	B	Label	5
Age	C	Numeric	5
Dept	D	Label	6
Trade	E	Label	9
Years	F	Numeric	5

Build the database shown in Figure 6-1 by following the steps listed in the Summary of Keystrokes—PROJS-6 in the Project Summary at the end of this project.

SORTING A DATABASE

The information derived from a database is easier to work with and more meaningful if the records are arranged in sequence on the basis of one or more fields. Arranging the records in sequence is called **sorting**. Figure 6-2 illustrates the difference between unsorted data and the same data in ascending and descending sequence. Data that is in sequence from lowest to highest in value is in **ascending sequence**. Data that is in sequence from highest to lowest in value is in **descending sequence**.

DATA IN NO PARTICULAR SEQUENCE	DATA IN ASCENDING SEQUENCE	DATA IN DESCENDING SEQUENCE
7	1	9
5	3	7
9	5	5
1	7	3
3	9	1

FIGURE 6-2 Data in various sequences

The Sort Menu

To sort a database, enter the command /Data Sort (/DS). The Sort menu displays in the control panel at the top of the screen, and the sort settings sheet displays in place of rows 1 through 10 in the worksheet (Figure 6-3). The commands available in the Sort menu are described in Table 6-2.

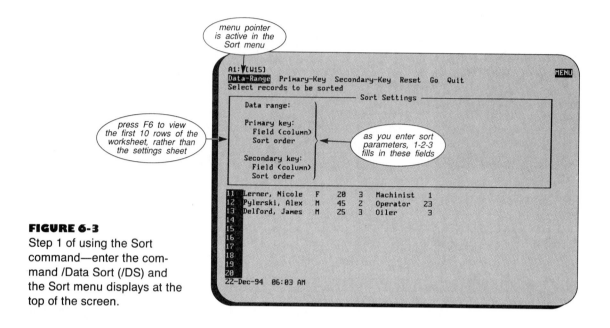

FIGURE 6-3

Step 1 of using the Sort command—enter the command /Data Sort (/DS) and the Sort menu displays at the top of the screen.

TABLE 6-2 A Summary of Commands in the Sort Menu

COMMAND	FUNCTION
Data-Range	Prompts you to specify the range of the database to sort.
Primary-Key	Prompts you to enter the field (column) you want to sort the records on and the sequence.
Secondary-Key	Prompts you to enter a second field (column) you want to sort on within the primary-key field, and the sequence for the secondary-key field. Used to *break ties* on the primary-key field.
Reset	Clears all sort settings.
Go	Causes the database to be sorted on the basis of the sort settings.
Quit	Quits the Data command and returns control to READY mode.

To illustrate the use of the Data Sort command, we will first sort the database in Figure 6-1 into ascending sequence on the basis of the employee name field (column A). Next, we will sort the same database on years of seniority (column F) within the sex code (column B). That is, the sex code will be the primary-key field and years of seniority will be the secondary-key field.

Sorting the Records by Employee Name

With the menu pointer active in the Sort menu (Figure 6-3), do the following:

1. Enter the data range.
2. Enter the primary-key field.
3. Enter the Go command.

To enter the data range, type the letter D for Data-Range. The **data range** defines the fields and records to be sorted in the database. The data range almost always encompasses *all* the fields in *all* the records below the column headings, although it can be made up of fewer records or fewer fields. Be aware, however, that if you do not select all the fields (columns) in the database, the unselected fields will not remain with the records they belong to and the data will get mixed up.

When you type the letter D for Data-Range, 1-2-3 responds by displaying the prompt message "Enter data range: A1" on the input line. Use the arrow keys and Period key to select the range A4..F13 as shown in Figure 6-4. Press the Enter key and the Sort menu shown at the top of the screen in Figure 6-3 reappears on the screen.

The next step is to enter the primary-key field. With the Sort menu on the screen and the cell pointer at A4, type the letter P for Primary-Key. 1-2-3 responds by displaying the prompt message "Primary sort key: A4" on the input line. Since column A is the employee name field and the cell pointer is in column A, press the Enter key. As shown in Figure 6-5, 1-2-3 responds with a second prompt message requesting the desired sequence of the sort. Type the letter A for ascending sequence and press the Enter key.

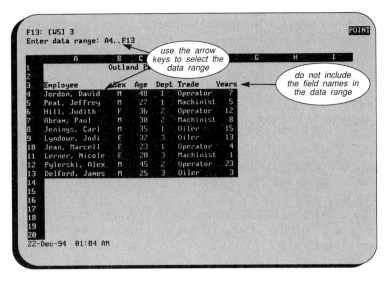

FIGURE 6-4 Step 2 of using the Sort command—enter the data range. The data range usually encompasses all the fields in all the records of the database.

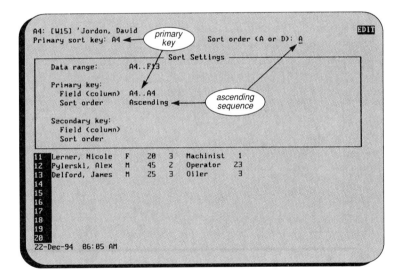

FIGURE 6-5 Step 3 of using the Sort command—enter the primary key and desired sequence for sorting the database by employee name.

To complete the sort, type the letter G for Go. 1-2-3 sorts the records and displays them in ascending sequence according to employee name. Following the completion of the Go command, control returns to READY mode as shown in Figure 6-6. Whereas the records in Figure 6-1 are in no particular sequence, the same records in Figure 6-6 are now in ascending sequence by employee name.

To complete this portion of the project, save and print a hard copy of the sorted database. Save the database using the file name PROJS-6A. Print the database following the same procedures used in the previous projects.

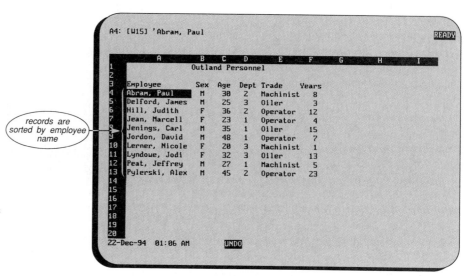

FIGURE 6-6 The database sorted by employee name in ascending sequence after typing the letter G for Go

Sorting the Records by Years of Seniority within Sex Code

In this example, we will use two sort keys. Our goal is to order the records so that the secondary-key field, years of seniority (column F), is ordered in descending sequence within the primary-key field, sex code (column B). We will sort the primary-key field into ascending sequence. Therefore, the female with the most years of seniority will be at the top of the list, and the male with the least seniority will be at the bottom of the list. This nested sorting always assumes that the primary-key field contains duplicate values.

To start this portion of the project, load the original database PROJS-6 (Figure 6-1) into main memory and enter the command **/Data Sort** (/DS). With the menu pointer active in the Sort menu (Figure 6-3), type the letter D for Data-Range. Next, select all the records in the database (A4..F13) as shown in Figure 6-4. Press the Enter key and the Sort menu shown earlier in Figure 6-3 reappears on the screen.

After the data range is set, enter the primary-key field. To accomplish this, type the letter P for Primary-Key. Move the cell pointer to column B (sex code) and press the Enter key. Type the letter A for ascending sequence. The primary-key field selections are shown on the input line in Figure 6-7. Press the Enter key to finalize the primary-key selections.

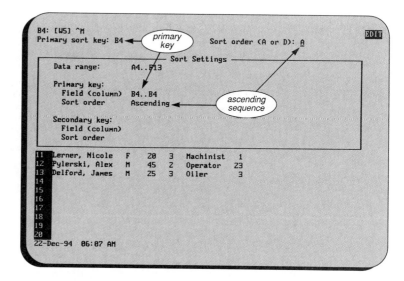

FIGURE 6-7 Entering the primary key and desired sequence for sorting the database by years of seniority within sex code

Type the letter S for Secondary-Key. 1-2-3 responds by displaying a prompt message on the input line requesting the secondary key. Move the cell pointer to column F, the one that contains the years of seniority, and press the Enter key. In response to the second prompt message on the input line, leave the D for descending sequence. The secondary-key field selections are shown in Figure 6-8. Press the Enter key to return control to the Sort menu.

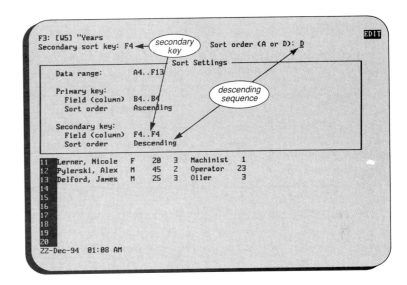

FIGURE 6-8
Entering the secondary key and desired sequence for sorting the database by years of seniority within sex code

To complete the sort, type the letter G for Go. 1-2-3 sorts the records and places them in ascending sequence according to the sex-code field in column B. Within the sex code, the records are in descending sequence according to the years of seniority in column F. This is shown in Figure 6-9. Following the completion of the Go command, 1-2-3 displays the sorted records and returns to READY mode.

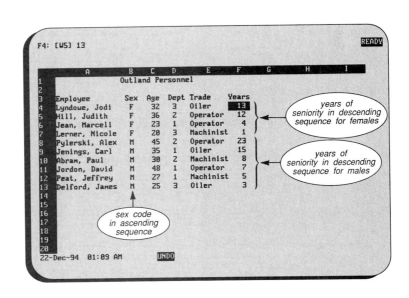

FIGURE 6-9
The database sorted by years of seniority within sex code

Save and print a hard copy of the sorted database. Use the file name PROJS-6B.

QUERYING A DATABASE

◆ One of the most powerful aspects of a DBMS is its capability to select records from a database that match specified criteria. This activity is called **querying a database**. Records that match the criteria can be highlighted, copied to another part of the worksheet, or deleted.

The Query Menu

To query a database, enter the command /**D**ata **Q**uery (/DQ). The Query menu displays in the control panel at the top of the screen, and the query settings sheet displays in place of rows 1 through 6 in the worksheet (Figure 6-10). The function of each of the Query commands is described in Table 6-3.

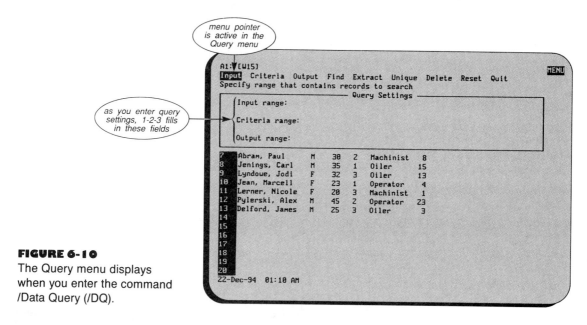

FIGURE 6-10
The Query menu displays when you enter the command /Data Query (/DQ).

TABLE 6-3 A Summary of Commands in the Query Menu

COMMAND	FUNCTION
Input	Prompts you to enter the range of the database to be queried. Usually the entire database is selected.
Criteria	Prompts you to enter the range of cells that includes the conditions for record selection. The conditions are entered into the worksheet off to the side or below the database.
Output	Prompts you to enter a range of cells to which records can be copied. The Output range is defined in the worksheet off to the side or below the database.
Find	Moves the cell pointer to the first record in the database that passes the test. The cell pointer moves one record at a time as you press the Up Arrow or Down Arrow key. When you invoke the Find command, the cell pointer extends to include the entire record. Pressing the Esc key or Enter key cancels the search.
Extract	Copies all selected records from the database to the Output range. The records that pass the test are selected from the database. Records that fail the test are not copied to the Output range.
Unique	Same as the Extract command, except that it copies only the first of any duplicate records.
Delete	Deletes all records from the database that pass the test.
Reset	Resets the Input, Output, and Criteria settings.
Quit	Quits the Data command and returns control to READY mode.

The Find Command

The Find command is used to search for records in the database that meet certain criteria. The command highlights the first record in the database that passes the test and continues to highlight records that pass the test as you press the Up and Down Arrow keys. If no more records pass the test in the direction you are searching, the computer beeps at you and the last record meeting the criteria remains highlighted.

With the database PROJS-6 (Figure 6-1) in main memory, let's search for records representing males who work in department 2 (Sex = M AND Dept = 2). To complete the search, do the following:

1. Choose an unused area off to the side of the database and set up the criteria.
2. Type the command /**D**ata **Q**uery (/DQ) and enter the Input range.
3. Enter the Criteria range.
4. Type the letter F for Find.

The first step in setting up the Criteria range is to select an unused area of the worksheet. Let's begin the Criteria range at cell H3. Copy cell B3 (Sex) to cell H3 and cell D3 (Dept) to cell I3. You can bypass the Copy command and enter the field names through the keyboard, but the field names in the Criteria range must agree exactly with the field names in the database, or the search won't work properly. To ensure that they are the same, it's best to use the Copy command.

Under each field name in the Criteria range, enter the value for which you want to search. In our example, we want to search for males who work in department 2. Therefore, enter the letter M in cell H4. (1-2-3 considers lowercase m and uppercase M to be the same in a Criteria range.) In cell I4, enter the label 2 (^2 or "2 or '2). These entries for the Criteria range are shown in Figure 6-11. The Criteria range must contain at least two rows—the field names in the first row and the criteria in the second row.

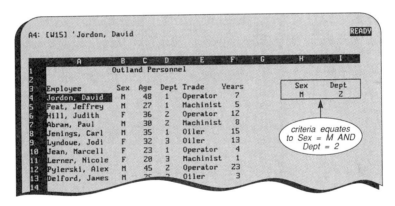

FIGURE 6-11   Step 1 of using the Find command—enter the criteria in unused cells off to the side of the database before issuing the Data Query command.

After building the Criteria range, enter the command /**D**ata **Q**uery (/DQ). The Query menu displays as shown in Figure 6-10. Type the letter I for Input and use the arrow keys to select the entire database (A3..F13). This is shown in Figure 6-12. The field names in row 3 must be included in the Input range. Press the Enter key.

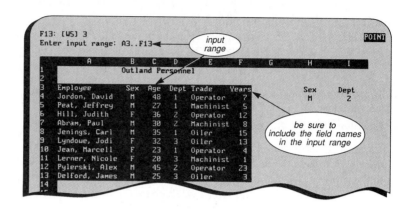

FIGURE 6-12
Step 2 of using the Find command—enter the command /Data Query Input (/DQI). Enter the Input range, which should encompass all the fields in all the records of the database, including the field names at the top.

Earlier, the Criteria range (H3..I4) was set up. Now it must be selected. Therefore, type the letter C for Criteria. Select the range H3..I4 as illustrated in Figure 6-13 and press the Enter key.

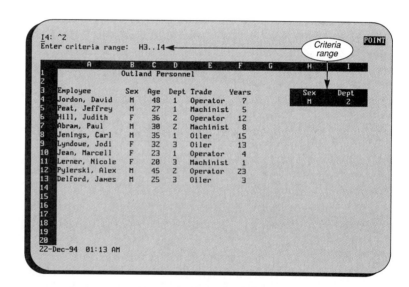

FIGURE 6-13
Step 3 of using the Find command—select the Criteria range.

Next, type the letter F for Find. As shown in the top screen of Figure 6-14, the first record that passes the test (Sex = M AND Dept = 2) is highlighted. Press the Down Arrow key and the next record that passes the test is highlighted. This is shown in the bottom screen of Figure 6-14. If you press the Down Arrow key again, the computer will beep at you because there are no more records that pass the test below the highlighted one. If you press the Up Arrow key, the previous record that passed the test is highlighted again.

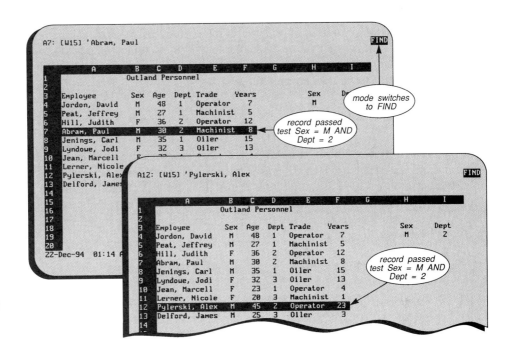

FIGURE 6-14
Step 4 of using the Find command—use the Up and Down Arrow keys to highlight the next record that passes the criteria.

After typing the letter F to invoke the Find command, you can move the elongated cursor to the very first record by pressing the Home key. You can move it to the last record by pressing the End key. These two keys allow you to start the search at the top or the bottom of the database. To terminate the Find command, press the Enter key or the Esc key to return to the Data Query menu.

While the Find command is still active, you can edit the record that is highlighted. Use the Right Arrow and Left Arrow keys to move from one field to another. Because the entire record is highlighted, the cell pointer does not move to the different fields when you use the arrow keys. However, you can determine the field location of the cell pointer because the cell address displays at the top of the screen on the status line. The blinking underline cursor that is active in the current cell also indicates the location of the cell pointer. When the cell address of the field you want to change displays in the upper left corner of the control panel, you can retype the contents or use the F2 key to edit them. If you decide the original values were correct before pressing the Enter key to complete the change, you can press the Esc key to discard the change.

To complete this portion of this project, save and print the database and criteria. Use the file name PROJS-6C.

More About the Criteria Range

The way you set up the Criteria range determines which records pass the test when you use the Find command. The following paragraphs describe several different examples of valid field names and logical expressions within a Criteria range.

No Conditions If the Criteria range contains no values below the field names, all the records pass the test. For example, if you use the Criteria range at the right, then all the records in the Input range pass the test and the Find command highlights every record in the Input range, one at a time.

Sex	Trade

Conditions with Labels The values below the field names in the Criteria range can be labels, numbers, or formulas. For example, if you want to select all the records in the database that represent employees who are operators, use the criteria at the right. In this example Operator is a label. If you use the Find command, this Criteria range causes 1-2-3 to use the condition Trade = Operator to evaluate each record. If the condition is true, the record passes the test and it is highlighted. If Trade does not equal Operator, the record fails the test and it is bypassed.

Trade
Operator

More than one type of trade can be listed in the Criteria range. For example, if you want to select records that represent employees who are operators or employees who are oilers (Trade = Operator OR Trade = Oiler), you can set up a Criteria range with the entries at the right. In this example, the Criteria range is three rows long.

| Trade |
| Operator |
| Oiler |

The global characters question mark (?) and asterisk (*) can be used within labels. The asterisk (*) means *any characters at this position and all remaining positions*. The question mark (?) means *any character at this position*. These **global characters** are also called **wild-card characters**. For example, the Criteria range at the right causes all records whose trade begins with the letter O to be selected. In our database, records with the trade of oiler or operator pass the test. The remaining records fail the test.

| Trade |
| O* |

The Criteria range at the right causes all records to be selected that represent employees whose trade is five characters long, begins with the letter O, and ends with the letters er. With regard to the placement of wild-card characters in a label, the question mark (?) can be used in any character position. The asterisk (*) can be used only at the end of a label.

| Trade |
| O??er |

Labels can also be preceded by the tilde (˜) to exclude a match. To select the records representing employees that work in any department other than department 3, you may use the criteria at the right. The department numbers in our database are labels, not numbers. The tilde (˜) can only precede labels. Table 6-4 summarizes the special symbols that may be used with labels in a Criteria range.

| Dept |
| ˜3 |

TABLE 6-4   A Summary of Special Symbols That Can Be Used with Labels in a Criteria Range

SYMBOL	MEANING	EXAMPLE
*	Any characters at this position and all remaining positions	Tr*
?	Any character at this position	M??T
˜	Not	˜F

Conditions with Numbers   If you want to select records that represent employees who are 30 years old, enter the criteria in the entry at the right. In this example, 1-2-3 uses the expression Age = 30 to determine if each record passes the test when the Find command is used. It is invalid to begin a number with any of the special characters we described earlier for labels, like *, ?, and ˜.

| Age |
| 30 |

Conditions with Formulas   Formula criteria are entered into the Criteria range beginning with a plus sign (+). The plus sign is followed by the address of the cell of the first record immediately below the specified field name in the Input range. The cell address is followed by a relational operator and the value to which to compare the field name. (Table 4-3 in Project 4 contains a list of the valid relational operators.) If you want to select all records that represent employees who are older than 25, use the criteria at the right.

| Age |
| +C4>25 |

The cell address C4 is the first cell in the database below the field name Age (Figure 6-15). Since C4 is a relative cell address, 1-2-3 adjusts the row as it goes through the database, passing and failing records. Hence, when you invoke the Find command, cell address C4 is used only to evaluate the first record. Thereafter, the 4 in C4 is adjusted to 5, 6, and so on, as each record in the database is evaluated.

In the previous example, the formula $+C4>25$ was shown in the cell below the field name Age. Actually, when a condition containing a formula is assigned to the cell, 0 or 1 displays. The number displayed in the cell assigned the formula $+C4>25$ depends on the value in cell C4. If it is greater than 25, then 1 (true) displays. If C4 contains a value less than or equal to 25, then 0 (false) displays. You can use the command /**R**ange **F**ormat **T**ext (/RFT) to display the formula in the Criteria range, rather than the numeric value 0 or 1.

Compound conditions may be formed by using the logical operators #AND#, #OR#, and #NOT#. (Table 4-4 in Project 4 provides an explanation of their meaning.) In the following example, all records are selected that meet the criteria Age < 37 AND Years ≥ 10.

Age
$+C4<37\#AND\#+F4>=10$

The compound condition may include numeric fields that are not directly under the field name. In this case, C4 refers to the Age field and F4 refers to the Years field.

Mixing Conditions with Formulas and Labels   If the criteria require both a label and a formula, use multiple field names. For example, if you wanted to find all records in the employee database that represent operators with more than 10 years of seniority (Trade = Operator AND Years > 10), use the criteria at the right.

Trade	Years
Operator	$+F4>10$

To select records that meet the criteria Trade = Operator OR Years > 10, use the entry at the right. Because the expressions Operator and $+F4>10$ are in different rows, 1-2-3 selects records that represent employees who are operators or have more than 10 years of seniority.

Trade	Years
Operator	
	$+F4>10$

The Delete Command

You can use the Delete command in the Data Query menu to delete all records that pass the test described in the Criteria range. As each record is deleted, all those below it move up toward the top of the database. Since the Delete command physically removes records from the database, it is strongly recommended that before executing this command, you save the database to disk.

The Extract Command

The Extract command copies data from the records that pass the test to the designated fields in the Output range. The Output range is a group of cells off to the side or below the database. The first row of the Output range includes duplicates of the field names in the Input range that you want to extract. This command is very powerful because it allows you to build a database that is a subset of the original one. The subset database can be printed, saved as a new database, or queried like any other database.

Again, load the employee database PROJS-6 (Figure 6-1) into main memory. Assume that your manager wants you to generate a list of all those employees who meet the criteria:

Age ≥ 27 AND NOT(Dept = 3) AND Years < 10

In the list, include the employee name, department, and sex code of all the records that pass the test.

To complete the extract, do the following:

1. Choose an area off to the side of the database and set up the criteria.
2. Choose an area below the database and set up an area to receive the extracted results.
3. Invoke the command /**D**ata **Q**uery (/DQ) and enter the Input range.
4. Enter the Criteria range.
5. Enter the Output range.
6. Type the letter E for Extract.

The criteria for this query involve three fields—Age, Dept, and Years. Use the cells in the range G3 through I4 for the Criteria range. Copy the three field names Age, Dept, and Years from the database in row 3 to cells G3, H3, and I3. The first condition in the previously stated criteria is Age ≥ 27. Therefore, in cell G4, enter the formula +C4>=27. This is shown in Figure 6-15. (Cells G4 through I4 have been formatted to the Text type so that the formulas display, rather than the numeric values 0 or 1.) The second condition is NOT(Dept = 3). Therefore, in cell H4, enter ~3. The condition for the third field is Years < 10. In cell I4, enter +F4<10.

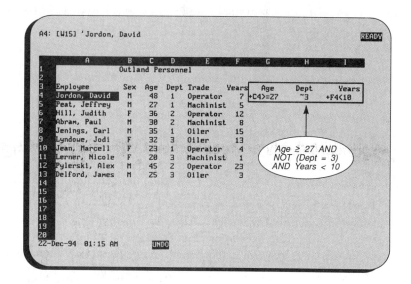

FIGURE 6-15
Step 1 of using the Extract command—enter the criteria in unused cells off to the side of the database.

The next step is to set up the Output range. This involves copying the names of the fields at the top of the database (row 3) to an area below the database. Since we want to extract the employee name, department, and sex code, copy the three field names to row 16 as illustrated in Figure 6-16.

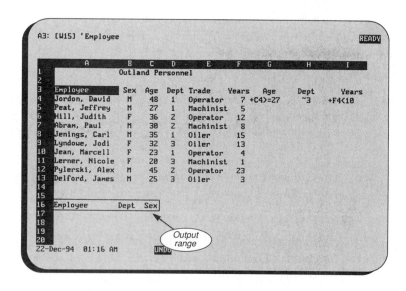

FIGURE 6-16
Step 2 of using the Extract command—copy the field names for the Output range below the database.

Enter the command /**D**ata **Q**uery (/DQ). The Query menu shown at the top of the screen in Figure 6-10 displays. Type the letter I for Input. Use the arrow keys to select the entire database, including the field names in row 3 (A3..F13). The Input range is shown in Figure 6-17. Press the Enter key.

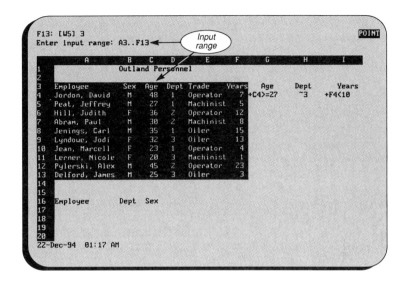

FIGURE 6-17

Step 3 of using the Extract command—enter the command /Data Query (/DQ) and enter the Input range. The Input range usually encompasses all the fields in all the records of the database, including the field names.

With the menu pointer in the Query menu, type the letter C for Criteria. Select the Criteria range G3..I4 as shown in Figure 6-18. Press the Enter key.

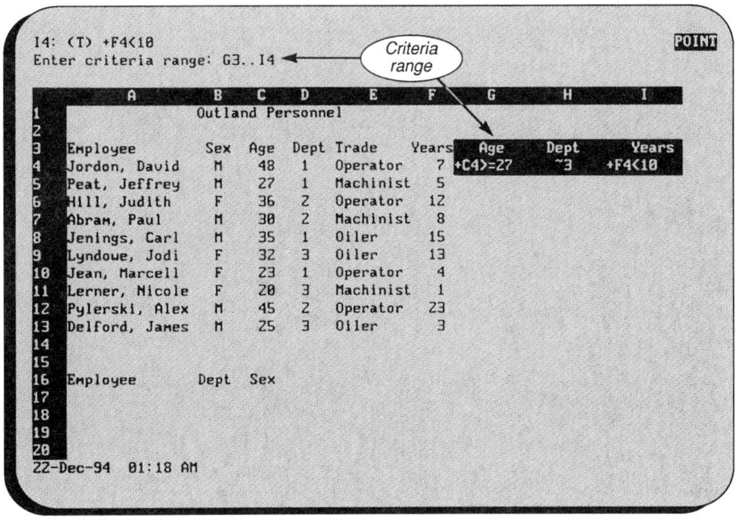

FIGURE 6-18

Step 4 of using the Extract command—enter the Criteria range.

Now type the letter O for Output. Select the range A16..C16 (Figure 6-19). Press the Enter key.

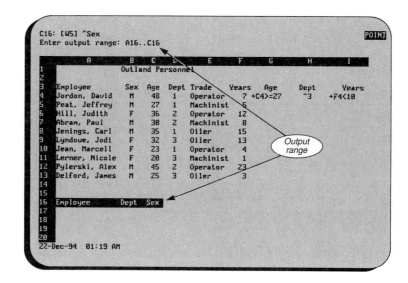

FIGURE 6-19
Step 5 of using the Extract command—enter the Output range.

After the Input, Criteria, and Output ranges are set, type the letter E for Extract. This causes 1-2-3 to select the records that meet the criteria specified in the range A3..I4. For each record selected, it copies the employee name, department, and sex code to the next available row beneath the field names in the Output range. Type the letter Q to quit the Data Query command. The results of the extract display below the database as shown in Figure 6-20. Save and print the database, criteria, and records extracted. To save the database, use the file name PROJS-6D.

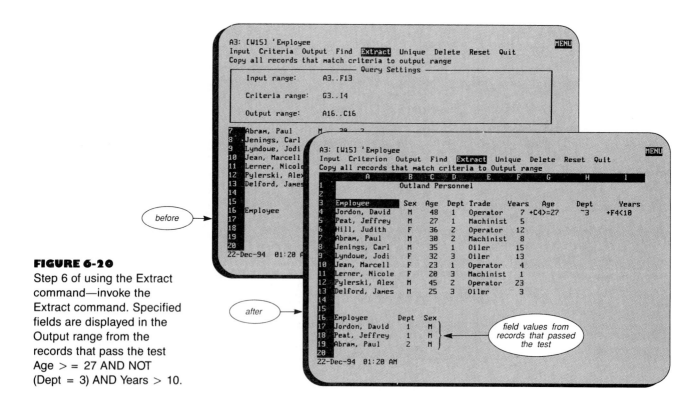

FIGURE 6-20
Step 6 of using the Extract command—invoke the Extract command. Specified fields are displayed in the Output range from the records that pass the test Age > = 27 AND NOT (Dept = 3) AND Years > 10.

In the previous example, the Output range was defined to be the row containing the field names (A16..C16). When the Output range is defined in this fashion, any number of records can be extracted from the database. The alternative is to define a rectangular Output range. In this case, if more records are extracted than rows in the Output range, 1-2-3 displays the diagnostic message "Too many records for Output range".

THE DATABASE FUNCTIONS

◆ 1-2-3 has seven functions for evaluating numeric data in the database. The functions, which are similar to the statistical functions discussed in Project 4, are described in Table 6-5.

TABLE 6-5 Database Statistical Functions

FUNCTION	FUNCTION VALUE
DAVG(I,O,C)	Returns the average of the numbers in the Offset column (O) of the Input range (I) that meet the criteria (C).
DCOUNT(I,O,C)	Returns the number of nonempty cells in the Offset column (O) of the Input range (I) that meet the criteria (C).
DMAX(I,O,C)	Returns the largest number in the Offset column (O) of the Input range (I) that meet the criteria (C).
DMIN(I,O,C)	Returns the smallest number in the Offset column (O) of the Input range (I) that meet the criteria (C).
DSTD(I,O,C)	Returns the standard deviation of the numbers in the Offset column (O) of the Input range (I) that meet the criteria (C).
DSUM(I,O,C)	Returns the sum of the numbers in the Offset column (O) of the Input range (I) that meet the criteria (C).
DVAR(I,O,C)	Returns the variance of the numbers in the Offset column (O) of the Input range (I) that meet the criteria (C).

The purpose of these functions is to return a statistic, like the average, on the values in the column of the records that meet the specified criteria. For example, with the database in Figure 6-1 in main memory, let's compute the average age of the male employees and the average age of the female employees.

The first step is to set up the criteria for each average. For the average age of females, use the criteria shown in cells H3 and H4 in Figure 6-21. Likewise, for the average age of males, use the criteria shown in cells I3 and I4. Next, enter the labels that identify the averages. This is shown in cells A16 and A17 in Figure 6-21.

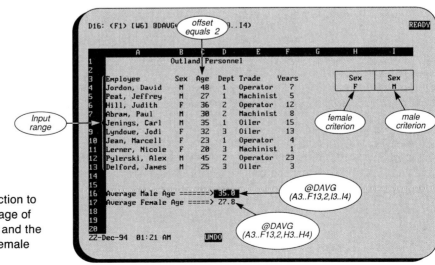

FIGURE 6-21
Using the DAVG function to display the average age of the male employees and the average age of the female employees

You can now assign the DAVG function to cells D16 and D17. This function has three arguments—Input range, offset, and Criteria range. Since the arguments in the function define the ranges, this function does not require that the ranges be defined through the Data Query command.

Set the Input range to the entire database (A3..F13). The offset argument defines the field in the database to be used in the computation. The offset of the leftmost field (Employee) is 0. The offset of the Sex field is 1. The offset of the Age field is 2, and so on. Hence, use the value 2 for the offset argument in the DAVG function. The third argument is the range of cells that make up the criteria—H3..H4 for females and I3..I4 for the males.

With the cell pointer at D16, enter the function @DAVG(A3..F13,2,I3..I4). This causes the average age of the male employees to display in cell D16. Press the Down Arrow key and enter @DAVG(A3..F13,2,H3..H4). This function causes the average age of the female employees to display in cell D17. Format cells D16 and D17 to the Fixed type with one decimal position. The effect of entering these two functions and formatting the results is shown in Figure 6-21. To complete this portion of the project, save and print the database, criteria, and averages. Save the database using the file name PROJS-6E.

THE LOOKUP FUNCTIONS

◆   Three functions that we have not yet discussed are the CHOOSE, VLOOKUP, and HLOOKUP functions. These three functions are called **lookup functions** because they allow you to look up values in a list or a table that is part of the worksheet.

The CHOOSE Function

The CHOOSE function selects a value from a list on the basis of an index. The general form of the CHOOSE function is @CHOOSE($x,y_0,y_1,y_2,...,y_n$), where the value of x determines the value in the list (y_0, y_1, y_2, ..., y_n) to store in the cell. If x equals 0, the first value (y_0) is stored in the cell. If x equals 1, the second value (y_1) is stored in the cell, and so on. The list can contain values, quoted strings, cell addresses, formulas, range names, or a combination of these.

Consider the partial worksheet in Figure 6-22. The table in the range E1..E7 contains costs. B1 is assigned the index that determines the value in the list that the function returns. The CHOOSE function is assigned to cell B3. It is entered as follows: @CHOOSE(B1,0,E2,E3,E4,E5+.02,E6*.95,E7,.46). Since B1 is equal to 3, the CHOOSE function returns the fourth value in the list—the value of cell E4.

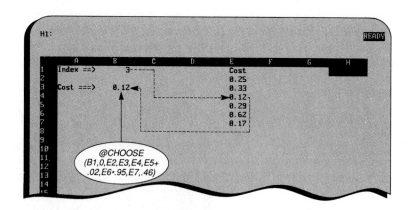

FIGURE 6-22

Using the CHOOSE function to select a value from the list of arguments following the index

If you change the value of B1 to some other number between 0 and 7, the function will store a different value in B3. If the value in B1 exceeds the number of items in the list, the diagnostic message "ERR" is assigned to B3. An index value of zero in cell B1 causes the CHOOSE function to assign zero to B3. If cell B1 is assigned a value of 7, the function returns the value .46 from the list and stores it in cell B3.

The VLOOKUP and HLOOKUP Functions

The VLOOKUP and HLOOKUP functions are useful for looking up values in tables, like tax tables, discount tables, and part tables. The general form of the VLOOKUP function is @VLOOKUP(x,range,offset). The first argument, x, is called the search argument. It is compared to values in the leftmost column of the multiple-column table defined by the second argument, range. The leftmost column of the range is called the range column. Offset defines the column from which a value is returned when a hit is made in the range column. A hit occurs when a value is found in the range column that is closest to but not greater than the search argument x.

The offset in the VLOOKUP function can be zero or positive. The offset value of the range column is zero. A positive offset causes a value to be selected from a column to the right of the range column.

While the VLOOKUP function looks up values in a table arranged vertically, the HLOOKUP function looks up values in a table arranged horizontally. Vertical tables are used more often than horizontal tables.

Consider the top screen of Figure 6-23. Column B contains a list of student test scores. A grade scale table is in the range F5..G9. Look up the corresponding letter grade in the grade scale table for each student test score and assign it to the appropriate cell in column D. For example, a test score of 78 returns the letter grade C; a test score of 99 returns the letter grade A. To look up the letter grades for the student test scores, enter the function @VLOOKUP(B5,$F$5..$G$9,1) in cell D5, the location of the letter grade for student number 1035.

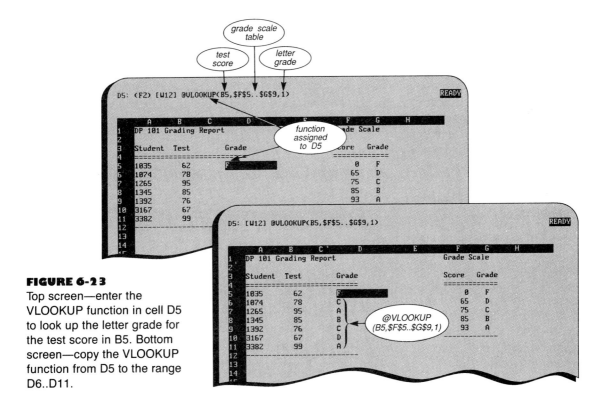

FIGURE 6-23
Top screen—enter the VLOOKUP function in cell D5 to look up the letter grade for the test score in B5. Bottom screen—copy the VLOOKUP function from D5 to the range D6..D11.

The first argument in the VLOOKUP function is cell B5, the test score for student number 1035. The second argument, $F$5..$G$9, defines the grade scale table. The third argument, 1, is the offset. It instructs 1-2-3 to assign the corresponding value in the grade scale table that is located one column to the right of the range column—column F.

Copy the VLOOKUP function in cell D5 to the range D6..D11. As the copy takes place, the first argument in the VLOOKUP function, B5, is adjusted to B6, B7, B8, and so on. The result of copying the VLOOKUP function is shown in the bottom screen of Figure 6-23. In this case, the VLOOKUP function in cells D5 through D11 returns the letter grades that correspond to the student test scores.

THE SEARCH AND REPLACE COMMANDS

◆ The /**R**ange Search (/RS) command is used to locate a string in labels and formulas within a specified range of the worksheet. A **string** consists of a series of characters that make up a cell entry. Use the Find command to locate a string. Use the Replace command to locate and replace one string with another.

The Find Command

To illustrate the use of the Find command, let's locate the string Oiler in the Outland Personnel worksheet shown in Figure 6-1. To find the string Oiler, do the following:

1. Enter the command /**R**ange Search (/RS).
2. Select the range A4..F13 to search.
3. Type the word `Oiler` as shown in the top screen of Figure 6-24. 1-2-3 does not differentiate between uppercase and lowercase letters. Hence, Oiler and oiler are the same.
4. Type the letter L for Labels. As shown in the bottom screen of Figure 6-24, you have three selections: Formulas, Labels, and Both. The Labels command tells 1-2-3 to search only those cells containing labels in the worksheet. Formulas means 1-2-3 will search cells containing only formulas. The command Both instructs 1-2-3 to search cells that contain either labels or formulas.
5. Type the letter F for Find as shown in the top screen of Figure 6-25.

   1-2-3 begins the search at the upper left cell of the specified range. It continues the search down and to the right. When 1-2-3 finds the word Oiler, it highlights the cell as shown in the bottom screen of Figure 6-25. Type the letter N to locate the next occurrence of Oiler. Type the letter Q to Quit the search and return 1-2-3 to READY mode.

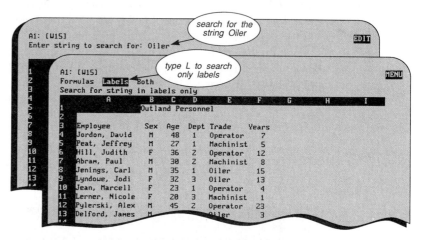

FIGURE 6-24 Initiating a search

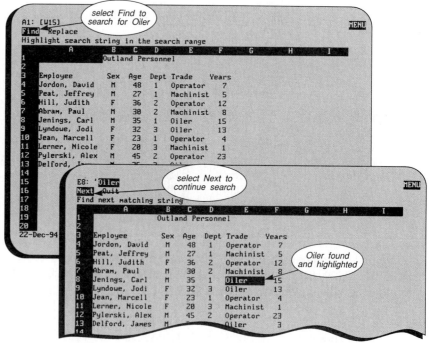

FIGURE 6-25 Completing the search

The Replace Command

The Replace command is similar to the Find command, except that the search string is replaced by a new string. To illustrate how the Replace command works, let's replace all occurrences of the word Oiler with Boiler. To initiate this command, follow the first four steps described for the Find command in the previous section (Figure 6-24).

With the top screen of Figure 6-25 displayed, type the letter R for Replace, instead of F for Find. 1-2-3 responds by displaying the prompt message "Enter replacement string:". Type the word Boiler as shown in the top screen of Figure 6-26 and press the Enter key. When 1-2-3 displays the menu shown in the middle screen of Figure 6-26, type the letter R for Replace. The first occurrence of Oiler is replaced with Boiler and 1-2-3 continues to search the worksheet. When it finds the next occurrence of Oiler, it redisplays the menu shown in the middle screen of Figure 6-26. This next occurrence is not changed until you select one of the commands. The bottom screen of Figure 6-26 shows all occurrences of Oiler changed to Boiler.

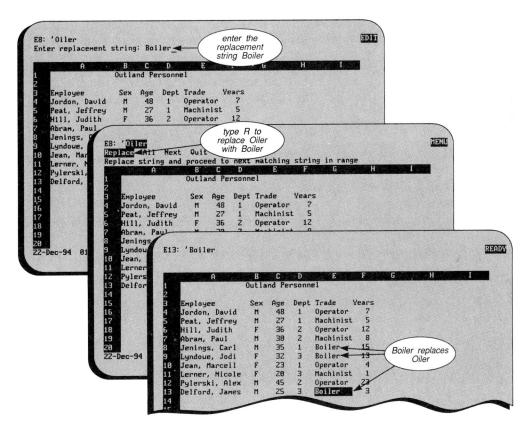

FIGURE 6-26   Completing a string replacement

Table 6-6 describes the functions of the Replace commands available in the middle screen of Figure 6-26.

TABLE 6-6   A Summary of the Commands in the Range Search Replace Menu

COMMAND	FUNCTION
Replace	Replaces the highlighted string and highlights the next cell containing the search string.
All	Replaces all remaining occurrences of the search string.
Next	Finds the next occurrence of the search string without changing the cell that is highlighted.
Quit	Stops the search and returns 1-2-3 to READY mode.

PROJECT SUMMARY

In this project you learned how to sort and query a worksheet database. The database was sorted in two different ways, first by employee name and then by years of seniority within sex code. Querying a database involves searching for records that meet a specified criteria. The selected records can be highlighted, extracted, or deleted.

Powerful database functions can be used to generate information about the database. In this project you were introduced to the lookup functions. These functions are used to return a value from a list or table. Finally, we discussed the Search and Replace. All the activities that you learned for this project are summarized in the Quick Reference following the Appendix. The following is a summary of the keystroke sequence we used in Project 6.

SUMMARY OF KEYSTROKES — PROJS-6 (Figure 6-1)

STEPS	KEY(S) PRESSED	RESULTS
1	/WCS16←	Sets width of column A to 16.
2	→/WCS5←	Sets width of column B to 5.
3	→/WCS5←	Sets width of column C to 5.
4	→/WCS6←	Sets width of column D to 6.
5	→→/WCS5←	Sets width of column F to 5.
6	F5 B1←Outland Personnel↓	Enters report title in B1.
7	↓←Employee→	Enters column A title in A3.
8	^Sex→	Enters column B title in B3.
9	"Age→	Enters column C title in C3.
10	^Dept→	Enters column D title in D3.
11	Trade→	Enters column E title in E3.
12	"Years←	Enters column F title in F3.
13	F5 A4←Jordon, David→^M→48→^1→Operator→7←	Enters Jordon's record in row 4.
14	F5 A5←Peat, Jeffrey→^M→27→^1→Machinist→5←	Enters Peat's record in row 5.
15	F5 A6←Hill, Judith→^F→36→^2→Operator→12←	Enters Hill's record in row 6.
16	F5 A7←Abram, Paul→^M→30→^2→Machinist→8←	Enters Abram's record in row 7.
17	F5 A8←Jenings, Carl→^M→35→^1→Oiler→15←	Enters Jenings's record in row 8.
18	F5 A9←Lyndowe, Jodi→^F→32→^3→Oiler→13←	Enters Lyndowe's record in row 9.
19	F5 A10←Jean, Marcell→^F→23→^1→Operator→4←	Enters Jean's record in row 10.
20	F5 A11←Lerner, Nicole→^F→20→^3→Machinist→1←	Enters Lerner's record in row 11.
21	F5 A12←Pylerski, Alex→^M→45→^2→Operator→23←	Enters Pylerski's record in row 12.
22	F5 A13←Delford, James→^M→25→^3→Oiler→3←	Enters Delford's record in row 13.
23	Home	Moves the cell pointer to A1.
24	/FSPROJS-6←	Saves the database worksheet as PROJS-6.

SUMMARY OF KEYSTROKES —
Sorting PROJS-6 by Employee Name (Figure 6-6)

STEPS	KEY(S) PRESSED	RESULTS
1	/FRPROJS-6↵	Retrieves the database worksheet PROJS-6.
2	/DS	Enters the Sort command.
3	DA4.F13↵	Selects A4..F13 as the data range.
4	PA4↵A↵	Selects column A as the primary key for ascending sort.
5	G	Sorts records in range A4..F13.
6	/PPRA1.F13↵AGPQ	Prints the database worksheet.
7	/FSPROJS-6A↵	Saves the database worksheet as PROJS-6A.

SUMMARY OF KEYSTROKES —
Sorting PROJS-6 by Years of Seniority within Sex Code (Figure 6-9)

STEPS	KEY(S) PRESSED	RESULTS
1	/FRPROJS-6↵	Retrieves the database worksheet PROJS-6.
2	/DS	Enters the Sort command.
3	DA4.F13↵	Selects A4..F13 as the data range.
4	PB4↵A↵	Selects column B as the primary key for ascending sort.
5	SF4↵↵	Selects column F as the secondary key for ascending sort.
6	G	Sorts records in range A4..F13.
7	/PPRA1.F13↵AGPQ	Prints the database worksheet.
8	/FSPROJS-6B↵	Saves the database worksheet as PROJS-6B.

SUMMARY OF KEYSTROKES —
Finding Records That Meet the Criteria Sex = M AND Dept = 2 (Figure 6-14)

STEPS	KEY(S) PRESSED	RESULTS
1	/FRPROJS-6↵	Retrieves the database worksheet PROJS-6.
2	F5 B3↵/C↵H3↵	Copies B3 to H3.
3	F5 D3↵/C↵I3↵	Copies D3 to I3.
4	F5 H4↵^M→^2↵	Enters label M in H4 and label 2 in I3.
5	/DQ	Enters the Query command.
6	IA3.F13↵	Selects A3..F13 as the input range.
7	CH3.I4↵	Selects H3..I4 as the criteria range.
8	F↓↓	Finds records that meet criteria.
9	Esc Esc Esc Esc	Quits the Find command.
10	/PPRA1.I13↵OMR77↵QAGPQ	Prints the database worksheet.
11	/FSPROJS-6C↵	Saves the database worksheet as PROJS-6C.

SUMMARY OF KEYSTROKES —
Extracting Records That Meet the Criteria Age > = 27
AND NOT (Dept = 3) AND Years < 10 (Figure 6-20)

STEPS	KEY(S) PRESSED	RESULTS
1	/FRPROJS-6←	Retrieves the database worksheet PROJS-6.
2	[F5] C3←/C←G3←	Copies C3 to G3.
3	→/C←H3←	Copies D3 to H3.
4	→→/C←I3←	Copies F3 to I3.
5	→↓+C4>=27→`~3→+F4<10←	Enters criteria in G4..I4.
6	/RFT←←←	Formats G4..I4 to Text.
7	[F5] A3←/C←A16←	Copies A3 to A16.
8	[F5] D3←/C←B16←	Copies D3 to B16.
9	[F5] B3←/C←C16←	Copies B3 to C16.
10	/DQ	Enters the Query command.
11	IA3.F13←	Selects A3..F3 as the input range.
12	CG3.I4←	Selects G3..I4 as the criteria range.
13	OA16.C16←	Selects A16..C16 as the output range.
14	EQ	Extracts records from the input range and places them in the output range. Quits the Extract command.
15	/PPRA1.I20←OMR77←QAGPQ	Prints the database worksheet.
16	/FSPROJS-6D←	Saves the database worksheet as PROJS-6D.

SUMMARY OF KEYSTROKES —
Using the Database Function DAVG (Figure 6-21)

STEPS	KEY(S) PRESSED	RESULTS
1	/FRPROJS-6←	Retrieves the database worksheet PROJS-6.
2	[F5] B3←/C←H3.I3←	Copies B3 to H3..I3.
3	[F5] H4←`F→`M←	Enters the labels F and M in H4 and I4.
4	[F5] A16←Average Male Age =======>↓	Enters row title in A16.
5	Average Female Age =====>←	Enters row title in A17.
6	[F5] D16←@DAVG(A3.F13,2,I3.I4)↓	Enters DAVG function for males in D16.
7	@DAVG(A3.F13,2,H3.H4)↑	Enters DAVG function for females in D17.
8	/RFF1←↓←	Formats D16..D17 to Fixed.
9	/PPRA1.I17←AGPQ	Prints the database worksheet.
10	/FSPROJS-6E←	Saves the database worksheet as PROJS-6E.

The following list summarizes the material covered in Project 6.

1. A **database** is an organized collection of data.
2. The data related to a person, place, or thing is called a **record**.
3. The data items that make up a record are called **fields**.
4. Each row in a worksheet can be used to store a record.
5. Each column in a worksheet can be used to store a field.

6. The row immediately above the first record contains the **field names**.
7. A **database management system (DBMS)** is a software package that is used to create a database and store, access, sort, and make additions, deletions, and changes to that database.
8. **Sorting** rearranges the records in a database in a particular sequence on the basis of one or more fields.
9. Data that is in sequence from lowest to highest is in **ascending sequence**.
10. Data that is in sequence from highest to lowest is in **descending sequence**.
11. To sort a database, enter the command **/D**ata **S**ort (/DS). Enter the data range and the sort keys. To complete the sort, enter the Go command.
12. The **data range** defines the fields and records to be sorted in the database. The data range for a sort is usually all the records in the database. Never include the field names in the data range.
13. A sort key, like the primary key, is assigned a column and a sort sequence.
14. Selecting records in a database on the basis of a specified criteria is called **querying a database**. Records that match the criteria can be highlighted, copied to another part of the worksheet, or deleted.
15. To query a database, enter the command **/D**ata **Q**uery (/DQ).
16. Before you enter the Data Query command, the criteria should be present in the worksheet. If you use an Output range, the field names for the Output range should also be present in the worksheet.
17. The Find command highlights records that pass the criteria.
18. To apply the Find command to a database, use the Data Query command to define the Input range and Criteria range. Finally, type the letter F for Find.
19. The criteria used to pass records include the field names and the values to which the field names are compared. Field names can be compared to labels, numbers, and formulas.
20. **Global**, or **wild-card**, **characters** are allowed in labels in the criteria. The two valid wild-card characters are the asterisk (*), which means *any characters in this position and all remaining positions*, and the question mark (?), which means *any character at this position*. The question mark (?) can be used anywhere in the label. The asterisk (*) can be used only at the end of a label.
21. A label preceded by a tilde (˜) in the criteria range negates the condition.
22. The criteria can include the logical operators AND, OR, and NOT.
23. The Delete command in the Data Query menu is used to delete selected records from the database.
24. The Extract command is used to copy selected records from the database to the Output range.
25. 1-2-3 includes database statistical functions to generate information about the database.
26. The **lookup functions**, CHOOSE, VLOOKUP, and HLOOKUP allow you to look up values in a list or table that is part of the worksheet.
27. A **string** consists of a series of characters that make up a cell entry.
28. To search for a string or replace a string with another in the worksheet, use the command **/R**ange **S**earch (/RS).

S T U D E N T   A S S I G N M E N T S

STUDENT ASSIGNMENT 1: True/False

Instructions: Circle T if the statement is true and F if the statement is false.

T F   1. The Reset command in the Sort menu resets the database back to its original sequence.
T F   2. The series of numbers 1, 3, 4, 5, 6 is in ascending sequence.
T F   3. A database management system is a worksheet.
T F   4. A database is an organized collection of data.
T F   5. The Extract command copies selected records to the Output range.
T F   6. To query a database, you must first select unused cells off to the side or below the database and set up the criteria.
T F   7. A sort key is identified by any cell in the column containing the field by which you want to sort.
T F   8. In a sort operation, the secondary-key field has a higher priority than the primary-key field.
T F   9. The tilde (˜) is used to OR a condition in the Criteria range.
T F 10. The wild-card character asterisk (*) may be used only at the front of a label that is part of the criteria.

Student Assignment 1 (continued)

T F 11. A Criteria range consisting of field names and empty cells below the field names will cause all the records in the database to be selected.

T F 12. The Criteria range must contain at least two rows and two columns.

T F 13. The DAVG function returns the average number of records in the database.

T F 14. The Offset column is relative to the leftmost field in the Input range.

T F 15. The database functions require that you define the Input range and Criteria range by invoking the Data Query command.

T F 16. It is required that the field names in the Output range be the same as the field names in the Input range.

T F 17. The /Range Search (/RS) command causes 1-2-3 to search for a string from right to left in the worksheet, one row at a time.

T F 18. The VLOOKUP and HLOOKUP functions are the same, except that VLOOKUP verifies the search of the table and HLOOKUP does not.

T F 19. An Offset column value of zero causes the VLOOKUP function to return the value in the range column that is closest to but not greater than the search argument.

T F 20. The Offset column in the VLOOKUP function cannot be negative.

STUDENT ASSIGNMENT 2: Multiple Choice

Instructions: Circle the correct response.

1. Which one of the following series of numbers is in ascending sequence?
   a. 1, 2, 3, 4, 5
   b. 5, 4, 3, 2, 1
   c. 1, 3, 5, 3, 1
   d. none of these

2. Which one of the following commands in the Query menu is used to highlight records?
   a. Extract
   b. Find
   c. Unique
   d. Criteria

3. To properly execute the Find command, the _____ and _____ range must be set.
   a. Input, Output
   b. Data-Range, Output
   c. Input, Criteria
   d. Data-Range, Criteria

4. Which one of the following characters represent *any character in this position*?
   a. tilde (˜)
   b. number sign (#)
   c. question mark (?)
   d. asterisk (*)

5. To copy all records that satisfy the criteria to the Output range, use the _____ command.
   a. Find
   b. Delete
   c. Extract
   d. Output

6. Which one of the following database functions returns the number of nonempty cells in the Offset column (O) of the records in the Input range (I) that meet the Criteria range (C)?
   a. DMAX(I,O,C)
   b. DAVG(I,O,C)
   c. DCOUNT(I,O,C)
   d. DVAR(I,O,C)

7. If a database has four fields, the rightmost column has an Offset value of _____ .
   a. 5
   b. 4
   c. 3
   d. 0

8. Which one of the following functions is used to search a columnar table?
   a. VLOOKUP
   b. CHOOSE
   c. SEARCH
   d. HLOOKUP

STUDENT ASSIGNMENT 3: Understanding Sorting

Instructions: Enter the database in the following figure and save it as STUS6-3. Sort the seven records on the basis of the problems that follow. Begin each problem by loading STUS6-3. Print the original worksheet and each sorted worksheet. Save each sorted worksheet as STUS6-3x where x is equal to the problem number.

1. Sort the database into descending sequence by cost.
2. Sort the database by district within division. Both sort keys are to be in ascending sequence.
3. Sort the database by department within district within division. All three sort keys are to be in descending sequence. (Hint: First sort on division. Next, sort *only* the first division by department within district. Continue sorting each division separately.)
4. Sort the database into descending sequence by division.
5. Sort the database by department within district within division. All three sort keys are to be in ascending sequence. (Hint: See the hint in problem 3.)

DIVISION	DISTRICT	DEPARTMENT	COST
2	1	2	1.21
1	2	2	2.22
2	1	3	1.57
1	2	1	3.56
1	1	1	1.11
2	1	1	1.45
1	2	3	2.10

STUDENT ASSIGNMENT 4: Understanding Criteria

Instructions: Write the criteria required to select records from the database in Figure 6-1 according to the following problems. To help you better understand what is required for this assignment, we have answered the first problem.

1. Select records that represent male employees who are less than 25 years old.

Criteria:

Sex	Age
M	+C4<25

2. Select records that represent employees whose trade is machinist or oiler.

Criteria:

3. Select records that represent employees whose last names begin with P or who work in department 2.

Criteria:

Student Assignment 4 (continued)

4. Select records that represent female employees who are at least 30 years old and have at least 10 years of seniority.

Criteria:

5. Select records that represent male employees or employees who are at least 30 years old.

Criteria:

6. Select records that represent male machinist employees who are at least 28 years old and whose last names begin with P.

Criteria:

STUDENT ASSIGNMENT 5: Understanding Database and Lookup Functions

Instructions: Load 1-2-3 and perform the following tasks.

1. Consider Figure 6-21 on page L243. Write a database function and the criteria that will assign to the current cell the number of years of seniority for the female employee with the maximum years of seniority. Use a Criteria range of I3..I4.
2. Consider Figure 6-21. Write a database function and the criteria that will assign to the current cell the average years of seniority of the male employees. Use a Criteria range of I3..I4.
3. Consider Figure 6-21. Write a database function and the criteria that will assign to the current cell the sum of the ages of the female employees. Use a Criteria range of I3..I4.
4. Consider Figure 6-21. Write a database function and the criteria that will assign to the current cell the average years of seniority for both the male and female employees. Use a Criteria range of I3..I4.
5. Consider Figure 6-22 on page L244. Use the CHOOSE function to assign cell B3 twelve times the cost in column E. Select the cost in column E on the basis of the index value in cell B1.
6. Consider the VLOOKUP function in the top screen of Figure 6-23 on page L245. Complete the following problems independently and write down the results displayed in column D:
   a. Decrease all test scores in column B by 10 points.
   b. Increase all test scores in column B by 10 points.
   c. Reset the test scores in column B to their original values and change the offset argument in the VLOOKUP function to zero.

STUDENT ASSIGNMENT 6: Building and Sorting a Database of Prospective Programmers

Instructions: Load 1-2-3 and perform the following tasks.

1. Build the database illustrated in the following figure. Use the field sizes listed in the table.
2. Save and print the database. Use the file name STUS6-6.
3. Sort the records in the database into decending sequence by name. Print the sorted version.
4. Sort the records in the database by years within sex. Select descending sequence for the sex code and ascending sequence for the years. Print the sorted version.

Field Descriptions for the Prospective Programmer Database

FIELD NAME	COLUMN	TYPE OF DATA	SIZE
Name	A	Label	16
Sex	B	Label	5
Age	C	Numeric	5
Years	D	Numeric	7
BASIC	E	Label	7
COBOL	F	Label	7
C	G	Label	5
RPG	H	Label	5
123	I	Label	5
DBASE	J	Label	7

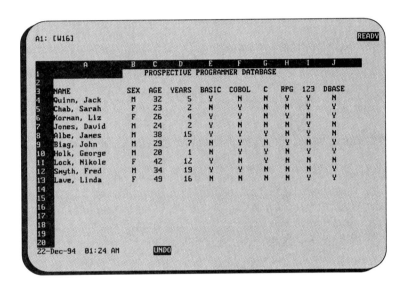

STUDENT ASSIGNMENT 7: Finding Records in the Prospective Programmer Database

Instructions: Load 1-2-3 and perform the following tasks.

1. Load the database created in Student Assignment 6 (STUS6-6). This worksheet is illustrated in the figure in Student Assignment 6.
2. For the Criteria range, copy row 3 (A3..J3) to row 15 (A15..J15).
3. In columns E through J of the database, the letter Y indicates that a prospective programmer knows the language or software package identified by the field name. The letter N indicates no experience with the language or software package. Find records that meet the following criteria. Treat each set of criteria in problems a through e separately.
   a. Find all records that represent prospective programmers who are male and can program in COBOL.
   b. Find all records that represent prospective programmers who can program in BASIC and RPG and use 1-2-3.
   c. Find all records that represent prospective male programmers who are at least 29 years old and can use dBASE.
   d. Find all records that represent prospective programmers who know 1-2-3 and dBASE.
   e. Find all records that represent prospective programmers who know at least one programming language and can use 1-2-3 or dBASE. (Hint: Your Criteria range should have 9 rows; including the field names.)
   f. All prospective programmers who did not know dBASE were sent to a seminar on the software package. Use the Find command to locate the records of these programmers and change the entries from the letter N to the letter Y under the field name dBASE. Save and print the database and the accompanying Criteria range. Use the file name STUS6-7.

STUDENT ASSIGNMENT 8: Extracting Records from the Prospective Programmer Database

Instructions: Load 1-2-3 and perform the following tasks.

1. Load the database created in Student Assignment 6 (STUS6-6). This worksheet is illustrated in the figure in Student Assignment 6.
2. For the Criteria range, copy row 3 (A3..J3) to row 15 (A15..J15). For the Output range, copy the field names NAME, SEX, and AGE (A3..C3) to K3..M3. Change the widths of column K to 16, column L to 5, and column M to 5. Extract the three fields from the records that meet the criteria in problems a through e. Treat each extraction in problems a through e separately. Print the worksheet after each extraction.
    a. Extract from records that represent prospective programmers who are male.
    b. Extract from records that represent prospective programmers who can program in BASIC and RPG.
    c. Extract from records that represent prospective male programmers who are at least 30 years old and can use 1-2-3.
    d. Extract from records that represent prospective programmers who know RPG and dBASE.
    e. Extract from records that represent prospective programmers who do not know how to use any programming language.
3. Save the database with the Criteria range specified in 2e. Use the file name STUS6-8.

STUDENT ASSIGNMENT 9: Property Tax Rate Table Lookup

Instructions: Load 1-2-3 and perform the numbered tasks to build the worksheet shown in the following figure. This worksheet uses the VLOOKUP function in cell C5 to look up the tax rate in the tax table in columns F and G. The VLOOKUP function employs cell C3 as the search argument. From the tax rate, the tax amount due in cell C7 can be determined.

1. Change the widths of column A to 11, column C to 13, and column F to 10. Leave the widths of the remaining columns at 9 characters.
2. Enter the title, column headings, and row identifiers.
3. Format cells C3 and C7 and range F4..F9 to the Comma (,) type with two decimal positions. Enter 57900 in cell C3. Format cell C5 and range G4..G9 to the Percent type with one decimal position.

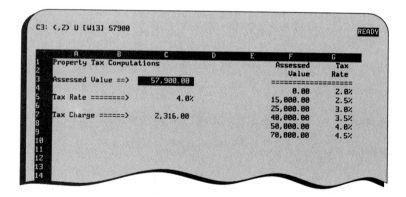

4. Enter the table values in the range F4..G9.
5. Assign the function @VLOOKUP(C3,F4..G9,1) to cell C5.
6. Assign the formula +C3*C5 to cell C7. This cell displays the tax amount due.
7. Test the worksheet to ensure that the VLOOKUP function is working properly.
8. Use the command /Worksheet Global Protection Enable (/WGPE) to enable (turn on) cell protection. Unprotect cell C3.
9. Save the worksheet. Use the file name STUS6-9.
10. Determine the tax rate and tax charge for the following assessed valuations: $9,850.00; $40,000.00; $62,550.00; $42,500.00; and $452,750.00. Remember that commas are not allowed in a numeric entry. Print the worksheet for each assessed valuation.

APPENDIX

Command Structure Charts for Release 2.2

This appendix includes structure charts for each of the commands in the Main menu of Release 2.2. The purple commands indicate features added in Release 2.2.

The Worksheet Command

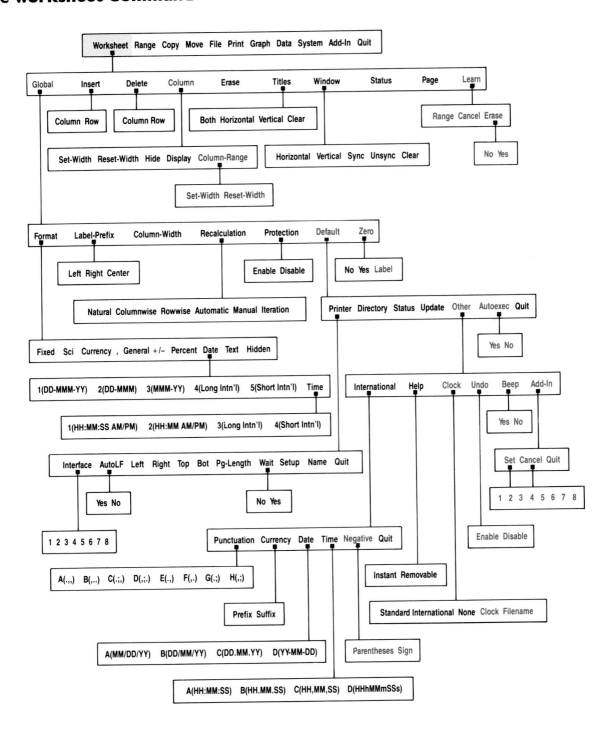

The Range Command

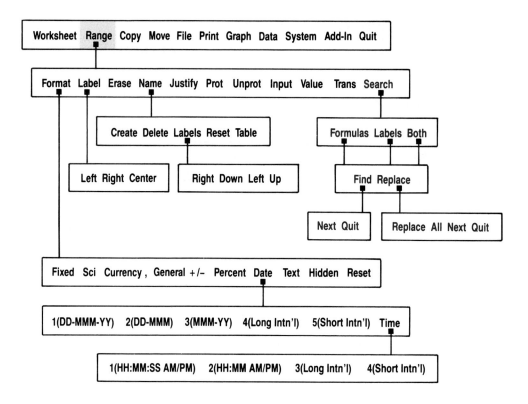

The Copy and Move Commands

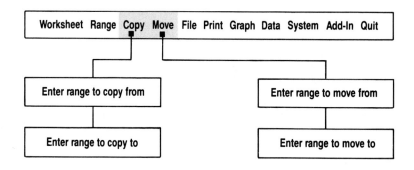

The File Command

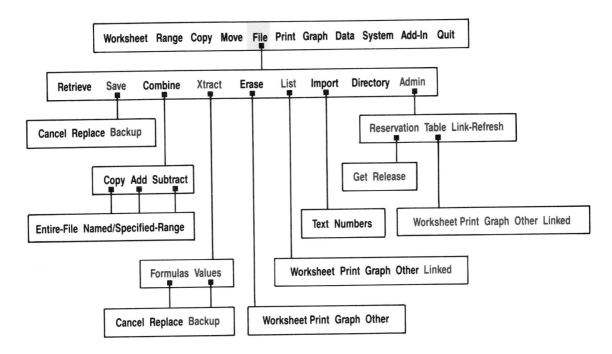

The Print Command

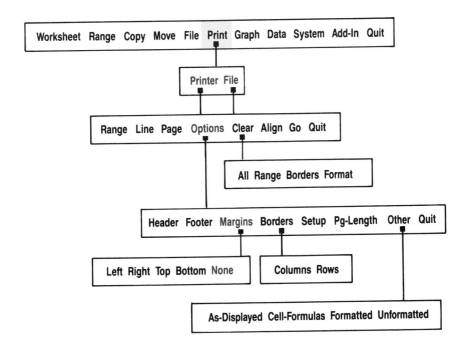

The Graph Command

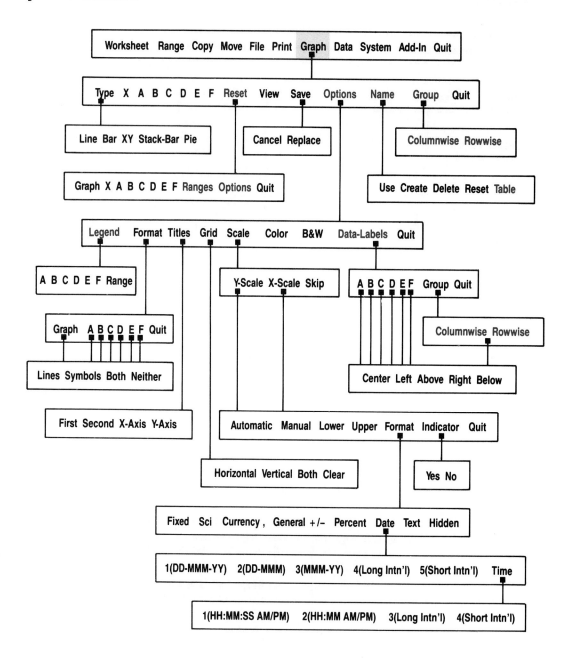

The Data Command

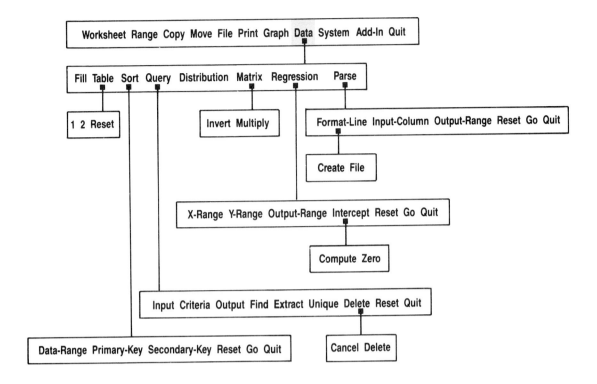

The System Command

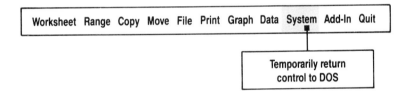

The Add-In Command

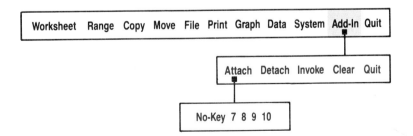

The Quit Command

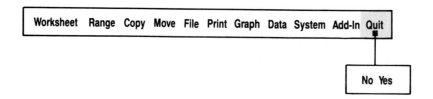

The PrintGraph Command

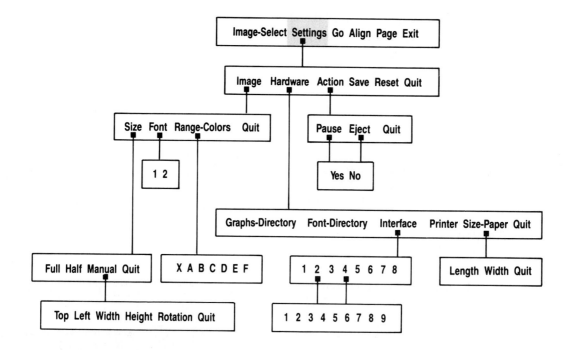

For each of the projects, we have provided the fundamental Lotus 1-2-3 activities in an easy-to-use quick reference format. This convenient reference tool is divided into three parts—activity, procedure, and description. All of the activities that you learn in each project are covered in the Quick Reference for that project. The numbers in parentheses that follow each activity refer to the page number on which the activity is first discussed in the text.

You can use these Quick References as study aids or to quickly recall how you complete an activity. The Quick Reference is a valuable and time-saving tool, and we encourage you to use it frequently.

QUICK REFERENCE — PROJECT 1

ACTIVITY	PROCEDURE	DESCRIPTION
START 1-2-3 (L2)	Type 123 Press ↵	Loads the 1-2-3 program into main memory.
MOVE CELL POINTER ONE CELL AT A TIME (L5)	↓ ↑ → ←	Press arrow keys to move cell pointer.
MOVE CELL POINTER MORE THAN ONE CELL AT A TIME (L15)	Press F5 Enter destination cell Press ↵	Use the GOTO command (F5) to move cell pointer to any cell in the worksheet including a cell which does not appear on the screen.
SAVE (L21)	Press / Type F Type S Enter file name Press ↵	Enters file name at the Save prompt. If the file name exists, type R to replace it.
PRINT SCREEN IMAGE (L25)	Press Print Screen	Prints exactly what you see on the screen.
CORRECT ERRORS ON INPUT LINE (L26)	Press Backspace	Erases character to left of cursor.
EDIT CELL CONTENTS (L27)	Press F2	Before pressing F2, move cell pointer to cell with error. Press ← or → to move cursor to character to correct. Toggle on overtype and type correct character.
UNDO (L30)	Press Alt-F4	Restores worksheet data and settings to what they were the last time 1-2-3 was in READY mode.
ERASE CELL CONTENTS (L31)	Press / Type R Type E Press ↵	Erases the contents of a cell.
ERASE WORKSHEET (L31)	Press / Type W Type E Type Y	Erases the worksheet in main memory. This command does not erase the worksheet from disk.
HELP (L31)	Press F1	Temporarily suspends the current activity and displays help. Press Esc key at any time to return to READY mode.
QUIT 1-2-3 (L32)	Press / Type Q Type Y	Quits 1-2-3 and returns control to DOS.

QUICK REFERENCE — PROJECT 2

ACTIVITY	PROCEDURE	DESCRIPTION
LOAD (L45)	Press / Type F Type R Select file name Press ↵	Use arrow keys to select file name.
CHANGE WIDTH OF ALL COLUMNS (L48)	Press / Type W Type G Type C Enter width Press ↵	Type the global width or use Left and Right Arrow keys to enter the global width.
CHANGE WIDTH OF ADJACENT COLUMNS (L50)	Press / Type W Type C Type C Type S Select columns Press ↵ Enter width Press ↵	Use Left and Right Arrow keys to select the columns. Type the width or use Left and Right Arrow keys to enter the width.
CHANGE WIDTH OF ONE COLUMN (L50)	Press / Type W Type C Type S Enter width Press ↵	Type the width or use Left and Right Arrow keys to enter the width.
FORMAT NUMERIC VALUES OVER A RANGE (L52)	Press / Type R Type F Select format Select decimal places Select range Press ↵	Select decimal places only if requested.
REPEAT CHARACTERS (L57)	Press \ Enter character(s) Press ↵	Character(s) will repeat throughout cell.
COPY (L58)	Press / Type C Enter source range Press ↵ Enter destination range Press ↵	Cell references in formulas are adjusted as copy takes place.
PRINT (L74)	Press / Type P Type P Select print range Press ↵ Type A Type G Type P Type Q	1-2-3 remembers the last print range entered.

QUICK REFERENCE — PROJECT 3

ACTIVITY	PROCEDURE	DESCRIPTION
FORMAT NUMERIC VALUES GLOBALLY (L95)	Press / Type W Type G Type F Select format Select decimal places Press ←	Select decimal places only if requested.
INSERT ROWS OR COLUMNS (L100)	Press / Type W Type I Type R or C Select range Press ←	If inserting rows, all rows including the one cell pointer is on, are pushed down. If inserting columns, all columns including the one cell pointer is on, are pushed to the right.
DELETE ROWS OR COLUMNS (L102)	Press / Type W Type D Type R or C Select range Press ←	Make sure rows or columns to be deleted do not include data referenced elsewhere in formulas.
FREEZE TITLES (L105)	Press / Type W Type T Type B or H or V	Type B for both row and column titles. Type H for only column titles. Type V for only row titles.
MOVE (L106)	Press / Type M Enter source range Press ← Enter destination range Press ←	When moving a range containing a formula or function that references cell addresses, the referenced cell addresses are not changed relative to the new position, unless they refer to cells within the moved range.
INVOKE ALLWAYS (L126)	Press / Type A Type I Select ALLWAYS Press ←	If a function key has been assigned to ALLWAYS, hold down the Alt key and press the assigned function key.
CHANGE FONT IN ALLWAYS (L128)	Press / Type F Type F Select font Press ← Select range Press ←	Use arrow keys to select the desired font.
SHADE CELLS IN ALLWAYS (L131)	Press / Type F Type S Select shade Select range Press ←	The shade can be light, dark, solid, or clear. The shortcut key is Alt-S.

(continued)

QUICK REFERENCE — PROJECT 3 (continued)

ACTIVITY	PROCEDURE	DESCRIPTION
BOLDFACING CELLS IN ALLWAYS (L132)	Press / Type F Type B Type S Select range Press ↵	The shortcut key is Alt-B.
UNDERLINING CELLS IN ALLWAYS (L133)	Press / Type F Type U Select underline Select range Press ↵	The shortcut key is Alt-U.
OUTLINING CELLS IN ALLWAYS (L134)	Press / Type F Type L Type O Select range Press ↵	The shortcut key is Alt-L.
CHANGE WIDTHS OF COLUMNS AND HEIGHTS OF ROWS IN ALLWAYS (L136)	Press / Type W Select column or row Type S Enter width or height Press ↵	Type the width or height or use arrow keys to enter the width or height.
PRINT IN ALLWAYS (L137)	Press / Type P Type R Type S Select range Press ↵ Press G	1-2-3 remembers the last print range entered.
ZOOM IN ALLWAYS (L138)	Press / Type D Type Z Select size	The size can be tiny, small, normal, large, or huge. The shortcut key to reduce the size is F4. The shortcut key to increase the size is Alt-F4.

QUICK REFERENCE — PROJECT 4

ACTIVITY	PROCEDURE	DESCRIPTION
NAME A RANGE (L157)	Press / Type R Type N Type C Enter name Press ↵ Enter range Press ↵	A range name can consist of up to 15 characters.
LABEL NAMES (L162)	Press / Type R Type N Type L Select adjacent cell Enter range Press ↵	An adjacent cell is to the right, down, to the left, or up.
DATA FILL (L163)	Press / Type D Type F Enter range Enter start Enter step Enter stop Press ↵	Range or stop value terminates data fill.
DATA TABLE 1 (L169)	Press / Type D Type T Type 1 Enter range Press ↵ Enter input cell Press ↵	Press F8 to recalculate a data table.
DATA TABLE 2 (L169)	Press / Type D Type T Type 2 Enter range Press ↵ Enter input cell-1 Press ↵ Enter input cell-2 Press ↵	Assigns formula to evaluate to upper left corner cell of range. Press F8 to recalculate a data table.
NAME MACRO (L171)	Press / Type R Type N Type C Enter name Press ↵ Enter range Press ↵	A range name can consist of up to 15 characters.

QUICK REFERENCE — PROJECT 4 (continued)

ACTIVITY	PROCEDURE	DESCRIPTION
INVOKE A MACRO (L171)	Alt-(macro name)	An alternative method for executing a macro is to press Alt-F3 and select the macro from the menu of range names.
SPLIT WINDOWS (L175)	Move cell pointer to split location Press / Type W Type W Type H or V	Type H for horizontal split. Type V for vertical split. Type /WWC to switch from two windows back to one window. Press F6 to deactivate current window and activate the other one.
CELL PROTECTION (L176)	Press / Type W Type G Type P Type E	This command sequence protects all cells. Use the /Range Unprotect (/RU) command to unprotect cells into which data is to be entered.

QUICK REFERENCE — PROJECT 5

ACTIVITY	PROCEDURE	DESCRIPTION
BUILD GRAPH (L193)	Press / Type G Type T Select graph type Enter ranges	Selects between line, bar, XY, stack-bar, and pie.
VIEW GRAPH (L194)	Press / Type G Type V	The shortcut key to view current graph is F10.
GRAPH OPTIONS (L196)	Press / Type G Type O Select option	Use the Options menu to select legends, formats, titles, grid, scale, color, B&W, and data-labels.
NAME GRAPH (L196)	Press / Type G Type N Type C Enter graph name Press ↵	A graph name can consist of up to 15 characters.
SAVE GRAPH SETTINGS (L197)	Press / Type F Type S Enter file name Press ↵	Graph settings are saved with the worksheet. Enter file name at the Save prompt.
SAVE PIC FILE (L197)	Press / Type G Type S Enter file name Press ↵	A PIC file is a snapshot of the current graph.
PRINT PIC FILE (L198)	Quit 1-2-3 Load PGRAPH Type I Highlight graph name Press ↵ Type A Type G Type P	When a graph name is highlighted, use the Spacebar to mark and unmark for printing. A number sign (#) to the left of a graph name indicates it is marked for printing.
ADD GRAPH TO WORKSHEET USING ALLWAYS (L213)	Press / Type G Type A Select graph name Press ↵ Enter range Press ↵	Press F10 to display graph in worksheet rather than crosshatched design.
RESIZING GRAPH USING ALLWAYS (L215)	Press / Type G Type S Select graph name Press ↵ Type R Enter range Press ↵ Type Q	Up to 20 graphs can be added to the worksheet.

QUICK REFERENCE — PROJECT 6

ACTIVITY	PROCEDURE	DESCRIPTION
SORT RECORDS (L230)	Press / Type D Type S Type D Select data range Press ↵ Type P Select sort key Press ↵ Select sort sequence Press ↵ Type G	If a secondary key is involved in the sort, enter it immediately after the primary sort key is entered.
FIND RECORDS (L235)	Press / Type D Type Q Type I Select input range Press ↵ Type C Select criteria range Press ↵ Type F	The criteria is entered into worksheet before initiating the query. After typing F, use arrow keys to find the next record that meets the criteria. Press ↵ or Esc to return to Data Query menu.
EXTRACT RECORDS (L239)	Press / Type D Type Q Type I Select input range Press ↵ Type C Select criteria range Press ↵ Type O Select output range Press ↵ Type E	The criteria is entered into worksheet before initiating the query. The column headings for the output range are entered before initiating the query.
SEARCH (L246)	Press / Type R Type S Select range Press ↵ Enter search string Press ↵ Select search type Type F Type N	Search type may be F for Formulas, L for Labels, or B for Both. Typing Q during the search activity returns 1-2-3 to READY mode.
REPLACE (L247)	Press / Type R Type S Select range Press ↵ Enter search string Press ↵ Select search type Type R Enter replace string Press ↵ Type R	Search type may be F for Formulas, L for Labels, or B for Both. To replace all occurrences, type A rather than R after entering the replace string. Typing Q during the replace returns 1-2-3 to READY mode.